DOUGLAS COOPER
UND DIE MEISTER DES KUBISMUS
AND THE MASTERS OF CUBISM

DOUGLAS COOPER
UND DIE MEISTER DES KUBISMUS
AND THE MASTERS OF CUBISM

Text und Katalog von/Text and catalogue by
Dorothy M. Kosinski

Mit einem Beitrag von/With a contribution by
John Richardson

KUNSTMUSEUM BASEL
THE TATE GALLERY LONDON

Diese Publikation erscheint
aus Anlass der Ausstellung «Douglas Cooper
und die Meister des Kubismus»
im Kunstmuseum Basel.
22. November 1987 – 17. Januar 1988.

Übersetzung der Texte von D. Kosinski und
J. Richardson: Hans Jürg Kupper

Photolithos: Schwitter AG, Basel
Graphische Gestaltung: Peter Köhler
Satz und Druck: Gissler Druck Basel
Einband: Buchbinderei Flügel, Basel

ISBN 3-7204-0052-2

INHALTSVERZEICHNIS
TABLE OF CONTENTS

VORWORT
FOREWORD

«Je lègue au Kunstmuseum de Bâle en témoignage de mon admiration pour la superbe collection d'œuvres cubistes de Picasso et Gris réunies dans ce musée le dessin par Picasso pour *Les Demoiselles d'Avignon* (1907)», bestimmte Douglas Cooper am 16. November 1983 – viereinhalb Monate vor seinem Tod – in seinem Testament. Diese generöse letztwillige Verfügung brachte das Kunstmuseum in den Besitz einer zweiten bedeutenden Studie zu Picassos revolutionärem Gemälde; die erste Kompositionsskizze zu den *Demoiselles d'Avignon* (Zervos, II, 19) war bekanntlich 1967 als Geschenk des Künstlers nach Basel gekommen.

Dieses Studienblatt ist im übrigen nicht das einzige Werk Picassos in der Öffentlichen Kunstsammlung Basel, das sich einst im Besitze von Douglas Cooper befunden hatte. Auch das 1967 aus dem Kunsthandel erworbene Gemälde *Femme au chapeau, assise dans un fauteuil* von 1941 (Zervos, II, 374) hat Ende der fünfziger Jahre vorübergehend ihm gehört.

Die Ausstellung *Douglas Cooper und die Meister des Kubismus* ist als Hommage an den Kenner, Apologeten und Sammler des Werkes von Braque, Gris, Léger und Picasso gedacht und möge als Zeichen der Dankbarkeit diesem Freund unseres Museums gegenüber verstanden werden. Die Bewunderung, die Douglas Cooper für die kubistischen Bestände des Kunstmuseums hegte, bringen wir ebenfalls der von ihm zusammengetragenen Sammlung entgegen. Was für eine faszinierende Fülle von Querbezügen ergeben sich zwischen diesen Aquarellen, Zeichnungen, Collagen sowie druckgrafischen Blättern und den kubistischen Gemälden, die Basel zu einem wesentlichen Teil den Schenkungen von Raoul LaRoche verdankt!

Den grosszügigen Leihgebern, die uns ermöglicht haben, diese zwei hervorragenden kubistischen Sammlungen auf Zeit unter einem Dach zu vereinen, gelte deshalb unser erstes Dankeswort.

Herzlich gedankt sei aber auch Frau Dr. Dorothy Kosinski, Kuratorin der Douglas Cooper Collection: Sie hat die Ausstellung nicht nur angeregt, sondern ihre

"Je lègue au Kunstmuseum de Bâle en témoignange de mon admiration pour la superbe collection d'œuvres cubistes de Picasso et Gris réunies dans ce musée le dessin par Picasso pour *Les Demoiselles d'Avignon* (1907)." Thus instructed Douglas Cooper in his will on November 16, 1983, four and a half months before his death. This generous bequest brought thereby, a second important study for Picasso's revolutionary painting into the Kunstmuseum's collection. The other sketch for the *Demoiselles* (Z, II, 19) came to Basel as a gift from the artist in 1967.

This study is, moreover, not the only work by Picasso, now in the Kunstmuseum's collection, which was once in Douglas Cooper's possession. The 1941 painting, *Femme au chapeau, assise dans un fauteuil,* (Z, II, 374), purchased in 1967, had briefly belonged to Cooper in the late 1950s.

The exhibition, *Douglas Cooper and the Masters of Cubism,* is conceived as an hommage to this connoisseur, apologist and collector of works by Braque, Gris, Léger and Picasso, and may be understood, as well, as a sign of our museum's gratitude vis-à-vis this friend. The admiration which Cooper had for the Cubist holdings in the Kunstmuseum, we, likewise, hold for the collection which he himself formed. What a fascinating abundance of cross-relationships arise between these watercolors, drawings, collages, as well as prints, and the Cubist paintings which Basel owns in large part thanks to the gift of Raoul LaRoche!

The generous lenders who have enabled us to temporarily bring together under one roof, these two outstanding Cubist collections, deserve our first word of thanks.

Our sincere thanks are extended as well to Dr. Dorothy Kosinski, Curator of the Douglas Cooper Collection. She not only suggested the exhibition, but energetically promoted its realization throughout, and wrote the accompanying catalogue.

Finally we thank John Richardson for the relevation of a chapter of Picasso's life which the artist had kept as

Realisierung in jeder Beziehung tatkräftig gefördert und den sie begleitenden Katalog verfasst.

John Richardson schliesslich verdanken wir die Enthüllung eines von Picasso als Geheimnis gehüteten Kapitels aus seinem Leben. Der Vorabdruck dieses Beitrages in der amerikanischen Zeitschrift *House & Garden* hat weltweites Aufsehen erregt und die Aufmerksamkeit auf unsere Ausstellung gelenkt.

secret. The appearance of this contribution in the American magazine *House & Garden* caused a worldwide sensation and helped to focus attention on our exhibition.

Christian Geelhaar

DANK DER AUTORIN
AUTHOR'S ACKNOWLEDGMENTS

Ich möchte meine Dankbarkeit William McCarty-Cooper gegenüber aussprechen. Dieses Projekt hätte ohne seine Grosszügigkeit und seine volle Unterstützung nie verwirklicht werden können.

Andere Personen waren der Realisierung dieses Kataloges und dieser Ausstellung ebenfalls sehr dienlich. Mein Dank geht an Leonard Lauder für sein grosses Interesse und seine Unterstützung. Ich kam erst dank des Vertrauens, das Angelica Zander Rudenstine mir schenkte, dazu, mit der Sammlung Douglas Cooper zu arbeiten. Ihr guter Rat, welcher so hilfreich war während der Vorbereitung von Katalog und Ausstellung, habe ich sehr geschätzt. Im weiteren geht mein Dank an Christian Geelhaar, Direktor des Basler Kunstmuseums, für sein Interesse, und seine Wertschätzung von Douglas Cooper's Beitrag als Sammler und Gelehrter.

Die Grosszügigkeit von John Richardson ist nicht nur sein Essai über Picasso und Gay Lespinasse, sondern sie bestand auch darin, dass er sein kostbares Wissen aus erster Hand über Cooper's Leben, Arbeit und das Zustandekommen der Sammlung, mit mir zu teilen bereit war. Caroline Brooke übernahm, neben anderen Nachforschungen, die schwierige Aufgabe, Douglas Cooper's voluminöse Bibliographie zusammenzutragen. Hansjörg Kupper war äusserst präzise in seiner Übersetzung meines Textes.

Meinem Ehemann, Thomas Krähenbühl, gilt mein Dank für seine unermüdliche Unterstützung und seine Ratschläge für die Ausformulierung und die eigentliche Ausführung dieses Projektes.

Nicolas Olsberg und seine Mitarbeiter des Getty Center for the History of Art and the Humanities machten mir in grosszügiger Weise das Cooper Archiv zugänglich. Ich danke ebenfalls Clive Phillpot und seinen Mitarbeitern in der Museum of Modern Art Library, New York.

Für die Vorbereitung des Katalogs haben mir viele Kollegen, Freunde und Bekannte unschätzbare Informationen und Unterstützung gewährt: John Barratt, V. Beston von Marlborough Fine Art, London, Emily

I wish to express my gratitude to William McCarty-Cooper. Without his generosity and enthusiastic support, this project could never have been realized.

Other people were instrumental to the realization of this catalogue and exhibition as well. My thanks to Leonard Lauder for his keen interest and support. It is due to the generous vote of confidence of Angelica Zander Rudenstine that I first came to work with The Douglas Cooper Collection. Her good counsel, so helpful throughout the preparation of the catalogue and exhibition, is deeply appreciated. I extend my thanks, as well, to Dr. Christian Geelhaar, Director of the Kunstmuseum Basel, for his interest in and appreciation of Douglas Cooper's contribution as collector and scholar.

John Richardson not only contributed the essay about Picasso and Gaby Lespinasse, but was also extraordinarily generous in sharing his valuable information about and first-hand insight into Cooper's life, work and the formulation of the collection. Caroline Brooke undertook the somewhat daunting task of assembling Cooper's vast bibliography and assisted me in other researches, as well. Hans Jürg Kupper was extremely meticulous in his translation of my text.

My husband, Thomas Krähenbühl, was unstinting in his advice and very real assistance in the formulation and execution of this project.

Nicholas Olsberg and his staff at the Getty Center for the History of Art and the Humanities very generously made the Cooper archive available to me. My thanks as well to Clive Phillpot and his staff at Museum of Modern Art Library, New York.

In the preparation of the catalogue, many individuals, friends and colleagues, generously provided invaluable information or assistance: John Barratt, V. Beston at Marlborough Fine Art, London, Emily Braun, Sarah Fox-Pitt at The Tate Gallery Archives, Susan Galassi, Maurice Jardot of The Galerie Louise Leiris, Valdina de Königsberg, Adrien Maeght, Lionel Prejger, Sabine Rewald, Shari Rhodes, Hortensia von Roda, Eleanore Saidenberg, Gert Schiff and Gary Tinterow.

Braun, Sarah Fox-Pitt von den Tate Gallery Archives, Susan Galassi, Maurice Jardot von der Galerie Louise Leiris, Paris, Valdina de Königsberg, Adrien Maeght, Lionel Prejger, Sabine Rewald, Shari Rhoads, Hortensia von Roda, Eleanore Saidenberg, Gert Schiff und Gary Tinterow.

Ich möchte ebenfalls meine Wertschätzung für die sorgfältigen und intelligenten Ratschläge und Arbeiten von Véronique Tabibzadeh ausdrücken, welche die Restaurierung der Werke der Sammlung übernahm.

Mein Dank gilt auch folgenden Mitarbeitern des Kunstmuseums Basel für ihre Arbeit: Paul Berger, Martin Bühler, Samuel Gugger, Klaus Hess und Laura Weidacher.

Schliesslich bin ich allen Leihgebern der Ausstellung zu Dank verpflichtet, besonders Churchglade Ltd. Ohne ihre Grosszügigkeit hätte dieses Projekt nie verwirklicht werden können.

I would also like to express my appreciation of the careful and intelligent advice and work of Veronique Tabibzadeh concerning conservation of works on paper in the Collection.

I extend my thanks, as well, to the following members of the staff at the Kunstmuseum Basel for their work: Paul Berger, Martin Bühler, Samuel Gugger, Klaus Hess and Laura Weidacher.

Finally, I would like to express my gratitude to all of the lenders to the exhibition, especially Churchglade Ltd., without whose generosity this project could never have been realized.

Dorothy M. Kosinski

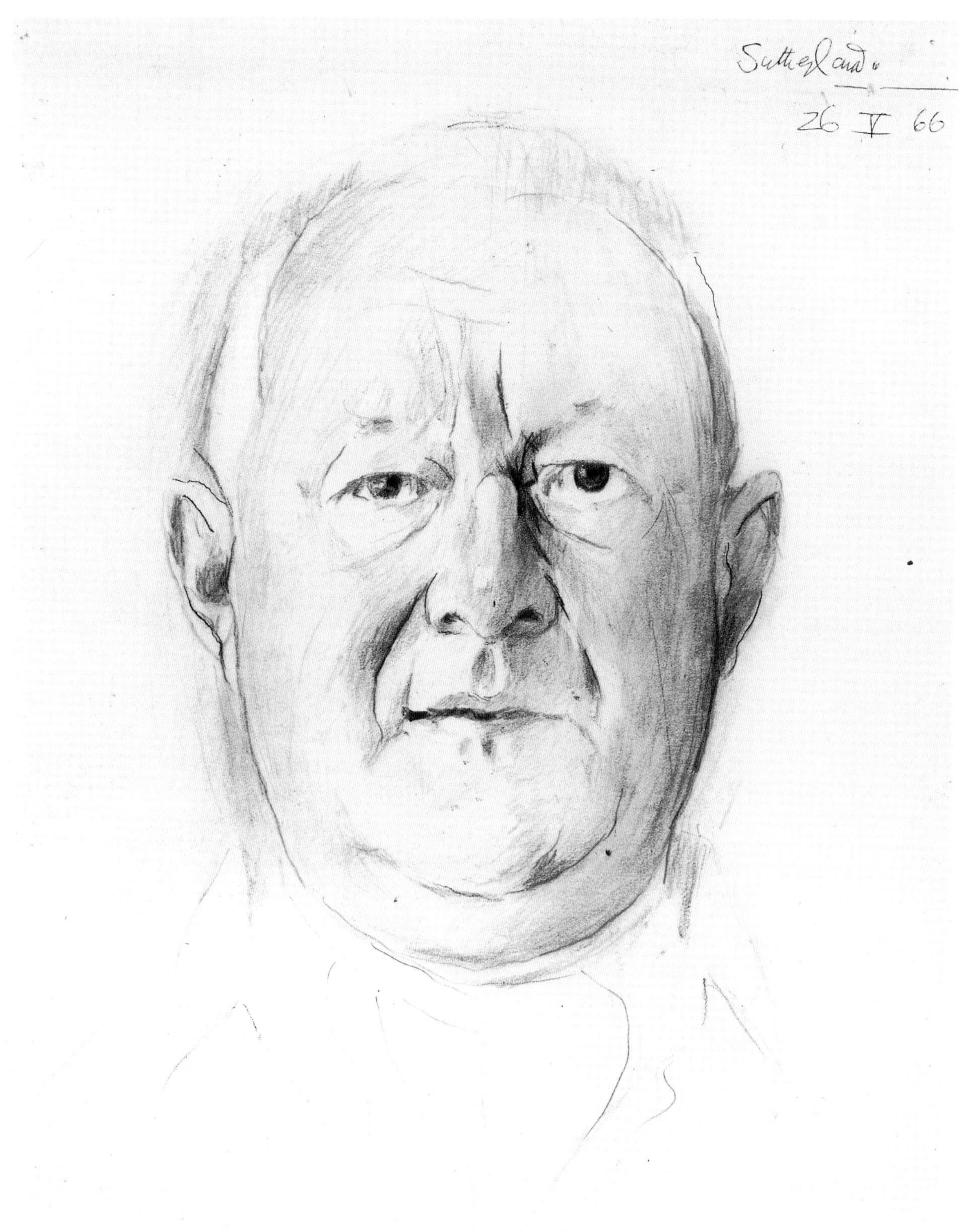

81 GRAHAM SUTHERLAND
(Porträt Douglas Cooper; Portrait of Douglas Cooper) 1966

DOUGLAS COOPER

Von Douglas Cooper (1911–1984) und seiner Bedeutung als Kunstkenner, -freund und -historiker ein adäquates Bild zeichnen kann nur, wer sich eingehend mit seiner Sammlung und seinen zahlreichen Schriften befasst. Cooper war nicht nur ein besessener und weitsichtiger Sammler, sondern auch ein imposanter Gelehrter und gefürchteter Kritiker. Er zeigte sich als Mann von grosser Kraft und grosser Gegensätzlichkeit. Seine Schriften – stets streitfreudig, wenn nicht streitsüchtig – verraten verblüffende geistige Weite; in ihnen befasste er sich vor allem mit der Kunst des 20. Jahrhunderts, doch äusserte er sich auch ausführlich zur Kunst und Literatur des neunzehnten Jahrhunderts (etwa in Büchern über Georges Seurat, Vincent van Gogh, Edouard Manet, Henri de Toulouse-Lautrec, Edgar Degas, Henri Rousseau und Paul Gauguin) und zu so unterschiedlichen Künstlern wie Peter Paul Rubens, Wilson Steer, Richard Parkes Bonington, Richard Wilson und Jacques-Louis David. Die grosse Leidenschaft seines Lebens aber, die über fünfzig Jahre lang – etwa von 1932 bis zu seinem Tod 1984 – seine Sammlung, sein Forschungsgebiet und sogar seine Freundschaften prägte, war der Kubismus.

Cooper wurde in eine wohlhabende englische Familie hineingeboren, die vor Generationen ihr Vermögen in Australien gemacht hatte. Seine Entfremdung von diesem familiären und nationalen Hintergrund wurde sozusagen das Begleitmotiv seines Lebens. Als Anglophobe konnte er sogar borstig werden, wenn man ihn für einen Australier hielt. In den dreissiger Jahren zeichnete er viele seiner Artikel mit dem von Lord Alfred Douglas hergeleiteten Pseudonym "Douglas Lord". Eine Zeitlang bewohnte Cooper das Haus Groom Place Nummer 8 in London, dessen Einrichtung

---

Bemerkung:
Die folgenden Abkürzungen sind im Text und in den Bemerkungen verwendet worden: DC Nummern = von Cooper verwendete Nummern in seiner Archivkartei; Neue DC Nummern = Nummern von Inventaren, welche nach Coopers Tod erstellt wurden; Ms. = Manuskript; *TLS* = *The Times Literary Supplement*; Z = Christian Zervos, *Pablo Picasso*, Paris, Cahiers d'art, 1932 bis heute, vol. 1–33.

An accurate picture of Douglas Cooper's (1911–1984) significance as connoisseur and art historian emerges only through an examination of both his art collection and his voluminous bibliography. He was not only a perspicacious and avid collector but was, as well, a formidable critic and scholar. Cooper is revealed, as a man of great intensity and extremes. His writings – often contentious, and sometimes viciously so, and always competitive – reveal an astonishing intellectual breadth. He wrote most of all on 20th century art, but also extensively on art and literature of the 19th century (including books on Georges Seurat, Vincent Van Gogh, Edouard Manet, Henri de Toulouse-Lautrec, Edgar Degas, Henri Rousseau and Paul Gauguin), and on artists as varied as Peter Paul Rubens, Wilson Steer, Richard Parkes Bonington, Richard Wilson and Jacques-Louis David. Clearly, however, the passion of his life for over fifty years – from about 1932 until his death in 1984 – defining his collection, constituting the subject of his scholarship and forming even his friendships, as well, was Cubism.

Cooper was born into an upper middle class family, whose fortune had been made, generations back, in Australia. Cooper's estrangement from familial and national background became, as it were, a lifelong theme. He bristled if ever misidentified as Australian. In the thirties he signed may of his articles with the pseudonym "Douglas Lord", inspired by Lord Alfred Douglas. Cooper had lived for some time at 8 Groom Place in London, in a house decorated with furniture designed by the painter Francis Bacon. After the War he shared a house at 18 Edgerton Terrace with Lord Amulree, a noted gerontologist and friend since Cambridge. Cooper's education at the prestigious public

---

Note:
The following abbreviations are used within the text and notes: DC numbers = work numbers assigned by Cooper on archival cards; New DC numbers = numbers from inventories assembled subsequent to Cooper's death; Ms. = Manuscript; *TLS* = *The Times Literary Supplement*; Z = Christian Zervos, *Pablo Picasso*, Paris, Cahiers d'art, 1932-present. vols.1–33.

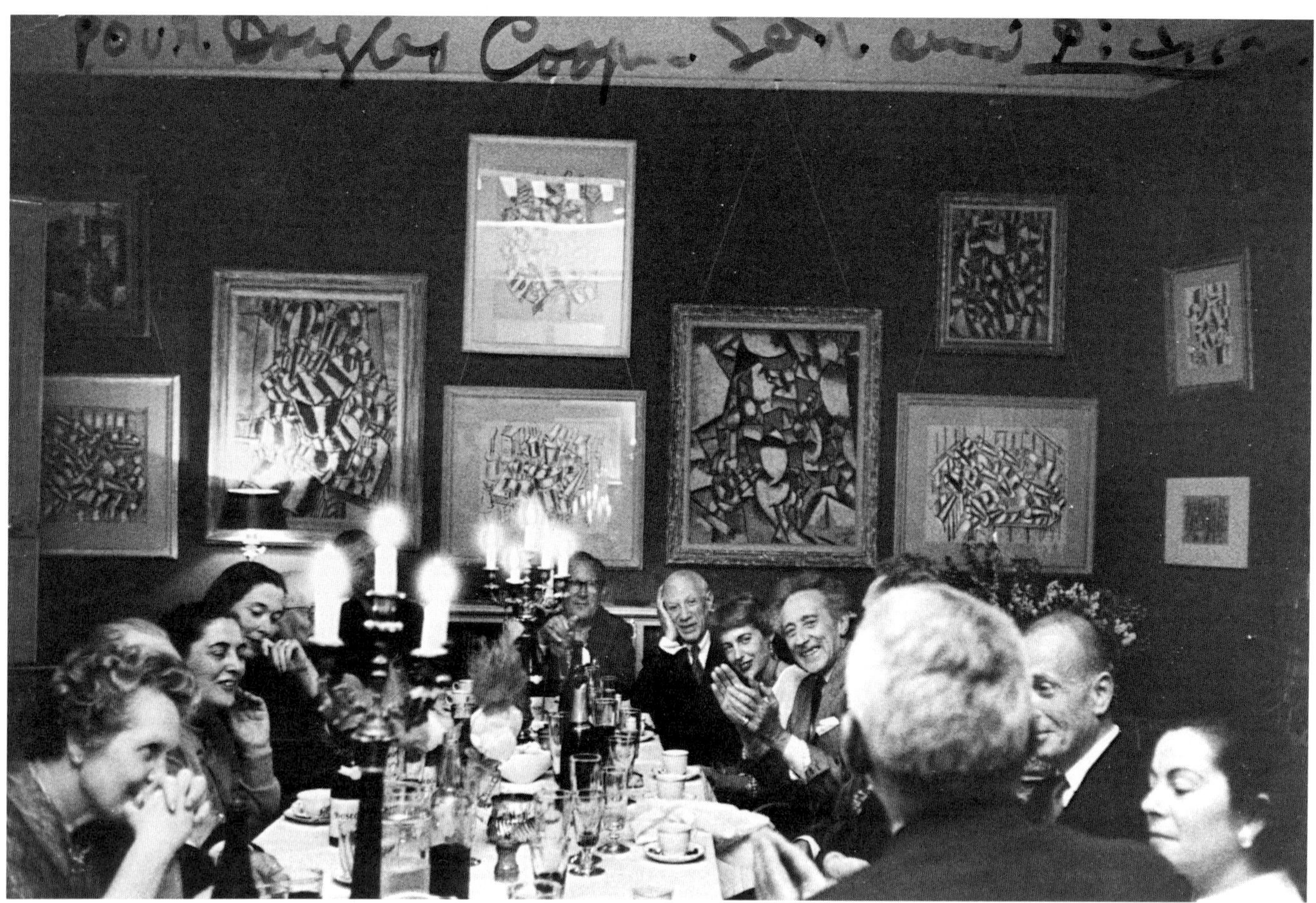

Château de Castille, ca.1955, Diner nach einem Stierkampf. Fotographie beschriftet: "Pour Douglas Cooper, son ami Picasso". Teilnehmer (sichtbare) von links nach rechts: Mme. Zette Leiris; unbekannte Dame; Mme. Jean Hugo; John Richardson; Cooper; Picasso; Mme. Françine Weisweiler; Jean Cocteau; Michel Leiris; unbekannte Dame; Jean Hugo (mit dem Rücken zur Kamera). Werke von Léger, von links nach rechts: *Les toits de Paris*, 1912 (DC122); *Deux femmes couchées*, 1913; *Stilleben*, 1914 (DC86); Stilleben auf einem Tisch, 1914 (DC73, jetzt im Metropolitan Museum of Art, New York); *Nature morte*, 1913 (No.30); *Landschaft*, 1913 (DC52); *Contrastes de forme*, 1913 (DC13); *Deux femmes couchées*, 1913 (DC14, jetzt im Metropolitan Museum of Art, New York); nicht identifiziert; Entwurf für einen Vorhang, *La création du monde*, 1922 (DC16).

Château de Castille, ca.1955, Dinner following bull fight. Photograph inscribed: "Pour Douglas Cooper, son ami Picasso". Participants (visible) left to right: Mme. Zette Leiris; unknown woman; Mme. Jean Hugo; John Richardson; Cooper; Picasso; Mme. Françine Weisweiler; Jean Cocteau; Michel Leiris; unknown woman; Jean Hugo (back to camera). Works by Léger, left to right: *Les toits de Paris*, 1912 (DC122); *Deux femmes couchées*, 1913; *Still-life*, 1914 (DC86); *Still-life on a table*, 1914 (DC73, now Metropolitan Museum of Art, New York); *Nature morte*, 1913 (No.30); *Landscape*, 1913 (DC52); *Contrastes de formes*, 1913 (DC13); *Deux femmes couchées*, 1913 (DC14, now Metropolitan Museum of Art, New York); not identified; Design for curtain, *La création du monde*, 1922 (DC16).

der Maler Francis Bacon entworfen hatte. Nach dem Krieg liess er sich in der Nummer 18, Edgerton Terrace, nieder, zusammen mit Lord Amulree, dem bekannten Gerontologen und Freund aus der Studienzeit in Cambridge. Coopers Ausbildung, die in Repton, der berühmten Public School, begonnen hatte, setzte sich – jeweils etwa ein Jahr – eben in Cambridge, dann an der Sorbonne und der Universität Freiburg im Breisgau fort. Während des Krieges diente er in einer französischen Ambulanzfahrer-Einheit; seine Erlebnisse zeichnete er auf in einem zusammen mit Denys Freeman geschriebenen Buch, *The Road to Bordeaux*, welches dann die Regierung auszugsweise als Pamphlet gegen Panik in Kriegssituationen nachdrucken liess. In der Folge erhielt Cooper eine Offiziersstelle in der Royal Air Force, wo er auch nachrichtendienstliche Aufgaben zu übernehmen hatte, so etwa – wegen seiner sprachlichen Fähigkeiten – Verhöre; ausserdem musste er, da er Kunsthistoriker war, die Fine Arts Commission in Sachen Bezeichnung und Schutz wichtiger Kunstdenkmäler beraten sowie konfiszierte Kunstwerke repatriieren. Während eines Ferienaufenthaltes 1949 in Südfrankreich – zusammen mit Lord Amulree und John Richardson – entdeckte er das baufällige Château de Castille in Argilliers, Gard, kaufte es und bewohnte es bis 1977; in diesem Jahr zog er um nach Monte-Carlo, wo er bis zu seinem Tod am ersten April 1984 ansässig blieb. Grund für den Umzug war vor allem das traumatische Erlebnis eines kapitalen Diebstahls, dem 27 Kunstwerke (noch längst nicht alle wieder aufgetaucht) zum Opfer fielen. Dank Coopers Sammlung, aber auch dank der farbigen und umstrittenen Persönlichkeit des durch unzählige Publikationen, Ausstellungen und Vorträge bekanntgewordenen Sammlers wurde das Schloss zum Anziehungspunkt, ja zu einem eigentlichen Wallfahrtsort für ein Kunstpublikum aller Art.[1]

In den dreissiger Jahren begann Cooper konsequent seine Sammlung kubistischer Kunst, welche um 1945 annähernd endgültige Gestalt annehmen sollte, aufzubauen, gemäss seinem 1932 gefällten Entscheid, ein Drittel seiner Erbschaft (ungefähr 100 000 Pfund)

school, Repton, was continued with a year or so each at Cambridge, the Sorbonne, and the University of Freiburg. His experiences serving with a French ambulance unit during the war are recorded in *The Road to Bordeaux* written with Denys Freeman, part of which was reprinted by the government as a pamphlet against panic in wartime situations. Cooper subsequently obtained a commission with the Royal Air Force. His assignments included a stint with intelligence; interrogation (because of his linguistic skills); and (drawing upon his art background) consultation with the Fine Arts Commission attempting to identify important works of art and buildings, and to protect them from destruction, and also to repatriate confiscated works of art. In 1949, on holiday with Lord Amulree and John Richardson, he discovered and purchased the dilapidated Château de Castille in Argilliers, Gard. The Château was home until 1977 when he moved to Monte Carlo where he lived until his death on April 1, 1984. This move was inspired, in large part, by the trauma of a major theft in which 27 works of art were stolen (many still not recovered). Cooper's art collection, but also his own colorful and controversial personality, well known through innumerable publications, exhibitions and lectures, served to make the Château de Castille a pilgrimage stop for members of the art world and others as well.[1]

Cooper's collection of Cubist works of art was very much formed by 1945. He collected consistently during the 1930s, fulfilling thereby his decision taken in 1932 to devote one-third of his inheritence (ca. 100 000 £) to amassing a collection devoted to the four major Cubist artists – Picasso, Braque, Gris and Léger, representing every phase of their development from 1906 or 1907 until 1914, , in all of their primary media – painting, drawing, papiers collés, prints and sculpture, and including the entire range of their subject matter – figures, landscapes and still lives.

It seems clear that Cooper had, from the outset, a well-defined notion of his collection and, as it were, its historical importance. Cooper, in fact, wrote exten-

dafür zu verwenden; geplant war ein Ensemble von Werken der vier Hauptkubisten – Picasso, Braque, Gris und Léger – , in dem jede Phase ihrer Entwicklung von 1906/7 bis 1914 vertreten sein sollte, aber auch das ganze Spektrum der Sujets (Figur, Landschaft, Stilleben) und alle von ihnen hauptsächlich gewählten Medien (Malerei, Zeichnung, Graphik, Plastik, Skulptur).

Sicher hatte Cooper von Anfang an eine klare Vorstellung von der Art und gewissermassen auch von der historischen Bedeutung seiner Sammlung, schrieb er doch viel und oft über private wie öffentliche Kunstsammlungen.[2]

Schon früh übte der Sammler Samuel Courtauld grosse Faszination auf Cooper aus. Dessen Frau sei, wie erzählt wird, der Dreizehnjährige anlässlich eines Konzerts vorgestellt worden, und zwar durch seinen Onkel Gerald Cooper, der ein Gönner des Streichorchesters war. Wieder zuhause habe er verkündet, er sei von Frau Courtauld eingeladen, sich ihre Bilder anzusehen; den Vorschlag seiner Mutter, ihn dorthin zu begleiten, quittierte er aber mit einem glatten "Nein!" und der Bemerkung, sie sei zu spiessbürgerlich. Onkel Geralds Einfluss auf Coopers Entwicklung ist nicht nur an dieser Anekdote abzulesen. Er, ein bekannter, hervorragender Musikologe und, wie könnte es anders sein, ein Sammler von Purcell-Autographen, nahm Cooper 1921 auch in Vorstellungen des Diaghilew-Balletts mit – und schulte so vielleicht als erster seinen Blick.

Aus Coopers Einleitung im 1954 erschienenen Katalog der Courtauld-Sammlung ist viel von seinem Selbstverständnis als Sammler kubistischer Kunst herauszulesen. Er hebt lobend die Kohärenz und durchgehend hohe Qualität der Sammlung hervor und führt dies auf Courtaulds unbestechliche Haltung und sein eigenständiges Urteil in einer Zeit zurück, in der in England zurückgebliebener Geschmack und regelrechte Ignoranz herrschten.

Die Courtauld-Sammlung ist hauptsächlich eine Sammlung von Post-Impressionisten... Und es ist

sively about private art collectors and also about public collections.[2]

Samuel Courtauld captured Cooper's imagination early on. At about age thirteen he had apparently been introduced by his uncle Gerald Cooper to Mrs. Courtauld at a performance by the string orchestra which the uncle supported. Young Cooper apparently returned home and announced that he had been invited by Mrs. Courtauld to see her pictures, shunning his mother's suggestion that she accompany him with a terse "No!" and the bald statement that that she was too much a philistine. Uncle Gerald's impact on Cooper's development goes beyond this single introduction. He was himself a noted and brilliant musicologist, a scholar and also, significantly, a collector of Purcell manuscripts. It was Uncle Gerald, too, who invited Cooper to performances of Diaghilev Ballets in 1921, providing the first stimulus of his visual acumen.

One can infer a great deal about Cooper's self-concept as collector of Cubism from his introduction to the 1954 catalogue of the Courtauld Collection. He lauds the coherence and uniformly high quality of Courtauld's collection, attributing this achievement to the collector's single-minded focus and exercise of independent judgement in the context of the lagging taste or downright ignorance of the English.

The Courtauld Collection is essentially a collection of post-Impressionist works... And it is particularly significant that the Collection centres around the work of a few great individuals – Cézanne, Degas, Manet, Renoir, Seurat, Toulouse-Lautrec and Van Gogh ...Many aspects of the development of these masters are represented – perhaps more strikingly than in any other private collection – and the group of works by each shows him at the height of his powers. Therein lies the uniqueness of this collection, and we can only marvel at the remarkable understanding shown by Mr. and Mrs. Courtauld in selecting the finest works and the greatest artists of the period.[3]

besonders bezeichnend, dass sie sich um die Werke einiger weniger grosser Persönlichkeiten – Cézanne, Degas, Manet, Renoir, Seurat, Toulouse-Lautrec und van Gogh – gruppiert… Viele Aspekte in der Entwicklung dieser Meister kommen – wohl in keiner anderen Privatsammlung so eindrücklich wie hier – zur Darstellung, und jede Werkgruppe zeigt ihren Schöpfer auf der Höhe seiner Kunst. Darin liegt die Einzigartigkeit dieser Sammlung, und wir können nur staunen über den aussergewöhnlichen Kunstverstand, den Herr und Frau Courtauld in der Wahl der besten Werke und der grössten Künstler dieser Epoche bewiesen.[3]

In einer längeren Anmerkung zu dieser Einleitung wird vielleicht noch deutlicher, dass Cooper eigentlich auf einen Vergleich von Courtauld, dem innovativen Post-Impressionisten-Sammler, mit Cooper, dem extravaganten Kubisten-Sammler, zielt:

> *Bis etwa 1939 setzte englischer Geschmack moderne Kunst gleich mit Bonnard, Vuillard, Rouault, Matisse (nach 1918), Derain, Modigliani und Utrillo, mit Künstlern also, die schon vor 1920 vom Fry-Bell-Kreis anerkannt worden waren. Moderne Kunst hatte offenbar traditionell, dekorativ und leicht verständlich zu sein, um akzeptiert zu werden. Und so sammelte denn niemand Fauves oder Kubisten; vielleicht wurden gelegentlich einzelne Picassos, Braques oder Gris gekauft, doch faktisch nie von einem Museum; und bezeichnenderweise entstand nicht einmal eine repräsentative Matisse-Sammlung in der Zwischenkriegszeit. Am traurigsten aber stimmt, dass niemand (weder ein Privatsammler noch ein Museumsdirektor) auf dem Plan erschien, der fähig gewesen wäre, Meisterwerke französischer Kunst des 20. Jahrhunderts mit demselben sicheren Urteil und Geschmack auszuwählen, welche Samuel Courtauld im Hinblick auf die Kunst des 19. Jahrhunderts bewiesen hatte.*[4]

Als 1954 der Katalog der Courtauld-Sammlung publiziert wurde, lebte Cooper schon fast zwei Jahre

But it is, perhaps, in a longish footnote in this introduction, that Cooper suggests most clearly the implicit comparison between Courtauld the innovative collector of post-Impressionism and Cooper the outré collector of Cubism:

> *The taste of the English in modern art, until about 1939, was for Bonnard, Vuillard, Rouault, post-1918 Matisse, Derain, Modigliani and Utrillo, artists who had been accepted in the Fry-Bell circle before 1920. Modern art, in order to be acceptable, had to appear traditional, decorative and easy to understand. Thus no-one collected Fauve or Cubist pictures; very occasionally single pictures by Picasso, Braque or Juan Gris might be bought by a collector, virtually never by a museum; and, significantly, not even one representative collection of works by Matisse was formed between the two wars. Saddest of all, however, no successor (neither a private collector nor a museum director) appeared who was capable of choosing masterpieces of French art of the twentieth century with the same certainty of judgment and the same breadth of taste as Samuel Courtauld had shown in regard to the nineteenth century.*[4]

Cooper had, by the time of the publication of the Courtauld Catalogue in 1954, been living in the Château de Castille in Argilliers in the south of France for nearly two years. He uses his thorough and scholarly catalogue of the Courtauld collection as a vehicle to express his contempt for the English art world and to firmly set himself apart from it. This was by no means an isolated diatribe, but rather one more manifestation of his ongoing warfare with the English. The 1950s, in fact, were dominated somewhat by Cooper's well-publicized involvement in "The Tate Affair", a protracted battle on the part of a number of trustees, staff members and affiliates of the Museum, to gain the removal of its director, John Rothenstein. Cooper's own collection becomes, as it were, the fulfillment of the formula implicit in his praise of Courtauld: the focus on a

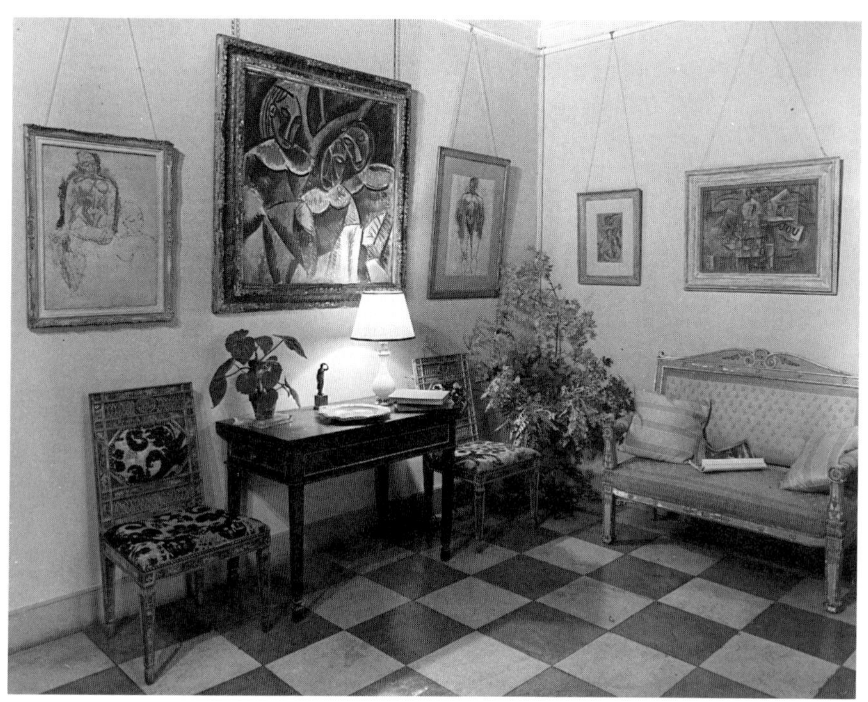

Château de Castille, ca. 1955, Werke von Picasso, von links nach rechts: *Sitzender Akt; Trois masquées, Drei Frauen unter einem Baum*, 1906–07 (jetzt im Musée Picasso, Paris); *Stehender weiblicher Akt*, 1906–07 (No. 50); *Stehende Figur*, 1907; *Stilleben mit toten Vögeln*, 1912 (DC34; Z II* 339)

Château de Castille, ca. 1955, works by Picasso, left to right: *Seated nude; Trois masquées, Three woman under a tree*, 1906–07 (now Musée Picasso, Paris); *Standing female nude*, 1906–07 (No. 50); *Standing figure*, 1907; *Still-life with Dead Birds*, 1912 (DC34; Z II* 339)

auf Schloss Castille in Argilliers. Der wissenschaftlich stichhaltige Katalog ist ihm auch Mittel, seiner Geringschätzung der englischen Kunst-Welt Ausdruck zu geben und sich klar davon abzugrenzen. Diese Schmähung war kein Einzelfall, vielmehr ein weiteres Kapitel in der fortlaufenden Geschichte seiner Anglophobie. Ein Akzent der fünfziger Jahre war auch die in der Öffentlichkeit sehr beachtete Rolle, welche Cooper in der sogenannten «Tate-Affäre» spielte, einem langwierigen Kampf, geführt von einem Teil der Bevollmächtigten und Mitarbeiter sowie von anderen interessierten Kreisen, mit dem Ziel, den Direktor der Tate, John Rothenstein, abzusetzen. Als Sammler wendet Cooper sozusagen die Formel an, welche er implizit mit seinem Lob Cour-

seminal movement (in this case Cubism rather than post-Impressionism) and an in depth representation of the great masters (now Picasso, Braque, Gris and Léger) through examples of their finest works. He provides the proper historical context for his own spectacular entry into collecting with his acquisitions between the wars of "difficult" Cubist works of art.

Almost thirty years later, in his introduction for the catalogue accompanying *The Essential Cubism* exhibition at The Tate Gallery, entitled: "Early Purchasers of True Cubist Art", Cooper chose to focus on the role of dealers and collectors in the recognition and appreciation of what he meticulously defined as "True Cubist Art". His discussion, beginning with the "Pioneer"

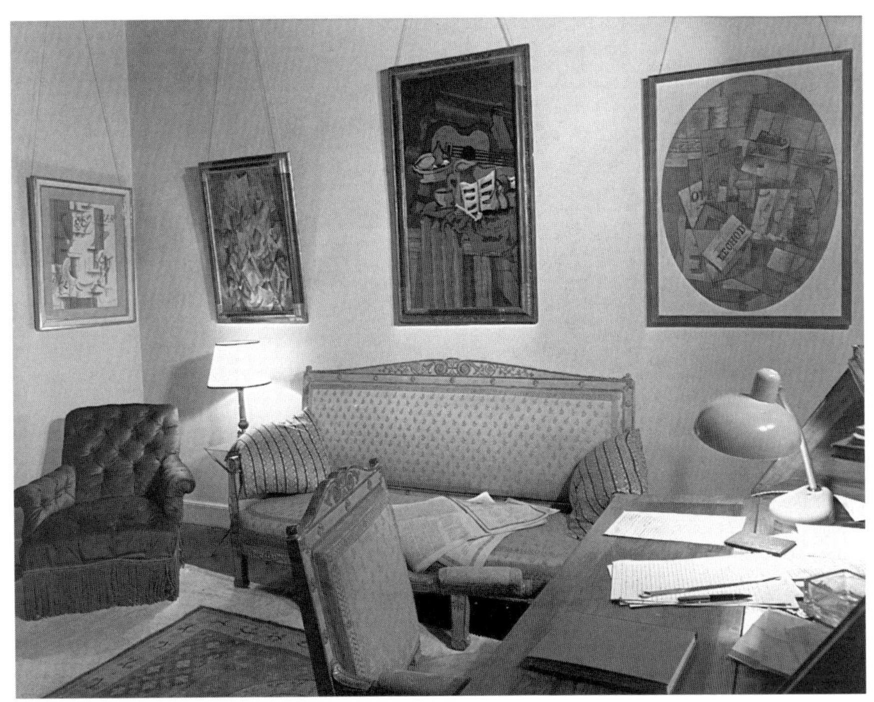

Château de Castille, ca.1955, Werke von Georges Braque, von links nach rechts: *Fruchtschale und Glas*, 1912 (No.5); *Stilleben mit Metronom*, 1909–10 (DC1); *Das Studio: Tisch mit Gitarre, Frucht und Pfeife*, 1924 (DC66); *Stilleben mit Glas und Zeitung*, (DC58).

Château de Castille, ca.1955, works by Georges Braque, left to right: *Fruit-dish and Glass*, 1912 (No.5); *Still-life with Metronome*, 1909–10 (DC1); *The Studio: Table with Guitar, fruit and pipe*, 1924 (DC66); *Still-life with a Glass and Newspaper*, 1913 (DC58).

taulds aufgestellt hatte: Konzentration auf eine zukunftsträchtige Richtung (anstatt Post-Impressionismus nun Kubismus), weitgehend vertreten durch die grossen Meister (hier also Picasso, Braque, Gris und Léger) und durch beste Beispiele ihres Schaffens. Mit dem Erwerb «schwieriger» kubistischer Werke in der Zwischenkriegszeit stellt er sein spektakuläres Début als Sammler in einen adäquaten historischen Zusammenhang.

In seiner Einleitung im Katalog zur Ausstellung *The Essential Cubism* in der Tate Gallery, betitelt «Early Purchasers of True Cubist Art», hebt Cooper fast dreissig Jahre später die Rolle der Händler und Sammler auf dem Weg der Anerkennung und Wertschätzung von, wie er es peinlich genau definiert, «wahrer kubistischer

dealers and collectors of 1907–20 and then covering "Later Enthusiasts and Collectors", provides not only the historical framework for Cubism, but the background, as well, for his own role as collector.[5] The dispersal of private collections during the twenties and thirties – for instance, those of John Quinn, Pierre Faure, Dr. Reber, or Jacques Zoubaloff – made accessible a number of important pictures to the interested collector. And so, Cooper frames his own historical position:

> *This was the situation at the beginning of the 1930s, as I discovered for myself when I first began to be deeply involved with twentieth-century art, and in particular with the painting of the true Cubists. It was a*

Kunst» hervor. Indem er die «Pioniere» unter den Händlern und Sammlern im Zeitraum von 1907 bis 1920 und dann die «späteren Kunstfreunde und Sammler» würdigt, steckt er nicht nur den historischen Rahmen für den Kubismus allgemein ab, sondern schafft auch einen Hintergrund für sich und seine eigene Rolle als Sammler.[5] Die Veräusserung privater Sammlungen in den zwanziger und dreissiger Jahren – zum Beispiel jene von John Quinn, Pierre Faure, Dr. Reber oder Jacques Zoubaloff – machte dem interessierten Sammler den Erwerb manches wichtigen Werkes möglich. In diesem historischen Kontext umreisst Cooper seine Stellung folgendermassen:

> *Die beginnenden dreissiger Jahre waren, wie ich selbst herausfand, als ich mich intensiv mit der Kunst des 20. Jahrhunderts, speziell mit den Werken wahrer Kubisten, zu beschäftigen anfing, für den Sammler und Käufer besonders günstig, weil der erste Boom zu einer schrecklichen und lang andauernden Baisse verkommen war mit dem Resultat, dass die Preise für die vier Meister des Kubismus, welche in den späten zwanziger Jahren wegen der wachsenden Nachfrage des amerikanischen Markts in die Höhe geschnellt waren, nun wieder fielen. Diese Situation nützte ich, so gut ich konnte, aus und begann 1932 wahre kubistische Werke in der Absicht zu kaufen, eine eigene umfassende Sammlung aufzubauen. Durch diese Tätigkeit, die mir zum lebenslangen Abenteuer wurde, kam ich nicht nur in Kontakt mit den genannten Künstlern (ausser mit Gris, der schon tot war), sondern auch mit vielen der erwähnten Händler und Sammler.*[6]

Cooper machte sich erstaunlich intensiv und speditiv ans Sammeln, nützte günstige Marktlagen aus und setzte sein neuerworbenes Vermögen so geschickt ein, dass er innerhalb nur eines Jahrzehnts eine verblüffend umfassende, exquisite Sammlung zusammenbrachte. Betrachtet man Coopers Sammeltätigkeit, ist tatsächlich weder eine bedeutende Veränderung noch eine

> *favourable moment for a collector to buy because the earlier boom had turned into a terrible and long-lasting slump, with the result that the prices for paintings by the four masters of Cubism had again fallen, having been pushed upwards in the later 1920s by a growing demand for the American market. I took advantage of the situation for myself as best I could and in 1932 began to buy true Cubist paintings with the intention of forming a substantial collection of my own. This pursuit became for me the adventure of a lifetime and led to my coming to know not only the artists concerned (apart from Gris, who was already dead) but also a great many of the dealers and collectors I have mentioned.*[6]

Cooper launched his collection with amazing intensity and rapidity, exploiting favourable market conditions and his new found capital, to establish within the short span of a decade, a collection of staggering depth and sophistication. Indeed, in studying Cooper's collecting, no fascinating metamorphosis or abrupt change is discernable. Rather, the drama unfolds in the thirties when Cooper amassed the core of the Collection reflecting his single-minded focus on what he himself later termed "true Cubism" or the "essential Cubism". Subsequent sales, exchanges or acquisitions were aimed at upgrading and refining the collection, or were simply, the result of mundane considerations such as the need for capital or the lack of space.[7]

Cooper profited from the few years in the 1930s, during which he worked with Freddie Mayor at The Mayor Gallery in London, making contacts with the artists and major collectors and other dealers, as well, which proved important to him in the years that followed.[8] For instance, in April 1936 Cooper organized an exhibition of works from Galerie de l'Effort Moderne. During 1936 and over the next several years he purchased approximately 8 works by Léger from Léonce Rosenberg, the owner of the Galerie. He also, while with Mayor, became acquainted with G. F. Reber

abrupte Abweichung vom Konzept auszumachen, vielmehr entwickelt sich alles folgerichtig, und, noch in den dreissiger Jahren, kommt der feste Kern der Sammlung zusammen, welcher spiegelt, was Cooper später «wahrer» oder «essentieller» Kubismus genannt hat. In der Folge dienten Verkäufe, Tauschgeschäfte oder Erwerbungen der Abrundung oder Qualitätsverbesserung der Sammlung oder wurden einfach nur getätigt aufgrund von Raum- oder Geldmangel oder andern praktischen Überlegungen.[7]

Cooper profitierte auch von seiner Zusammenarbeit mit Freddie Mayor in der gleichnamigen Londoner Galerie in den dreissiger Jahren, kam er doch, was ihm später sehr nützte, in Kontakt mit Künstlern, wichtigen Sammlern und Händlern.[8] Zum Beispiel organisierte er im April 1936 eine Ausstellung mit Werken aus der Galerie de l'Effort Moderne, von deren Besitzer, Léonce Rosenberg, er im selben Jahr, wie auch in den folgenden Jahren, ungefähr acht Légers erwarb. Den Händler und Sammler G. F. Reber, von dem er später manches Werk erstand, lernte er ebenfalls in den wenigen Jahren bei Mayor kennen. Cooper macht es sich zur Aufgabe, Ausstellungen zusammenzustellen, so mit Werken von Cocteau, Klee, Miró, Picasso und den anderen Kubisten.[9] Als er die Mayor Gallery verliess, zog er sein investiertes Kapital in Form von Werken aus den Beständen ab. Einige dieser Werke, darunter Gouachen von Miró, Cocteau-Zeichnungen und Arbeiten von Paul Klee, bildeten eine Basis, die Cooper zu handeln erlaubte, wenn er – was oft geschah – den Kubisten-Kern seiner Sammlung aufstocken wollte.

Die leider unvollständigen Akten der dreissiger Jahre bieten dennoch Einblick in ein Jahrzehnt, das hinsichtlich der Quantität wie der Qualität der Erwerbungen aussergewöhnlich ist; zudem entsteht aufgrund der Provenienz der Werke eine historisch bedeutsame Liste von Sammlern und Händlern.[10]

Unter den frühesten Erwerbungen befindet sich die Bleistiftzeichnung *Frauenkopf, Schatulle und Apfel* von Picasso aus den Jahr 1909 (Nr. 54), 1933 bei der Londoner Arnold Haskell Gallery gekauft. 1934 folgten

the dealer-collector from whom he subsequently purchased many works. Cooper devoted himself to assembling exhibitions of works by Cocteau, Klee, Miró, Picasso, and the other Cubists.[9] When Cooper left the Gallery he withdrew his financial interest in the form of stock. Some of these works, including gouaches by Miró, Cocteau drawings and works by Paul Klee formed a base for Cooper's collection, frequently traded to make another addition to the Cubist core.

An examination of the unfortunately incomplete collection records of the 1930s reveals a decade extraordinary in terms of the sheer volume of acquisition, the quality of the individual objects, but fascinating, as well, because of the sources of the works of art, constituting an historically significant list of collectors and dealers.[10]

Among the earliest acquisitions is the pencil drawing by Picasso, *Head of Woman, Casket and Apple*, 1909, (No. 54) purchased from the Arnold Haskell Gallery in London in 1933. In 1934 two more Picassos followed: a 1909 charcoal and ink, *Head* and a 1901 crayon sketch of a soldier, both purchased from Alfred Flechtheim.[11] The same year Cooper acquired the Léger oil, *Animated landscape: Man with a Dog,* 1921, from Flechtheim.[12] Two more Picassos followed in 1935 from Flechtheim: a 1912 oil, *Still-life with Dead Birds* and a 1905 watercolor, an Ex-Libris for Guillaume Apollinaire.[13]

The collection of Jacques Zoubaloff, sold at auction in Paris at the Hôtel Drouot in November 1935 was an important source for a number of Cooper's purchases: another Léger oil, *Animated landscape: Man with a Dog*, 1921, as well as the following works by Juan Gris: a 1919 oil, *Seated Harlequin*[14], a 1922 gouache, *Harlequin with guitar,* a 1919 pencil drawing of *Seated Harlequin with guitar,* a 1920 pencil drawing, *Still-life: Guitar, Book and Newspaper,* and the 1911 pencil drawing, *Still-life with Cup and Glass* (No. 13). Cooper also acquired three Picassos in 1935: two from André Level at the Galerie Percier, Paris: a 1920 gouache, *Guitar on a table* and a charcoal drawing from the

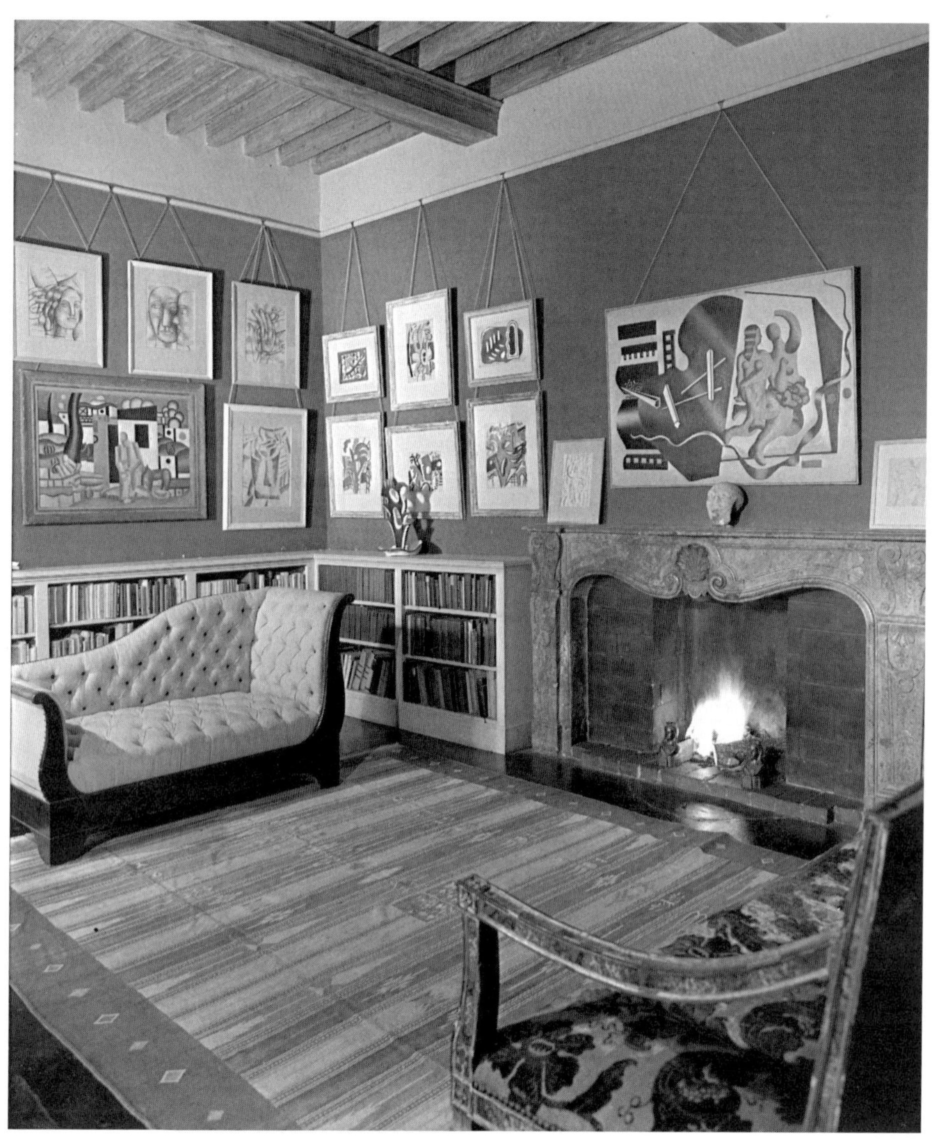

Château de Castille, ca.1955, Werke von Léger, von links nach rechts, obere Reihe: *Ohne Titel* (DC178); *Les deux figures* (DC177); *Ohne Titel* (DC176); *Ohne Titel*, 1936 (DC71); nicht identifiziert. Von links nach rechts, untere Reihe: *Paysage animé*, 1921; *Dessin pour la "Partie de Cartes", Fragment*, 1916–17 (DC91); *Coq bleu* (DC69); *Paysage*, 1937; *Coq rouge*, (DC68); *Studie für "Les foreurs"*, 1916 (DC56); *Deux danseuses*, 1929; *Porträt von Philippon*, 1915 (DC188).

Château de Castille, ca. 1955, works by Léger, left to right at top: *Untitled* (DC178); *Les deux figures* (DC177); *Untitled* (DC176); *Untitled*, 1936 (DC71); *Untitled* (DC 77); unidentified. Left to right at bottom: *Paysage animé*, 1921; *Dessin pour la "Partie de Cartes", Fragment*, 1916–17 (DC91); *Coq bleu* (DC69); *Paysage*, 1937; *Coq rouge*, (DC68); *Study for "Les foreurs"*, 1916 (DC56); *Deux danseuses*, 1929; *Portrait of Philippon*, 1915 (DC188).

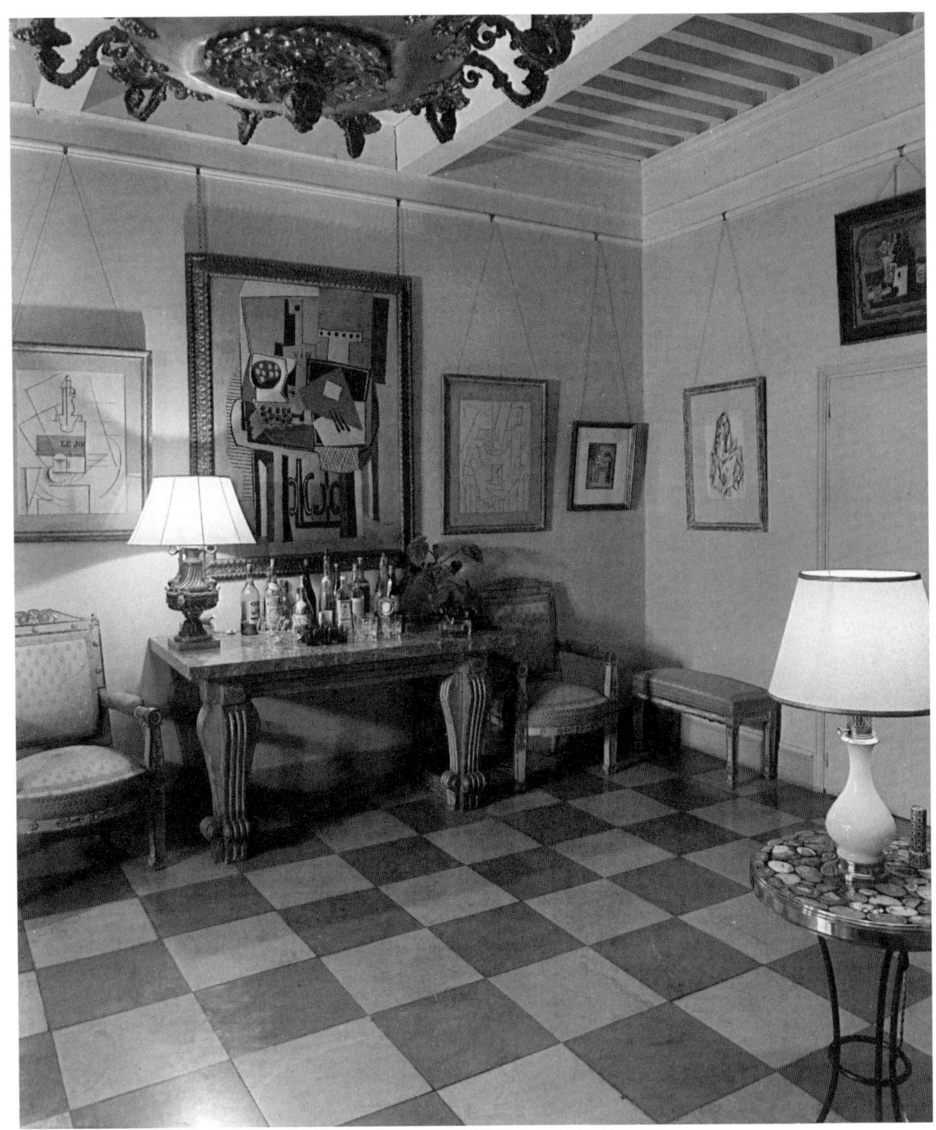

Château de Castille, ca.1955, Werke von Picasso, von links nach rechts: *Flasche, Becher und Zeitung*, 1912–14 (Z II** 397); *Stilleben auf einem Guéridon*, 1922–23 (DC67; Z IV 441); *Stilleben mit Tisch und Birnenschale*, 1912 (No.58); *Gitarre mit Fruchtschale auf einem Tisch*, 1920 (DC100); *Sitzende Frau mit einem Buch*, 1909 (DC40; Z II** 722); *Stilleben mit Girlanden*, 1918 (DC98).

Château de Castille, ca.1955, works by Picasso, left to right: *Bottle, cup and newspaper*, 1912–14 (Z II** 397); *Still-life on a Guéridon*, 1922–23 (DC67; Z IV 441); *Still-life with Table and Dish of Pears*, 1912 (No.58); *Guitar with Fruit-dish on a Table*, 1920 (DC100); *Seated woman with a Book*, 1909 (DC40; Z II** 722); *Still-life with Garlands*, 1918 (DC98).

zwei weitere Picassos: die Kohle/Tusch-Zeichnung *Kopf* von 1909 und die Kreidestudie eines Soldaten von 1901, beide erworben von Alfred Flechtheim,[11] dem Cooper im selben Jahr noch das Ölbild *Paysage animé – L'homme au chien (Belebte Landschaft – Mann mit Hund)*, 1921, von Léger[12] und ein Jahr später zwei weitere Picassos abkaufte, nämlich das Ölbild *Stilleben mit toten Vögeln* von 1912 und ein Aquarell, ein Ex-Libris für Guillaume Apollinaire, von 1905.[13]

Die im November 1935 bei Hôtel Drouot in Paris versteigerte Sammlung von Jacques Zoubaloff war eine wichtige Quelle für Cooper, der noch ein Léger-Ölbild, *Paysage animé – L'homme au chien (Belebte Landschaft – Mann mit Hund)* von 1921 sowie die folgenden Werke von Gris erwarb: *Sitzender Harlekin*, 1919, Öl,[14] *Harlekin mit Gitarre*, 1922, Gouache, und die Bleistiftzeichnungen *Sitzender Harlekin mit Gitarre*, 1919, *Stilleben: Gitarre, Buch und Zeitung*, 1920, und *Stilleben mit Tasse und Glas*, 1911 (Nr. 13). 1935 kaufte Cooper auch drei Picassos: zwei bei André Level von der Galerie Percier, Paris, nämlich die Gouache *Gitarre auf einem Tisch* und die Kohlezeichnung *Der Tisch des Künstlers*, beide von 1920, sowie, von Paul Rosenberg, das Ölbild *Stilleben mit Gitarre und Fruchtschale* von 1932.[15]

1936 kamen in die Sammlung: drei Ölbilder von Braque, drei Ölbilder von Gris zusammen mit einer Aquarell/Kohle-Arbeit, zehn Ölbilder und Gouachen von Léger und drei Arbeiten auf Papier von Picasso.[16] Unter den Ölbildern von Braque befand sich das bedeutende *Stilleben mit Metronom*, 1909/10, erworben vom Londoner Sammler E. L. T. Mesens. Alle drei Ölbilder von Gris stammten aus Kahnweilers Galerie Simon, Paris.[17] Die Aquarell/Kohle-Arbeit *Stilleben: Gitarre und Glas*, 1913, wurde dem Sammler Zak abgekauft. Léonce Rosenberg und die Galerie de l'Effort Moderne waren die Quelle von mindestens vier Léger-Werken aus den Jahren 1913/4, darunter *Nature morte* (Nr. 30)[18]. Ein weiteres Werk mit dem Titel *Contrastes de formes* wurde wieder bei Kahnweilers Galerie Simon erworben.[19] Fünf Werke, von Léger direkt gekauft, kamen nun zur Gouache *Composition* von 1934, wel-

same year, *The Artist's Table* and a 1932 oil, *Still-life with Guitar and Fruit-dish*, from Paul Rosenberg.[15]

1936 saw the acquisition of 3 oils by Braque, 3 Juan Gris oils and one watercolor and charcoal, 10 Léger oils and gouaches and 3 works on paper by Picasso.[16] Among the Braque oils was the important 1909–10, *Still-life with Metronome*, acquired from the collector, E.L.T. Mesens in London. The three oils by Juan Gris were all acquired from Kahnweiler's Galerie Simon, Paris. The watercolor and charcoal, *Still-life: Mandolin and glass*, 1913, was obtained from the collector Zak.[17] Léonce Rosenberg and the Galerie de l'Effort Moderne in Paris was the source for at least four 1913–14 works by Léger, including *Nature morte* (No. 30).[18] Another 1913 *contrastes de formes* was obtained from Kahnweiler's Galerie Simon.[19] Five additional works were obtained directly from the artist joining a 1934 gouache, *Composition,* which Léger had given Cooper already in 1934.[20] The Picassos obtained in 1936 included the ink drawing, *Standing Woman*, 1911–12 (No. 56) purchased from Renou & Colle, Paris.[21]

Cooper was extraordinarily active in 1937. His purchases included three works by Braque: one papier collé and two oils. Works by Juan Gris included two works on paper: a watercolor and charcoal and a pencil drawing as well as four oils. Cooper acquired at least fifteen works by Léger in 1937: seven gouaches, seven works on paper, and one oil. These acquisitions included the drawing for *La Partie de Cartes*, 1916–17 (No. 33). Cooper added 13 works by Picasso to his collection this year: 6 oils, 2 watercolors, 1 gouache, one papier collé, one ink drawing, one pencil drawing and a charcoal.[22] These works include the following works in this exhibition: *Still-life with Table and Dish of Pears*, 1912, *Still-life with Peaches and Playing Cards,* 1914, and *The Cardplayer*, 1914 (Nos. 58, 62, 63). Cooper did infrequently purchase at auction during this year: from Christie's in London, Hôtel Drouot, Paris, or Rain's Auction House in New York. His primary sources were dealers and a few private collectors, in London, Paris or

che der Künstler Cooper schon im Entstehungsjahr gegeben hatte.[20] Unter den 1936 erworbenen Picassos befand sich auch die Tuschzeichnung *Stehende Frau* von 1911/12 (Nr. 56), gekauft bei Renou & Colle, Paris.[21]

1937 war Cooper aussergewöhnlich aktiv; unter den Käufen waren drei Braques, ein Papier collé und zwei Ölbilder, sowie sechs Gris, eine Aquarell/Kohle- und eine Bleistift-Arbeit auf Papier und vier Ölbilder. Im selben Jahr kamen mindestens fünfzehn Légers in die Sammlung: sieben Gouachen, sieben Arbeiten auf Papier und ein Ölbild; unter diesen Werken befand sich auch die Zeichnung zu *La Partie de Cartes (Die Kartenspieler)* von 1916/7 (Nr. 33). Neuerwerbungen waren auch dreizehn Picassos: sechs Ölbilder, zwei Aquarelle, eine Gouache, ein Papier collé sowie je eine

the United States. He purchased from Jeanne Bucher Galerie, Paris, Earl Horter, Philadelphia, Pierre Loeb, Paris, Pierre Matisse, New York, G. F. Reber, Lausanne, Renou et Colle, Paris, Léonce Rosenberg, Paris, Galerie Simon, Paris, the Zak Collection, and Zwemmer Gallery, London.

The collector/dealer, Gottlieb Friedrich Reber, emerges as one of Cooper's most crucial sources of Cubist pictures, especially of works by Picasso. In 1938 Cooper matched his 6 purchases of the previous year, with five additional Picassos and one work by Juan Gris.[23] The 5 works by Picasso included: *Woman and Harlequin*, 1915, (No. 65), and *Still-life: mandolin and Gueridon*, 1921 (No. 73).[24] The following year Cooper obtained 4 additional Picassos from Reber including: *Standing female nude*, 1906–07, (No. 50),

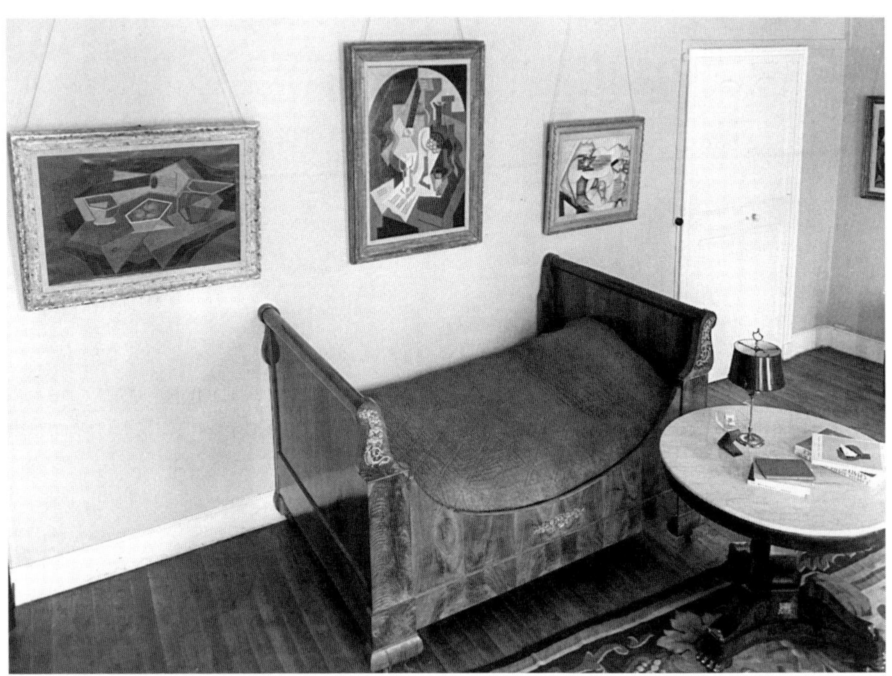

Château de Castille, ca.1955, Werke von Juan Gris, von links nach rechts: *Stilleben: Gitarre, Dreieck und Fruchtschale*, 1926 (DC49); *Stilleben mit Mandoline*, 1919 (DC85); *Stilleben: Gitarre und Glas*, 1913.

Château de Castille, ca.1955, works by Juan Gris, left to right: *Still-life: Guitar, Set-Square and Fruit-dish*, 1926 (DC49); *Still-life with Mandoline*, 1919 (DC85); *Still-life: Guitar and Glass*, 1913.

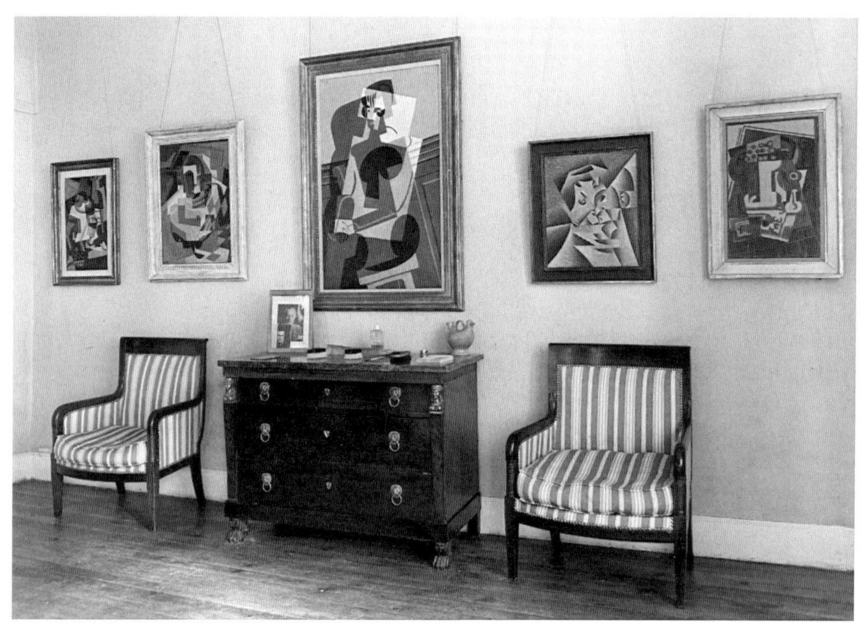

Château de Castille, ca.1955, Werke von Juan Gris, von links nach rechts: *Fruchtschale und Weinflasche*, 1917 (DC107); *Harlekin*, 1917; *Porträt von Madame Josette Gris*, 1916 (DC84); *Porträt der Mutter des Künstlers*, 1912 (DC97); *Stilleben mit Fruchtschale*, 1918.

Château de Castille, ca.1955, works by Juan Gris, left to right: *Fruit-dish and Bottle of Beaune*, 1917 (DC107); *Harlequin*, 1917; *Portrait of Madame Josette Gris*, 1916 (DC84); *Portrait of the Artist's Mother*, 1912 (DC97); Still-life with Fruit-dish, 1918.

Tusch-, Bleistift- und Kohlezeichnung.[22] Daraus stammen die folgenden Werke in dieser Ausstellung: *Stilleben mit Tisch und Birnenschale*, 1912, *Stilleben mit Pfirsichen und Spielkarten*, 1914, und *Der Kartenspieler* (Nr. 58, 62, 63) aus demselben Jahr. Gelegentlich kaufte Cooper in dieser Zeit auch auf Auktionen, so bei Christie's in London, bei Hôtel Drouot, Paris, oder bei Rain's Auction House, New York. Hauptquelle für ihn aber waren Händler sowie einige private Sammler in London, Paris oder den Vereinigten Staaten. Er kaufte bei der Jeanne Bucher Galerie, Paris, von Earl Horter, Philadelphia, Pierre Loeb, Paris, Pierre Matisse, New York, G. F. Reber, Lausanne, bei Renou & Colle, Paris, bei der Galerie Simon, Paris, der Zak Collection und der Zwemmer Gallery, London.

Wohl eine von Coopers wichtigsten Quellen war

and *Bottle of Bass and Guitar*, 1912 (No. 60).[25] In 1939 Cooper purchased, as well, a Juan Gris oil, *Guitar on a Table*, 1916. In addition, in 1945, Cooper purchased another Gris oil, *Landscape at Beaulieu*, 1916 and two works by Léger including: *Study for Still-life with Bust*, 1924 (No. 41).[26]

Cooper had apparently met Reber during his years at the Mayor Gallery,in London, in the early thirties. Reber, a German collector/dealer, had already before 1914 formed a major collection of French 19th Century masters. It was after 1921 that he began to exchange this material in order to form a major collection of Cubist works of art and later works by Picasso, Braque, Léger and Gris.[27]

In addition to this string of purchases from Reber, Cooper made, in the final years of this decade, other

der Sammler und Händler Gottlieb Friedrich Reber, besonders was Werke von Picasso betrifft; fünf solche kamen 1938 von ihm – nebst einem Werk von Gris[23] –; sie ergänzten die sechs Picassos, die Cooper schon im Vorjahr erworben hatte. Unter den genannten fünf befanden sich: *Frau und Harlekin*, 1915 (Nr. 65) und *Stilleben mit Mandoline auf einem Tisch*, 1921 (Nr. 73).[24] Im folgenden Jahr kaufte Cooper vier weitere Picassos von Reber, darunter *Stehender weiblicher Akt* von 1906/7 (Nr. 50) und *Eine Flasche «Bass» und Gitarre* von 1912 (Nr. 60).[25] 1939 erwarb er auch ein Ölbild von Juan Gris, *Gitarre auf einem Tisch* von 1916; 1945 folgte ein weiteres Ölbild von Gris, *Landschaft bei Beaulieu*, 1916, sowie zwei Werke von Léger; dabei war die *Studie für «Stilleben mit Büste»* von 1924 (Nr. 41).[26]

Offenbar wurde Cooper mit dem Deutschen Reber während seinen Jahren – es waren die frühen dreissiger – in der Londoner Mayor Gallery bekannt. Reber hatte schon vor 1914 eine bedeutende Sammlung von französischer Kunst des 19. Jahrhunderts aufgebaut. Nach 1921 aber begann er diese Bestände zu veräussern, um eine ebenso bedeutende Sammlung kubistischer Kunst und späterer Werke von Picasso, Braque, Léger und Gris zusammenbringen zu können.[27]

Neben dieser Reihe von Werken, welche er von Reber erworben hatte, fügte Cooper in den letzten Jahren dieses Jahrzehnts noch weitere seiner Sammlung hinzu. 1938 wurde in der Mayor Gallery ein bedeutendes Ölbild von Braque, *Landschaft bei La Ciotat*, von 1907 (nun in der Sammlung des Museum of Modern Art, New York) gekauft. Aus gleicher Quelle stammten auch drei Werke von Gris[28] und, aus der Galerie Jeanne Bucher, zwei Bleistiftzeichnungen desselben Künstlers, nämlich *Stilleben: Teekanne und Glas*, 1916 (Nr. 16), und *Stilleben: Der Tabaksbeutel*, 1918 (Nr. 19). Dazu kamen noch, ebenfalls von Gris, zwei bedeutende Ölbilder: *Häuser an der Place Ravignan*, 1911, von der Galerie Percier (André Level), und *Porträt der Mutter des Künstlers*, 1912, von der Galerie de Beaune, Paris, weiter, im Jahr 1938, von der Galerie Simon, vier Légers, darunter *Stehender Akt*, 1911 (Nr. 28).[29] Aus

additions to his collection, as well. In 1938, the major Braque oil, *Landscape at la Ciotat*, 1907, (presently in the collection, Museum of Modern Art, New York) was purchased from the Mayor Gallery. The Mayor Gallery was the source, as well, for three works by Juan Gris.[28] From the Galerie Jeanne Bucher came two Gris pencil drawings: *Still-life: Teapot and Glass*, 1916, (No. 16) and *Still-life: The Tobacco pouch*, 1918, (No. 19). In addition, he acquired two major Gris oils: *Houses in the Place Ravignan*, 1911, from Galerie Percier, André Level and *Portrait of the Artist's Mother*, 1912, from Galerie de Beaune, Paris. Four Légers entered the collection in 1938, including *Standing nude*, 1911, (No. 28) from Galerie Simon.[29] *Two Figures*, 1920, (No. 35) was purchased, as well, in 1938, from an undetermined source. Two Picassos were purchased from Pierre Loeb in 1938 including *Head of a Man*, 1908, (No. 52).[30]

Among Cooper's significant purchases in 1939, beyond those from Reber already mentioned was the Juan Gris, *Still-life with Bottle and Cigars*, 1912, (No. 14) from Ronald Fleming.[31]

Cooper's collecting by no means ceased in 1940. Indeed, he continued to assiduously pursue those specific works which would complement and complete the collection he had already, so rapidly, amassed. On the other hand, subsequent acquisitions would never match the staggering volume of purchases during the 1930s. Important works by Georges Braque were added in the forties and fifties. For instance, *Big Trees at l'Estaque*, 1908, oil, was purchased from Paul Adamidi Frasheri Bey in 1945. The first Cubist collage, *Fruit-dish and Glass*, 1912, was purchased in 1946 (No. 5). Two ink drawings which were reproduced as illustrations in Reverdy's periodical *Nord-Sud*, *Still-life: Fruit-dish and Newspaper*, 1919, and *Still-life with Guitar on a Table*, 1917, entered the collection respectively in 1943 from the Redfern Gallery, London and in 1946 from St. George's Gallery, London (Nos. 7 and 6). Several major oil paintings followed during the fifties.[32] From the Marlborough Gallery, London, in 1955, came four

unbestimmter Quelle stammten die ebenfalls 1938 erworbenen *Zwei Figuren* von Léger, 1920 (Nr. 35). Im gleichen Jahr wurden von Pierre Loeb noch zwei Picassos gekauft; der eine war *Männerkopf*, 1908 (Nr. 52).[30]

Zu Coopers wichtigen Käufen des Jahres 1939, abgesehen von den schon erwähnten von Reber, gehörte Gris' *Stilleben mit Flasche und Zigarren*, 1912 (Nr. 14), erworben von Roland Fleming.[31]

Natürlich hörte auch 1940 Cooper nicht auf zu sammeln, ja er blieb unablässig auf der Suche nach ganz bestimmten Werken, die seine Sammlung, die er schon – und zwar so rasch – zusammengebracht hatte, ergänzen und vervollständigen würden. Vermochten die ab jetzt gemachten Erwerbungen jene der dreissiger Jahre an schierer Quantität auch nie zu übertreffen, so kamen doch in den vierziger und fünfziger Jahren wichtige Werke von Braque hinzu; so etwa wurde 1945 von Paul Adamidi Frasheri Bey das Ölbild *Grosse Bäume bei L'Estaque* von 1908 gekauft, und 1946 kam die erste kubistische Collage, *Fruchtschale und Glas*, 1912 (Nr. 5), in die Sammlung. Zwei Tuschzeichnungen, die als Illustrationen in Reverdys Zeitschrift *Nord–Sud* erschienen waren, nämlich *Stilleben: Fruchtschale und Zeitung*, 1919, und *Stilleben mit Gitarre auf einem Tisch*, 1917, wurden 1943 bei der Redfern Gallery, London, respektive 1946 bei der St. George's Gallery, London, erworben (Nr. 7 und 6). In den fünfziger Jahren folgten mehrere bedeutende Ölbilder[32], und 1955 kamen von der Londoner Marlborough Gallery vier wichtige Arbeiten auf Papier, darunter *Stehender Akt*, 1907 (Nr. 1), und *Stilleben mit Würfel*, 1912 (Nr. 4).[33]

1950 erstand Cooper von Miss Evie Hone aus Rathfarnham, Irland, das bedeutende Ölbild *Gitarre auf einem Stuhl* von 1913.[34] Mindestens vier der Zeichnungen in dieser Ausstellung (Nr. 10, 11, 17 und 18) wurden in den fünfziger Jahren und sogar noch bis 1966 erworben.

Auch Coopers Léger-Bestände wuchsen von den vierziger zu den sechziger Jahren beständig. Einige dieser Werke sind in der Ausstellung unter den Num-

important works on paper including: *Standing Nude*, 1907, (No. 1), and *Still-life with Dice*, 1912 (No. 4).[33]

In 1950 Cooper purchased the important Juan Gris oil, *Guitar on a chair*, 1913, from Miss Evie Hone, in Rathfarnham, Ireland.[34] At least four of the drawings in this exhibition (Nos. 10, 11, 17 and 18) were purchased in the 1950s and as late as 1966.

Similarly, Cooper's Léger holdings continued to grow from the forties through the seventies. Some of the works included in this exhibition, purchased during these decades, include (Nos. 29, 31, 37, 39, 41, and 42). Of course, in 1954 Cooper commissioned the monumental *Trapeze Artists* for the staircase at the Château de Castille (now in the National Gallery of Australia).[35]

Throughout the forties on through the seventies, works by Picasso continued to flow into the collection in the form of major works, as well as prints, ceramic plates, sculptures and personal mementos. *Still-life with Chocolate Pot*, 1909, (No. 53) was purchased from Reid & Lefevre, London, 1953. *Bearded Man playing a Guitar*, 1914, *Composition with Violin*, 1912, *Still-life: Glass and Bottle of Bass*, 1914, and *Boy with a Popsicle, 1938*, (Nos. 64, 59, 61 and 74) were all purchased in the 1950s. The *Study for the "Demoiselles d'Avignon"* (now in the Kunstmuseum, Basel, No. 51) was given to Cooper by the artist in 1959. In 1962–63 the loggia wall in the garden at the Château of Castille, was decorated with subjects derived from Picasso's notebooks (Nos. 75, 76, 77, 79 and 80). In 1978 Cooper purchased a series of watercolors, letters and archival material as well, which document Picasso's love affair in 1916 with Mlle. Gaby Lespinasse (Nos. 66, 67 and 68). The 1920, *Pierrot and Harlequin*, (No. 71) was purchased at Sothebys, London, at the Paul Rosenberg sale in 1979. One of Cooper's last purchases was the 1909 *Still life: Sugar Bowl and Fan* (No. 55), at Sothebys, New York, November 1983.[36]

Cooper's collection was by no means devoted exclusively to the four major Cubists. Indeed, the Collection reflects the broadest notion of Cubism, as

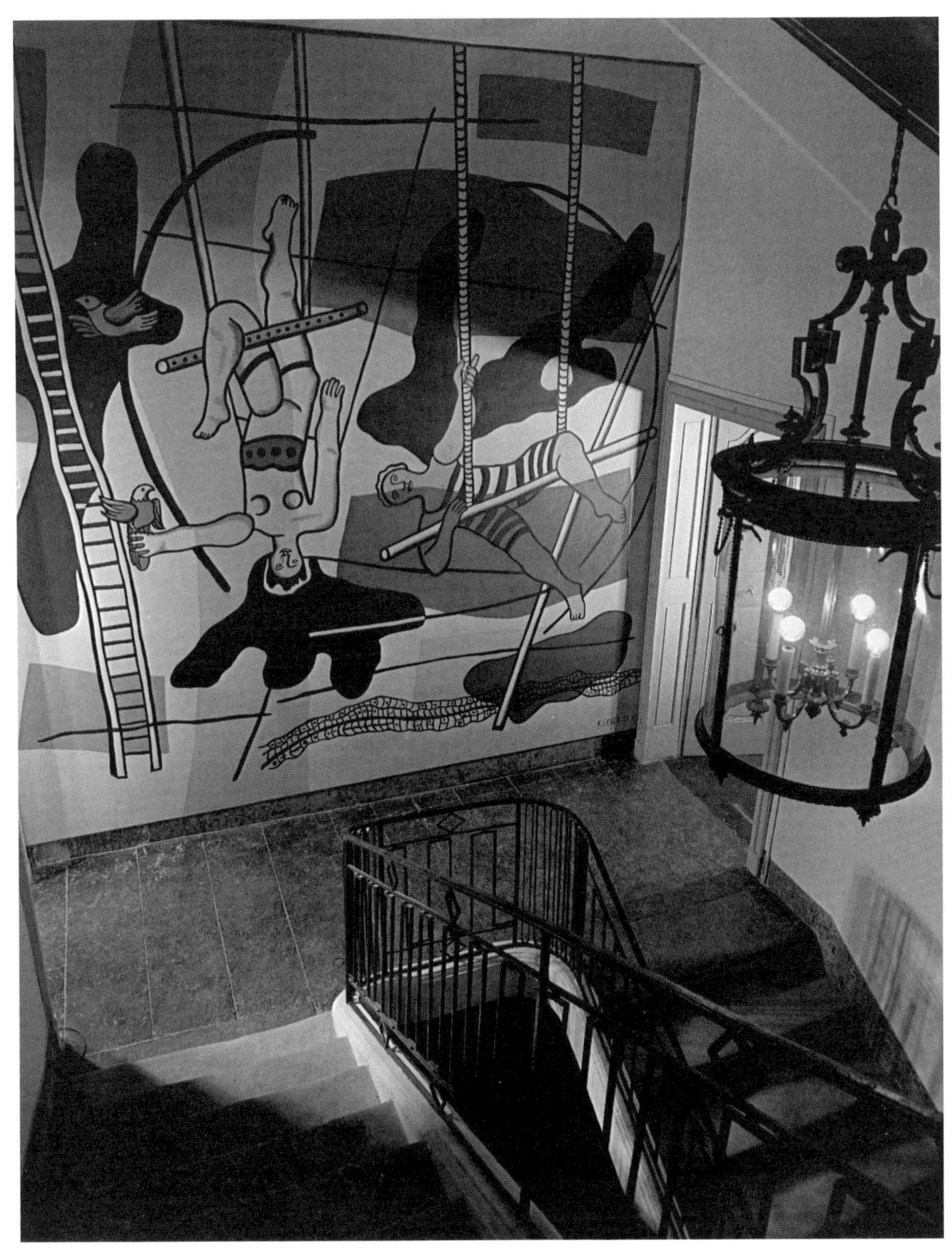

Château de Castille, ca.1955, Fernand Léger, *Der Trapezkünstler*, 1951.

Château de Castille, ca.1955, Fernand Léger, *The Trapeze Artists*, 1951.

mern 29, 31, 37, 39, 41 und 42 zu finden. Nicht vergessen seien die monumentalen *Trapezkünstler*, welche Cooper 1954 für das Treppenhaus auf Schloss Castille in Auftrag gab und die sich heute in der National Gallery of Australia befinden.[35]

Von den vierziger bis zum Ende der siebziger Jahre strömten unablässig Werke von Picasso in die Sammlung: grössere Arbeiten wie auch Graphik, Keramik, plastische Werke und persönliche Erinnerungsstücke. *Stilleben mit Schokoladenkanne*, 1909 (Nr. 53), wurde 1953 bei Reid & Lefevre, London, erworben; ebenfalls in den fünfziger Jahren *Bärtiger Mann, Gitarre spielend*, 1914, *Komposition mit Violine*, 1912, *Stilleben: Glas und eine Flasche «Bass»*, 1914, und *Knabe mit Eislutscher*, 1938 (Nr. 64, 59, 61 und 74). 1959 erhielt Cooper vom Künstler die *Studie zu den «Demoiselles d'Avignon»* (heute Kunstmuseum Basel) (Nr. 51). In den Jahren 1962–63 wurde die Loggia-Wand des Schlosses mit Sujets aus Picassos Skizzenbüchern gestaltet (s. Nr. 75, 76, 77, 79 und 80). 1978 erwarb Cooper eine Serie von Aquarellen sowie Briefe und Materialien, welche Picassos Liebesaffäre mit Gaby Lespinasse im Jahre 1916 dokumentieren (s. Nr. 66, 67 und 68). *Pierrot und Harlekin* von 1920 (Nr. 71) wurde in London auf der Sotheby-Auktion der Sammlung Paul Rosenberg 1979 erstanden. Eine von Coopers letzten Erwerbungen – vom November 1983, ebenfalls bei Sotheby, New York – war das *Stilleben: Zuckerdose und Fächer* von 1909 (Nr. 55).[36]

Coopers Sammlung war alles andere als nur auf die vier Hauptkubisten beschränkt, ja sie spiegelt sogar einen überaus weiten Kubismus-Begriff, was zum Beispiel in der Ausstellung *The Cubist Epoch* im Los Angeles County Museum und im Metropolitan Museum of Art 1970–71 zum Ausdruck kam. So zeigt denn auch diese Ausstellung zwei Arbeiten auf Papier von Henri Laurens: *Kopf*, 1919, und *Kubistischer Kopf*, 1919 (Nr. 26 und 27). Cooper besass auch mehrere plastische Werke dieses Künstlers.[37] Die Ausweitung ins Internationale, wie sie Cooper für den Kubismus in *The Cubist Epoch* leistete, spiegelt auch die in diese Ausstellung aufgenommene

presented, for instance, in *The Cubist Epoch*, exhibition at the Los Angeles County Museum and The Metropolitan Museum of Art in 1970–71. The present exhibition includes two works on paper by Henri Laurens: *Head*, 1919, and *Cubist Head*, 1919, (Nos. 26 and 27). Cooper owned, as well, several sculptures by Laurens.[37] Similarly, the small drawing by Otto Gutfreund included in this exhibition (No. 21) reflects the international scope which Cooper brought to Cubism in *The Cubist Epoch*. Gutfreund, a Czech sculptor, was influenced by the Cubists, especially the sculpture of Laurens and Lipchitz.[38]

Cooper's collection, in fact, extended far beyond Cubism, including works by a broad array of artists. A 1952 letter to Curt Valentin heralds the "nearing completion" of the Château de Castille, mentioning three rooms devoted to Picasso, and one each: Gris, Léger, Miró and Klee, and two or three others devoted to assorted artists of the modern school.[39]

Indeed, pursuing an interest which developed while working at the Mayor Gallery, Cooper formed a significant collection of works by Klee and Miró. Much of this material was, over the years, gradually traded or sold in the process of upgrading and refining the Cubist collection. The room of Mirós at the Château de Castille in the fifties dwindled to two works: *Paysan Catalan au repos (Catalan Peasant Resting)*, 1936 and the maquette for *Programme, Ballets Russes de Monte-Carlo*, 1933 (No. 49).[40] Similarly, now only three works by Paul Klee remain in the collection: *Der Berg der heiligen Katze*, 1923, *Seiltänzer*, 1923 and *Blume und Früchte*, 1927 (Nos. 23, 24 and 25), the others having been exchanged or sold in order to enhance the Cubist collection.[41] Cooper's serious interest in Klee is also evident in his bibliography, specifically in the 1949 monograph *Paul Klee*, published by Penguin.[42]

The "assorted masters of the modern school", very often artists with whom Cooper was personally acquainted, included: César, Cocteau, Giacometti, Guttuso, Hockney, Hugo, Marini, Masson, Matisse, Modigliani, de Staël, and Sutherland and Ubac.[43] It

kleine Zeichnung von Otto Gutfreund (Nr. 21), einem tschechischen Bildhauer, der von den Kubisten, besonders von Laurens und Lipchitz, beeinflusst war.[38]

Eigentlich ging Coopers Sammlung, da sie ein breites Spektrum von Künstlern umfasste, weit über den Kubismus hinaus. In einem Brief von 1952 an Curt Valentin, in dem die «baldige Fertigstellung» von Schloss Castille angekündigt wird, erwähnt Cooper drei Picasso-Räume, je einen Gris-, Léger-, Miró- und Klee-Raum sowie zwei, drei andere, in denen verschiedene Künstler der Moderne vereint seien.[39]

Tatsächlich verfolgte er ein Interesse, das auf die Zeit seiner Arbeit in der Mayor Gallery zurückging, weiter und brachte eine bedeutende Sammlung von Werken Klees und Mirós zusammen. Vieles davon wurde über die Jahre hinweg getauscht oder verkauft zugunsten der Kubisten-Sammlung und der Steigerung ihrer Qualität. Von den Werken, die der Miró-Raum auf Schloss Castille einst beherbergte, blieben gerade noch zwei: *Paysan catalan au repos (Rastender katalanischer Bauer)*, 1936, und *Maquette «programme ballets russes de Monte-Carlo»*, 1933 (Nr. 49).[40] Ähnlich erging es den Klees: nur noch drei befinden sich nun in der Sammlung, nämlich *Der Berg der heiligen Katze*, 1923, *Seiltänzer*, 1923, und *Blume und Früchte*, 1927 (Nr. 23, 24 und 25); die übrigen waren eingetauscht oder verkauft worden.[41] Coopers ernsthaftes Interesse an Klee zeigt sich auch in seinen Schriften, speziell in der 1949 als Penguin-Buch erschienenen Monographie *Paul Klee*.[42]

Unter den «verschiedenen Künstlern der Moderne» fanden sich zumeist solche, mit denen Cooper persönlich bekannt war, so César, Cocteau, Giacometti, Guttuso, Hockney, Hugo, Marini, Masson, Matisse, Modigliani, de Staël, Sutherland und Ubac.[43] Diese Liste liest sich wohl keineswegs zufällig so – spiegelt also nicht einfach Bekanntschaften und Freundschaften, die zufällig entstanden –, sondern sie bezeugt recht eigentlich Coopers vorherrschendes Interesse am Figurativen im Gegensatz zum rein Abstrakten.[44] Nicht dass Cooper einfach nur Werke dieser Künstler sammelte oder von ihnen Geschenke oder Erinnerungs-

seems, however, that this roster of artists is not random, that is, does not merely reflect the coincidence of acquaintance and friendship, but does bespeak Cooper's dominant interest in the figurative as opposed to the purely abstract.[44] Very frequently Cooper not only collected works by these artists, or received mementos or gifts, but also wrote books, catalogues or articles about their works.[45]

It is worthwhile to discuss briefly Cooper's relationship to Nicolas de Staël and to Graham Sutherland. Cooper came to know de Staël quite well while living in Argilliers. In a letter to Curt Valentin he writes: "our new chum here is Nicolas de Staël, who lives here and calls about once a week. Despite his painting which I find ridiculous and horrible, he is actually very nice. And he seems to be making a lot of money."[46] In light of this rather cynical comment, it is ironic that de Staël became an element in "The Tate Controversy". Sutherland and Cooper both resigned in 1956 from a committee planning an exhibition of the artist's work at the Whitechapel Gallery, because John Rothenstein, Director of the Tate Gallery, had also been appointed to that committee. Though Cooper articulated his withdrawal in terms of a defense of the recently deceased de Staël, it was clearly but another episode in a long standing feud with Rothenstein. This was a very public quarrel indeed, involving investigations of the Museum by the House of Commons and the Treasury. Another aspect of this affair was Sutherland's resignation in 1954 from his position as trustee of the Tate.[47] The most notorious incident surely, receiving abundant and amusing coverage in the press, occurred on November 3, 1954 at the opening of a Diaghilev exhibition at Forbes House, at which time, Rothenstein was provoked to punch Cooper in the jaw.

It would seem, therefore, that Cooper had a close relationship with his comrade-in-arms, Sutherland. Sutherland painted a major portrait of Cooper in 1967, the same year as the retrospective exhibition at the Haus der Kunst in Munich, for which Cooper contributed an essay. A pencil study for this portrait is

stücke erhielt, vielmehr – und das war sehr oft der Fall – schrieb er Bücher, Katalogbeiträge und Artikel über ihr Schaffen.[45]

Lohnend ist, in aller Kürze über Coopers Beziehung zu Nicolas de Staël und Graham Sutherland zu sprechen. Als Cooper in Argilliers lebte, lernte er de Staël ziemlich gut kennen. In einem Brief an Curt Valentin schreibt er: «Unser neuer Kamerad hier ist Nicolas de Staël, er lebt hier und kommt ungefähr einmal die Woche vorbei. Trotz seiner Malerei, die ich absurd und entsetzlich finde, ist er eigentlich sehr nett. Und anscheinend verdient er einen Haufen Geld.»[46] Hinsichtlich dieser doch ziemlich bissigen Bemerkung scheint es Ironie des Schicksals zu sein, dass de Staël in der «Tate-Kontroverse» eine Rolle spielte. 1956 traten Sutherland und Cooper aus dem Planungskomitee für eine de Staël-Ausstellung in der Whitechapel Gallery aus, weil John Rothenstein, der Direktor der Tate Gallery, auch in diese Kommission berufen worden war. Obwohl Cooper deutlich sagte, sein Austritt sei ein Zeichen der Solidarität mit dem kürzlich verstorbenen Künstler, war dies doch offensichtlich nur eine weitere Episode der schon lange andauernden Fehde mit Rothenstein, eines von wahrlich grosser Publizität begleiteten Streits, im Laufe dessen es auch zu Untersuchungen durch das Unterhaus und das Finanzministerium kam. Ein weiterer Aspekt dieser Affäre war 1954 der Rücktritt von Graham Sutherland als Bevollmächtigter der Tate Gallery.[47] Das bekannteste der unrühmlichen Ereignisse – von der Presse ausführlich und mit Witz abgehandelt – fand am 3. November 1954 an der Eröffnung einer Diaghilew-Ausstellung im Forbes House statt, als sich Rothenstein so provoziert fühlte, dass er Cooper einen Kinnhaken versetzte.

Man sollte also meinen, dass Cooper in sehr enger Beziehung zu seinem Kampfgefährten Sutherland stand. Der Künstler malte auch 1967 ein grösseres Porträt von ihm, im selben Jahr also, da er eine Retrospektive im Haus der Kunst in München hatte, für die Cooper einen Aufsatz schrieb. Eine Bleistiftstudie zum erwähnten Porträt befindet sich in dieser Ausstellung (Nr. 81).

included in this exhibition (No. 81). Their friendship, however, deteriorated into a vituperative and public quarrel. This profound shift in opinion is clear in the contrast between Cooper's earlier writings on Sutherland and an unpublished essay, probably written in 1978. The latter, focused as a review of an exhibition, *Portraits by Graham Sutherland*, organized by John Hayes at the National Portrait Gallery in June 1977, scathingly attacks Sutherland's art and character, and particularly disowns his own portrait by the artist.[48]

Cooper had, as well, a profound and sustained interest in art of the nineteenth century, manifest most of all in his extensive writings. At his death he had nearly completed a revised catalogue raisonné of the paintings of Paul Gauguin. His bibliography, for instance, includes numerous articles on and reviews concerning Cézanne.[49] The collection, however, maintained its focus on the 20th century and the Cubists in particular. He did briefly own a work by Cézanne, an oil by Courbet, a drawing by Delacroix, as well as two small bronzes by Daumier and 35 portrait medals by David d'Angers.[50]

Like Cooper's collection, his concept of Cubism emerged in sophisticated form early on, and though refined, was not essentially altered in later years. His notion of Cubism might best be described as hierarchical. He insisted upon the uniqueness and personal significance of the contributions of Picasso and Braque. He did, however, recognize Gris and Léger too, but in a more limited way, as true Cubists. Other artists were relegated to a entirely different and decidedly lesser plateau. Thereon, Cooper based his tenet that Cubism was not a style, and could therefore never be successfully adopted by other artists, nor transformed into the idiom of a school. Cooper's insistence upon the intuitive, non-formulaic essence of Cubism, precludes, as well, philosophical or theoretical interpretations. The quintessence of Cubism, in Cooper's formal analysis, is the shift in 1911 from a perceptual to a conceptual approach to reality. Cooper attributed great significance to the development of papier collé in late 1912,

Die Freundschaft gerann aber zu einem gehässigen und in aller Öffentlichkeit geführten Streit. Dieser tiefgehende Gesinnungswandel wird denn auch deutlich in der Gegensätzlichkeit von Coopers früheren Schriften über Sutherland und einem wahrscheinlich 1978 geschriebenen und unpublizierten Aufsatz; in diesem – gedacht als Besprechung der von John Hayes in der National Portrait Gallery realisierten Ausstellung *Portraits by Graham Sutherland* im Juni 1977 – reitet Cooper eine verletzende Attacke gegen Sutherlands Kunst und Charakter und erkennt vor allem seinem Porträt alle Qualitäten ab.[48]

Cooper besass auch ein tiefes und nie nachlassendes Interesse an der Kunst des 19. Jahrhunderts, was vor allem in seinen zahlreichen Schriften ersichtlich wird. Bei seinem Tode hatte er beinahe den revidierten Catalogue Raisonné der Malerei von Paul Gauguin fertiggestellt. Auch finden sich, zum Beispiel, etliche Artikel und Besprechungen zu Cézanne.[49] Die Sammlung allerdings konzentrierte sich weiterhin auf das 20. Jahrhundert und im speziellen auf die Kubisten. Cooper besass jedoch kurze Zeit ein Werk von Cézanne sowie ein Ölbild von Courbet, eine Delacroix-Zeichnung, zwei kleine Bronzen von Daumier und 35 Porträtmedaillen von David d'Angers.[50]

Anspruchsvoll war von Anfang an nicht nur Coopers Sammlung, sondern auch seine Auffassung von Kubismus, die, obwohl sie noch differenziert wurde, sich doch im wesentlichen in den späteren Jahren nicht veränderte. Sie kann am besten als hierarchisch beschrieben werden. Cooper besteht auf der Einzigartigkeit und der individuellen Bedeutung von Picasso und Braque. Zwar erkennt er auch Gris und Léger als wahre Kubisten an, allerdings in beschränkterem Masse. Andere Künstler werden auf einen gänzlich verschiedenen und entschieden minderen Platz verwiesen. Coopers Überzeugung war nämlich, dass der Kubismus kein Stil sei und dass er deshalb auch nicht von andern Künstlern mit Erfolg übernommen werden, noch eine Schule begründen könne. Coopers Insistieren auf dem intuitiven Wesen des Kubismus, dem jede Formel-

insisting on Braque's innovatory role in the exploration of this new technique. These points are clearly presented in the major publications *The Cubist Epoch*, 1971 and *The Essential Cubism*, 1983. They are articulated however, already in Cooper's earlier writings, in catalogues, articles and reviews.

In his 1955 review of Christopher Gray's book, *Cubist Aesthetic Theories*, Cooper emphasizes the crucial difference between the four major Cubists and their followers: "Had Mr. Gray devoted more time to studying the evolution of the Cubist movement, he would have seen that the group of Braque, Gris, Léger and Picasso stands in contrast to the group of La Section d'Or around Gleizes, Metzinger, Delaunay and Villon, not least because, as the name implies, the latter were indeed, guided by theory and mathematical calculation, whereas the former relied on intuition."[51]

Cooper nearly mythologizes the creation of Picasso and Braque, likening their collaboration between the fall of 1909 and the spring of 1913, with that of Monet and Renoir between 1868 and 1874.[52] Gris ("was accepted by the two originators as a Cubist painter in their own sense of the term") and Léger ("can be said to have painted a series of Cubist works") were only cautiously accepted by Cooper as "true" Cubists.[53] The artists of the Cubist Movement (he names Gleizes, Villon, Hayden, Marcoussis, Metzinger, Lhote and Le Fauconnier) are dismissed, "in terms of Cubism, were pathetic".[54]

Cooper took great pains to define the time period and evolutionary phases of Cubism, eschewing, however, the traditional nomenclature ("analytic", "hermetic", "synthetic", "rococo") which implied distinct stylistic developments.

> *With today's hindsight, I see an extensive movement growing up around "true" Cubism, developing and changing fast, and then falling apart. Therefore, to my mind, the divisions which count are historical rather than stylistic and may be said even to cut across the stylistic phases. For that reason I prefer to borrow the*

haftigkeit fremd sei, schliesst auch theoretische oder philosophische Interpretationen aus. Die Quintessenz des Kubismus liegt, nach Coopers formaler Analyse, im Wandel von einer perzeptionellen zu einer konzeptionellen Sicht der «Wirklichkeit». Für ihn war die Entwicklung des Papier collé Ende 1912 von grosser Bedeutung, und er bestand auf Braques führender Rolle im Erforschen dieser neuen Technik. All dies wurde klar dargelegt in den zwei grossen Publikationen *The Cubist Epoch* von 1971 und *The Essential Cubism* von 1983, war aber auch schon in Coopers früheren Schriften, in Katalogen, Artikeln und Besprechungen formuliert worden.

In seiner 1955 erschienenen Besprechung von Christopher Grays Buch *Cubist Aesthetic Theories* betont Cooper den entscheidenden Unterschied zwischen den vier Haupt-Kubisten und ihren Anhängern oder Nachfolgern: «Hätte Herr Gray der Entstehung der kubistischen Richtung mehr Zeit gewidmet, hätte er erkannt, dass Braque, Gris, Léger und Picasso sich völlig von der Gruppe La Section d'Or um Gleizes, Metzinger, Delaunay und Villon unterscheiden, nicht zuletzt weil, wie der Name Goldener Schnitt schon impliziert, diese sich an Theorie und mathematische Berechnung hielten, während die erstgenannten ganz auf ihre Intuition vertrauten.»[51]

Beinah mythologisiert Cooper die Leistung von Picasso und Braque, vergleicht er doch ihre Zusammenarbeit zwischen Herbst 1909 und Frühling 1913 mit jener von Monet und Renoir zwischen 1868 und 1874.[52] Gris («der von den zwei Begründern als Kubist in ihrem Sinn akzeptiert wurde») und Léger («der immerhin eine Reihe kubistischer Werke gemalt habe») wurden von Cooper nur sehr zurückhaltend als «wahre» Kubisten anerkannt.[53] Über die Künstler kubistischer Richtung (er nennt Gleizes, Villon, Hayden, Marcoussis, Metzinger, Lhote und Le Fauconnier) geht er hinweg – sie seien «im Sinn des Kubismus bloss rührend».[54]

Cooper bemühte sich sehr, die Periode und die Phasen der Entstehung und Entwicklung des Kubismus zu definieren, vermied jedoch die traditionelle Terminologie

> *terminology which is generally used in discussing the evolution of Renaissance art, that is to say ''early,'' ''high,'' and ''late.'' The ''early'' phase of Cubism, as I see it, runs from the end of 1906 till the summer of 1910; it was a period of necessary experiment by Picasso and Braque alone and led to their first major achievements before any Cubist movement had started. The period of ''high'' Cubism which followed was shorter, lasting only two years, from the summer of 1910 till the winter of 1912.*[55]

Cooper consistently stresses a gap between the ''intuitive'' Cubism of Picasso and Braque and the ''methodical, theoretical, and sometimes mathematical form'' of the works of the Cubist followers[56] In *The Essential Cubism*, Cooper writes:

> *By their very nature, as we have seen, Cubist paintings are essentially personal in character and bear the mark of an individual personality. They are, indeed, intimate records of a way of life and allow us an insight into the surrounding in which the original Cubist artists lived and worked. So, in conclusion, it seems appropriate to quote once again Juan Gris's enlightening comment that Cubism was ''not a manner'' but ''a state of mind''.*[57]

It is interesting that Cooper acknowledges the role of Daniel-Henry Kahnweiler, as friend and pioneering dealer, in isolating the true Cubists from the confusing *mêlée* of competition and theories:

> *... from 1907 onwards, he was instrumental in carrying out their policy of remaining aloof from the crowd. This book, is, therefore, a personal though authoritative interpreation of the views of those who confined themselves to pure creative painting and refused to dabble in theories or art politics.*[58]

Cooper's ''reading'' of Cubism in terms of a shift from the empirical to the conceptual is by no means innova-

logie («analytisch», «hermetisch», «synthetisch», «Rokoko»), die bestimmte stilistische Entwicklungen impliziere.

> *Aus heutiger Distanz sehe ich eine grosse Bewegung rund um den «wahren» Kubismus entstehen, sich entwickeln, sich schnell verändern und auseinanderfallen. Daher meine ich, dass es historische, nicht stilistische Gliederungen sind, die gelten, ja dass sich diese mit jenen überschneiden. Aus diesem Grund brauche ich lieber die Terminologie, welche man üblicherweise auf die Kunst der Renaissance anwendet, nämlich «früh», «hoch» und «spät». Die «frühe» Phase des Kubismus erstreckt sich, meiner Ansicht nach, von Ende 1906 bis Sommer 1910; dies war notwendigerweise eine experimentelle Phase, in der allein Picasso und Braque zu ersten grossen Lösungen kamen, und dies auch bevor irgendeine kubistische Bewegung ihren Ausgang genommen hätte. Die folgende Phase des «Hochkubismus» war kürzer; sie dauerte nur zwei Jahre, von Sommer 1910 bis Winter 1912.*[55]

Beständig betont Cooper die Kluft zwischen dem «intuitiven» Kubismus von Picasso und Braque und der «methodischen, theoretischen und gelegentlich mathematischen Form» der Werke bei den Kubismus-Anhängern.[56] In *The Essential Cubism* schreibt er:

> *Wie wir gesehen haben, sind kubistische Werke ihrer Natur nach von wesentlich individueller Art und tragen den Stempel einer einzigartigen Persönlichkeit. So stellen sie denn auch intime Zeugnisse einer Lebensweise dar und erlauben uns Einblick in die Bedingungen, mit denen sich die ersten Kubisten im Leben und in ihrer Arbeit auseinandersetzen mussten. So scheint es angemessen, abschliessend noch einmal Juan Gris' erhellende Bemerkung zu zitieren, Kubismus sei «kein Stil», sondern «eine Geisteshaltung».*[57]

Interessant zu sehen ist, dass Cooper Daniel Henry Kahnweilers Rolle als Freund der Kubisten und Pionier

tive, but rather partakes of an approach and vocabulary utilized already by a long line of apologists of Cubism, including, most prominently Kahnweiler.[59] Cooper's presentation of Cubism as "conceptual", his explanation of its use of forms without "descriptive" or mimetic purpose, hinging upon a redefinition of "representational", must be understood in terms of his battle to combat a lack of understanding and accusations of "pure abstraction". Cooper reacted furiously to suggestions that Cubism was abstraction without subject matter. In 1946 in a critique of John Russell's book on Braque, Cooper explains the "representational" quality of Cubism:

> *Admittedly the Cubist form of representation was not imitative of nature, but it was highly "representational", a word we must be careful not to confuse with "naturalistic". The fundamental pictorial problem is how to represent on a canvas which has only two dimensions solid bodies which have three. This has, generally speaking, been solved by artists in one of two ways, which I will call the empirical and the conceptual – the representation of what the artist sees, and the representation of what the artist knows.*[60]

Cooper's attitude was that of a crusader on behalf of Cubism, explaining it to and defending it from a misapprehending public. His defense of Cubism was often linked to his vituperative appraisal of the indifference or ignorance of the English art public and the hopeless backwardness of English art. Indeed, some of the untoward vehemence, even possessiveness, of Cooper's stance must be seen in terms of his own highly emotional and protracted struggle with his native land.[61] It seems clear, for instance, that Cooper's inability to give more than lukewarm praise to John Golding's *Cubism*, 1959, (which originated as a doctoral thesis under Cooper's own direction), stems from his own intense involvement with Cubism, a subject which he had championed with a crusader's zeal. One cannot help but suspect that Cooper found it more than a

unter den Händlern, der die «wahren» Kubisten vom Klüngel der Theoretiker und Konkurrenten trennte, anerkennt:

> *...seit 1907 half er ihnen wesentlich, ihr Ziel, sich von der Menge wegzuhalten, zu verfolgen. So ist denn dieses Buch eine persönliche, doch massgebende Interpretation der Ansichten jener, die sich nur auf das rein Schöpferische der Malerei konzentrierten und ein oberflächliches Theoretisieren oder Mitmischen in der Kunst-Politik von sich wiesen.*[58]

Coopers «Interpretation» des Kubismus als Wandel vom Empirischen zum Konzeptionellen ist keineswegs neu, sondern schliesst sich in der Betrachtungsweise und im Vokabular der langen Reihe der Apologeten des Kubismus, in der Kahnweiler herausragt, an.[59] Wenn Cooper den Kubismus als «konzeptionell» darstellt und wenn er erklärt, dass in der Anwendung des Formenvokabulars keinerlei «deskriptives» oder mimetisches Ziel verfolgt werde – wobei er sich allerdings auf eine Neu-Definition des «Gegenständlichen» (des Repräsentierenden) stützt –, dann muss dies als Teil seines Kampfes gegen mangelndes Verständnis und gegen den Vorwurf der «reinen Abstraktion» verstanden werden. Cooper reagierte heftig auf Hypothesen wie: Kubismus sei Abstraktion ohne Inhalt. 1946 erläutert er in einer Besprechung von John Russells Buch über Braque die «gegenständliche» (repräsentierende) Natur des Kubismus:

> *Die kubistische Art der Darstellung ahmt zugegebenermassen die Wirklichkeit nicht nach, aber sie «repräsentiert» sie in hohem Grade; sie ist «repräsentierend», was nicht mit «naturalistisch» verwechselt werden sollte. Das bildnerische Grundproblem ist, wie man auf einer zweidimensionalen Leinwand dreidimensionale Körper darstellen kann. Dies wurde, allgemein gesprochen, von den Künstlern auf zweierlei Art gelöst – auf die empirische und die konzeptionelle, wie ich sie nenne; die Darstellung (Repräsentation)*

bit difficult to fully acknowledge the merits of Golding's thorough study of Cubism, because it represented, in effect, the book that he himself envisioned writing about the subject dominant in his own life.[62]

The most coherent framework for the story of Cooper the collector-scholar and for the presentation of the individual works in this exhibition is a set of four "monographs" on the major Cubists – Braque, Gris, Léger and Picasso – through which Cooper's acquisitions and writings may be juxtaposed and woven together. The formation of Cooper's collection, so quick and intense during the thirties, and based upon a concept or subject that did not radically change subsequently, precludes a meaningful structure based upon a chronology of his acquisitions and deaccessions, or upon the growth or clarification of his guiding idea. This "monographic" organization offers, as well, a glimpse of the broader context of Cooper's entire collection including oils and sculptures, in which the works on paper selected for this exhibition must be situated.[63] A selection of works on paper from the collection reflects a real concentration of this material, revealing the depth of Cooper's appreciation of the nuances of the artists' development and his understanding of the significance of different media within the context of Cubism.

also dessen, was der Künstler sieht, und die Darstellung dessen, was er weiss.[60]

Cooper war ein Kämpfer für den Kubismus und gegen das Unverständnis, dem er in der Öffentlichkeit begegnete. Als Apologet des Kubismus attacktierte er auch oft in einem Atemzug die Indifferenz und Ignoranz des englischen Kunstpublikums sowie die hoffnungslose Rückständigkeit der englischen Kunst. Einiges von Coopers Widerspenstigkeit und Heftigkeit, ja von seinem Besitzanspruch, hängt natürlich auch damit zusammen, dass er nie mit seiner Heimat zurande kam und auf sie immer höchst emotional reagierte.[61] Klar scheint auch, dass seine Unfähigkeit, John Goldings *Cubism* von 1959 nicht mehr als nur lauwarm zu loben – das Werk entstand als Doktorarbeit unter seiner eigenen Leitung –, von seinem überaus starken Engagement für den Kubismus herrührte, für eine Sache, die er mit dem Eifer eines Kreuzritters verfocht. Man muss geradezu vermuten, dass der Grund, weshalb Cooper es alles andere als leicht fand, die Verdienste von Golding und sein so gründliches und grossartiges Buch über den Kubismus anzuerkennen, darin liegt, dass es eigentlich das Buch war, welches er selbst so gerne geschrieben hätte: über das Thema eben, das sein Leben bestimmte.[62]

Der Geschichte von Douglas Cooper, dem Sammler und Wissenschaftler, und der Vorstellung der einzelnen Werke in dieser Ausstellung soll ein klarer Rahmen, gebildet aus «Monographien» der vier Hauptkubisten – Braque, Gris, Léger und Picasso –, gegeben werden, innerhalb dessen auch Coopers Erwerbungen mit seinen Schriften konfrontiert und in Beziehung gebracht werden können. Da seine Sammlung in den dreissiger Jahren so rasch und intensiv heranwuchs und stets von einem kaum sich wandelnden Leitbild oder Thema bestimmt wurde, verbietet sich nun auch eine Betrachtungsweise, welche auf eine Chronologie von Coopers Anschaffungen und Veräusserungen oder auf dem Werden oder der Klärung seiner Leitidee basieren

1 The author wishes to acknowledge the kind generosity of John Richardson, who allowed two interviews and who also wrote an interesting contribution for this catalogue (see pages 183–196). See, as well, Richardson's biographical tribute to Cooper, "Remembering Douglas Cooper", *The New York Review of Books*, April 25, 1985, pp. 24–26, which provides a thumbnail but first hand account of Cooper's life. Also see Richardson's "Château des Cubistes," *l'Oeil*, April 1954, pp. 18–25 and "Cubists among the Columns," *Vanity Fair*, July 1984, pp. 50–61.

2 *The Courtauld Collection* (with Anthony Blunt), London: University of London, Athlone Press, 1954; "Le Musée de Ceret, Musée de Saint-Tropez, Musée de Bagnols – Musées des petites villes du Midi de la France", *L'Oeil*, no. 1, 1955, pp. 21–26; "How to Collect Pictures and Influence People," *Sunday Times*, 10.7.62, pp. 14–15 and 17; *Great Private Collections*, New York: MacMillan, 1963; *Great Family Collections*, New York: MacMillan, 1965; *Gertrude Stein, Picasso and Juan Gris*, Ottawa: National Gallery of Canada, 1971; and in his introduction to *The Essential Cubism, Braque, Picasso and Their Friends, 1907–1920 (curated by Cooper and Gary Tinterow)* London, *The Tate Gallery, 1983, entitled: "Early Purchasers of True Cubist Art."*

3 *In The Courtauld Collection*, Cooper writes:

Thus although the episode of Impressionism is represented here, the Courtauld Collection as a whole looks foward. In fact it illustrates, in a way that no other private collection can claim to do, that vital phase in the history of French nineteenth-century art when the old artistic idiom was dying and the new one was being evolved.(p. 11)

Yet the making of the Courtauld Collection – at least so far as the French pictures are concerned – was a cardinal event in the history of English taste... But no other English collector has shown the breadth of taste or the discrimination of Courtauld, and none has equalled his achievement. The Courtauld Collection was unique in England at the time when it was made; it is still unique today.(p. 11)

And the importance, for England, of Courtauld as a collector is that his enthusiasm was whole-hearted, that he was prepared to trust his own judgment, and that his taste was wide enough to embrace the whole period from 1860 till 1900.(p. 13)

But it is a measure of Courtauld's own "love" and artistic insight that, during those years when Fry's influence and prestige were at their highest, he ignored the views of the self-appointed leaders of taste and was able to build up an extremely intelligent and well-balanced collection of Impressionist and post-Impressionist paintings by following the counsels of his own judgement. (p. 59)

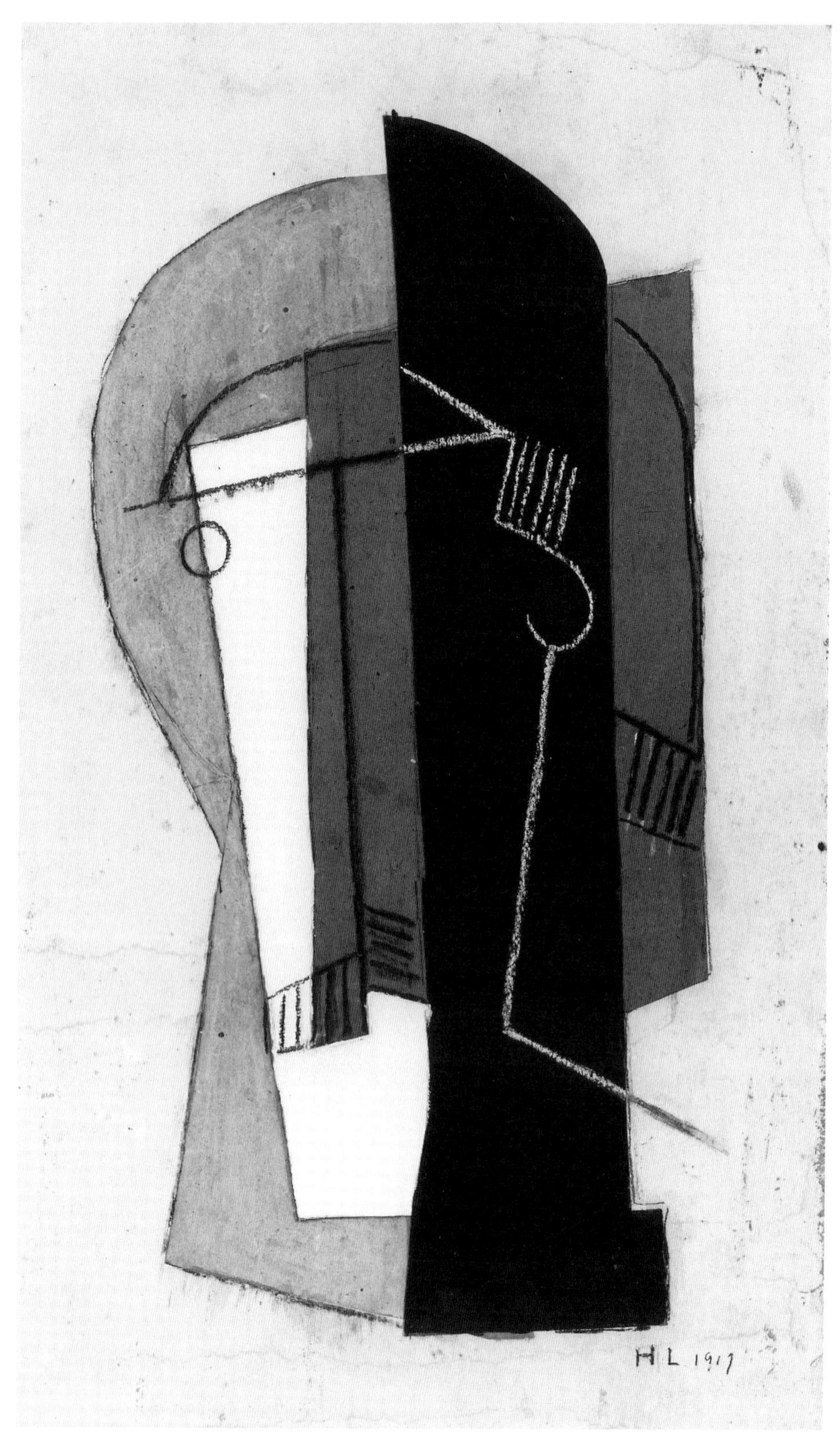

26 HENRI LAURENS
(Kopf; Head) 1919 (?)

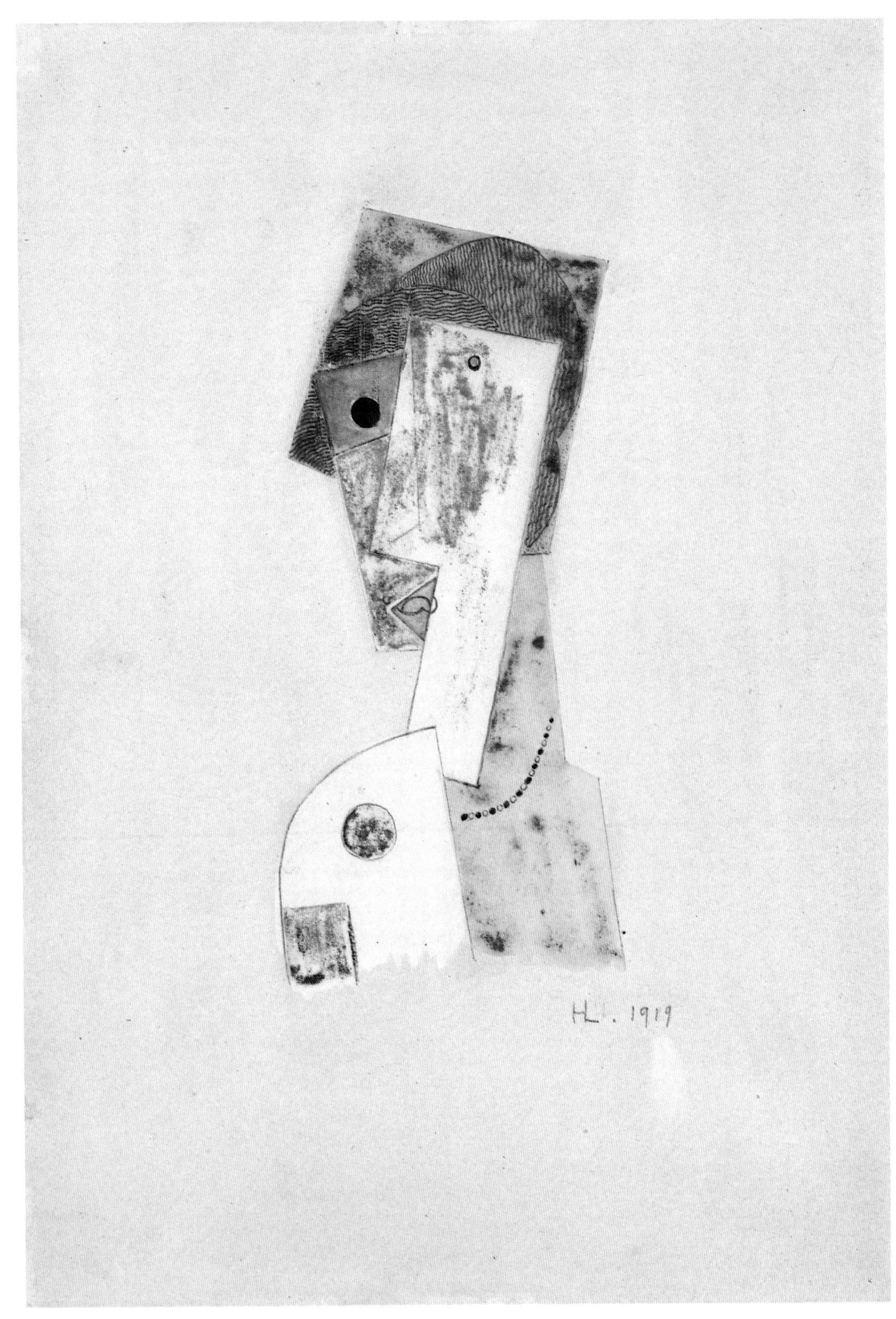

27 HENRI LAURENS
(Kubistischer Kopf; Cubist Head) 1919

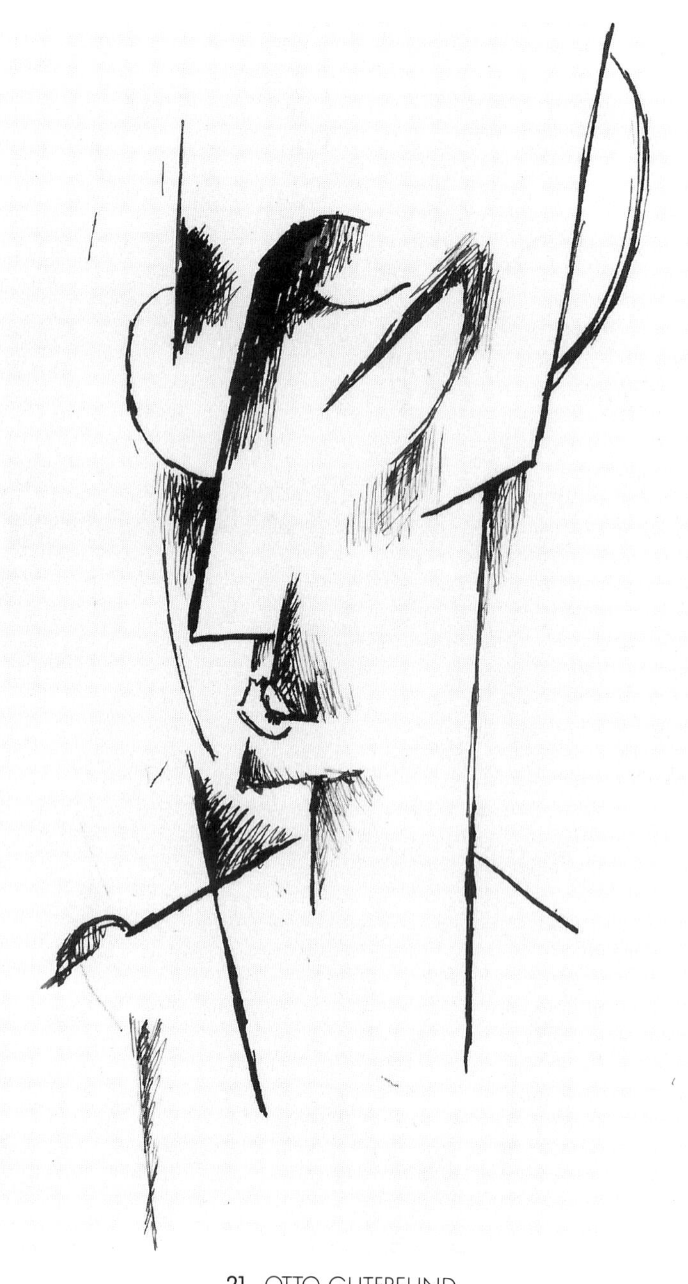

21 OTTO GUTFREUND
(Kopf; Head) (1911)

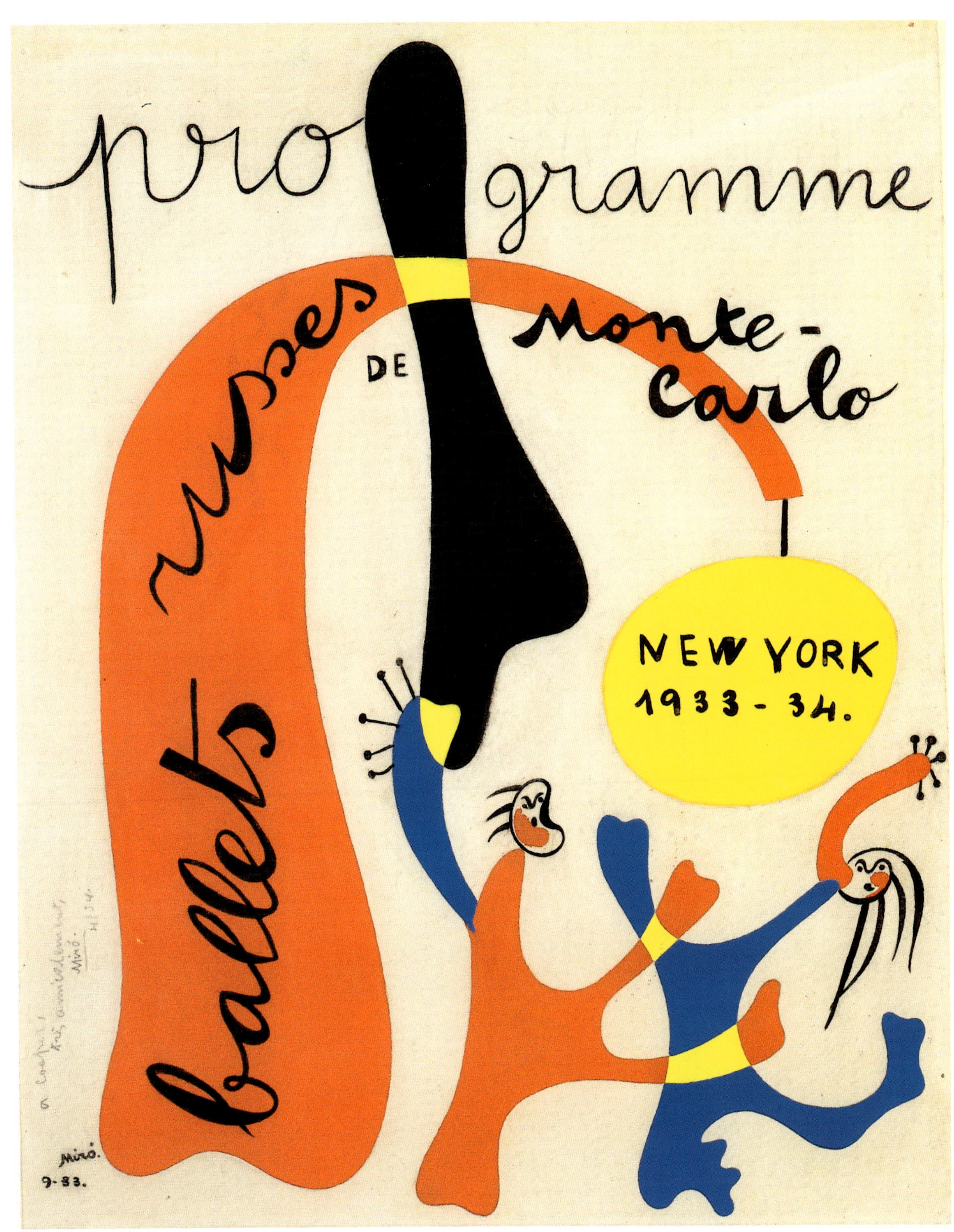

49 JOAN MIRO
Programme, Ballets Russes de Monte-Carlo, New York, 1933–34 (Maquette)

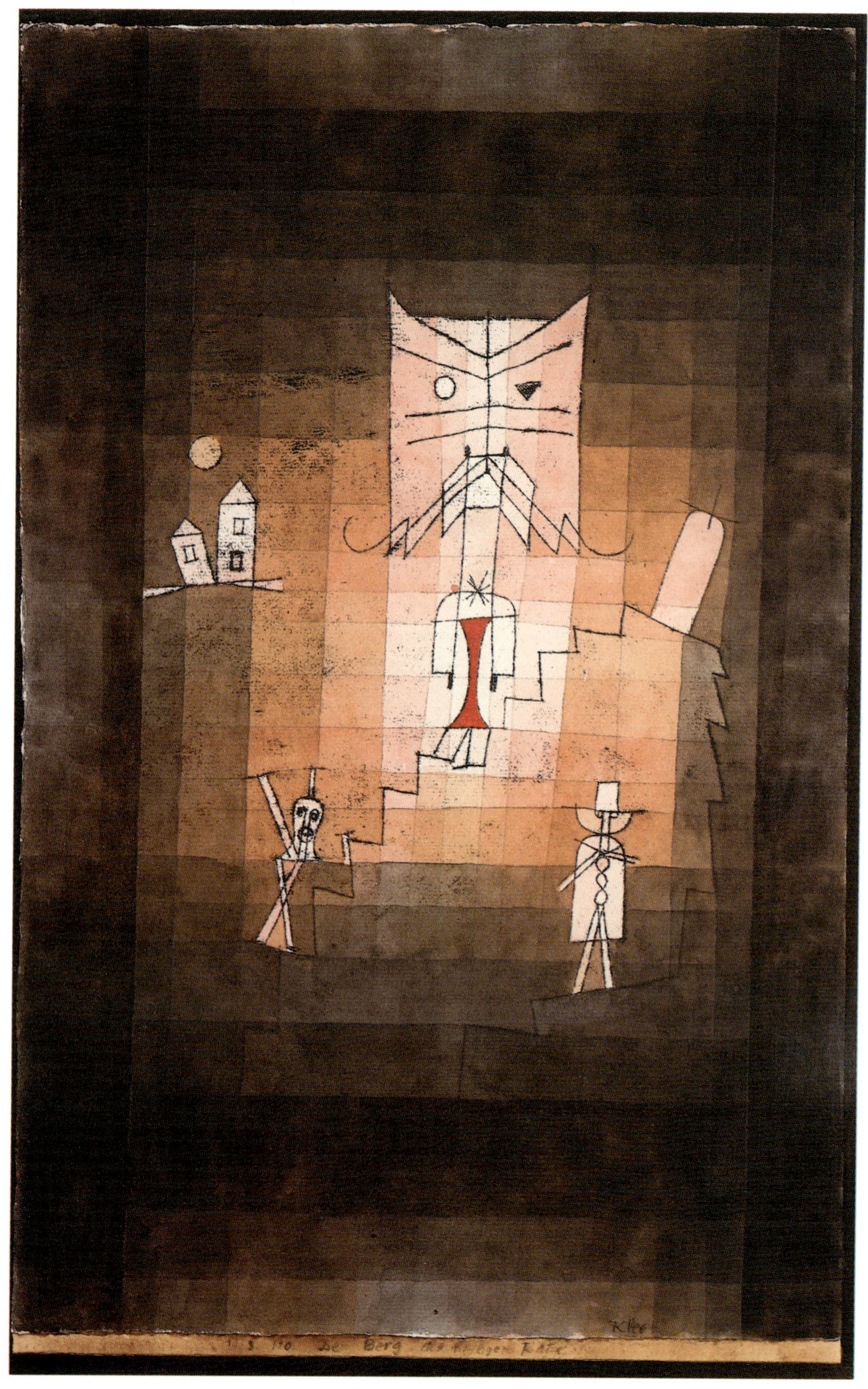

23 PAUL KLEE

Der Berg der heiligen Katze (The Mountain of the Sacred Cat) 1923

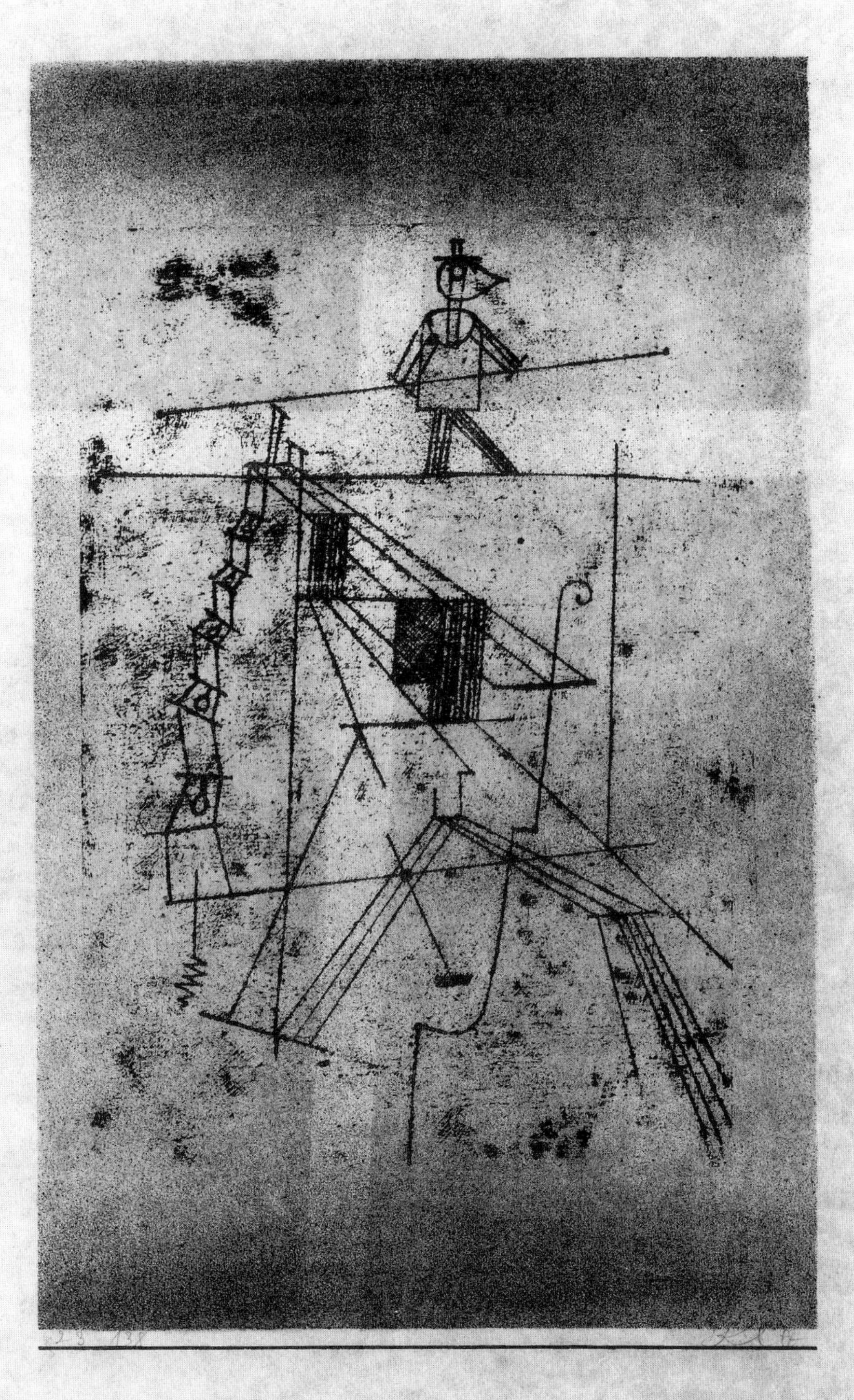

24 PAUL KLEE
(Seiltänzer; Tight Rope Walker) 1923

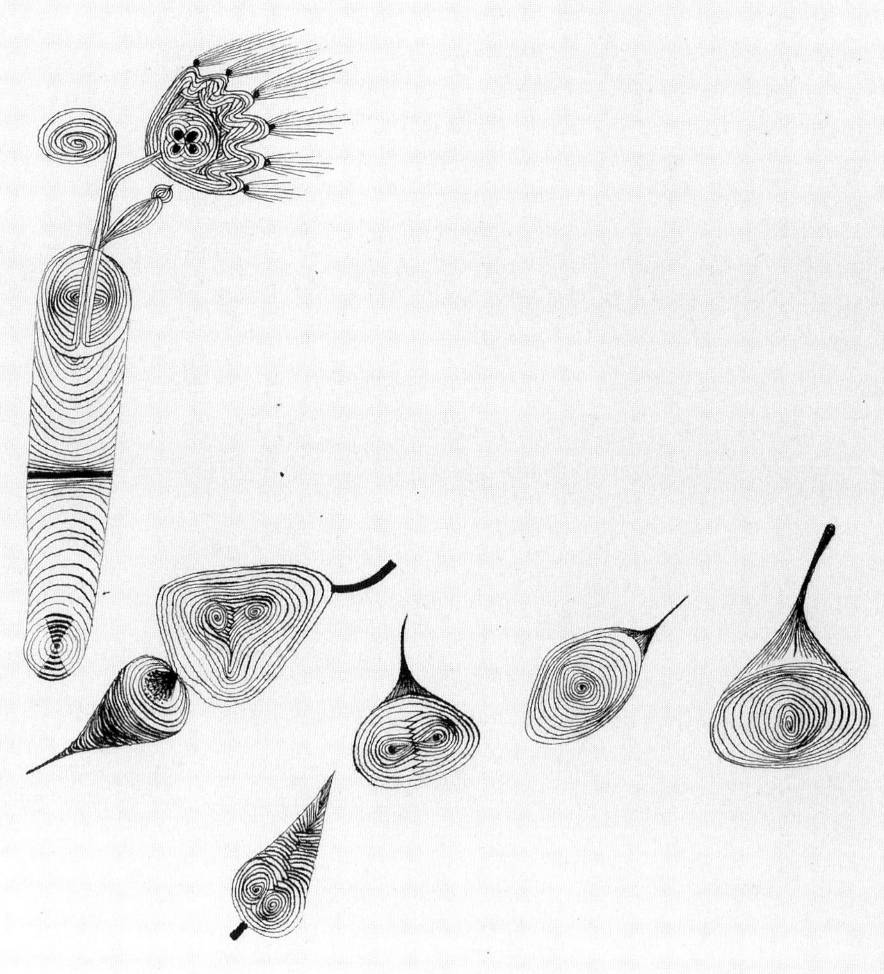

25 PAUL KLEE
Blume und Früchte (Flowers and Fruits) 1927

würde. Eine «monographische» Struktur, wie hier, gibt zudem Einblick in die grösseren Zusammenhänge von Coopers Sammlung als Ganzem, welche auch Ölbilder und plastische Werke umfasst und in welcher der Platz der Arbeiten auf Papier, die ja für diese Ausstellung ausgewählt worden sind, zu bestimmen ist.[63] Eine solche Auswahl kommt zwar einer Einengung des gesamten Materials, aber auch einer Konzentration gleich, die Coopers tiefes Verständnis für die Feinheiten einer schöpferischen Entwicklung, wie auch seine Erkenntnis der Bedeutung, welche die verschiedenen Medien im Kontext des Kubismus haben, aufzeigen kann.

1 An dieser Stelle möchte sich die Schreibende herzlich bei John Richardson für die zwei Interviews, die er gewährte, für seinen interessanten Beitrag in diesem Katalog (s. S. 183–196) und vor allem für seine stets bewiesene Freundlichkeit und Grosszügigkeit bedanken. S. a. Richardsons Hommage an Cooper, "Remembering Douglas Cooper", *The New York Review of Books*, 25. April 1985, S. 24–26, eine knappe biographische Studie aus erster Hand. S. a. Richardsons «Château des Cubistes», *l'Oeil*, April 1954, S. 18–25, und "Cubists among the Columns", *Vanity Fair*, Juli 1984, S. 50–61.

2 *The Courtauld Collection* (zusammen mit Anthony Blunt), London: University of London, Athlone Press, 1954; «Le Musée de Céret, Musée de Saint-Tropez, Musée de Bagnols – Musées des petites villes du Midi de la France», *l'Oeil*, Nr. 1, 1955, S. 21–26; "How to Collect Pictures and Influence People", *Sunday Times*, 10.7.1962, S. 14–15 und 17; *Great Private Collections*, New York, Macmillan, 1963; *Great Family Collections*, New York, Macmillan, 1965; *Gertrude Stein, Picasso and Juan Gris*, Ottawa, National Gallery of Canada, 1971; s. a. "Early Purchasers of True Cubist Art" in der Einleitung zu *The Essential Cubism, Braque, Picasso, and Their Friends, 1907–1920*, curated by Douglas Cooper and Gary Tinterow, London, The Tate Gallery, 1983.

3 In *The Courtauld Collection* schreibt Cooper:
Und auch wenn hier die Zeit des Impressionismus vertreten ist, ist die Courtauld-Sammlung als Ganzes doch in die Zukunft gerichtet, ja sie veranschaulicht auf eine Weise, wie es keine zweite Privatsammlung vermöchte, jene wichtige Phase der französischen Kunst des 19. Jahrhunderts, in der alte künstlerische Ausdrucksweisen verschwanden und neue entwickelt wurden (S. 11).
Doch der Aufbau der Courtauld-Sammlung war – zumindest was die französische Kunst angeht – ein Markstein in der Geschichte des

4 *Ibid.*, p. 59, note 4.

5 *The Essential Cubism*, p. 31: Cooper once again emphasizes England's niggardly reticence vis-à-vis French twentieth century art. "In Germany, Italy and, of course, England, where Augustus John was still more highly valued than Matisse and Picasso, no collectors of true Cubist painting existed either before or after the war."

6 *Ibid.*, p. 31

7 Works were sold, for instance, to finance Léger's largescale painting, *The Trapeze Artists*, and the wall by Picasso at Castille in 1963. Other works were sold before the move to Monte Carlo in 1977. Works in the collection were included in sales at Sothebys in New York in 1968 and 1969 and in London at Sothebys in 1974 and 1978.

8 Cooper's affiliation with Mayor did not last long, as the natural conflict between his lack of interest in the workings of the art dealer and Mayor's focus on making the gallery commercially viable soon became apparent.

9 Braque, Picasso, Léger, Masson, Miró, Ernst, Klee and Metzinger were among the artists included in an exhibition which opened on April 20, 1933. Other artists exhibited that year included: Max Ernst (June 8 – July 1), Joan Miró (July). In 1934 paintings by Paul Klee were shown, opening January 16. "Twentieth Century Classics", including works by Braque, Gris, Léger and Picasso, opened on February 20. On September 26 an exhibition of Picasso drawings from 1900–1934 opened. The first exhibition of 1935 included paintings by Gris, Léger and Picasso. An exhibit of paintings by Klee opened on May 29; Drawings by Cocteau on December 4th. On July 9, 1936, an exhibition of "Abstract Paintings by American Artists" arranged by the Gallery of Living Art, New York University opened. In November a Juan Gris exhibition opened. 1936 closed with an exhibit of gouaches and small oils by a variety of artists including: Klee, Miró and Graham Sutherland. In February 1937 works by Matisse, Picasso, and Braque were included in a group show of leading English and French artists.

10 Many records were discarded at moments of personal upheaval in Cooper's life, certainly at the time of the move from Castille in Argilliers to Monte-Carlo in 1977. A sizeable archive, however, including Cooper's correspondence, manuscripts and library is now housed at The Getty Center for the History of Art and the Humanities, Los Angeles, California.

11 *Head*, 1909: Z, II**, 716.

englischen Geschmacks... Aber kein zweiter englischer Sammler hat bis jetzt solch grossen Kunstverstand und Geschmack wie Courtauld bewiesen, und keiner kommt an seine Leistung heran. Die Courtauld-Sammlung war einzigartig in England zur Zeit ihrer Entstehung – und sie ist es noch immer (S. 11).
Für England liegt Courtaulds Bedeutung als Sammler auch darin, dass er in seiner Begeisterung aufrichtig war, dass er stets seinem eigenen Urteil vertraute und dass er aufgrund seines ästhetischen Verständnisses eine ganze Periode – 1860–1900 – begreifen konnte (S. 13). «Liebe» zur Sache und künstlerischer Scharfblick waren Courtaulds Massstab, und so ignorierte er zu einer Zeit, da Frys Einfluss und Prestige am grössten waren, die Ansichten der selbsternannten Dirigenten des Geschmacks und konnte, indem er sich auf sein eigenes Urteil verliess, eine ausserordentlich kluge und gut gewichtete Sammlung impressionistischer und postimpressionistischer Kunst aufbauen (S. 59).

4 ibid., S. 59, Anm. 4.

5 *The Essential Cubism,* S. 31: Wieder unterstreicht Cooper die schäbige Zurückhaltung der Engländer gegenüber der französischen Kunst des 20. Jahrhunderts: «In Deutschland, Italien und natürlich auch in England, wo man Augustus John immer noch höher einschätzte als Matisse und Picasso, existierten weder vor noch nach dem Krieg Sammler wahrer kubistischer Kunst.»

6 ibid., S. 31.

7 Zum Beispiel wurden Werke verkauft, damit Légers grossformatige *Trapezkünstler* und die Picasso-Wand auf Schloss Castille 1963 finanziert werden konnten. Wieder andere wurden vor dem Umzug nach Monte-Carlo veräussert. Werke aus der Sammlung erschienen auf Auktionen bei Sotheby in New York (1968 und 1969) und London (1974 und 1978).

8 Coopers Verbindung mit Mayor dauerte nicht sehr lang, denn es wurde bald klar, dass sein Desinteresse am Kunsthandel mit Mayors Konzentration auf die wirtschaftliche Rentabilität der Galerie natürlich unvereinbar war.

9 Braque, Picasso, Léger, Masson, Miró, Ernst, Klee und Metzinger waren u.a. die Künstler, welche eine am 20. April 1933 eröffnete Ausstellung vereinigte. Weitere dieses Jahr gezeigte Künstler waren: Max Ernst (8. Juni–1. Juli), Joan Miró (Juli). 1934 wurden, ab 16. Januar, Werke von Klee präsentiert, ab 20. Februar «Meisterwerke des 20. Jahrhunderts», darunter Werke von Braque, Gris, Léger und Picasso, ab 26. September Zeichnungen von Picasso aus den Jahren 1900–1934. Die erste Ausstellung 1935 brachte Gris,

12 This work was given to Daniel-Henry Kahnweiler in 1937 when Cooper learned that Flechtheim had, in fact, had no right to the work.

13 *Still-life with Dead Birds* (Z, II*, 339). The Ex-Libris was sold to Curt Valentin in 1937, in exchange for a Paul Klee, *Märchen*, 1929.

14 Sold to Galerie Beaune, Paris in 1938.

15 *Guitar on a Table* (Z, VI, 1414) was sold in 1946 to Galerie Allard, Paris and *The Artist's Table* was sold in 1952. *Still-life with Guitar and Fruit-dish*: Z, VII, 375.

16 Two of the Braques, *Pipe, apples and glass*, 1933 and *Glass and apples* of the same year, were subsequently sold in 1939 to the Mayor Gallery in London.

17 *Guitar and compotier*, 1921 (traded with the same Gallery the following year for a 1917 *Harlequin* by Gris.), *Still-life: Carafe and glass*, 1919 (subsequently sold in 1951) and *Still-life with guitar and fruit-dish* 1926.

18 One 1914 *Still-life* (oil), and two 1913 gouache: *Two reclining Women* and *Study of a Woman in Red and Green*, the latter given to the artist in 1954 in exchange for *The Trapeze Artists,* painted for the staircase of the Château de Castille at Argilliers.

19 Traded with Berggruen in 1957 for two other 1913 gouaches.

20 These included three gouaches and an oil dated 1936 all entitled *Composition* (An oil and a gouache were sold to the Mayor Gallery, London in 1938.) and a 1913 oil entitled *Landscape*.

21 The others were: *Seated Woman with a Book*, 1909, watercolor and ink (Z, II**, 722) purchased from Zwemmer Gallery, London (sold in 1974), *The Guitariste*, a 1912–13 pencil drawing (Z, II**, 394) from Pierre Loeb (sold to G. Leuthal in 1958).

22 Three Braques: *Guitar and Glass*, 1913, papier collé (sold to Mayor Gallery in 1946); *Guitar, fruit, pipe and a notebook of music*, 1924, oil, from G. F. Reber; from the Philadelphia artist-collector-dealer, Earl Horter, *The Guéridon: Newspaper, bottle, glass*, 1913 oil (to Acquavella Gallery 1969).

Two Gris drawings: a watercolor and charcoal, *Still-life: guitar and glass*, 1913 from the Zak collection; and a 1919 pencil drawing from Jeanne Bucher, *Apple, glass and knife*. (Both were sold to or traded with Berggruen in 1957.)

Four Gris oils: two at Christie's, London, 23, April 1937, Nos. 39 and 41 respectively, the 1916 *Portrait of Mme. Josette Gris* (Given to the

Léger und Picasso zusammen; es folgten: ab 29. Mai Bilder von Klee, ab 4. Dezember Zeichnungen von Cocteau, ab 9. Juli – nun 1936 – "Abstract Paintings by American Artists", eine von der Gallery of Living Art, New York University, zusammengestellte Schau, und im November eine Gris-Ausstellung. Das Jahr 1937 endete mit Gouachen und kleinformatigen Ölbildern von Klee, Miró, Graham Sutherland u.a. Im Februar 1937 wurden Werke von Matisse, Picasso, Braque und anderen führenden französischen und englischen Künstlern zu einer Gruppenausstellung vereinigt.

10 Viele Dokumente wurden zu Zeiten persönlicher Krisen in Coopers Leben vernichtet; so bestimmt auch 1977, dem Jahr des Umzugs von Argilliers nach Monte-Carlo. Allerdings befindet sich heute ein ansehnliches Archiv im Getty Center for the History of Art and the Humanities in Los Angeles, California; es beherbergt Coopers Briefe, Manuskripte und Bibliothek.

11 *Kopf,* 1909 (Z, II**, 716)

12 Dieses Werk wurde 1937 Daniel-Henry Kahnweiler übergeben, als Cooper erfahren hatte, dass Flechtheim kein Anrecht darauf besass.

13 *Stilleben mit toten Vögeln* (Z, II*, 339). Das Exlibris wurde 1937 an Curt Valentin verkauft im Austausch gegen einen Klee, *Märchen,* 1929.

14 1938 verkauft an die Galerie Beaune, Paris.

15 *Gitarre auf einem Tisch* (Z, VI, 1414) wurde 1946 an die Galerie Allard, Paris, verkauft; *Der Tisch des Künstlers* wurde 1952 veräussert. *Stilleben mit Gitarre und Fruchtschale*: Z, VII, 375.

16 Zwei der Braque-Werke, *Pfeife, Äpfel und Glas* und *Glas und Äpfel,* beide von 1933, wurden 1939 der Mayor Gallery, London, verkauft.

17 *Gitarre und Fruchtschale,* 1921 (mit derselben Galerie im folgenden Jahr getauscht gegen einen *Harlekin,* 1917, von Gris), *Stilleben: Karaffe und Glas,* 1919 (verkauft 1951), und *Stilleben mit Gitarre und Fruchtschale,* 1926.

18 Ein *Stilleben* (Öl) von 1914 und zwei Gouachen von 1913, *Zwei liegende Frauen* und *Studie einer Frau in Rot und Grün;* letztere wurde dem Künstler im Austausch gegen die *Trapezkünstler* für das Treppenhaus des Schlosses Castille gegeben.

19 1957 mit Berggruen getauscht gegen zwei andere Gouachen von 1913.

Prado in gratitude for his election to that Museum's *patronato.* Cooper also gave the Prado Picasso's *Still-life with Pigeons,* 1912, and the palette which the artist used while working on the *Déjeuner sur l'herbe* series; and the 1919, *Still-life with mandoline* (sold to the Pittsburgh collector, G. D. Thompson in 1955.); and from Pierre Matisse the 1913, *Still-life with violin and guitar.* (With Galerie Simon, Cooper traded the 1921 oil, *Guitar and Compotier,* for *Harlequin,* 1917, oil.)

Fifteen works by Léger: 4 gouaches created that year were obtained directly from the artist: *The Blue Cock, Composition: Butterflies and Flower, The Red Cock,* and *Composition* (exchanged in 1958 with Galerie Louise Leiris for *Construction Worker, Legs - No. 45 -). 3 gouaches were purchased from Pierre Loeb: Still-life,* 1913, *Three reclining women,* 1913 (disposed of the same year) and *Still-life with alarm clock,* 1914. 3 works on paper came from Jeanne Bucher, Paris: a pencil sketch for *Animated landscape: Man with Dog,* 1921, an ink and wash sketch for *The Sappers,* 1916, (Both of these were sold to or exchanged with Berggruen in 1957), and a 1918 watercolor, *The Mason.* 4 works from Léonce Rosenberg: a two-part wash drawing for *The Card Players,* 1916–17 (later sold to Eugene Thaw); another pencil and wash drawing for *The Card Players,* 1916–17 (No. 33); a 1920 watercolor, *Composition; and the 1924 oil, Still-life with a Bust.* In addition, Cooper purchased a pencil drawing of the curtain design for *Le Création du monde,* 1922, at Rain's Auction House in New York.

Fifteen works by Picasso: *Head,* 1913 purchased at Hôtel Drouot, Paris (in 1974, sold at Sotheby Parke Bernet); *Head of Man,* 1907, watercolor, (Z, II**, 716) from Zwemmer Gallery (disposed of the following year); *Still-life with Peaches and Playing Cards,* 1914, from Galerie Simon (No. 62); *The Student,* 1917–18, oil, (Z, III, 104) from Pierre Matisse (subsequently sold in 1974); *Standing woman,* 1911–12, ink, (No. 56), and *The Card Player,* 1914, pencil (No. 63) from Renou and Colle in Paris; *Seated Woman,* 1909, oil (Z, II*, 176) (to Eardley Krollys in 1939) and *Still-life , 1913, pencil and papiers collés (probably to Berggruen in 1957 for papier collé, Violin,* 1912, (No. 59) from Earl Horter; and from Dr. G. F. Reber: 4 oils: *Three female nudes under a tree (Three masks),* 1907, (Z, II*, 53, now in The Musée Picasso, Paris), *Nude in an armchair,* 1909, (Z, II*, 174) and *The Clarinet Player,* 1911 (Z, II*, 288, now in the Thyssen Collection, Lugano), and *Still-life with Guitar, Grapes and Bottle,* 1922–23, (Z, IV, 441) and one gouache: *Table in front of a window,* 1919.

23 The Gris was a 1917 oil, *Fruit-dish with a bottle of Beaune* (now in the Neumann Collection?).

24 The other 3 works by Picasso included: *Two Women,* 1920, pastel, (Z, IV, 56) *Guitar and fruit-dish on table,* 1920, (Z, IV, 214) *Head of a woman,* 1921, oil (Z, IV, 357).

20 Dazu gehörten drei Gouachen und ein Ölbild (datiert 1936), alle mit dem Titel *Komposition* (ein Ölbild und eine Gouache wurden 1938 der Mayor Gallery, London, verkauft), und ein Ölbild mit dem Titel *Landschaft* von 1913.

21 Die andern: *Sitzende mit Buch,* 1909, Aquarell und Tusche (Z, II**, 722), erworben von der Zwemmer Gallery, London (verkauft 1974), *Der Gitarrist,* 1912–13, Bleistift (Z, II**, 394) von Pierre Loeb (1958 verkauft an G. Leuthal).

22 Drei Braques: *Gitarre und Glas,* 1913, Papier collé (1946 verkauft an die Mayor Gallery); *Gitarre, Obst, Pfeife und ein Notenheft,* 1924, Öl, von G. F. Reber; von Earl Horter, dem Künstler, Sammler und Händler in Philadelphia, *Das Tischchen: Zeitung, Flasche, Glas,* 1913, Öl (1969 an die Acquavella Gallery).

Zwei Gris-Zeichnungen: Stilleben: *Gitarre und Glas,* 1913, Aquarell/Kohle, von der Zak-Sammlung; *Apfel, Glas und Messer,* 1919, Bleistift, von Jeanne Bucher. (Beide verkauft an oder getauscht mit Berggruen, 1957).

Vier Ölbilder von Gris: zwei bei Christie's (London, 23. April 1937, Nr. 39 und 40), *Porträt Josette Gris,* 1916 (dem Prado geschenkt als Dank für seine Wahl ins patronato des Museums. Cooper schenkte dem Prado auch Picassos *Stilleben mit Tauben,* 1912, sowie die Palette, die der Künstler bei der Arbeit an der *Déjeuner sur l'Herbe*-Serie gebrauchte), und *Stilleben mit Mandoline,* 1919 (1955 an G. D. Thompson, den Sammler in Pittsburgh, verkauft); von Pierre Matisse das *Stilleben mit Violine und Gitarre,* 1913. (Mit der Galerie Simon tauschte Cooper das Ölbild *Gitarre und Fruchtschale,* 1921, gegen *Harlekin,* 1917, Öl.)

Fünfzehn Werke von Léger: Vier in diesem Jahr geschaffene Gouachen, direkt vom Künstler erworben, *Der blaue Hahn, Komposition: Schmetterlinge und Blume, Der rote Hahn* und *Komposition* (1958 getauscht mit der Galerie Louise Leiris für *Bauarbeiter, Beine* – Nr. 45 –). Drei Gouachen von Pierre Loeb: *Stilleben,* 1913, *Drei liegende Frauen,* 1913 (im gleichen Jahr veräussert), und *Stilleben mit Wecker,* 1914. Drei Arbeiten auf Papier kamen von Jeanne Bucher, Paris: eine Bleistiftskizze für *Paysage animé: l'homme au chien (Belebte Landschaft, Mann mit Hund),* 1921, eine Tuschskizze für *Die Sappeure,* 1916 (diese beiden wurden verkauft an oder getauscht mit Berggruen, 1957), und ein Aquarell *Der Maurer,* 1918. Vier Werke von Léonce Rosenberg: eine zweiteilige Tuschzeichnung für *Die Kartenspieler,* 1916–17 (später verkauft an Eugene Thaw), eine Bleistift/Tuschzeichnung wieder für *Die Kartenspieler,* 1916–17 – Nr. 33 –, ein Aquarell *Komposition,* 1920, und das Ölbild *Stilleben mit Büste,* 1924. Dazu kaufte Cooper bei Rain's Auction House, New York, den Entwurf für den Vorhang von *La Création du Monde,* 1922.

25 In 1939 Cooper's acquisitions from Reber included the following Picassos: *Bacchus,* 1908, ink (apparently a gift from Reber); *Man and Woman,* 1921, pastel on board (Z, IV, 224) (sold to Berggruen in 1953?).

26 The other Léger purchased from Reber in 1945 was: *Composition: musical instruments,* 1925. *Study for "Still-life with Bust",* 1924 (No. 41) relates to the 1924 oil purchased from Léonce Rosenberg in 1937. (Collection records indicate purchase from Erna Reber, G. F. Reber's wife. Reber died July 15, 1959.)

27 See Cooper, *The Essential Cubism,* p. 30 concerning Reber. Reber was, at the same time, actively guiding the formation of another major Cubist/modernist collection, that of Ingeborg Eichmann, school-mate of Reber's daughter, and daughter of a wealthy paper manufacturer in the Sudetan Land. She had a serious interest in art and had written a substantial thesis on the Douanier Rousseau. Reber introduced Cooper and Eichmann, who formed a friendship and traveled together to the United States in 1937. Correspondence with Curt Valentin, March 5, 1954, indicates that this friendship continued at least into the 1950s; Cooper mentions that Eichmann had recently visited Castille. (See Archives, the Museum of Modern Art, Library, New York.)

28 Works by Juan Gris acquired from the Mayor Gallery in 1938: *Grapes and glass,* 1921, pencil; *Guitar with sheet music,* 1923, ink; *Bottle and Glass,* 1919, oil (sold to Mayor Gallery in 1946).

29 Other Légers acquired from the Galerie Simon in 1938: *Nude reclining,* 1907, ink; *Male figure,* 1908, ink.

30 Also acquired from Pierre Loeb in 1938: Picasso, *Still-life with garlands,* 1918, oil (Z, III, 142).

31 Another Gris obtained from Ronald Fleming in 1939: *The Book,* 1924, oil (sold in 1950 to Hannover Gallery). Cooper bought a 1924 Gris oil entitled *Harlequin,* from Willi Raeber in Basel. Directly from Picasso came a 1938 pastel, *Portrait of a woman* (sold to Mayor Gallery in 1946).

32 Braque oils purchased in 1950s: *Still-life with bunch of grapes,* 1918, from Tooth & Son, London in 1950, *Still-life with guitar,* 1918 from César de Hauke in 1958 (Date from receipt in collection records; *The Essential Cubism* however states 1960), and *Studio VIII,* purchased directly from the artist ca. 1955.

33 Two other works from Marlborough 1955: *Carafe, bottle and newspaper,* 1913, charcoal (no. 164, Nicole Worms de Romilly and Jean Laude, *Braque le Cubisme, 1907–1914,* Paris, Maeght, 1982 [sold to Berggruen in 1956]), and *Bottle of Marc,* 1912–13, collage and charcoal (Worms de Romilly and Laude, no. 127).

Fünfzehn Werke von Picasso: *Kopf,* 1913, gekauft bei Hôtel Drouot, Paris (1974 verkauft bei Sotheby Parke Bernet), *Männerkopf,* 1907, Aquarell (Z, II**, 716), von der Zwemmer Gallery (veräussert im folgenden Jahr), *Stilleben mit Pfirsichen und Spielkarten,* 1914, von der Galerie Simon – Nr. 62 –, *Der Student,* 1917–18, Öl (Z, III, 104), von Pierre Matisse (1974 verkauft), *Stehende Frau,* 1911–12, Tusche – Nr. 56 –, und *Der Kartenspieler,* 1914, Bleistift – Nr. 63 –, von Renou & Colle, Paris, *Sitzende Frau,* 1909, Öl (Z, II*, 176; an Eardly Krollys, 1939) und *Stilleben,* 1913, Bleistift und Papiers collés (wahrscheinlich an Berggruen 1957 für das Papier collé *Komposition mit Violine,* 1912 – Nr. 59 –) von Earl Horter, Philadelphia; vier Ölbilder von Dr. G. F. Reber: *Drei Akte unter einem Baum (Drei Masken),* 1907 (Z, II*, 53; heute Musée Picasso, Paris), *Akt im Lehnstuhl,* 1909 (Z, II*, 174), *Der Klarinettist,* 1911 (Z, II*, 288; heute in der Sammlung Thyssen, Lugano), und *Stilleben mit Gitarre, Trauben und Flasche,* 1922–23 (Z, IV, 441), sowie eine Gouache, *Tisch vor einem Fenster,* 1919.

23 Von Gris: *Fruchtschale mit einer Flasche Beaune,* 1917, Öl (heute in der Sammlung Neumann?).

24 Die drei andern Picassos: *Zwei Frauen,* 1920, Pastell (Z, IV, 56), *Gitarre und Fruchtschale auf Tisch,* 1920 (Z, IV, 214) und *Frauenkopf,* 1921, Öl (Z, IV, 357).

25 Zu Coopers Erwerbungen von Reber 1939 gehörten die folgenden Picassos: *Bacchus,* 1908, Tusche (anscheinend ein Geschenk von Reber) und *Mann und Frau,* 1921, Pastell auf Karton (Z, IV, 224; anscheinend 1953 verkauft an Berggruen).

26 Der zweite Léger von Reber: *Komposition: Musikinstrumente,* 1925. *Studie für «Stilleben mit Büste»,* 1924 (Nr. 41) steht in Bezug zum Ölbild von 1924, erworben von Léonce Rosenberg, 1937. (Sammlungsakten deuten Kauf von Erna Reber, G. F. Rebers Frau, an. Reber starb am 15. Juli, 1959).

27 Zu Reber, s. Cooper, *The Essential Cubism,* S. 30. Gleichzeitig war Reber massgebend beteiligt am Aufbau einer andern bedeutenden Sammlung von Kubisten und weiteren Künstlern der Moderne, jener von Ingeborg Eichmann, der Tochter eines wohlhabenden Papierfabrikanten in den Sudeten und Schulfreundin von Rebers Tochter. Ihr Interesse an Kunst(geschichte) war ernsthaft, hatte sie doch schon eine beachtliche Dissertation über Rousseau, den Zöllner, geschrieben. Reber machte Cooper mit ihr bekannt; sie befreundeten sich und reisten 1937 zusammen in die Vereinigten Staaten. Wie aus dem Briefwechsel mit Curt Valentin hervorgeht, dauerte ihre Freundschaft bis gut in die fünfziger Jahre. Cooper erwähnt, dass Eichmann kürzlich Castille besucht habe. (Archiv, Museum of Modern Art, Library, New York)

Many graphic works were purchased in the 1950s and 1960s including *Standing Nude,* 1907, etching (No. 2).

34 No. 64, *The Essential Cubism.*

35 Légers acquired in 1945 included: *View of Paris,* 1912, oil, from Reid and Lefevre. In 1949, Léger himself was the source for *Portrait of Philippon,* 1915, pencil, *Study for "The City",* 1919, watercolor, *Composition,* 1929, ink, *Head of a man,* 1931, ink and *The Elephants,* 1949, gouache. Cooper continually purchased graphics by Léger.

36 Additional purchases of works by Picasso, 1940s – 1970s: In 1944, *Seated nude,* 1906, wash was purchased from The Mayor Gallery(?). In 1950, Cooper purchased a 1917 pencil, *Interior* from the Galerie Louise Leiris. From Edouard Loeb in 1955, Cooper purchased *Bottle of Bass,* 1913, blue chalk and saw dust (traded to Reid & Lefevre the same year).

37 *Femme Cubiste,* terra cotta; *Femme accroupie au voile,* 1930, terra cotta (Galerie Simon label: *Femme accroupie,* 1930, 2/6 (in black on sculpture), no: 1139(?)3/2, photo no. 7575); *Femme couchée (de face),* 1921, bronze (Galerie Louise Leiris, no. 6741/4 and stamped 4/8 in metal, purchased 21 March 1959); and *Femme couchée (de dos),* 1921, bronze (Galerie Simon, no. 6741/1). Cooper not only devoted a sizeable section to Laurens in *The Cubist Epoch,* London: Phaidon (in association with the Los Angeles County Museum of Art and the Metropolitan Museum of Art, New York) 1970, but included thirteen works by that artist in *The Essential Cubism,* 1983.

38 Douglas Cooper, *The Cubist Epoch,* pp. 247–248.

39 April 16, 1952 letter to Curt Valentin, in Archives, The Museum of Modern Art, Library, New York.

40 *Paysan catalan au repos,* (Catalan Peasant Resting) painted on copper, was purchased from Pierre Matisse on March 2, 1937. Five other works by Miró were purchased at the same time: *Two Women,* 1935, oil (DC22 sold to Mayor Gallery June 1938), *Lovers,* 1934, pastel (DC23 sold in 1955 to Galerie Maeght), *Figure,* 1935, gouache (DC30 sold to Mayor Gallery Dec. 1946), *Bird, Shooting Star and Landscape* 1935, gouache (DC31 sold to Klaus Perls July 1964) and *Figure,* 1934, pencil and gouache (sold in 1961). He obtained other Mirós from Pierre Matisse as well. Later in June of 1937 he acquired *Composition,* 1937, gouache on paper (DC80 sold to Kornfeld in June 1966), *Composition,* 1937, gouache on black paper (DC76, sold to Klaus Perls, June 1965), *Composition,* 1937, gouache on black paper (DC79 sold to Klaus Perls June 1965). In July of the previous year Cooper purchased *Figure,* 1935,

28 *Trauben und Glas,* 1921, Bleistift, *Gitarre mit Noten,* 1923, Tusche, und *Flasche und Glas,* 1919, Öl (verkauft an die Mayor Gallery 1946).

29 Andere Erwerbungen von der Galerie Simon 1938: *Liegender Akt,* 1907, Tusche; *Männliche Figur,* 1908, Tusche.

30 Auch von Loeb: Picassos *Stilleben mit Girlanden,* 1918, Öl (Z, III, 142).

31 Ein weiterer Gris von Ronald Fleming, 1939: *Das Buch,* 1924, Öl (1950 an die Hannover Gallery verkauft). Cooper kaufte ein Ölbild von Gris, *Harlekin,* 1924, von Willi Raeber, Basel. Direkt von Picasso kam *Frauenporträt,* 1938, Pastell (1946 verkauft an die Mayor Gallery).

32 Erworbene Braque-Ölbilder in den fünfziger Jahren: *Stilleben mit Trauben,* 1918, von Tooth & Son, London, 1950, *Stilleben mit Gitarre,* 1918, von César de Hauke, 1958 (Datum auf Quittung in Sammlungsakten; *The Essential Cubism* hingegen hat 1960), und *Studio VIII,* direkt vom Künstler, ca. 1955.

33 Die andern zwei von Marlborough: *Karaffe, Flasche und Zeitung,* 1913, Kohle (Nr. 164, Nicole Worms de Romilly und Jean Laude, *Braque le Cubisme, 1907–1914,* Paris, Maeght, 1982 [verkauft an Berggruen 1956]) und *Flasche Marc,* 1912–13, Collage/Kohle (Worms de Romilly und Laude, Nr. 127).
Viel Grafik wurde in den fünfziger und sechziger Jahren erworben, darunter *Stehender Akt,* 1907, Radierung (Nr. 2).

34 Nr. 64, *The Essential Cubism.*

35 Léger-Erwerbung, 1945: *Ansicht von Paris,* 1912, Öl, von Reid & Lefevre. Von Léger direkt, 1949: *Porträt von Philippon,* 1915, Bleistift, *Studie für «Die Stadt»,* 1919, Aquarell, *Komposition,* 1929, Tusche, *Männerkopf,* 1931, Tusche, und *Die Elephanten,* 1949, Gouache. Cooper erwarb regelmässig Grafik von Léger.

36 Weitere Picasso-Käufe, vierziger bis siebziger Jahre: *Sitzender Akt,* 1906, Tusche, von der Mayor Gallery 1944, *Intérieur,* 1917, Bleistift, von der Galerie Louise Leiris 1950, *Flasche «Bass»,* 1913, blaue Kreide und Sägemehl, von Edouard Loeb 1955 (getauscht mit Reid & Lefèvre im selben Jahr).

37 *Femme Cubiste,* Terrakotta, *Femme accroupie au voile,* 1930, Terrakotta [Galerie Simon-Etikett: *Femme accroupie,* 1930, 2/6 (in Schwarz auf dem Werk), no: 1139 (?) 3/2, photo no. 7575], *Femme couchée (de face),* 1921, Bronze (Galerie Louise Leiris, no. 6741/4, bezeichnet 4/8 im Metall, erworben 21. März 1959) und *Femme* gouache (DC63 sold to Klaus Perls June 1965) and *Figure at the Window,* 1935, gouache (DC25). Other Mirós which Cooper acquired included: *Composition,* 1933, gouache, from Miró himself (DC48), *Star, Planet, Moon, Woman and Landscape,* 1935, gouache, frpm Pierre Loeb in July 1936 (DC28 sold to Klaus Perls in June 1965), *Woman,* 1935, gouache also from Loeb in 1936 (DC61 sold to Klaus Perls in June 1965), *Signs and Figurations,* 1935, gouache (DC62 also from Loeb in 1936 sold to the Mayor Gallery June 1938), *Figures,* 1937, ink (DC75 from Loeb in 1937 sold to Kornfeld in June 1966), *Statue,* 1925, oil, at auction from Rain's Galleries, New York, February 1937 (DC26 sold to Mayor Gallery December 1946) and *Woman Chasing Bird,* 1928, pencil, purchased at Christie's London, April 1937 (Pertinsot Sale) disposed of in 1939. Cooper wrote an introduction to *Joan Miró,* a series of wood cuts with a poem by Paul Eluard, published by Berggruen in 1958.

41 For instance, *Harlekin auf der Brücke,* watercolor and ink, 1920 (DC190 purchased from the Klee Gesellschaft in 1949) (see John Richardson's "A Cache of Klees", *Vanity Fair,* February 1987) was traded to Eleanore Saidenberg in 1955 for a *Pierrot* by Picasso. Mrs. Saidenberg very kindly informed me that the Pierrot in question was a gouache, with a portrait of Picasso as a boy on the reverse, which she purchased from Ludwig Charell in May, 1955. The Klee was unfortunately subsequently been stolen from Mrs. Saidenberg.

Many of Cooper's Klees were sold or exchanged with Heinz Berggruen during the fifties. *Der Ballon im Fenster (The Balloon through the Window),* watercolor, 1929 (DC223 purchased from the Klee Gesellschaft in 1947), *Golf von Y,* watercolor and other media, 1925 (DC194 purchased from the Klee Gesellschaft in 1949), *Märchen,* 1929, watercolor on gesso on canvas (DC144 purchased from Curt Valentin at the Buchholz Gallery, New York, April 1939 in exhcange for the Picasso "Ex Libris for Apollinaire".) and *Befestigte Düne bei Baltrum (Fortified Dunes on Baltrum)* watercolor, 1923, (DC145 purchased from the artist in 1945?) were all sold to Berggruen in April of 1955. Six more Klees were sold to Berggruen in 1956: *Barockbildnis (Baroque Portrait),* 1920, gouache and ink (DC9 purchased from Alfred Flechtheim in 1934), *Flora Noctis,* 1939, gouache (DC170 purchased from the artist), *Südliche Gärten (Southern Gardens),* 1919, watercolor on paper (DC171 gift from the artist), *Architektur im Orient* 1929, watercolor on paper (DC193, bought from the Klee Gesellschaft in 1949), *Bauchredner und Rufer im Moor (Ventriloquist and Crier in the Bog),* 1923, watercolor (DC153 purchased from Lily Klee in 1946), and *Garten in der tunesischen Europäerkolonie, St. Germain (Garden in the European Quarter of St. Germain, Tunis),* 1914, watercolor (DC152 Gift by Lily Klee, 1945). In September 1957 Cooper exchanged *Stilleben mit dem Würfel (Still-life with Dice),* 1923, watercolor (DC146, bought in 1945) with Berggruen. At least 3 works by Klee were exchanged

couchée (de dos), 1921, Bronze (Galerie Simon, no. 6741/1). Cooper widmete Laurens nicht nur einen ansehnlichen Abschnitt in *The Cubist Epoch*, London, Phaidon, in association with the Los Angeles County Museum of Art, and the Metropolitan Museum of Art, New York, 1970, sondern nahm auch dreizehn Werke des Künstlers in *The Essential Cubism* auf.

38 Cooper, *The Cubist Epoch,* S. 247–248.

39 Brief vom 16. April 1952 an Curt Valentin, Archiv, Museum of Modern Art, Library, New York.

40 *Paysan catalan au repos (Rastender katalanischer Bauer),* auf Kupfer gemalt, wurde am 2. März 1937 von Pierre Matisse erworben. Gleichzeitig wurden fünf weitere Werke von Miró gekauft: *Zwei Frauen,* 1935, Öl (DC22 verkauft an die Mayor Gallery, Juni 1938), *Liebespaar,* 1934, Pastell (DC23 verkauft an die Galerie Maeght, 1955), *Figur,* 1935, Gouache (DC30 verkauft an die Mayor Gallery, Dezember 1946), *Vogel, Sternschnuppe und Landschaft,* 1935, Gouache (DC31 verkauft an Klaus Perls, Juli 1964) und *Figur,* 1934, Bleistift/Gouache (verkauft 1961). Er erwarb noch andere Mirós von Pierre Matisse. Im Juni 1937 kaufte er *Komposition,* 1937, Gouache auf Papier (DC80 verkauft an Kornfeld, Juni 1966), *Komposition,* 1937, Gouache auf schwarzem Papier (DC76 verkauft an Klaus Perls, Juni 1965). Im Juli des vorigen Jahres erwarb Cooper *Figur,* 1935, Gouache (DC63 verkauft an Klaus Perls, Juni 1965) und *Figur am Fenster,* 1935, Gouache (DC25). Weitere erworbene Mirós: *Komposition,* 1933, Gouache, direkt von Miró (DC48), *Stern, Planet, Mond, Frau und Landschaft,* 1935, Gouache, von Pierre Loeb, Juli 1936 (DC28 verkauft an Klaus Perls, Juni 1965), *Frau,* 1935, Gouache, auch von Loeb, 1936 (DC61 verkauft an Klaus Perls, Juni 1965), *Zeichen und Gestalten,* 1935, Gouache (DC62 auch von Loeb, 1936, verkauft an die Mayor Gallery, Juni 1938), *Figuren,* 1937, Tusche (DC75 von Loeb, 1937, verkauft an Kornfeld, Juni 1966), *Statue,* 1925, Öl, auf Auktion bei Rain's Galleries, New York, Februar 1937 (DC26 verkauft an die Mayor Gallery, Dezember 1946) und *Frau und Vogel,* 1928, Bleistift, bei Christie's, London, April 1937 (Pertinsot-Sammlung), veräussert 1939. Cooper schrieb eine Einleitung zu *Joan Miró,* Holzschnitte mit einem Gedicht von Paul Eluard, hg. v. Berggruen 1958.

41 Zum Beispiel: *Harlekin auf der Brücke,* 1920, Aquarell/Tusche (DC190 erworben von der Klee-Gesellschaft, 1949 [s. John Richardson: "A Cache of Klees", *Vanity Fair,* Februar 1987], ging an Eleanore Seidenberg im Tausch für einen *Pierrot* von Picasso, 1955. Von Mrs. Saidenberg bekam ich freundlicherweise die Information, dass der besagte Pierrot eine Gouache mit einem Porträt von Picasso als Knabe auf der Rückseite gewesen sei; sie habe sie von Ludwig Charell im Mai 1955 erworben. Der Klee wurde ihr später leider gestohlen).

with Berggruen in April 1958 for Braque's *Still-life with guitar,* 1918, oil (DC308): *Feldfrüchte (Field produce),* 1931, watercolor (DC172 purchased form the artist), *Blau-Vogel-Kürbis (Bird and Gourd in Blue),* 1939, gouache (DC128 purchased from Lily Klee in 1946), *Mephisto als Pallas,* 1939, various media (DC173 purchased form the artist) along with Fernand Léger's *Study for "The Balcony",* 1913, gouache on paper (DC20 purchased form Léonce Rosenberg in 1936) and Juan Gris' *The Fruit-dish,* 1918, oil (DC125 purchased form L. Neumann, Basel 1945).

42 Another publication on Klee was Cooper's 1941 review of an exhibition at The Leicester Galleries entitled "Paul Klee: A Memorial", *The Listener,* March 13, 1941, p. 381. Cooper was slated to translate Will Grohmann's *Paul Klee*. In a December 5, 1953, letter to Curt Valentin he admits that he thinks it is "lousy". Another letter to Valentin dated April 27, 1954, offers amusing insight into his disposal of so many works by Klee: "I am not translating Grohmann's Klee. It is so bad and dreary that after 75 pages I could not go on. It has made me loathe Klee forever". (Archives, the Museum of Modern Art, Library, New York.)

43 Cooper owned three sculptures by César: *The Insect,* welded steel, *The Turkey*, bronze, and *Untitled*, welded steel.

Cooper's Giacomettis: a minor pencil drawing, *Bottles in the Studio*, 1949 (New DC122/243), and several etchings including, *Portrait,* 1949 (New DC95/137) and *Still-life with Bottles* (New DC134/263). There are, as well, two sculptures by Giacometti in the collection: a bronze *Portrait of Diego*, 1955 (New DC22/21; See exhibition catalogue, from Martigny, Fondation Pierre Gianadda, 1986, *Alberto Giacometti*, 16 may – 2 nov, page 275, no. 144. Cooper's bronze is signed and stamped 6/6); and a plaster of another version *Portrait of Diego in a Sweater,* 1953 (New DC106/228; see the bronze cast in the exhibition catalogue Martigny, 1986, p. 273, no. 129.)

Cooper had met Renato Guttuso through Picasso. At one time he owned many works by this prominent Italian Communist including: *Still-life*, 1946, watercolor and crayon (DC134 bought from the artist August 1946), *Crouching Nude*, 1946, ink (DC135 bought from the artist August 1946), *The Glass*, 1946, watercolor, (DC136 bought from the artist August 1946), *Gourd and Candle*, 1946, oil, (DC137 bought from the artist August 1946), *Reclining Nude*, 1946, chalk, (DC138 bought from the artist), *Seated Nude*, 1946, chalk, (DC139 gift from the artist) and *Head*, 1947, watercolor (DC157 gift from the artist). (Guttuso introduced quotations from Picasso in his work and included him, as well, in his "Conversation Pieces", such as *La Visite*, which included also Cézanne, Velasquez, Cranach, Rembrandt, Delacroix and Courbet.)

Cooper owned a number of prints by André Masson: *Sisyphus*, 1946 etching (DC114 purchased from the Galerie Simon November 1946), *The Boot*, 1946, lithograph (DC115 from Galerie Simon June

Viele Klees in Coopers Besitz wurden in den fünfziger Jahren verkauft an oder getauscht mit Heinz Berggruen. *Der Ballon im Fenster,* 1929, Aquarell (DC223 erworben von der Klee-Gesellschaft, 1947), *Golf von Y,* 1925, Aquarell/Mischtechnik (DC194 erworben von der Klee-Gesellschaft, 1949), *Märchen,* 1929, Aquarell auf Kreidegrund auf Leinwand (DC144 erworben von Curt Valentin in der Buchholz Gallery, New York, im April 1939 im Austausch gegen den Picasso «Ex Libris für Apollinaire») und *Befestigte Düne bei Baltrum,* 1923, Aquarell (DC145 erworben vom Künstler 1945?): alle im April 1955 an Berggruen verkauft; an ihn gingen 1956 sechs weitere Klees: *Barockbildnis,* 1920, Gouache/Tusche (DC9 erworben von Alfred Flechtheim, 1934), *Flora Noctis,* 1939, Gouache (DC170 erworben vom Künstler), *Südliche Gärten,* 1919, Aquarell auf Papier (DC171 Geschenk des Künstlers), *Architektur im Orient,* 1929, Aquarell auf Papier (DC193 erworben von der Klee-Gesellschaft, 1949), *Bauchredner und Rufer im Moor,* 1923, Aquarell (DC153 erworben von Lily Klee 1946) und *Garten in der tunesischen Europäerkolonie, St-Germain,* 1914, Aquarell (DC152 Geschenk von Lily Klee, 1945). Im September 1957 tauschte Cooper *Stilleben mit dem Würfel,* 1923, Aquarell (DC146 erworben 1945) mit Berggruen. Mindestens drei Klees wurden im April 1958 getauscht mit Berggruen gegen Braques *Stilleben mit Gitarre,* 1918, Öl (DC308), es waren dies: *Feldfrüchte,* 1931, Aquarell (DC172 erworben vom Künstler), *Blau – Vogel– Kürbis,* 1939, Gouache (DC128 erworben von Lily Klee, 1946), *Mephisto als Pallas,* 1939, Mischtechnik (DC173 erworben vom Künstler) zusammen mit Légers *Studie für «Den Balkon»,* 1913, Gouache auf Papier (DC20 erworben von Léonce Rosenberg, 1936) und Juan Gris' *Die Fruchtschale,* 1918, Öl (DC125 erworben von L. Neumann, Basel, 1945).

42 1941 schrieb Cooper noch eine Besprechung der Klee-Ausstellung in den Leicester Galleries mit dem Titel "Paul Klee: A Memorial" (*The Listener,* 13. März 1941, S. 381). Cooper war auch als Übersetzer von Will Grohmanns *Paul Klee* vorgesehen, das er aber, wie ein Brief an Curt Valentin vom 5. Dezember 1953 zeigt, für «lausig» hält. Ein weiterer Brief an Valentin – vom 27. April 1954 – wirft auf halbernste Weise Licht auf die vielen Veräusserungen von Klee-Werken: «Grohmanns Klee übersetze ich nicht. Es ist so schlecht und langfädig, dass ich nach 75 Seiten nicht mehr weiter konnte. Es hat mir Klee für immer verekelt» (Archiv, The Museum of Modern Art, Library, New York).

43 Cooper besass drei Plastiken von César: *Das Insekt,* Stahl, *Der Truthahn,* Bronze, und *ohne Titel,* Schweissstahl.

Coopers Giacomettis: eine kleinere Bleistiftzeichnung, *Flaschen im Atelier,* 1949 (Neue DC122/243), und einige Radierungen, darunter *Porträt,* 1949, und *Stilleben mit Flaschen* (Neue DC134/263). Auch zwei Giacometti-Plastiken gehören zur Sammlung: *Porträt Diego,* Bronze, 1955 (Neue DC22/21; s. Ausstellungskatalog der Fonda-1946), *The Spring,* 1946, lithograph (DC116 from Galerie Simon June 1946), *Portrait of Monsieur Kahnweiler,* 1946, lithograph (DC151 gift of Kahnweiler), *Self-portrait,* 1948, etching (DC165 gift of the artist).

Cooper owned only two works by Henri Matisse: *The Spanish Drawing,* 1915, charcoal [DC131 purchased from Marguerite D.(?)] and *Seated Dancer,* 1944 pencil drawing (DC143 gift from the artist; inscribed "à David Cooper"). He also owned a small bronze, *Venus* (Small Crouching Torso), 1908, numbered 1/10(?). Cooper apparently briefly owned a major Matisse studio. Though always regretting not keeping it, he nonetheless maintained that one could not allow oneself to be distracted from the main focus of a collection.

He owned a work by Modigliani *Nude,* ca. 1919, watercolor and pencil (DC148 purchased from St. George's Gallery 1945, sold to d'Arquian, 1951). One work by Henry Moore was included in the collection: *Drawing for a sculpture,* 1933, ink and wash (DC32, purchased from the artist 1933, sold to Leicester Galleries 1951).

The collection included a number of small sketches, gouaches and prints by De Staël.

Besides his own portrait and the preparatory study for it, Cooper owned a vast number of works by Sutherland, over thirty of which were disposed of in 1976, sold to the Redfern Gallery, London.

In addition, the collection included a few unrelated works: Pietro Consagra's, *Nude,* 1947, crayon on paper (DC164) and Pizzinato's, *Plant in front of a window,* 1947, pastel (DC180), both gifts from the artists; and two prints, one by Ernst Neizvestny another by Dimitrienko.

44 Cooper's bias against abstraction is surely manifest in his intense interest in Cubism. In a letter to Curt Valentin, November 24, 1953, he expresses his contempt for the works of Louise Bourgeois and generally derides "untalented American abstracts". (Letter in Archives, Museum of Modern Art, Library, New York).

45 In 1962, Cooper's appreciation of César was published in Amriswil by Bodensee-Verlag. In 1973 he wrote the catalogue for an exhibition of *César Le Novateur* at the Musée Réattu in Arles.

Cooper wrote about Guttuso in 1950 in a preface to an exhibition catalogue at the Hannover Gallery, London and in 1957 in an exhibition catalogue for ACA Galleries in New York.

Cooper wrote "Matisse and Gauguin" for the catalogue of a Matisse exhibition, *Henri Matisse, Das Goldene Zeitalter,* at the

tion Pierre Gianadda, Martigny 1986, *Alberto Giacometti,* 16. Mai–2. November, S. 275, Nr. 144. Die Bronze ist bezeichnet mit Signatur und Auflage 6/6); und eine Version von *Porträt Diego im Pullover,* 1953, Gips (Neue DC106/228; vgl. Ausstellungskatalog Martigny, 1986, S. 273, Nr. 129: der Bronzeguss davon).

Cooper lernte Renato Guttuso, den prominenten italienischen Kommunisten und Maler, durch Picasso kennen. Zeitweilig besass er viele Werke von ihm, so: *Stilleben,* 1946, Aquarell/Ölkreide (DC134 erworben vom Künstler, August 1946), *Kauernder Akt,* 1946, Tusche (DC135 erworben vom Künstler, August 1946), *Das Glas,* 1946, Aquarell (DC136 erworben vom Künstler, August 1946), *Kürbisflasche und Kerze,* 1946, Öl (DC137 erworben vom Künstler, August 1946), *Liegender Akt,* 1946, Kreide (DC138 erworben vom Künstler), *Sitzender Akt,* 1946, Kreide (DC139 Geschenk des Künstlers) und *Kopf,* 1947, Aquarell (DC157 Geschenk des Künstlers).
Guttuso verwendete in seinem Werk Zitate von Picasso und nahm seinen Freund in seine ‹Gruppenbilder› auf, so in *La Visite,* das auch Cézanne, Velàsquez, Cranach, Rembrandt, Delacroix und Courbet enthielt.

Cooper besass eine Anzahl grafischer Blätter von André Masson: *Sisyphus,* 1946, Radierung (DC114 erworben von der Galerie Simon, November 1946), *Der Stiefel,* 1946, Lithografie (DC115 von der Galerie Simon, Juni 1946), *Der Frühling,* 1946, Lithografie (DC116 von der Galerie Simon, Juni 1946), *Porträt Herr Kahnweiler,* 1946, Lithografie (DC151 Geschenk von Kahnweiler), *Selbstporträt,* 1948, Radierung (DC165 Geschenk des Künstlers).
In Coopers Besitz waren nur zwei Werke von Henri Matisse: *Die spanische Zeichnung,* 1915, Kohle (DC131 erworben von Marguerite D ?) und *Sitzende Tänzerin,* 1944, Bleistift (DC143 Geschenk des Künstlers; mit Widmung «à David Cooper»). Er besass auch die kleine Bronze *Venus* (kleine kauernde Figur), 1908, numeriert 1/10. Anscheinend besass Cooper kurze Zeit auch ein bedeutendes *Studio.* Obwohl er immer bereute, es nicht behalten zu haben, meinte er doch, dass man sich nicht von Hauptlinie und -ziel einer Sammlung abbringen lassen dürfe.
In der Sammlung waren auch: ein Modigliani, *Akt,* ca. 1919, Aquarell/Bleistift (DC148 erworben bei der St. George's Gallery 1945, verkauft an d'Arquian 1951), ein Henry Moore, *Zeichnung für eine Skulptur,* 1933, Tusche (DC32 erworben vom Künstler 1933, verkauft an die Leicester Galleries 1951) und eine Anzahl Skizzen, Gouachen und Grafik von de Staël.
Neben seinem Porträt und der vorbereitenden Studie dazu besass Cooper eine sehr grosse Anzahl Werke von Sutherland, von denen über dreissig 1976 an die Redfern Gallery, London, verkauft wurden.

Die Sammlung enthielt auch einiges ohne spezifischen Bezug, so: Pietro Consagras *Akt,* 1947, Ölkreide auf Papier (DC146), Pizzinatos *Pflanze vor dem Fenster,* 1947, Pastell (DC180) – beides Geschenke

Kunsthalle, Bielefeld, 1981. He reviewed an exhibition of Matisse and Moore at Galleries Lefevre in 1948 in *The Observer,* November 1948 (Ms., Getty Study Center); and in "Matisse without Masterpieces, an exhibition in Paris", in *The Times,* September 15, 1956.

In 1958 Cooper organized an exhibition of De Staël's work for the Musée Réattu in Arles. In 1962 Cooper's book, *Nicolas de Staël,* was published in London by Weidenfeld and Nicolson. "Nicolas de Stael: In Memoriam", appeared in the *Burlington Magazine,* no. 98, May 1956, p. 140–146.

Cooper published a major monograph on Sutherland: *The Works of Graham Sutherland,* London, 1961 and reissued in 1967. In 1965 Cooper contributed to the catalogue of an exhibition of Sutherland's works at the Galleria Civica de Arte Moderna in Torino.

46 Letter to Curt Valentin, November 24, 1953, Archives, The Museum of Modern Art, Library, New York.

47 In a February 5, 1954 letter to Curt Valentin, Cooper writes: "we are having a wonderful row with the Trustees and Director of The Tate and are hoping that any day now Sir John will have been thrown out. Graham has resigned with a wonderful splash... all of the papers are full of the dirt." (Archives, Museum of Modern Art, Library, New York.)

48 Cooper's essay for the 1967 Munich, Haus der Kunst exhibition glowed with praise. About Sutherland's portraiture Cooper specifically writes: "... he excells, because he does not simply attach importance to the element of facial 'likeness' but conceives of portraiture as another kind of 'nature study' in which he can embrace the human content as a whole. That is to say, Sutherland sees in bodily attitudes, as well as in the forms and convolutions of a face, the same sort of expression of character and of the toll of life's struggle as in the linear markings or formal and surface contrasts which constitute externally the individuality of a scarab beetle, a boulder of a mountain gorge." (p. 5 Ms.)
Cooper also penned a glowing praise of Sutherland upon the occasion of the artist's receipt of the Shakespeare Prize from Hamburg University, May 30, 1974.
In the unpublished essay Cooper writes about Sutherland as "a failure (there is no other word) as a portrait-painter." (p. 12 Ms.) Cooper attributed Sutherland's turn to portraiture to social advancement and financial reward. Cooper criticizes Sutherland's portraits for a lack of psychological insight: "... as paintings, his portraits are dry, crude and artificial. There was no emotional exchange between Sutherland and his sitter." (p. 12 Ms.) Finding slight praise only for Sutherland's portraits of Max Beaverbrook and Somerset Maugham, Cooper expresses his intense dislike for his own image painted by

der Künstler –, sowie zwei Drucke, einen von Ernst Neizvestny und einen von Dimitrienko.

44 Coopers Ablehnung der abstrakten Kunst wird kompensiert durch die intensive Hinwendung zum Kubismus. In einem Brief an Curt Valentin vom 24. November 1953 drückt er seine Verachtung für die Werke von Louise Bourgeois aus und spricht allgemein von den «untalentierten amerikanischen Abstrakten» (Brief im Archiv, Museum of Modern Art, Library, New York).

45 Coopers Würdigung Césars erschien 1962 im Bodensee-Verlag, Amriswil. 1973 verfasste er den Katalog für die Ausstellung *César Le Novateur* im Musée Réattu, Arles.
Über Guttuso schrieb Cooper 1950 in der Einleitung für den Ausstellungskatalog der Hannover Gallery, London, und 1957 in einem Ausstellungskatalog der ACA Galleries, New York.
Cooper schrieb den Artikel «Matisse und Gauguin» für den Katalog einer Matisse-Ausstellung in der Kunsthalle Bielefeld, 1981, *Henri Matisse, Das goldene Zeitalter*. Im November 1948 besprach er eine Ausstellung von Matisse und Moore in den Galeries Lefevre im *Observer* (Ms. Getty Study Center) und auch in der *Times* vom 15. September unter dem Titel "Matisse without Masterpieces, an exhibition in Paris" (Matisse ohne Meisterwerke, eine Ausstellung in Paris).
1958 organisierte Cooper eine Ausstellung von de Staëls Werk im Musée Réattu in Arles. 1962 erschien Coopers Buch *Nicolas de Staël* bei Weidenfeld und Nicolson, London. 1967 publizierte Norton, New York, ein weiteres Buch Coopers über den Künstler, und in der Nummer 98 des *Burlington Magazine* erschien im Mai 1956 "Nicolas de Staël: In Memoriam", S. 140–146.
Cooper publizierte eine grössere Monografie über Sutherland: *The Works of Graham Sutherland,* London 1961 (1967[II]). 1965 verfasste Cooper einen Beitrag für den Katalog zur Ausstellung von Werken Sutherlands in der Galleria Civica d'Arte Moderna in Turin.

46 Brief an Curt Valentin vom 24. November 1953, Archiv, Museum of Modern Art, Library, New York.

47 In einem Brief vom 5. Februar 1954 an Curt Valentin schreibt Cooper: «Wir haben den schönsten Krach hier mit den Bevollmächtigten und dem Direktor der Tate und hoffen, dass Sir John lieber heute noch als morgen rausgeschmissen wird. Grahams Rücktritt war ein Knall – die Zeitungen tönen dementsprechend» (Archiv, Museum of Modern Art, Library, New York).

48 Coopers Aufsatz für die Ausstellung 1967 im Haus der Kunst, München, strotzte vor Lob. Über Sutherlands Kunst des Porträtierens schreibt er im besonderen: «... er ist überragend, weil für ihn Ähnlichkeit nicht an erster Stelle kommt, sondern weil Porträtieren ihm eine Sutherland, and likens most of the artist's sitters to dead bodies ready for the embalmer.

The quarrel was apparently sparked by a misunderstanding about Sutherland's inclusion in an exhibition of masterpieces of the Ecole de Paris, planned for the Grand Palais, which however, never came to pass.

49 Cooper's writings on Cézanne include: "Paul Cézanne", a review of the exhibition at the l'Orangerie, *Burlington Magazine*, July 1936, pp. 32–35; a review of "Dessins de Paul Cézanne", by Adrien Chappuis, *Burlington Magazine*, March 1939, p. 149; "Cézanne in Aix", *The Listener*, July 23, 1953, p. 150; "Cézanne's Studio: American Gift to France," *The Times*, July 5?, 1953; "Two Cézanne Exhibitions at the Orangerie and the Tate," *Burlington Magazine*, no. 96, Nov–Dec 1954, pp. 344–349, 378–380; "Cézanne Studio now National Museum," *The New York Times*, July 11, 1954, p. 4; "Au Jas de Bouffan," *Oeil*, no. 2, 1955, pp. 13–16 and 46; "Cézanne's Chronology," *Burlington Magazine*, no. 98, Nov–Dec 1956, p. 449; "Cézanne's Vision of Provence," *The Times*, July 30, 1956, p. 3; and a review of Andrien Chappui's *Les dessins de Paul Cézanne au Cabinet des Estampes du Musée des Beaux-Arts de Bâle*, in *Master Drawings*, vol I, no. 4, 1963, pp. 54–56.

Note Cooper's article, "Courbet in Philadelphia and Boston," *Burlington Magazine*, no. 102, June 1960, pp. 244–245. He reviewed Michael Florisoone's *Delacroix* in "Publications received", in the *Burlington Magazine*, vol. 74, January–June 1939, p. xvii.

50 He owned one work by Paul Cézanne, *Préparatifs d'un festin*, ca. 1885, oil on canvas, purchased in 1933 from Pierre Loeb. This work (Venturi No. 586) was exchanged in 1935 with Paul Rosenberg for *Guitar and Fruit-dish*, 1932, by Picasso.

Cooper owned an important work by Gustave Courbet, *Femme endormie*, 1853, oil on canvas, which he purchased from P. M. Turner in London in 1943 and subsequently sold to Jacques Guérin in Paris in 1953 (DC150). In addition Cooper once owned a small pencil drawing by Delacroix, *Electra recognizing her brother*, purchased from Tooth and Co., in London in 1944. The Collection also includes two small bronze portrait busts by Daumier.

51 "Christopher Gray's *Cubist Aesthetic Theories*", *Times Literary Supplement*, April 29, 1955, p. 196; Though acknowledging that Gray's writing about the poets and their work was "perceptive and shows a good historical sense" (p. 3 Ms.), he found Gray's interdisciplinary thrust "obscuring" and especially objected to "his determined attempt to formulate "theories" where none existed."

weitere Art Natur-Studium ist, durch das er zu menschlicher Essenz vordringen kann. Das heisst, Sutherland sieht in Körperhaltungen wie in Gesichtszügen den gleichen Charakter-Ausdruck, den gleichen Stempel des Lebens wie in der Zeichnung oder den vielfältigen Formen, welche uns äusserlich die Eigenart eines Käfers oder der Flusssteine einer Bergschlucht beschreiben» (S. 5, Ms.).
Cooper brachte auch glühendes Lob zu Papier, als Sutherland am 30. Mai 1974 den Shakespeare-Preis der Hamburger Universität erhielt.
Im unpublizierten Aufsatz nennt Cooper Sutherland «einen (es gibt kein anderes Wort) Versager als Porträt-Maler» (Ms., S. 12). Nach Cooper habe Sutherland sich nur der Porträtkunst zugewandt, weil sozialer Aufstieg und finanzieller Ertrag winkten. Und er kritisiert an Sutherlands Porträts einen Mangel an psychologischer Tiefe: «... als Bilder sind sie trocken, grob und künstlich. Da gab es keinen emotionalen Dialog zwischen Künstler und Modell» (Ms., S. 12). Nur für Sutherlands Porträts von Max Beaverbrook und Somerset Maugham findet Cooper schwaches Lob, drückt dafür umso stärker seine Abneigung gegen das eigene Porträt aus und vergleicht die meisten von Sutherlands Porträtierten mit Leichen, die aufs Einbalsamieren warten.
Dem Streit liegt wohl ein Missverständnis über Sutherlands Teilnahme an einer Ausstellung von Meisterwerken der Ecole de Paris zugrunde, welche für das Grand Palais geplant war, aber nie zustande kam.

49 Unter Coopers Schriften zu Cézanne befinden sich: «Paul Cézanne», Besprechung einer Ausstellung in der Orangerie (*Burlington Magazine,* Juli 1936, S. 32–35), eine Besprechung von «Dessins de Paul Cézanne» von Adrien Chappuis (im *Burlington Magazine,* März 1939, S. 149), "Cézanne in Aix" (*The Listener,* 23. Juli 1953, S. 150), "Cézanne's Studio: American Gift to France" (*The Times,* 5. Juli 1953), "Two Cézanne Exhibitions at the Orangerie and the Tate" (*Burlington Magazine,* Nr. 96, November/Dezember 1954, S. 344–349, 378–380), "Cézanne's Studio now National Museum" (*The New York Times,* 11. Juli 1954, S. 4), «Au Jas de Bouffan» (*l'Oeil,* Nr. 2, 1955, S. 13–16 und 46), "Cézanne's Chronology" (*Burlington Magazine,* Nr. 98, November/Dezember 1956, S. 449), "Cézanne's Vision of Provence" (*The Times,* 30. Juli 1956, S. 3) und eine Besprechung von Adrien Chappuis' *Les dessins de Paul Cézanne au Cabinet des Estampes du Musée des Beaux-Arts de Bâle* in *Master Drawings,* Bd. I, Nr. 4, 1963, S. 54–56.
S. a. Coopers Artikel "Courbet in Philadelphia and Boston" (*Burlington Magazine,* Nr. 102, Juni 1960, S. 244–245). Er besprach auch Michael Florisoones *Delacroix* im *Burlington Magazine* (Nr. 74, Januar–Juni 1939, S. xvii).

50 Er besass ein Werk von Cézanne, *Preparatifs d'un festin (Vorbereitungen für ein Festmahl),* ca. 1885, Öl auf Leinwand, 1933 (p. 4 Ms.) Moreover, Cooper objected vehemently to Gray's emphasis of the connection between Fauvism and Cubism.

52 Cooper, *The Essential Cubism*, p. 11.

53 *Ibid.*, pp. 11–12 and 14. A decade earlier, in *The Cubist Epoch*, Léger did not quite make the cut. Cooper wrote: "Léger came near to being a ‹true› Cubist for a while, but he does not finally qualify as such because his pictorial purposes were too different from those of the creators." (p. 12, *The Cubist Epoch*).

54 In *The Cubist Epoch*, Cooper divides the artists of the Cubist Movment into three groups: "The rest of the many dependants fall into three groups: a) those who 'cubified' as a mannerism; b) a few who tried to make a scientific method out of Cubism and c) a greater number who used and transformed Cubism to achieve other (not always reconcilable) pictorial ends." (p. 12)

55 Cooper, *The Cubist Epoch*, p. 13

56 See Cooper's review of Guy Habasque's *Cubism*, Geneva and London, 1959, "Studies in Modern Painting", *Times Literary Supplement*, Friday, August 7, 1959, p. 456. Cooper also objected to "confusion about the stylistic development of Cubism and the misdating of works".

57 *The Essential Cubism*, p. 14.

58 In his review of Kahnweiler's, *The Rise of Cubism* (1956 English translation of the 1920 original, *Der Weg zum Kubismus*), in the *Times Literary Supplement*, June 8, 1956, p. 340 (p. 2 Ms.)

59 Cooper's argument clearly partakes of a neo-Kantian model which had been promulgated early on by apologists of Cubism including Léon Werth (*Picasso*, 1910), Michel Puy ("The Salon Des Indépendants" 1911), Roger Allard (*The Signs of Renewal in Painting*, 1912, Oliver-Hourcade (*The Tendency of Contemporary Painting*, 1913), Jacques Rivière (*Present Tendencies in Painting*, 1912), and Maurice Raynal ("Conception et Vision," in *Gil Blas*, August, 1912; and "What is Cubism," in *Comoedia Illustré*, December 1913) and most notably, Daniel-Henry Kahnweiler.

It is interesting to consider Cooper's approach to Cubism within the context of J. M. Nash's "The Nature of Cubism", *Art History*, no. 4, December 1980, pp. 435–447. Judging their theory as inadequate to explain the appearance of Cubist paintings, Nash attempts to refute the "neo-Kantian idealism" of Kahnweiler and the other apologists, with a Nietzschean derived notion of "Reality"articulated in *Du Cubisme*, 1912, by Gleizes and Metzinger. "According to this

erworben von Pierre Loeb. Das Werk (Venturi Nr. 586) wurde 1935 mit Paul Rosenberg getauscht für *Gitarre und Fruchtschale*, 1932, von Picasso.
In Coopers Besitz war auch ein wichtiges Werk von Gustave Courbet, *Femme endormie*, 1853, Öl auf Leinwand, 1943 erworben von P. M. Turner, London, und 1953 verkauft an Jacques Guérin, Paris (DC150). Auch besass Cooper eine kleine Bleistiftzeichnung von Delacroix, *Elektra erkennt ihren Bruder*, erworben bei Tooth & Co., London, 1944. Die Sammlung enthält auch zwei kleine Porträtbüsten in Bronze von Daumier.

51 "Christopher Gray's *Cubist Aesthetic Theories*" (*Times Literary Supplement*, 29. April 1955, S. 196). Obwohl er anerkannte, dass das, was Gray über die Dichter und ihr Schaffen schrieb, «scharfsinnig (sei) und gutes historisches Verständnis» zeige (Manuskript, S. 3), fand er doch seine interdisziplinäre Stossrichtung «verwirrend» und kritisierte besonders «seine entschlossenen Versuche, ‹Theorien› zu formulieren, wo keine zu formulieren sind» (Ms., S. 4). Überdies wehrte sich Cooper vehement gegen Grays Betonung einer Verbindung zwischen Fauvismus und Kubismus.

52 Cooper, *The Essential Cubism*, S. 11.

53 ibid., S. 11–12 und 14. Ein Jahrzehnt früher, in *The Cubist Epoch*, gelang Léger der Sprung noch nicht ganz. Cooper schrieb: «Léger war eine Zeitlang nahe dem, was einen wahren Kubisten ausmacht; als solcher gilt er aber letztlich nicht, weil sein Kunstwollen doch zu verschieden von jenem der Schöpfer des Kubismus war» (*The Cubist Epoch*, S. 12).

54 In *The Cubist Epoch* teilt Cooper die Künstler kubistischer Richtung in drei Gruppen ein: «Den Rest der vielen Anhänger kann man in drei Gruppen teilen: a) jene, die in kubistischer Manier ‹kubifizierten›, b) ein paar wenige, die versuchten, aus dem Kubismus eine wissenschaftliche Methode zu machen, und c) eine grössere Anzahl, die den Kubismus verwendeten und veränderten, um andere bildnerische (und nicht immer zu vereinbarende) Ziele zu erreichen» (S. 12).

55 Cooper, *The Cubist Epoch*, S. 13.

56 S. Coopers Besprechung von Guy Habasques *Cubism*, Genf und London 1959, "Studies in Modern Painting" (*Times Literary Supplement*, 7. August 1959, S. 456). Cooper wendet sich auch gegen die «Verwirrung, die bei der stilistischen Entwicklung des Kubismus» angerichtet wird, sowie gegen die «Falschdatierung von Werken».

57 *The Essential Cubism*, S. 14.

theory, reality is nothing but the fiction the crowd has grown accustomed to. The artist does not uncover the reality underlying appearances, he *makes* "reality" according to his individual "preexisting idea" and forces this image on everyone else. this is no rhetorical and woolly version of neo-Kantian idealism – it is its flat contradiction. (p. 439)... "The central concern of *Du Cubisme* is not with the formal properties of the image but with the distinctive character of its maker, the artist. (p. 440) Nash concludes: "It is ironical that history has decided that Gleizes and Metzinger are among the herd of Picasso's followers. But in their essay, I think they got it right. Because what Picasso and Braque dsicovered was not the impossible ultimate system to represent Reality – the Thing in Itself. What they achieved was the right and the freedom constantly to recreate appearance – to impose their vision on the world." (p. 443)
Could this model more easily accomodate Cooper's insistence upon the intuitive creative act of Braque and Picasso, his concept (borrowing a phrase from Gris) of Cubism as a "state of mind"?

See also Mark Roskill, *The Interpretation of Cubism*, Philadelphia, Art Alliance Press, 1985, pp. 154 ff, "Intermezzo, Traditional Approaches in Art History and the Problems of Cubism".

60 Cooper, "The Art of George Braque", *The Listener*, vol.35, April 25, 1946, p. 547.

61 See for instance "The Art Galleries", *The Listener*, November 10, 1938 in which Cooper lambasts modern English art for "incompetence", finding praise, among current exhibitions, only for those at Lefevre and Tooth & Son, which featured French art, Picasso, Miró, Rousseau, Bonnard, Cézanne, in particular.

In "Picasso-Matisse Exhibition", *Phoebus*, January – February 1946, pp. 45–46, Cooper delights in demonstrated the ignorance of the English art-going public in the face of an exhibition of Picasso and Matisse at the Victoria and Albert Museum:

The occasion has not been allowed to pass unchallenged; in fact it is almost true to say that such reserves of energy as are still possessed by the art-lovers of Great Britain – and they have been starved for six years – have been employed to produce a scandal as noisy and as pathetically irrelevant as that accompanying the first Post Impressionist Exhibition in London in 1910. A daughter of Holman Hunt has made speeches in the rooms of the exhibition attacking the art of Picasso as "Garbage Art"; Dr. D. S. MacColl and Professor Bodkin have pleaded in a letter to "The Times" that school-children who come to see "the majestic display of English funeral sculpture" from Westminster Abbey in the entrance halls of the same museum may be prevented from

58 *Times Literary Supplement,* 8. Juni 1956, S. 340 = Besprechung von Kahnweilers *Der Weg zum Kubismus* (1920) in der englischen Übersetzung von 1956, *The Way of Cubism* (S. 2, Ms.).

59 Mit seinen Argumenten gehört Cooper ganz klar zu jenen Apologeten des Kubismus, die schon früh ein neokantianisches Modell vertraten; unter ihnen: Léon Werth (*Picasso,* 1910), Michel Puy ("The Salon des Indépendants", 1911), Roger Allard (*The Signs of Renewal in Painting,* 1912), Oliver Hourcade (*The Thendency of Contemporary Painting,* 1913), Jacques Rivière (*Present Tendencies in Painting,* 1912), Maurice Raynal («Conception et Vision» in *Gil Blas,* August 1912; «Was ist Kubismus?» in *Comœdia illustrée,* Dezember 1913) und vor allem Daniel-Henry Kahnweiler.

Interessant ist, Coopers Kubismus-Begriff im Kontext von J. M. Nashs "The Nature of Cubism" (*Art History,* Nr. 4, Dezember 1980, S. 435–447) zu betrachten. Da ihre Theorien nicht taugten, das Entstehen kubistischer Kunst zu erklären, wollte Nash den «neokantianischen Idealismus» von Kahnweiler und anderen Apologeten mit einem von Nietzsche hergeleiteten – 1912 von Gleizes und Metzinger in *Du Cubisme* formulierten – «Realitäts»-Begriff widerlegen. «Nach dieser Theorie ist Realität nichts als eine Fiktion, an welche die Menge sich gewöhnt hat. Der Künstler deckt nicht die hinter den Erscheinungen liegende Wirklichkeit auf, sondern er *erschafft* ‹Realität› nach seinem Bild, nach seiner nur ihm eigenen ‹prae-existenten Idee›, und drängt es allen auf. Dies ist keine bloss rhetorische oder verschwommene Version des neokantianischen Idealismus – es steht in völligem Widerspruch zu ihm» (S. 439) ... «In *Du Cubisme* geht es zentral um die unverwechselbare Natur des Künstlers, des Schöpfers eines Bilds – und nicht um dessen formale Eigenschaften» (S. 440). Und Nash folgert: «Ironie der Geschichte ist, dass Gleizes und Metzinger zur Herde der Picasso-Anhänger gezählt werden. Mit ihrem Aufsatz aber, so glaube ich, hatten sie recht. Denn was Picasso und Braque entdeckten, war nicht die unmögliche endgültige Methode, Wirklichkeit darzustellen – das Ding an sich –, was sie errangen, war vielmehr das Recht und die Freiheit, Erscheinung beständig neu zu schaffen, um so ihre Vision der Welt aufzuprägen» (S. 443).

Fänden Coopers Bestehen auf dem intuitiven schöpferischen Akt bei Picasso und Braque und sein Begriff vom Kubismus als – um es in Gris' Worten zu sagen – «Geisteshaltung» nicht besser in diesem Modell Platz?

S. a. Mark Roskill, *The Interpretation of Cubism,* Philadelphia, Art Alliance Press, 1985, S. 154 ff., "Intermezzo, Traditional Approaches in Art History and the Problems of Cubism".

60 Cooper, "The Art of Georges Braque", *The Listener,* 25. April 1946, S. 547.

straying into the rooms devoted to "this crazy guying of humankind"; several newspapers have been running long discussions such as "Must we tolerate ugliness in ART?" or "Picasso: Genius or Hoax?". As a result the exhibition has obtained a quite disproportionate notoriety, has acquired an attraction as great as the circus and is visited by at least four thousand people a day.

62 "The Great Years of Cubist Vision," *Times Literary Supplement,* January 1, 1960. Cooper does find much to praise about Golding's book: its limited time span from 1906 and the *Demoiselles* to the outbreak of the war in 1914; the author's assertion that Cubism "never cohered into a real movement". Cooper states: "this is first and foremost a book about true Cubism as it evolved through intuition alone in the hands of Braque and Picasso... The publication of a comprehensive history and stylistic analysis of Cubist painting during the great years, especially a well-documented survey such as Mr. Golding's has compiled, is an important event because it fills a yawning gap on the library shelves."

Indeed, considering how closely Golding's book adheres to Cooper's viewpoint, in subject and structure, the grudging nature of Cooper's praise and the inclusion of harsh and mean-spirited criticism is somewhat surprising. Cooper writes about "the rigidity of the author's mind". He tempers his praise with the following caveat: "But his understanding is above all an intellectual and ratiocinatory process involving influences, scientific speculations and historical events. Mr. Golding has not a painter's eye... Somehow Mr. Golding gives the impression that he is writing about a school of painting from whose products he derives neither visual satisfaction nor enjoyment." Cooper seems to find Golding's appreciation of the differences between paintings by the essential Cubists and the peripheral artists somewhat lacking. "As instance, Mr. Golding's failure, or inability, to convey the essential difference in "quality" and pictorial significance between the inspired paintings of "the creators of true Cubism" and the banal mannerisms of their hangerson. Perhaps this is the consequence – or is it the cause? – of his unwillingness to define what constitutes true Cubist painting. To quote Apollinaire helps no one, for he did not always know himself what he was writing about, exploited poetic liberties, shifted his camp continuously and was not clear-minded or detached." (Again in 1972, in reviewing the second edition of the book, February 1972, *Books and Bookman,* "Profiting from Picasso", pp. 6–7, Cooper offers only grudging praise. While criticizing some minor errors or omissions he admits, "Nevertheless, this is an essentially serious and useful volume of critical interpretation. In fact, it is the only one of those under review which commands respect.") While Cooper's positive comments are founded on concrete aspects of the book, his biting criticism seems based more on a personal intolerance, perhaps on a suspicion that Golding did not fully appreciate his own insights.

61 S. z.B. "The Art Galleries", *The Listener*, 10. November 1938, wo Cooper die moderne englische Kunst der «Inkompetenz» bezichtigt und von den gegenwärtigen Ausstellungen nur für jene bei Lefevre und Tooth & Son Lob findet, die französische Kunst, insbesondere Picasso, Miró, Rousseau, Bonnard, Cézanne, zeigen.
In "Picasso – Matisse Exhibition", *Phoebus*, Januar–Februar 1946, S. 45–46, ergreift Cooper freudig die Gelegenheit einer Picasso und Matisse-Ausstellung im Victoria und Albert Museum, um die Ignoranz des englischen Kunstpublikums vorzuführen:

Das Ereignis durfte natürlich nicht ohne Widerspruch stattfinden, ja man kann geradezu sagen, dass ein solches Mass an Energie – wie es die Kunstfreunde Grossbritanniens immer noch besitzen, obwohl man sie seit sechs Jahren hungern lässt – mobilisiert wurde, dass das Resultat ein ebenso lauter und erbärmlich irrelevanter Skandal war, wie man ihn von der ersten Postimpressionisten-Ausstellung 1910 in London her kennt. Eine Tochter von Holman Hunt hielt in den Ausstellungsräumen Reden, in welchen sie Picassos Kunst als «Müllkunst» verunglimpfte. Dr. D. S. MacColl und Professor Bodkin riefen in Leserbriefen an die Times dazu auf, den Schulkindern, die in den Eingangshallen des Museums «die majestätische Schau englischer Grab-Skulptur» aus der Westminster Abbey besuchen wollen, den Zutritt zu den «dieser Karikierung der Menschheit» gewidmeten Räumen zu verwehren; mehrere Zeitungen brachten lange Diskussionen über Fragen wie «Müssen wir Hässlichkeit in der Kunst tolerieren?» oder «Picasso: Genie oder Scharlatan?». Als Folge davon hat die Ausstellung eine so unverhältnismässige Berühmtheit erlangt, dass sie – wie eine Zirkus-Attraktion – jeden Tag von mindestens viertausend Leuten besucht wird.

62 "The Great Years of Cubist Vision", *Times Literary Supplement*, 1. Januar 1960. Cooper hat vieles zu loben an Goldings Buch: Die Beschränkung auf die Zeit von 1906 und den *Demoiselles* bis zum Kriegsausbruch 1914; die vom Autor vertretene Ansicht, dass der Kubismus «sich nie in einer wirklichen Bewegung konsolidierte». Cooper stellt fest: «Es ist in erster Linie ein Buch über den wahren Kubismus, wie er einzig aus der Intuition heraus von Braque und Picasso entwickelt wurde ... Die Publikation einer umfassenden Geschichte und einer stilistischen Analyse der kubistischen Malerei der Blütezeit, besonders ein so gut dokumentierter Überblick, wie ihn Herr Golding zusammengebracht hat, ist ein wichtiges Ereignis, wird doch damit eine gähnende Lücke in den Bibliotheken gefüllt.»

Allerdingst ist – wenn man sieht, wie eng Goldings Buch sich in Thema und Struktur an Cooper hält – doch etwas überraschend, wie widerwillig Lob geäussert wird und wie scharf und bösartig die Kritik manchmal ausfällt. Cooper braucht das Wort von der «geistigen Unbeweglichkeit des Autors» und schwächt sein Lob ab durch folgenden Vorbehalt: «Sein Verständnis ist aber vor allem ein

63 An exhibition which would reassemble Cooper's collection beginning in the thirties and follow its subsequent refinement, is a project of a different scope, involving complex detective work tracing the many works which have been dispersed over the years (a procedure made especially difficult by the lacunae in the Collection records), as well as establishing criteria which would differentiate between the core of the collection and objects which passed through Cooper's hands in a more casual fashion.

intellektuelles, ein rationaler Prozess, der wissenschaftliche Theorie, historische Fakten und andere Einflüsse einbezieht. Herr Golding besitzt nicht das Auge des Malers... Irgendwie bekommt man den Eindruck, Herr Golding schreibe über eine Malschule, deren Produkte ihm weder visuelle Befriedigung noch Freude bereiten.» Cooper scheint auch zu bemängeln, dass Golding nicht genügend unterscheide zwischen Werken von wahren Kubisten und solchen von Künstlern des Umfelds. «Nehmen wir zum Beispiel Herrn Goldings Versagen – oder Unfähigkeit –, den grundlegenden Unterschied in ‹Qualität› und bildnerischer Bedeutung zwischen den inspirierten Werken der ‹Schöpfer des wahren Kubismus› und der banalen Manier ihrer Anhänger zu vermitteln. Vielleicht ist dies die Folge davon – oder ist es der Grund dafür? –, dass er nicht definieren will, was denn eigentlich wahre kubistische Kunst ausmache. Apollinaire zitieren hilft da niemandem, denn dieser wusste auch nicht immer, worüber er schrieb, auch machte er von seiner poetischen Freiheit ausführlich Gebrauch, wechselte beständig das Lager und war weder unvoreingenommen noch ein klarer Denker.» (Noch einmal, 1972, in seiner Besprechung der zweiten Auflage – "Profiting from Picasso", *Books and Bookmen*, Februar 1972, S. 6–7 –, spendet Cooper nur widerwillig Lob. Er kritisiert zwar kleinere Fehler oder Auslassungen, gibt aber doch zu: «Dennoch ist es ein grundsätzlich ernsthafter und nützlicher Band kritischer Interpretation. Und eigentlich ist es der einzige von denen, die zur Besprechung vorliegen, der Respekt verdient.») Während Coopers positive Bemerkungen konkrete Aspekte des Buches betreffen, scheint seine beissende Kritik eher auf persönlicher Überempfindlichkeit, vielleicht auch auf dem Verdacht zu gründen, Golding bringe seinen Erkenntnissen keine eigentliche Anerkennung entgegen.

63 Eine Ausstellung, die alles, was Cooper seit den dreissiger Jahren gesammelt hat, zusammenbringen würde, wäre ein Unterfangen von ganz andern Dimensionen; es verlangte nicht nur komplizierte Detektivarbeit bei der Suche nach einer grossen Anzahl von Werken, die über die Jahre in alle Winde zerstreut wurden (was wiederum besonders erschwert würde durch die Lücken im Archiv), sondern machte auch Kriterien notwendig, die einer Unterscheidung zwischen dem Kern der Sammlung und andern Werken, mit denen Cooper auf verschiedene Weise in Berührung kam, dienten.

GEORGES BRAQUE

Coopers Schriften über Braque und die Werke, die er von ihm erwirbt, zeigen, wie hoch er dessen Rolle als eigenständig Schaffender, ja Neuerer – denn er wirft Licht auf die schöpferische Beziehung zwischen Picasso und Braque 1907–13 – zur Zeit des entstehenden Kubismus einschätzt; er erkennt nicht nur die spezifische Eigenart von Braques Schaffen, sondern würdigt auch die Stärke des Spätwerks nach 1945.

Die Erwerbungen der dreissiger, vierziger und fünfziger Jahre spiegeln Coopers Fähigkeit, die wichtigen Schritte in Braques Entwicklung während und nach der Zeit des Kubismus wahrzunehmen und zu verstehen. Er besass ein bedeutendes Ölbild der fauvistischen Periode, *Landschaft bei La Ciotat* von 1907 (zur Chronologie von Coopers hauptsächlichen Anschaffungen s. S. 19–28). In den fünfziger Jahren kaufte er sowohl die Radierung wie die Zeichnung mit dem Titel *Stehender Akt*, beide von 1907 (Nr. 1 und 2), welche den Einfluss von Cézanne wie auch die Wirkung von Picassos *Demoiselles* auf Braque verraten. *Grosse Bäume bei L'Estaque*, gemalt im Sommer 1908, zeigt des Künstlers weitere Verarbeitung der Lehren Cézannes während eines Aufenthaltes in dem im Titel genannten, unweit von Marseille gelegenen Dorf. Das mehr als ein Jahr später, im Winter 1909–10 entstandene *Stilleben mit Metronom* ist Frucht der ersten Zeit intensiver Zusammenarbeit mit Picasso. Die Kohlezeichnung *Stilleben mit Würfel* von 1912 (Nr. 4) zeigt einen Braque, der sich über eine für den analytischen Kubismus typische komplexe Komposition den Kopf zerbricht. Cooper besass mehrere Papiers collés, von denen er eines, *Fruchtschale und Glas* (Nr. 5), entstanden im September 1912, immer behalten hat, gilt es doch als erstes Papier collé und bezeichnet zugleich den Beginn des synthetischen Kubismus. *Stilleben mit Gitarre auf einem Tisch*, gemalt im Herbst 1918, vertritt die Zeit der Entstehung eines eigenen Stils, der wohl kubistisches Vokabular benützt, sich aber auch von ihm abgrenzt. Zwar war Cooper Besitzer einer ganzen Anzahl von Werken Braques aus den zwanziger, dreissiger und noch späte-

Cooper's writings about Braque and his acquisitions of the artist's works reflect an appreciation of the artist's autonomous, even innovatory role during the formation of Cubism, clarifying the creative relationship between Picasso and Braque during the years 1907–1913; recognizing the intrinsic or characteristic qualities of his work and acknowledging the power of the artist's late production after 1945.

His acquisitions during the thirties on through the fifties reflect his perception of the significant moments of Braque's development during Cubism and afterward. Cooper owned a major oil representing Braque's Fauve period, *Landscape at la Ciotat*, 1907. (see pages 18–26 for the chronology of Cooper's major purchases.) In the 1950s he purchased the etching as well as the drawing of *Standing Nude*, 1907, (Nos.1 and 2) which reveal the influence of Cézanne as well as the impact of Picasso's *Demoiselles*. *Big Trees at l'Estaque*, painted in the summer of 1908 reflects Braque's further digestion of the lessons of Cézanne during his stay that year at that village not far from Marseille. *Still-life with Metronome*, painted more than a year later during the winter of 1909–1910, is a result of the first period of intense collaboration between Braque and Picasso. The charcoal, *Still-life with Dice*, from 1912, (No. 4) reveals Braque's puzzling over a complex composition typical of Analytic Cubism. Cooper owned several *papiers collés* by Braque, but always kept *Fruit-dish and Glass*, (No. 5) executed in September 1912, which is recognized as the first Cubist *papier-collé*, and marks the beginning of Synthetic Cubism. *Still-life with guitar on a table*, painted in the autumn of 1918, represents the emergence of Braque's own style which draws upon, but is distinct from the Cubist idiom. Cooper owned a number of works by Braque from the twenties, thirties or later, but considered the *Studio VIII*, 1952–55, as the monumental summation of the late work of this artist.

The two versions of *Standing Nude*, (Nos. 1 and 2) are among Braque's very few figural compositions during the period 1906–09.[64] In the catalogue for the

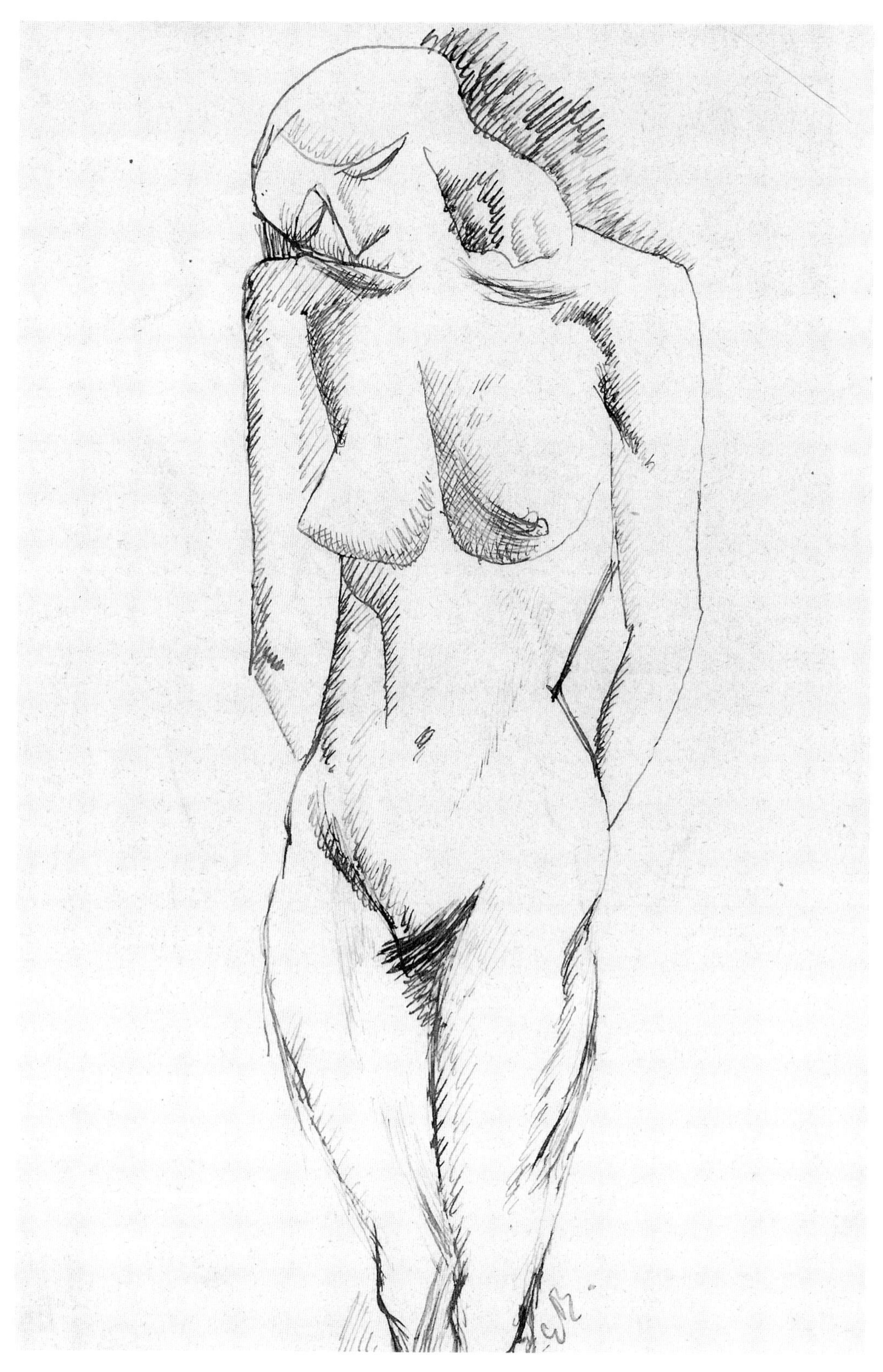

1 GEORGES BRAQUE
(Stehender Akt; Standing Nude) (1907)

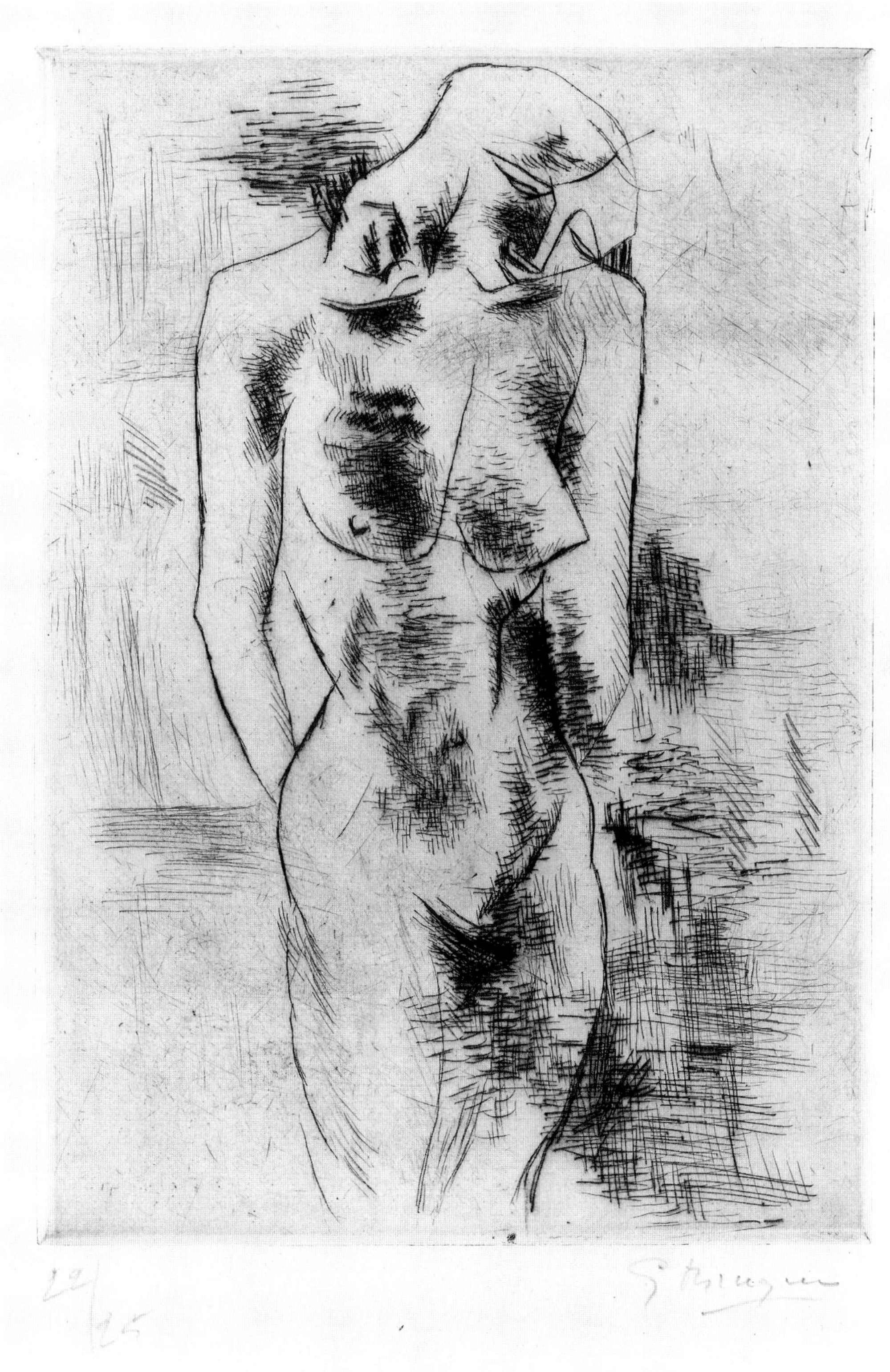

2 GEORGES BRAQUE
(Stehender Akt; Standing Nude) (1907)

ren Jahren, doch betrachtete er *Studio VIII*, 1952–55, als monumentale Summa des Spätwerks.

Die zwei Versionen von *Stehender Akt* (Nr. 1 und 2) gehören zu den sehr wenigen Figurenkompositionen Braques in den Jahren 1906–9.[64] Im Katalog zur Braque-Ausstellung 1956 in der Tate Gallery, London (s. Nr. 9: Maquette für den Katalog dieser Ausstellung), hebt Cooper den Einfluss hervor, den Cézanne auf Braques Werk von 1907/8 ausübte und der ihn vom Fauvismus wegbrachte. In einem Eintrag zum Ölbild *Akt* schreibt Cooper:

> *So ist es denn um so verständlicher, dass er eigentlich bereit sein musste für eine umfassendere Entdeckung von Cézanne, die, als es soweit war – 55 Bilder von Cézanne wurden 1907 im Salon d'Automne ausgestellt, und im selben Jahr waren 79 Aquarelle bei Bernheim Jeune zu sehen –, ihm (und den meisten seiner Freunde) die Augen öffnete für eine tiefere Sicht der Malerei. Sogleich wurde diese Erfahrung umgesetzt und resultierte in jenem Stilwandel, den ein Bild wie* Blick vom Hôtel Mistral *oder besser noch der* Akt *aufzeigen.*[65]

In der Erörterung von Braques *Akt* sieht Cooper die Wirkung von Picassos *Demoiselles* weniger im Stilistischen als im Konzeptionellen. «In diesem Bild scheint kaum etwas von der Behandlung der Figuren in den *Demoiselles* direkt beeinflusst zu sein.»[66] Das heisst, er ist der Auffassung, dass die Begegnung mit Picasso und den *Demoiselles* im Oktober oder November 1907 Braque eine neue Sicht der Lehren Cézannes und ihrer Anwendung vermittelt habe.[67]

> *Von da an hatte Braque intuitiv begriffen, dass das Ziel seiner Malerei nicht sein durfte, «eine Anekdote nachschaffen zu wollen, sondern eine Bildwirklichkeit zu erschaffen». Cézanne wies den Weg dahin, indem er bewies, dass es möglich war, Raum und Tiefe mittels der Farbe zu suggerieren und nicht durch das Trompe l'œil der Zentralperspektive. Sich vom Impressionismus*

1956 exhibition of Braque at the Tate Gallery in London, (see No. 9 in this catalogue, Braque's Maquette for the catalogue of this exhibition) Cooper emphasizes the impact of Cézanne on Braque's work of 1907–1908 drawing him away from fauvism. In an entry on the *Nude* oil painting Cooper writes:

> *It is thus all the more understandable that he should have been ready for the fuller revelation of Cézanne which, when it came – fifty-six pictures by Cézanne were shown at the Salon D'Automne of 1907, and in the same year seventy-nine of his watercolours were shown in the galleries of Bernheim Jeune – opened Braque's eyes (and indeed those of most of his friends) to a more profound approach to painting. Thereupon, as pictures like the* View from the Hotel Mistral *and even more the* Nude *prove, he began at once to modify his style in accordance with his enriched vision.*[65]

In this discussion of Braque's *Nude*, Cooper finds that the impact of Picasso's *Demoiselles* was not so much stylistic as conceptual. "There is little in the picture which looks as if it had been directly inspired by the handling of the figures in the *Demoiselles*."[66] That is, he understands Braque's meeting of Picasso and viewing of the *Demoiselles* in October or November of 1907, as offering to Braque a new way of understanding and dealing with the lessons of Cézanne.[67]

> *From that moment Braque realized intuitively that his purpose in painting should not be "to try to reconstitute an anecdotal fact, but to constitute a pictorial fact". Cézanne pointed the way to this realization by proving that it was possible to suggest space and recession by means of colour without recourse to the trompe-l'œil of scientific perspective. Above all, he had gone on from Impressionsim to pursue his "little sensation" of space consistently until he had found a means of reconciling this pictorially with the new insistence on respecting the flat surface of the canvas. But Cézanne, who was*

entfernend, suchte er vor allem seine «petite sensation» von Raum, so beständig, bis er Mittel fand, sie mit der hartnäckigen neuen Anerkennung der zweidimensionalen Bild-Oberfläche malerisch in Einklang zu bringen. Doch blieb Cézanne, der wesentlich ein Kind des 19. Jahrhunderts war, stets naturalistischer Tradition verhaftet, mit der Picasso hingegen schon gebrochen hatte, als Braque ihm begegnete; er hatte nämlich den wichtigsten Schritt schon getan: durch den Verzicht auf eine perzeptionelle zugunsten einer konzeptionellen Bildsprache. Historisch gesehen hatte er so an die Stelle des Naturalismus, der bis anhin galt, den Realismus als Ziel der Kunst gesetzt: natürlich nicht sozial-engagierten Realismus, sondern bildhaften – den Realismus einer Kunst ohne falschen Schein.[68]

Cooper unterstreicht das gemeinsame Schaffen und die enge Zusammenarbeit von Picasso und Braque, indem er ausführt: «Wir müssen uns davor hüten, ihre Leistungen säuberlich trennen oder die Bedeutung des einen gegen die des andern aufwiegen zu wollen.»[69] Aber da Braque sich vor Picasso mit Cézanne auseinandergesetzt habe, will Cooper in dessen Werk eine frühere Äusserung des Kubismus erkennen:

> *Zugegebenermassen hielten damals – und noch bis 1919 – die meisten Braque (der von Natur aus bescheiden und zurückhaltend ist) für einen Nachfolger oder Anhänger Picassos. Doch dank dem Beweismaterial, das uns heute zur Verfügung steht, wissen wir, dass diese Ansicht der Wahrheit entbehrt. Wir können das Entstehen des Kubismus in Braques Werk beobachten, bevor es bei Picasso auszumachen ist; wir können sehen, wo der Kubismus sich herleitet und so Cézanne als seinen natürlichen Vater bezeichnen; gleichzeitig erkennen wir, in welchem Masse die Erfahrung des Kubismus immer noch auf die Art des bildnerischen Ausdrucks von Braque und Picasso einwirkt.*[70]

essentially a child of the nineteenth cenury, always remained within the tradition of naturalism. Picasso, on the other hand, had already broken with this tradition when Braque met him, because he had already taken the major step of rejecting a perceptual in favour of a conceptual pictorial idiom. Thus, historically, he had substituted at that moment a pursuit of realism in art for the naturalism which had existed before: not, of course, social realism but pictorial realism, the realism of an art without make-believe.[68]

Cooper emphasizes the joint creation and close collaboration of Braque and Picasso, stating: "we must beware of trying to differentiate between their respective contributions or to weigh up the relative importance of the one against the other."[69] Yet, on the basis of Braque's precocious dialogue with Cézanne, he is willing to recognize an earlier manifestation of Cubism in that artist's work:

> *Admittedly, at the time – and indeed until 1919 – most people thought of Braque (who is by nature modest and retiring) as a follower of Picasso. But with all the evidence at our disposal nowadays we know that there is no truth in this view. We can see Cubism nascent in Braque's work before it occurs in that of Picasso, we can see whence it derives and thus proclaim Cézanne as its natural father, at the same time we can recognize the extent to which the Cubist experience still continues to affect both Braque's and Picasso's way of expressing themselves pictorially.*[70]

Similarly in his entry in the 1956 catalogue concerning his own picture *Big Trees at l'Estaque*, oil, summer 1908, Cooper clearly credits Braque with the earlier exploration of the Cubist idiom prior to 1909:

> *This picture and others if the series (colls Kunstmuseum, Basel; Museum of Modern Art, New York; Rump, Copenhagen; Rupf, Bern) should be compared with the landscapes painted by Picasso in Paris and at the*

Auch Coopers Eintrag im Katalog von 1956 zu dem ihm selbst gehörenden Ölbild *Grosse Bäume bei L'Estaque* gesteht Braque im Erforschen eines kubistischen Idioms von 1909 Priorität zu:

Dieses Bild sowie andere der Gruppe (in den folgenden Sammlungen: Kunstmuseum, Basel; Museum of Modern Art, New York; Rump, Kopenhagen; Rupf, Bern) sollte mit den von Picasso im selben Sommer in Paris und La Rue des Bois gemalten Landschaften verglichen werden (vide Zervos, op. cit., Bd. II (i), Nr. 72, 78–83). Ein solcher Vergleich macht den grossen Schritt vorwärts, den Braque plötzlich getan hatte, ersichtlich. Denn war Braque, in Cézannes Fussstapfen die Natur betrachtend, schon in gewissem Grade zur Facettierung (zum Beispiel im Vordergrund des hier besprochenen Bilds) und so zum Ausgangspunkt des Kubismus gelangt, fasste Picasso die Naturszene in beinah «primitiver» Sprache und komponierte seine Bilder mit höchst vereinfachten Formen; damit negierte er zwar die äussere Erscheinung, aber behielt doch mehr oder weniger einen einzigen Blickpunkt bei. Anerkanntermassen zog es Picasso in die gleiche Richtung wie Braque, doch kann nicht gesagt werden, seine Landschaften aus dieser Zeit enthielten «Kuben». Tatsächlich machte Picasso den Schritt, den Braque im Sommer 1908 gemacht hatte, erst ein Jahr später.[71]

Cooper besass die meisten graphischen Arbeiten von Braque.[72] *Stilleben mit Gin-Flasche auf einem Tisch (FOX)* (Nr. 3) ist eines von zwei Blättern, die Daniel Henry Kahnweiler im Entstehungsjahr, 1912, in einer Auflage von je hundert drucken liess. Diese Arbeit sollte wohl zusammen mit Picassos *Stilleben mit Marc-Flasche* (Nr. 57) ein Paar bilden. Cooper bespricht die Struktur dieser Drucke von Braque und Picasso im Hinblick auf die Mittel, welche sie während des Sommers 1911 in Céret in den Pyrenäen entwickelten, um ihre sehr hermetischen Kompositionen, die typisch sind für den Hochkubismus, zu klären:

Rue des Bois during the same summer (vide Zervos, op.cit., Vol II, (i), (Nos. 72, 78–83). This comparison reveals the great step forward that Braque had suddenly taken. For where Braque, looking at nature and following in the steps of Cézanne, had already resorted to a certain degree of faceting (e.g.in the foreground of the present picture), thereby arriving at the starting point of Cubism, Picasso was reducing the natural scene to almost "primitive" terms and composing his pictures with highly simplified forms, regardless of natural appearances, but nevertheless keeping more or less to a single view-point. Picasso was, admittedly, tending in the same direction as Braque, but still his landscapes of this date cannot be described as consisting of "cubes". In fact, Picasso did not catch up with the step that Braque took in the summer of 1908 until a year later.[71]

Cooper owned most of George Braque's prints.[72] *Still-life with a Bottle of Gin on a Table (Fox)* (No. 3) is one of two prints by the artist which were pulled in the period, in 1912, each in an edition of 100 printed by Daniel Henry Kahnweiler. This print may be considered one of a pair with Picasso's *Still-life with Bottle of Marc* (No. 57). Cooper discusses the structure of these two prints by Braque and Picasso in terms of the means they evolved during the summer of 1911 at Céret in the Pyrenées in order to bring clarity to their most hermetic compositions of this high Cubist period:

A linear scaffolding (clearly visible in their two great prints Bottle of Marc *and* Fox*, 1911–12) was made to indicate distances and to hold the composition together, while an associated structure of planes and cubes, over which realistic details were inscribed, gave volume and served to integrate spatially the foreground with the background.*[73]

The oval configuration of these prints, moreover, is comparable to the device used in the oils of this time to create a more compact pictorial structure. The etching

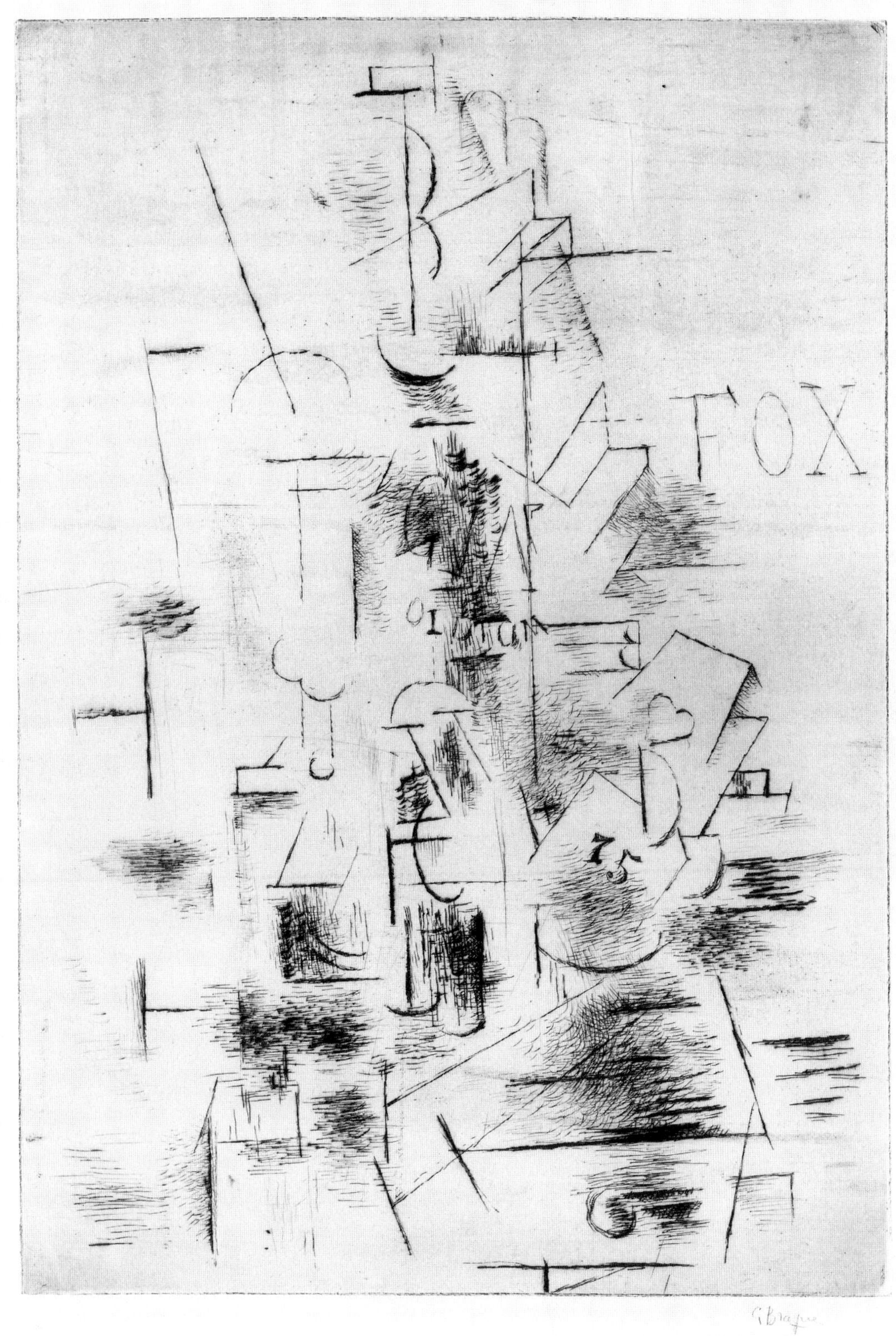

3 GEORGES BRAQUE

(Stilleben mit Gin-Flasche auf einem Tisch [FOX]; Still-life with Bottle of Gin on a Table [FOX]) (1911)

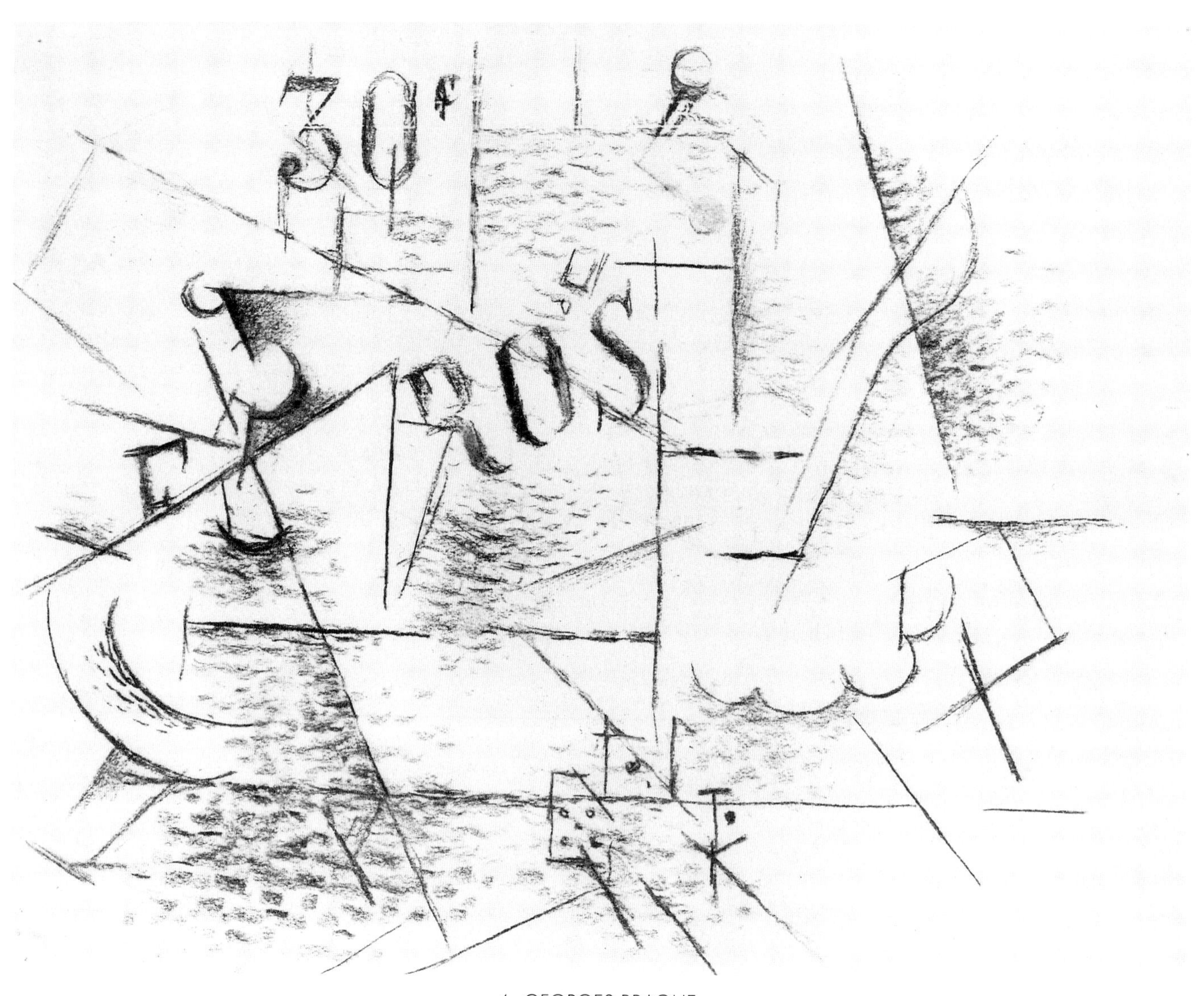

4 GEORGES BRAQUE
(Stilleben mit Würfel; Still-life with Dice) (Summer 1912)

> *Ein lineares Gerüst (klar sichtbar in ihren grossartigen Blättern* Marc-Flasche *und* Fox, *1911–12) wurde geschaffen, um Masse anzudeuten und die Komposition zusammenzuhalten, während ein dichtes Gefüge von Flächen und Kuben, dem realistische Details einbeschrieben wurden, Räumlichkeit verlieh und dazu diente, Vorder- und Hintergrund zu verklammern.*[73]

Die ovale Binnen-Komposition dieser Drucke kann überdies mit dem auch bei den Ölbildern aus dieser Zeit angewendeten Kunstgriff verglichen werden, eine kompaktere Bildstruktur zu schaffen. Auch der Effekt konzentrierter Nadelspuren in den Radierungen erinnert an die Malweise – voneinander abgesetzte gestrichelte Pinselzüge in verschiedener Dichte und Ausdehnung –, welche den Ölbildern taktile Oberflächenqualität verleiht und die Bildebenen untereinander differenziert.[74]

Die Komposition ist unverkennbar ein, wenn auch ätherisches, Stilleben: im Zentrum befindet sich die Flasche Gin «Old Tom» und links ein Glas mit Trinkhalm; unten auf dem Bild ist eine Tischschublade erkennbar, und rechts schwebt das Wort FOX (was den Schauplatz als die bei den Kubisten so beliebte Fox's English Bar in der Nähe des Gare St Lazare identifiziert). Auch in der Verwendung von Schablonenschrift wird Braque von Cooper als Neuerer angesehen.

> *Aber noch besser ersichtlich ist sie in Figurenkompositionen, etwa bei Picassos* Pfeifenrauchender Mann *oder Braques* Der Portugiese *(Kunstmuseum Basel), beide von 1911; in letzterem trat wahrscheinlich Schablonenschrift zum ersten Mal in Erscheinung. Diese Erfindung – die unerwartete Verwendung eines Werkzeugs der Dekorationsmaler – wurde sicher von Braque gemacht. In einem Stilleben Braques, entstanden in den ersten Monaten des Jahres 1910, erscheint eine Zeitung, deren Titel ausgeschrieben ist, doch dient die Schrift nur der Identifizierung der Form und spielt keine strukturelle Rolle in der Komposition. Vom Sommer 1911 an begannen Braque und, fast gleich-*

striations may be compared, as well, to the broken brush work which gives a tactile quality to the paintings' surfaces and creates differentiations between planes.[74]

The composition consists of an unmistakable but ethereal still-life: at the center is the bottle of Gin – Old Tom; at the left is a glass with drinking straw; at the bottom of the composition is a drawer of the table; to the right floats the word Fox (identifying the locale as Fox's English Bar near the Gare St. Lazare, so popular with the Cubists). The use of stenciled lettering is another instance in which Cooper credits Braque with an innovatory role:

> *But it is even more evident in figure compositions such as Picasso's* Man Smoking a Pipe *or Braque's* The Portugueuse *(Kunstmuseum, Basel), both of 1911, the latter being probably the first painting in which stenciled lettering made its appearance. This innovation – an unexpected application of a painter-decorator's stock-in-trade – was certainly made by Braque. In a still life by Braque of early 1910 a newspaper appears with its mast-head spelled out, but there the lettering serves simply to identify the form and plays no structural role in the composition. From the summer of 1911 on, however, Braque, and almost immediately Picasso, began to use words, letters and figures as an active pictorial element. That is to say, they treated them not simply as ornamental additions but chose those with an associative relevance to the subject of the picture, so that they contributed to the realism of the presentation. They also played a comparable role to the trompe-l'œil nail in Braque's 1909 still life by paradoxically emphasizing the schism between painting and reality. The lettering, Braque said, was a group of "forms which could not be distorted because, being themselves flat, they were not in space, and thus by contrast their presence in the picture made it possible to distinguish between objects situated in space and those which were not." In other words, the lettering emphasized the two-dimensional nature of the painted*

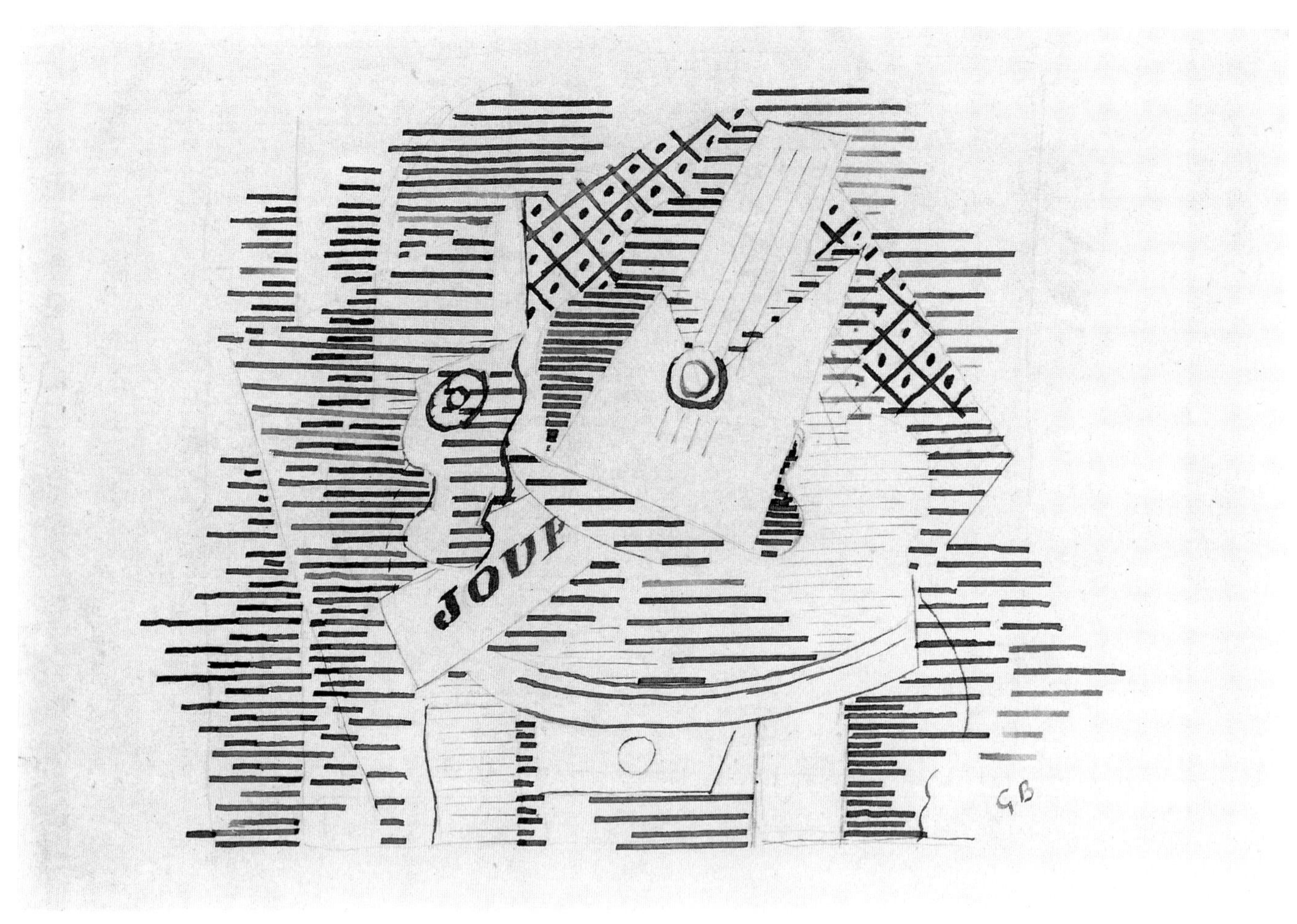

6 GEORGES BRAQUE
(Stilleben mit Gitarre auf einem Tisch; Still-life with Guitar on a Table) (1917)

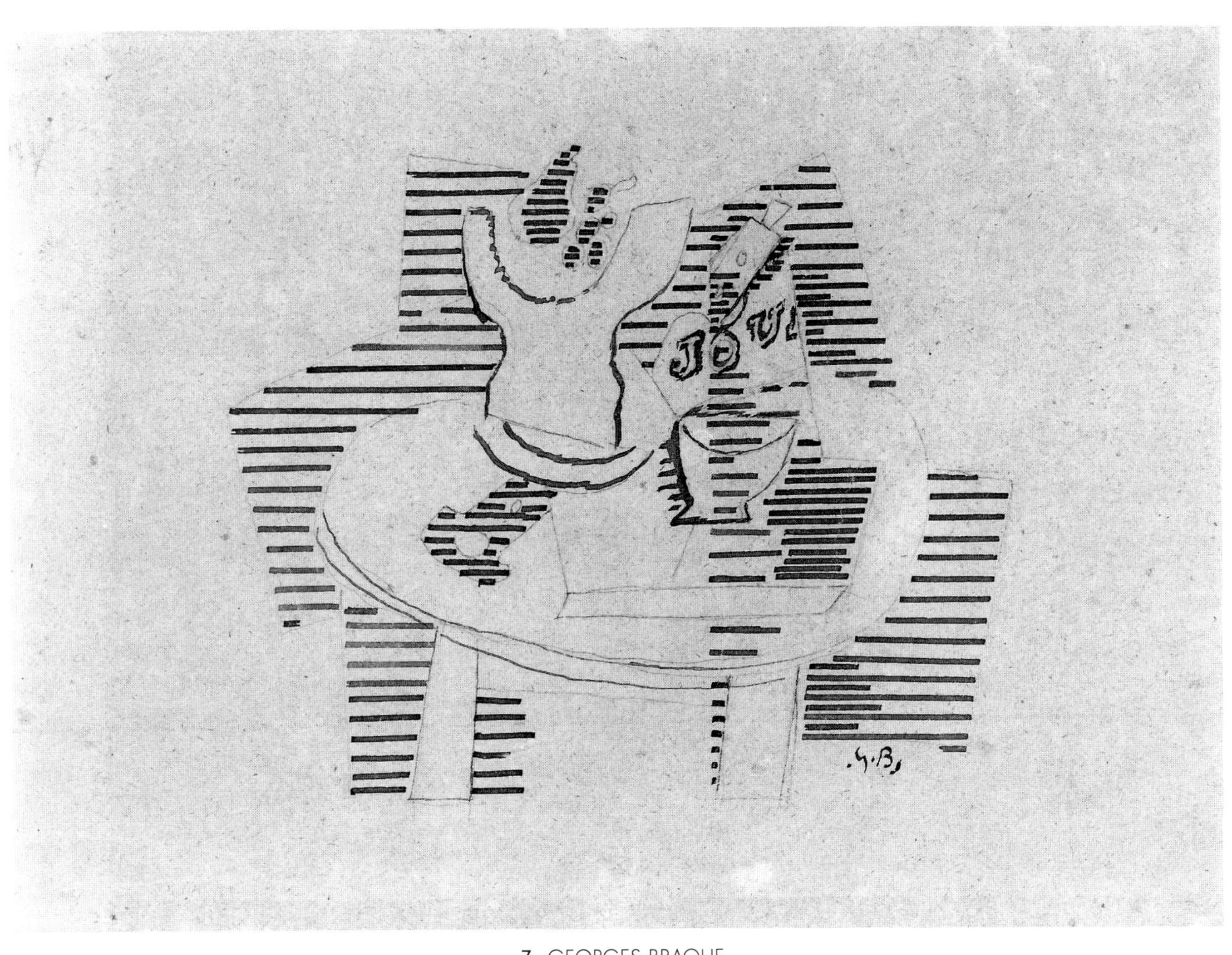

7 GEORGES BRAQUE
(Stilleben: Fruchtschale und Zeitung; Still-life: Fruit-dish and Newspaper) (1919)

zeitig, Picasso, Wörter, Buchstaben und Zahlen als aktive Bildelemente zu verwenden, das heisst, sie behandelten sie nicht bloss als dekoratives Beiwerk, sondern wählten solche von assoziativer Relevanz für das Sujet, so dass sie zum Realismus der Darstellung beitrugen. Sie spielten auch eine dem Trompe l'œil-Nagel in Braques Stilleben von 1909 vergleichbare Rolle, indem sie paradoxerweise die Kluft zwischen Bild und Wirklichkeit noch betonten. Die Buchstaben, sagte Braque, waren eine Gruppe von «Formen, die man nicht verformen konnte, weil, in sich flach, sie keine Räumlichkeit besassen; und so, als Kontrast, machte ihre Präsenz im Bild es möglich, zwischen im Raum eingebundenen und nichteingebundenen Dingen zu unterscheiden». Mit andern Worten unterstrichen die Buchstaben die Zweidimensionalität der Malfläche, fungierten aber auch als umgekehrtes Repoussoir und liessen den dinghaften Inhalt räumliche Züge annehmen.[75]

Die für Braques Ölbilder dieser Periode typischen ikonographischen und formalen Elemente charakterisieren auch das *Stilleben mit Würfel*, 1912 (Nr. 4), mit seinen Schablonenbuchstaben und Schablonenzahlen, dem illusionistisch gezeichneten Nagel mit Schatten und dem Würfel. Die Komposition zieht sich Richtung Blatt-Zentrum zusammen (oder, genauer vielleicht, strahlt von diesem Zentrum aus). Der Komplex linearer Elemente verliert seine Starre durch schuppenartig aufgetragene Kohlepartien, was den flackernden Flächen aus kleinen Pinselstrichen in Braques Malerei dieser Zeit sehr nahe kommt.

Das Blatt *Fruchtschale und Glas* (Nr. 5), das als erstes kubistisches Papier collé gilt, nimmt in der Literatur und in den Ausstellungen kubistischer Kunst eine prominente Stellung ein. Offenbar kaufte Braque das Papier mit der imitierten Holzmaserung (faux-bois), das er schon in Avignon in einem Schaufenster entdeckt hatte und mit dem er dieses und andere Papiers collés schuf, zwischen dem 3. und 12. November 1912 im

surface yet acted as a repoussoir in reverse to make the objective content assume a spatial connotation.[75]

Iconographic and formal elements typical of Braque's oil paintings of the same period also characterize *Still-life with Dice*, 1912, (No. 4), including stenciled numbers and letters, the illusionistically depicted nail with shadow and the dice. The composition draws together to the center of the paper (or perhaps, more acurately radiates out from that center). The complex of linear elements is softened through passages of fish-scale application of charcoal which is very similar to the flickering surface of small brushstrokes in his paintings of this period.

Fruit-dish and Glass, (No. 5) acknowledged as the first Cubist *papier-collé*, figures prominently in the literature and exhibitions of Cubist works of art. It was apparently at the village of Sorgues north of Avignon, during the few days between September 3 and 12, 1912, while Picasso had journeyed to Paris, that Braque bought the faux-bois paper which he had already spotted in the window of a shop in Avignon, and created this and other *papiers-collés* as well.[76]

Cooper saw the development of *papier collé* as marking the beginning of a new phase in Cubism which "inverts the structural procedure" of the earlier period. "This meant that, instead of breaking down a figure or an object into different fragments and facets, which when reassembled added up to a total image, they could begin with a range of purely pictorial elements – shaped forms and coloured planes, for instance – and endow them gradually, as the composition progressed, with an objective significance."[77]

Cooper links Braque's invention of *papier collé* to his sensitivity to the sensuous properties of the most ordinary objects, his attention to texture and surface in his works, and attributes this particular awareness of tactile values to Braque's formation as *peintre-décorateur*. In 1948 Cooper writes:

No single painter has lavished more care and technical mastery on describing in terms of oil paint the unas-

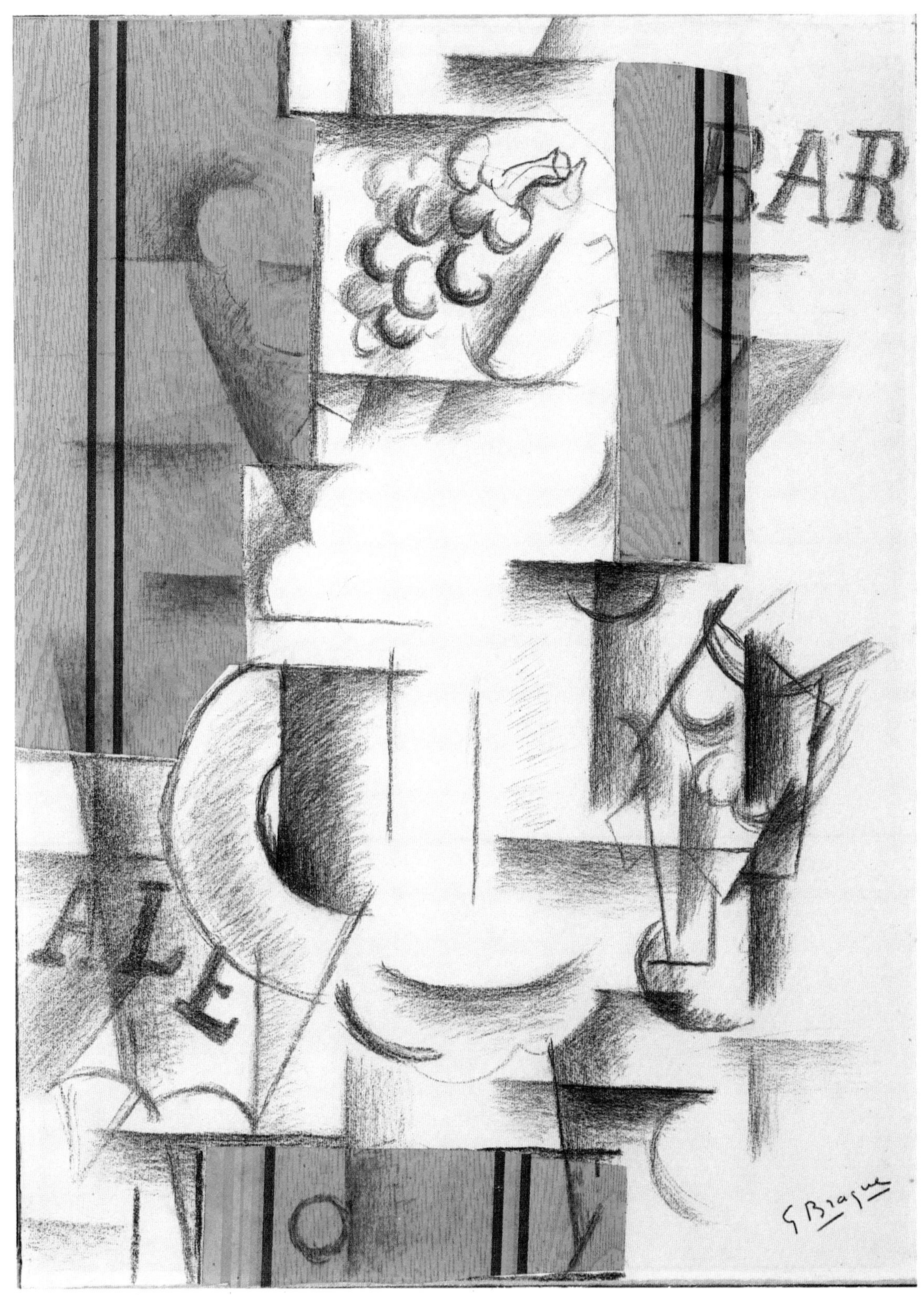

5 GEORGES BRAQUE
(Fruchtschale und Glas; Fruit-dish and Glass) (September 1912)

Dorf Sorgues nördlich von Avignon, zu einer Zeit also, da Picasso nach Paris gereist war.[76]

Cooper betrachtete die Entwicklung des Papier collé als Beginn einer neuen Phase des Kubismus, welche den «strukturellen Prozess» der vorhergehenden «umkehrte. Das bedeutete, dass sie [Braque und Picasso], anstatt eine Figur oder einen Gegenstand in verschiedene Fragmente oder Facetten zu zerlegen, welche, wieder zusammengefügt, ein ganzes Bild ergäben, dass sie also mit einer Reihe von reinen Bild-Elementen – bestimmten Formen und farbigen Flächen, zum Beispiel – anfangen konnten, um sie allmählich, im Lauf der Arbeit an der Komposition, mit dinghafter Bedeutung auszustatten.»[77]

Für Cooper hängt Braques Erfindung des Papier collé ganz eng zusammen mit seiner Sensibilität gegenüber den sinnlichen Eigenschaften gewöhnlichster Dinge sowie mit der Aufmerksamkeit, die er Textur und Oberfläche in seinem Werk schenkt; Braques besonderen Sinn für taktile Werte führt Cooper auf dessen Ausbildung zum Dekorationsmaler zurück. 1948 schreibt er:

> *Kein einziger Maler liess, im Medium Ölfarbe, mehr Sorgfalt und technische Meisterschaft der Schilderung jener anspruchslosen Dinge angedeihen, aus denen unser tägliches Leben besteht. Keiner liebte sie mehr oder kannte sie besser. Arbeitet Braque auch eher aus seinem Intellekt als aus seinem Gefühl heraus, haben doch in seiner Kunst sowohl lyrische Momente wie Sinnlichkeit Platz... Auch weiss Braque, vielleicht besser denn irgendeiner heute, um die Bedeutung taktiler Werte. «Es genügt nicht, das, was man malt, ansehen zu lassen. Man muss es auch berühren lassen.» Keiner hat ein grösseres Gefühl für das Stoffliche und wie es variiert werden kann; das zeigen sein brillant assoziationsreicher Einsatz von geklebten Papieren in den Jahren 1910–1914, seine Verwendung von Buchstaben, Zeitungen und Noten, die beständige und stets variierte Anwendung des «Maserns» bei Marmor und Holz oder seine Mischungen von Farbe mit Sägemehl oder Sand.*[78]

> *suming objects which compose our daily life. No painter has loved them more or known them better. Though Braque works with his intelligence rather than with his passions, his art is neither devoid of lyricism nor of sensuousness... Braque, too, knows better perhaps than anyone today the importance of tactile values. "Ce n'est pas assez de faire voir ce qu'on peint. Il faut encore le faire toucher." No one has a greater sense of matière and how it can be varied: for instance, his brilliantly evocative use of pasted papers in the period 1910–1914, his use of lettering, newspapers and sheets of music, the ever-varied though recurrent use of "graining" in marble and wood, the sand or sawdust which is often mixed with his paint.*[78]

Moreover, Cooper sees Braque's innovation of *papier collé* not only as a crucial turning point within the development of Cubism, but also as a decisive moment within the broader context of Braque's stylistic development.

> *Only subsequently, in 1918–1919, did Braque embark on a series of large-scale still-life compositions which are characterized by large relaxed forms, an overall looseness in the handling, and a richer, more varied, descriptive use of color attached to large planes – just as it had been in some of his papiers collés of 1913 and 1914...* Fruit-dish and Glass *had been made some six years previously and it was the root from which sprang a whole period of Braque's stylistic development leading up to this extraordinary later phase. That is what gives an unexpected degree of significance and importance within Braque's œuvre to this first papier collé and justifies its being described as one of his major imaginative achievements.*[79]

In his study of Braque's later work, *Braque: The Great Years*, Chicago, The Art Institute, 1972, Cooper underlines themes and techniques which had been developed in the earlier Cubist phase: the interaction of linear elements and planar passages (similar to the

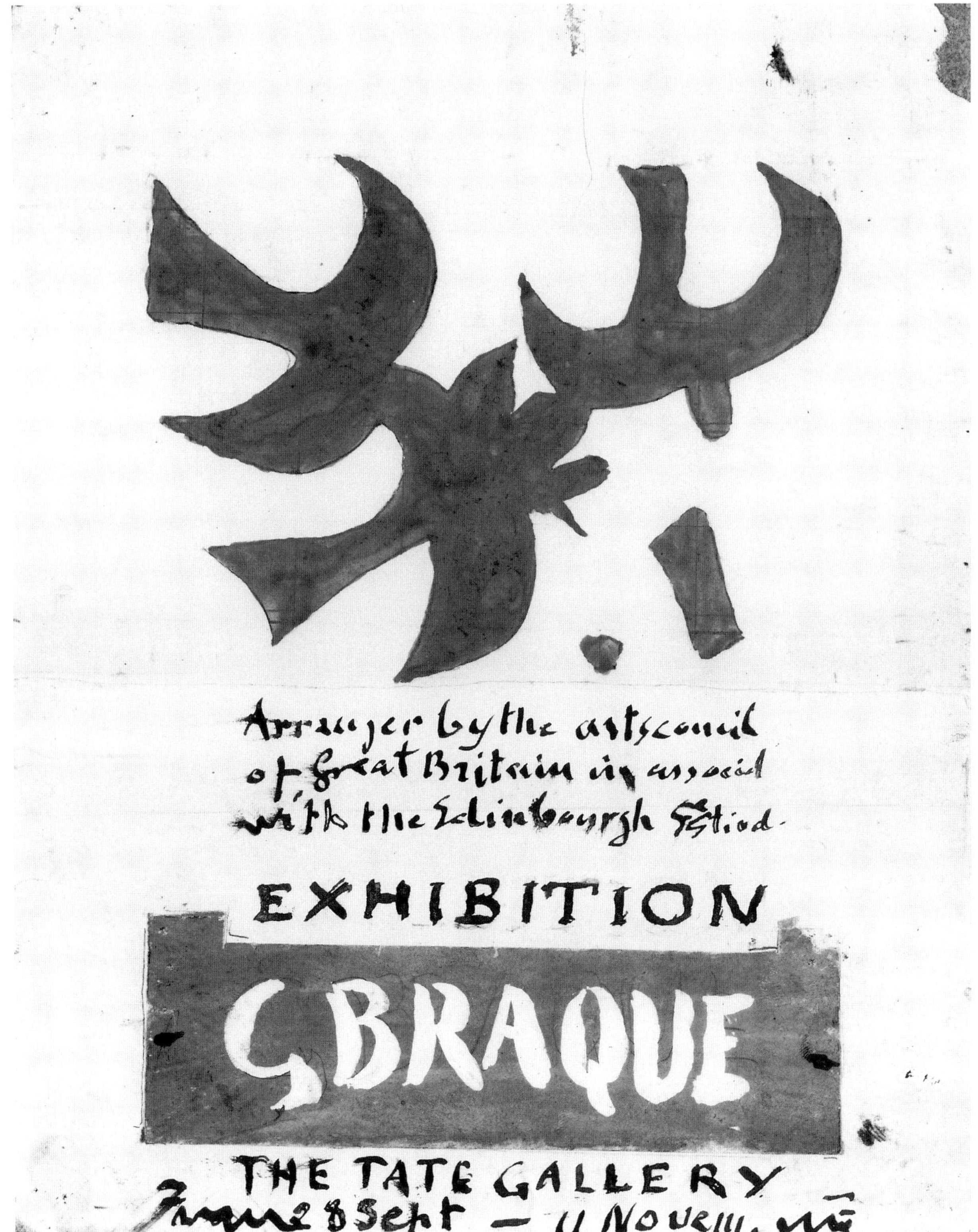

9 GEORGES BRAQUE
(Maquette für Katalog, Ausstellung Tate Gallery; Maquette for Catalogue, Tate Gallery Exhibition) (1956)

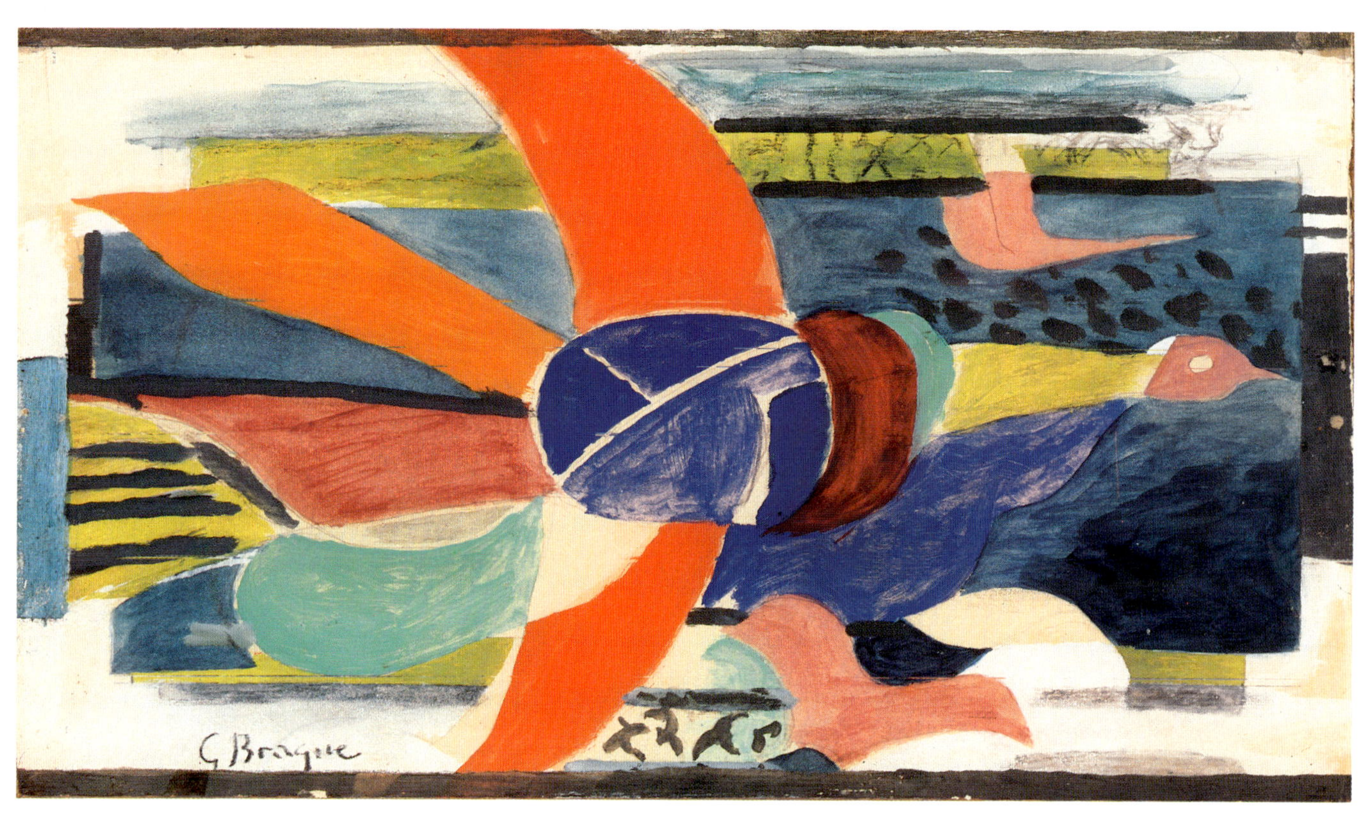

8 GEORGES BRAQUE
(Feuervogel; Fire Bird) (ca. 1954)

Überdies betrachtet Cooper Braques Erfindung des Papier collé nicht nur als Wendepunkt in der Entwicklung des Kubismus, sondern auch als entscheidendes Moment im weiteren Zusammenhang von Braques eigener stilistischer Entwicklung.

Erst später, 1918–1919, fing Braque eine Reihe grossformatiger Stilleben an, die gekennzeichnet sind durch grosse ruhige Formen, eine allgemeine Lockerheit der Machart und durch eine differenziertere und deskriptive Farbgebung in den grossen Flächen – genau das, was bei einigen Papiers collés der Jahre 1913 und 1914 zu sehen war... Fruchtschale und Glas *entstand ungefähr sechs Jahre früher; das Werk bildete den Ausgangspunkt einer langen Stilentwicklung, welche in dieser aussergewöhnlichen späteren Phase kulminierte. Deshalb kommt dem ersten Papier collé ein vielleicht unerwarteter Grad an Bedeutung und Wichtigkeit zu, und es verdient, als eine seiner schöpferischsten Leistungen bezeichnet zu werden.*[79]

In seiner Studie über Braques späteres Werk, *Braque: The Great Years*, Chicago, The Art Institute, 1972, hebt Cooper die Bedeutung der Themen und Techniken, welche in der früheren kubistischen Periode entwickelt worden waren, hervor: die Interaktion von linearen Elementen und flächigen Partien (welche an die raffinierte Kombination von Kohlezeichnung und geklebten Papieren in den früheren Papiers collés erinnert), das Spiel mit Textur, Struktur und kontrastierenden Oberflächen, die komplexe Wechselwirkung von wirklich und unwirklich, von Illusion und Realität.[80] Cooper schätzt die Reihe der *Studio*-Bilder als Höhepunkt in Braques Spätwerk ein; er selbst besass das monumentale *Studio VIII*, welches er um 1955 direkt vom Künstler erworben hatte.

64 S. William Rubin, "Cézannisme and the Beginnings of Cubism", in *Cézanne, The Late Years,* New York, The Museum of Modern Art, 1977, S. 170: «Während der Jahre 1906–09 machen

sophisticated combination of charcoal drawing and pasted papers in the earlier *papiers collés)*, the manipulation of texture and contrasting surfaces, the complex interplay of real and unreal, illusion and reality.[80] Cooper prized the Studio series as the grand culmination of Braque's late years, and himself owned the monumental *Studio VIII*, purchased directly from the artist ca. 1955.

64 See William Rubin "Cézannisme and the Beginnings of Cubism", in *Cézanne: The Late Years*, New York, The Museum of Modern Art, 1977, p. 170: "During the period 1906–09, Braque's four figure paintings represent less than six percent of his work, while landscapes make up more than three-fourths of it." The drawing and etching, the major oil, *Nude*, December 1907 – June 1908 in the Collection Alex Maguy, Paris, and the lost ink drawing, *Three Nudes*, early 1908 (all illustrated in Rubin's article, pages 170–171) (executed in just this order) demonstrate the profound impact of Cézanne's Bather compositions, Matisse's figural works such as *Blue Nude*, early 1907, The Baltimore Museum of Art, The Cone Collection, as well as Picasso's *Demoiselles d'Avignon*.

65 Cooper, *Georges Braque*, London: The Tate Gallery, 1956, p.8. In the same context, Cooper denies any significant impact of Matisse on Braque, and carefully differentiating Braque's work from that of the other Fauves ("it never showed any signs of the expressionist tendencies often apparent in the work of other members of the group"). Cooper is apparently inspired by the desire to find a place for Braque between the traditional polarity of Matisse and Picasso as masters of 20th century art. In the catalogue entry on p. 28, however, Cooper does acknowledge Braque's debt to Matisse, especially noting the impact of Matisse's *Blue Nude* of 1907.

66 Cooper, *Georges Braque*, 1956, p. 28.

67 See Edward Fry in "Cubism 1907–1908: An Early Eyewitness Account," *Art Bulletin*, 48, no. 1, March 1966, pp. 70–73 re. the encounter with Picasso: "more to accelerate and intensify Braque's exploration of Cézanne's ideas" than to "divert his thinking in any essential way." (p. 71)

William Rubin, in "Cézannisme and the Beginnings of Cubism" stresses that Braque's *Nude*, manifests the impact of Cézanne that is already evident in Braque's works (predominantly landscapes) since

Braques Figurenbilder weniger als sechs Prozent seines Schaffens aus; im Gegensatz dazu liegt der Anteil der Landschaften bei über drei Vierteln.» Die Zeichnung und die Radierung, das grosse Ölbild *Akt* (entstanden Dezember 1907 – Juni 1908; Sammlung Alex Maguy, Paris), und die verlorene Tuschzeichnung *Drei Akte* (Anfang 1908) – alle in dieser Reihenfolge entstanden und alle als Illustrationen zu Rubins Artikel erschienen – zeigen den grossen Einfluss von Cézannes Kompositionen mit Badenden, von Matisses Figurenbildern wie *Blauer Akt* (Anfang 1907; The Baltimore Museum of Art, The Cone Collection) sowie von Picassos *Demoiselles d'Avignon*.

65 Cooper, *Georges Braque*, London, The Tate Gallery, 1956, S. 8. Im gleichen Zusammenhang stellt Cooper einen bedeutenden Einfluss von Matisse auf Braque in Abrede, auch unterscheidet er sorgfältig zwischen dem Werk Braques und dem der anderen Fauves («nie waren darin Anzeichen von expressionistischen Tendenzen, oft sichtbar im Werk anderer Mitglieder der Gruppe, zu sehen»). Cooper ist anscheinend beflügelt vom Wunsch, für Braque einen Platz zwischen den zwei traditionellen Eckpfeilern der Kunst des 20. Jahrhunderts Matisse und Picasso zu finden. Im Katalogeintrag auf Seite 28, allerdings, anerkennt Cooper, dass Braque in Matisse' Schuld stand, und vermerkt vor allem den Einfluss von Matisse' *Blauem Akt* von 1907.

66 Cooper, *Georges Braque*, 1956, S. 28.

67 S. Edward Fry, "Cubism 1907–1908: An Early Eyewitness Account", *Art Bulletin*, 48, Nr. 1, März 1966, S. 70–73. Das Zusammentreffen mit Picasso «beschleunigte und intensivierte viel eher Braques Studium der Ideen Cézannes», als dass es «sein Denken auf irgendwelche grundsätzliche Weise in andere Bahnen lenkte» (S. 71).

William Rubin, in "Cézannisme and the Beginning of Cubism", unterstreicht, dass Braques *Akt* zwar schon den Einfluss von Cézanne zeige, dass dieser aber bereits seit 1906, vor allem in den Landschaften, ersichtlich sei. Tatsächlich bemerkt Rubin Elemente in seinen Bildern, welche auf «Braques Bindung an Cézanne weisen, dessen Werke er schon 1902 kennengelernt hatte und der bereits 1904 eine Rolle in seiner Entwicklung spielte» (S. 158).

68 Cooper, *Georges Braque*, 1956, S. 9.

69 ibid., S. 5. In *The Cubist Epoch*, S. 27, geht er den Kubismus immer noch als «gemeinsames Schaffen» an.

70 William Rubin liefert wohl das eindrücklichste und unerschütterlichste Argument für Braques Priorität in der Entwicklung des Kubismus; s. "Cézannisme and the Beginnings of Cubism":

1906. Indeed, Rubin notes elements of his paintings which point to "Braque's commitment to Cézanne, whose painting he had seen as early as 1902 and who was a factor in his development as early as 1904". (p. 158)

68 Cooper, *Georges Braque*, 1956, p. 9.

69 *Ibid.*, p. 5. In *The Cubist Epoch*, p. 27, he continues to approach Cubism as a "joint creation".

70 The most impressive and adamant argument in favor of Braque's earlier development of Cubism is that of William Rubin in "Cézannisme and the Beginning of *Cubism*":

We shall discover that the sudden reversal of direction popularly supposed to have taken place between Braque's late Fauve pictures and his earliest Cubist efforts is a myth; that Braque had already evolved significantly in the direction of Cubism before he met Picasso and that his progression from Fauvist to Cubist owes far less to Picasso – to the Demoiselles *in particular – than has been supposed. Indeed, we shall be forced to conclude that the earliest form of Cubism was less a "joint creation" of Picasso and Braque than an invention of Braque alone, extrapolated from the possibilites proposed by Cézanne. The place of Picasso (and thus, necessarily, of primitive art) in this specific development (up to the fall of 1908) will be reexamined, and he will be seen less as a contributor to the formal language of early Cubism than as a model of daring whose radical departures probably inspired the basically conservative Braque to take uncharacteristic chances. (p. 152)*

71 Cooper, *Georges Braque*, 1956, p. 28–29.

72 *Small Cubist Guitar*, 1909–1910, etching (Vallier, no. 2; Engelberts, no. 2), *Job*, 1911, dry-point (Vallier, no. 5; Engelberts, no. 4); *Fox*, 1911, dry point (Vallier, no. 6; Engelberts, no. 5); and *Composition (Nature Morte I)*, 1911, etching (Vallier, no. 8; Engelberts, no. 8) Edwin Engelberts, *Georges Braque – Catalogue de l'œuvre graphique original*, Geneva, 1958; Dora Vallier, *L'œuvre gravé de Braque*, Paris 1982).

73 Cooper, *The Cubist Epoch*, p. 52–53.

74 Dieter Koepplin, in *Kubismus, Zeichnungen und Druckgraphik*, Kunstmuseum Basel, 1969, no. 24, mentions a 1911 oil painting which relates to this etching (Richardson, *G. Braque*. 1960, illus .10) and a wash drawing which appears to be a study for the etching (D.-H. Kahnweiler, *Der Weg zum Kubismus*, Munich, 1959, illus. p. 65; F. Elgar, *Braque 1906–1920*, illus. no. 1).

75 *Ibid.*, p. 54–56.

Wir werden sehen, dass der plötzliche Richtungswechsel, der, wie gemeinhin angenommen wird, zwischen den späteren fauvistischen und den frühesten kubistischen Werken stattgefunden habe, ein Mythos ist, dass Braque sich deutlich in Richtung Kubismus entwickelt hatte, bevor er Picasso traf, und dass sein Fortschreiten von Fauvistischem zu Kubistischem viel weniger auf Picasso – und besonders auf die Demoiselles – zurückgeht, als bisher angenommen wurde. Ja wir werden zum Schluss kommen müssen, dass die früheste Form des Kubismus weniger eine «gemeinsame Schöpfung» von Picasso und Braque als eine Erfindung von Braque allein war, hergeleitet aus den bei Cézanne ablesbaren Möglichkeiten. Picassos Stellung (und so auch jene der primitiven Kunst) in dieser spezifischen Entwicklung (bis zum Herbst 1908) wird neu untersucht werden, und er wird weniger als Beiträger an das Formenvokabular des frühkubistischen Idioms als ein Vorbild an Wagemut angesehen werden, dessen radikale Neuanfänge wohl den grundsätzlich konservativen Braque dazu inspirierten, ungewohnte Wagnisse einzugehen» (S. 152).

71 Cooper, *Georges Braque*, 1956, S. 28–29.

72 *Kleine kubistische Gitarre*, 1909–10, Radierung (Vallier Nr. 2; Engelberts Nr. 2), *Job*, 1911, Kaltnadel (Vallier Nr. 5; Engelberts Nr. 4), *Fox*, 1911, Kaltnadel (Vallier Nr. 6; Engelberts Nr. 5) und *Komposition (Nature morte I)*, 1911, Radierung (Vallier Nr. 8; Engelberts Nr. 8). S. Edwin Engelberts, *Georges Braque, Catalogue de l'Oeuvre graphique originale*, Genf, Galerie Rauch, 1958; Dora Vallier, *L'Oeuvre gravée de Braque*, Paris, Flammarion, 1982.

73 Cooper, *The Cubist Epoch*, S. 52–53.

74 Dieter Koepplin, in *Kubismus, Zeichnungen und Druckgraphik*, Kunstmuseum Basel, 1969, Nr. 24, erwähnt ein Ölbild von 1911, welches mit dieser Radierung in Bezug steht (Richardson, *G. Braque*, 1960, Abb. 10), und eine Tuschzeichnung, die als Studie für die Radierung gelten kann (D.-H. Kahnweiler, *Der Weg zum Kubismus*, München 1959, Abb. S. 65; F. Elgar, *Braque 1906–1920*, Abb. Nr. 1).

75 ibid., S. 54–56.

76 Henry Hope, in *Georges Braque*, New York 1949, ist einer der ersten, der die Schöpfung des ersten Papier collé definitiv Braque zuschreibt. 1936 erwähnt Barr (*Cubism and Abstract Art*, S. 78) die «Erfindungskraft von Braque... Schon 1910 führte er in ein Stilleben einen perspektivisch gesehenen Nagel mit illusionistischem Schatten ein – ein Trick, ein *Trompe l'œil*. Im folgenden Jahr begann er Texturen zu imitieren und Buchstaben zu malen... 1912 wird die Veränderung der Sicht deutlich durch den neuen Gebrauch der *Collage*, das Aufkleben von Papierstreifen...» Cooper, in *Braque*,

76 Henry Hope in Georges *Braque*, New York, 1949, is among the first to definitively credit Braque with the creation of his first papier collé. In 1936 Barr (*Cubism and Abstract Art*, New York, Museum of Modern Art, 1936, p. 78) mentions the "inventiveness of Braque... As early as 1910 in a still life he had introduced a foreshortened nail with an illustionistic shadow, a trick, a *trompe-l'œil*. In the following years he began to paint imitation textures and letters... The difference in point of view is made clear by the addition in 1912 of *Collage*, the pasting of strips of paper..." In *Braque*, 1956, Cooper credits Braque with the invention of the *papier collé*, p. 11 and 35–36. In his essay, "Braque as Innovator: The First Papier Collé" in the 1982, Washington, National Gallery, *Braque, The Papiers Collés*, Cooper relates that it was during a visit of Braque and his wife Marcelle to the Château de Castille on September 7, 1957, that he learned "from the artist himself that this was the first *papier collé* he had made, and what is more that it had preceded by at least a week the first *papier collé* by Picasso." (p. 18)

77 Cooper, *The Essential Cubism*, p. 13.

78 *Braque: Paintings 1909–1947*, London: Drummond, 1948 p. 6; See as well, p. 11 and pp. 35–36 in Cooper, *Braque*, 1956.

79 Cooper, "Braque as Innovator: The First *Papier Collé*", in *Braque, The Papiers Collés*, p. 21.

80 Cooper's enthusiasm waned apparently in the thirties. In *La France Libre*, May 15, 1946, in "Georges Braque: l'Order et le Métier", Cooper contrasts his disappointment with Braque's works during the thirties and his renewed excitement when he once again revisited the artist's studio in 1945 (p. 66).

1956, würdigt Braque als Erfinder des Papier collé (S. 11, 35–36). In seinem Aufsatz "Braque as Innovator: The First Papier Collé" im Katalog der National Gallery Washington, *Braque, The Papiers Collés,* 1982, erzählt Cooper, dass, während eines Besuchs von Braque und seiner Frau Marcelle auf Schloss Castille am 7. September 1957, er «vom Künstler selbst» erfuhr, «dass dies das erste Papier collé war, das er gemacht hatte, und dass es überdies mindestens eine Woche vor Picassos erstem Papier collé entstanden war» (S. 18).

77 Cooper, *The Essential Cubism,* S. 13.

78 *Braque: Paintings 1909–1947,* London, Drummond, 1948, S. 6; s. a. S. 11 und S. 35–36 in Cooper, *Braque,* 1956.

79 Cooper, "Braque as Innovator: The First *Papier collé*", *Braque, The Papiers Collés,* S. 21.

80 Es scheint, dass Coopers Begeisterung in den dreissiger Jahren schwand. In «Georges Braques: l'Ordre et le Métier», *La France Libre,* 15. Mai 1946, stellt Cooper seine Enttäuschung über Braques Werk in den dreissiger Jahren seiner erneuten Begeisterung gegenüber, als er, 1945, den Künstler noch einmal im Atelier besuchte (S. 66).

JUAN GRIS

Die elf Werke von Juan Gris in dieser Ausstellung stellen nur einen kleinen Teil der einst bedeutenden Gris-Sammlung dar, die James Thrall Soby in seinem 1958 erschienenen Buch, welches die Ausstellungen in New York, Minneapolis, San Francisco und Los Angeles begleitete, als «eine der besten, die es gibt» würdigte.[81]

Gris' glühende Bewunderin, Gertrude Stein, behauptete, für den Künstler sei das «Stilleben eine Religion».[82] Cooper führt Gris' Ernst und Tiefe in der Darstellung alltäglicher Gegenstände auf sein Erbe, die spanische Kunsttradition, zurück:

> *Juan Gris war im wesentlichen ein Meister des Stillebens und als Maler – was Künstlertum wie Temperament betrifft – tief durchdrungen vom Geist spanischer Tradition. Vor seinen Stilleben denkt man weniger an Chardin oder Cézanne als an Zurbaràn, Velàsquez oder Melendez. Bei diesen findet man nämlich einen vergleichbar hohen Ernst und eine ähnliche Klarheit der Komposition; ja diese Künstler stellen die alltäglichsten Dinge mit einer Direktheit dar, wie sie auch Gris eigen ist.*[83]

Weiter begreift Cooper Gris' Beschränkung im Sujet als Mittel, den Blick auf gestalterische Probleme zu konzentrieren; auch erkennt er in der Eindringlichkeit, mit der sich Gris diesen Gegenständen zuwendet, einen tiefen Ausdruck des Menschseins, der ohne Symbol und ohne Anekdote auskommt.

> *Juan Gris brauchte die Gegenwart des Menschen in seinen Werken nicht: Die Gruppen von Hausgegenständen, die Thema seiner Malerei sind, vermochten von selbst die einfachen, alltäglichen Bedürfnisse des nicht anwesenden Menschen zu evozieren. Gris' Bilderwelt war erfüllt von solchen Gegenständen, und er wurde nie müde, sie darzustellen. Er befrachtete sie mit keinerlei Symbolik im Kontext seines Werks. Und dennoch kann man nicht anders als den ihnen innewohnenden Ausdruck des Menschlichen erkennen,*

The eleven works by Juan Gris included in this exhibition represent but a small fraction of what was a major Gris collection. Indeed, in his 1958 book which accompanied the exhibitions in New York, Minneapolis, San Francisco and Los Angeles, James Thrall Soby praises Cooper's Gris collection as "one of the finest in existence".[81]

Gris' ardent admirer, Gertrude Stein, claimed that for Gris "still life is a religion".[82] Cooper attributes the seriousness and profundity of Gris' rendering of his every day objects to his Spanish artistic heritage:

> *Juan Gris était essentiellement un maître de la nature morte et, en tant que peintre, profondément imprégné – au point de vue artistique aussi bien que par tempérament – de l'esprit de la tradition espagnole. Devant une de ses natures mortes, ce n'est pas à Chardin ou à Cézanne que l'on pense, mais plutôt à Zurbarán, Velásquez ou Melendez. Car dans leurs tableaux on retrouve une austérité et une netteté de composition comparables, et ces artistes nous présentent les objets familiers avec quelque chose de la même désinvolture que Gris.*[83]

Cooper, furthermore, understands Gris' limited range of subject matter as a means of narrowing and sharpening the focus on pictorial concerns, but also recognizes in Gris' earnest probing of these objects a profound expression of humanity, without recourse to symbol or anecdote.

> *Juan Gris n'avait pas besoin d'introduire une présence humaine dans ses compositions: ses groupes d'objets domestiques... qui servent de sujet à ses peintures suffisaient par eux-mêmes à évoquer les simples besoins quotidiens de quelque être invisible. Ces objets meublaient le monde pictural de Juan Gris et il ne se laissa jamais de les représenter. Gris ne les dotait d'aucune signification symbolique dans le contexte de son œuvre. Par contre, il est impossible d'ignorer la signification humaine qu'ils assumaient*

der dank Gris' Wissen um ihre formalen, taktilen, Nutz- und Assoziationswerte zustandekam. Er näherte sich ihnen in aller Offenheit, sah sie so, wie sie waren, und, mehr Realist als Idealist, wollte er sie weder schöner noch verführerischer machen, als sie in Wirklichkeit waren. Gris machte sich visuell vertraut mit ihren nur ihnen eigenen Formen und schuf sie buchstäblich wieder in ihrer ganzen Fülle. Es gibt weder Trompe l'œil noch Gemogel in Gris' Bildern. Und die Bedeutung seiner Werke für uns, ihr ewiger Wert als Malerei, liegt in der Aufrichtigkeit von Gris' künstlerischer Vision sowie in seiner erstaunlichen Beherrschung der neuen Bildsprache, die er allmählich erarbeitet und vervollkommnet hat, um seinen Bedürfnissen gerecht zu werden.[84]

Diese Auswahl von Arbeiten auf Papier aus der Cooper-Sammlung bietet einen ziemlich vollständigen Überblick über Gris' Werk von 1910–11 bis 1922–23, indem sie sowohl die Inhalte, mit denen er sich beschäftigte, als auch die verschiedenen Stadien seiner stilistischen und technischen Entwicklung veranschaulichen kann. Dominierendes Sujet ist das Stilleben, gewöhnliche Gegenstände des Alltags also: Krüge, Schalen, Teller und Gläser, Tassen, Schüsseln, Lampen, Messer, Tabaksbeutel, Teekannen, Weinflaschen, Gitarren und Violinen.

Stilleben mit Krug (Nr. 10) ist das früheste Werk dieser Gruppe, datiert 1910. Es wird bestimmt von dramatischem Helldunkel sowie vom Spiel des Lichts, in geometrisierten Formen, auf den Gegenständen – dem herabhängenden Tuch im Hintergrund, dem Teller, der Schale und dem Krug.[85] Charakteristisch für das *Stilleben mit Petrollampe* von 1911 (Nr. 11) ist der suchende andeutende Kontur der Gegenstände und die vom Blattrand merkwürdig gekappte Tischecke.[86]

Der Einfluss Cézannes ist im *Stilleben: Suppenschüssel und Glas* (Nr. 12) in verschiedenen Aspekten erkennbar: in der Art, wie die Hinterkante der Tischplatte heraufgezogen ist, anstatt räumlich in die Tiefe verlaufen zu dürfen (zur Verzerrung des Raums trägt auch die feh-

grâce à sa compréhension de leurs valeurs formelles, tactiles, utilitaires et associatives. Il les abordait franchement, les voyait tels qu'ils étaient et, étant plus réaliste qu'idéaliste, ne cherchait pas à les faire paraître plus beaux ou plus séduisants qu'ils ne l'étaient en réalité. Gris se familiarisait visuellement avec leurs formes individuelles et les recréait littéralement sur sa toile dans toute leur plénitude. Il n'y a ni trompe-l'œil, ni tricherie dans les peintures de Juan Gris. Et le sens de ses tableaux pour nous-mêmes, leur valeur éternelle en tant que peintures, résident dans la probité de sa vision artistique et dans son étonnante maîtrise du nouveau langage pictural qu'il a élaboré peu à peu et perfectionné pour répondre à ses besoins."[84]

This selection of works on paper from Cooper's collection offers a rather complete overview of Gris' work from 1910–11 through 1922–23, illustrating the subject matter which preoccupied him and the various stages of his stylistic and technical devlopment, as well. The dominant subject is the still-life, ordinary objects of everday life: pitchers, bowls, plates and glasses, cups, terrines, lamps, knives, tobacco pouches, tea pots, wine bottles, guitars and violins.

Still-life with Pitcher (No. 10), dating from 1910, is the earliest work of the group. The work is dominated by dramatic chiaroscuro and a play of geometricized patches of light on the surface of the objects-- the cloth hanging in the background, plate, bowl and vertical vessel.[85] *Still-life with Oil Lamp*, 1911, (No. 11) is characterized by the tentative or inflected contour of objects and an awkward cropping of the table corner by the edge of the paper.[86]

The impact of Cézanne is discernible in several aspects of *Still-life: Soup Terrine and Glass* (No. 12): the manner in which the back edge of the plane of the table is drawn upward rather than allowed to recede in space (the exclusion of any front edge of that table through the cropping of the image with the edge of the paper contributes to the spatial distortion), the way in which the rear edge of the supporting plane is discon-

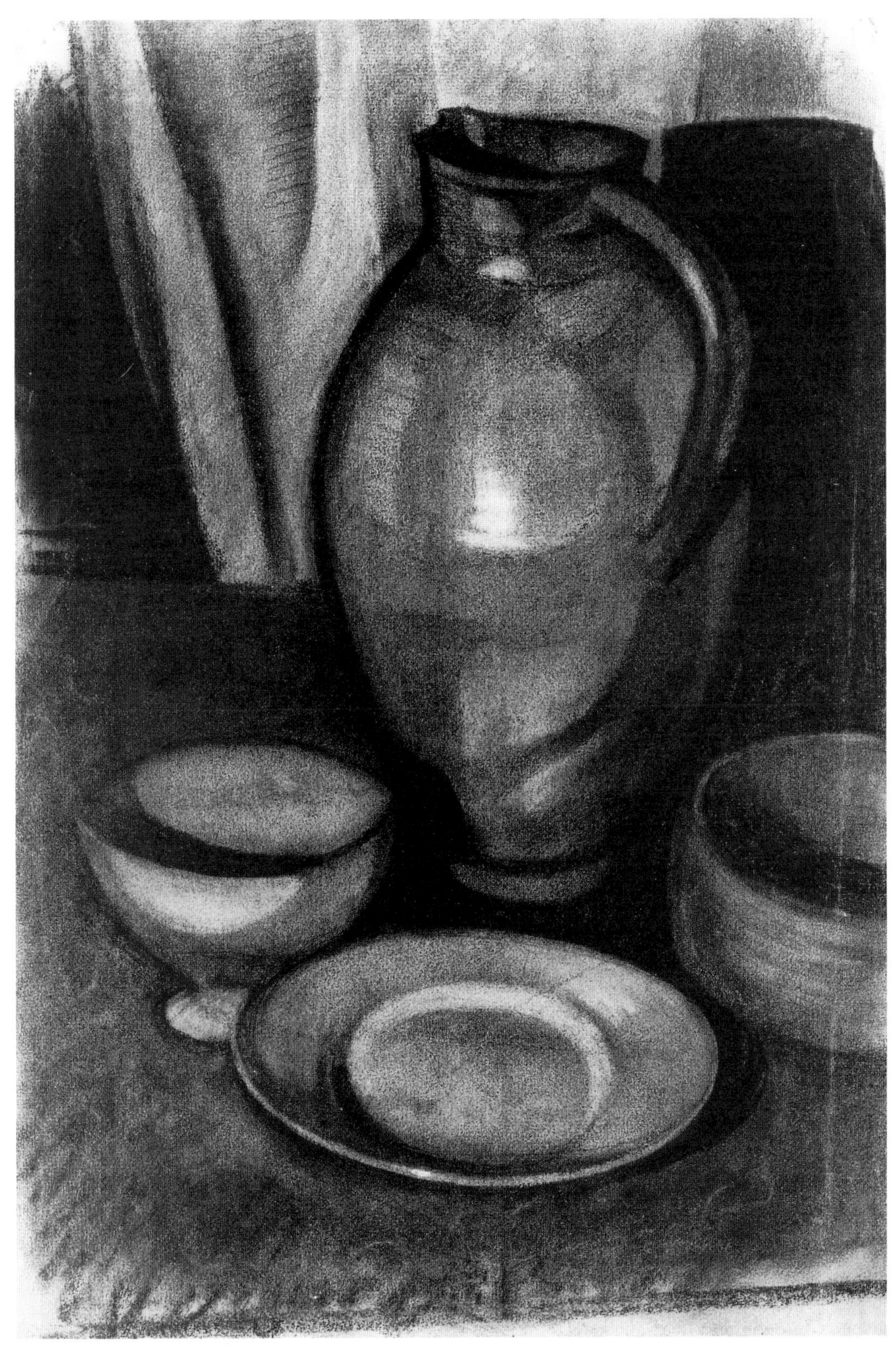

10 JUAN GRIS
(Stilleben mit Krug; Still-life with Pitcher) 1910

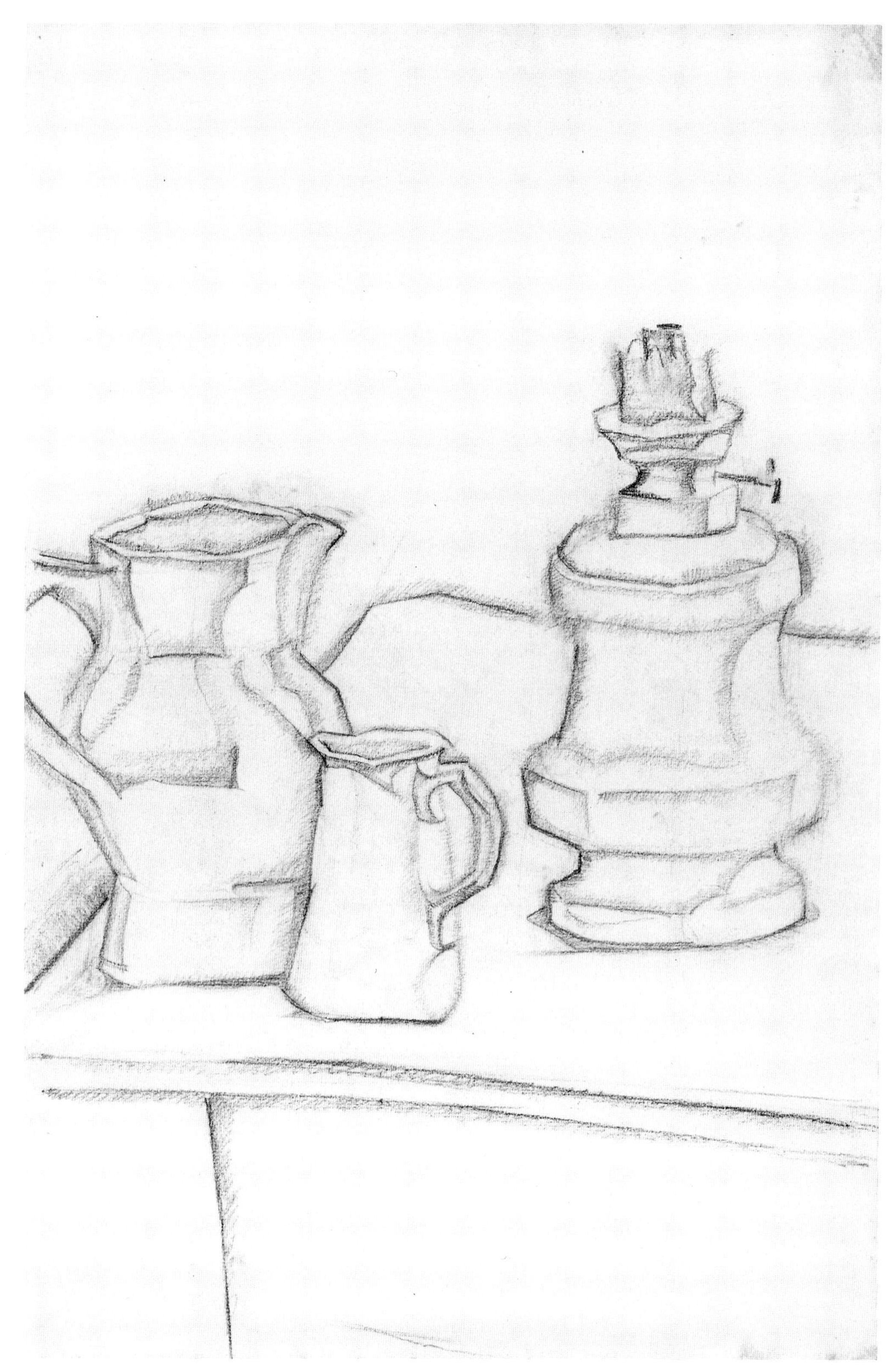

11 JUAN GRIS
(Stilleben mit Petrollampe; Still-life with Oil Lamp) (1911)

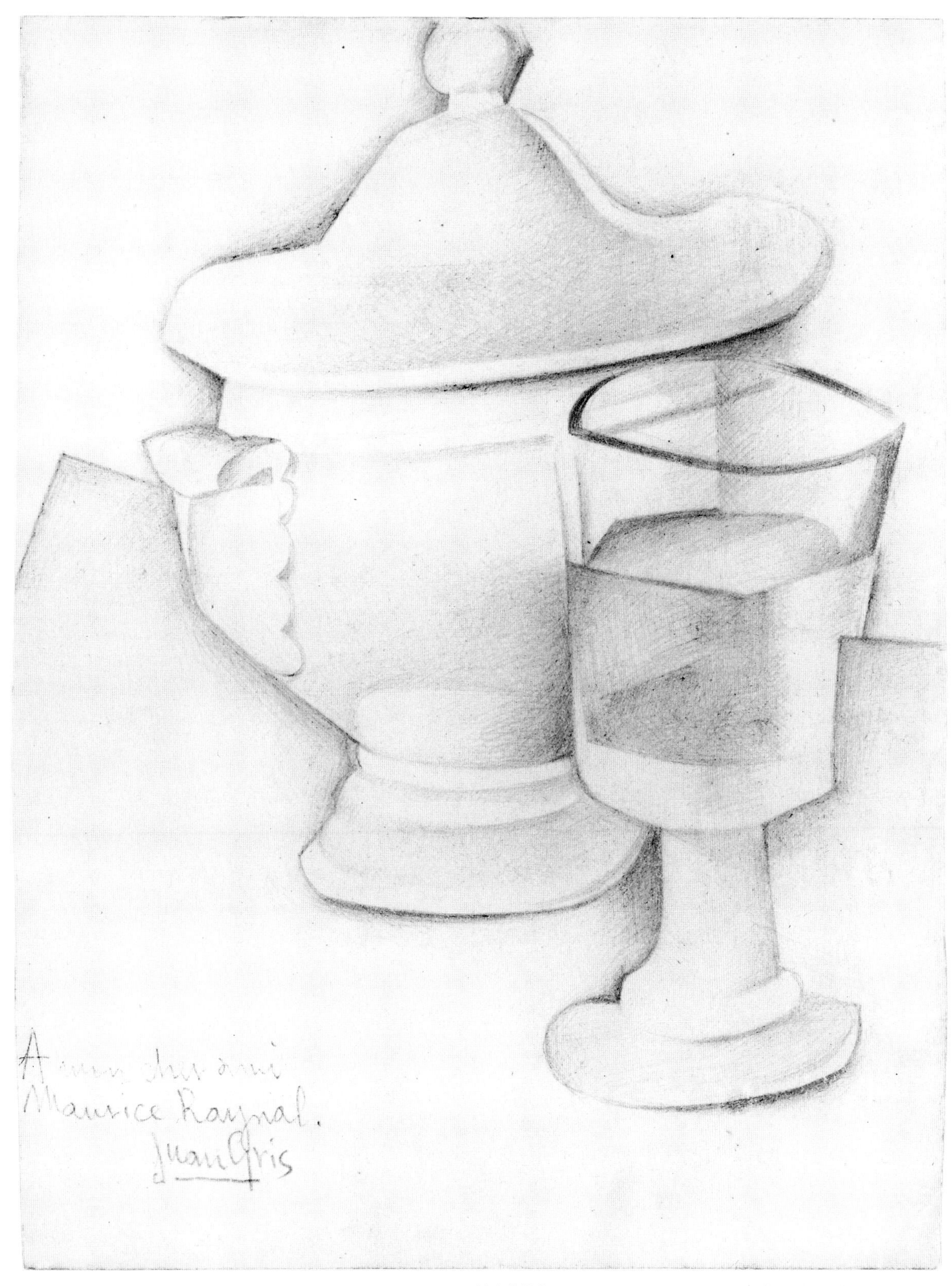

12 JUAN GRIS
(Stilleben: Suppenschüssel und Glas; Still-life: Soup Terrine and Glass) (1911)

lende, vom Blattrand abgeschnittene Vorderkante des Tisches bei), sowie in der Art, wie die Hinterkante der Tragfläche des Tischs unterbrochen ist und sogar die Form des Glases rechts durchschneidet oder «überlappt».[87]

Radikalere Abstraktion erscheint in Gris' Werk der Jahre 1911–12, als er die Lehren Cézannes verarbeitet und sich allmählich das kubistische Idiom der Werke Picassos und Braques aneignet. Im *Stilleben mit Tasse und Glas* von 1911 (Nr. 13) werden die Gegenstände fragmentiert und schweben unsicher in einem unklar definierten Raum, der sich aus von oben links nach unten rechts verlaufenden Diagonalen zusammensetzt. Durch die Fragmentierung des Glases können Teile des Fusses, des Stiels, der Stelle im Innern des Glases, wo der Kelch ansetzt, sowie der Aussen- und Innenseitenflächen des Glases simultan dargestellt werden, was Gris' Verständnis des analytischen Kubismus verrät.[88]

Die diagonalen Streifen in diesem Werk können als Lichtstrahlen gelesen werden, das heisst, dass dem immateriellen Element aggressive Form gegeben wird, welche Festes wie Leeres durchdringt und verändert. Cooper schreibt über Gris' Handhabung des Lichts: «Auch Gris braucht Licht (aus *einer* Quelle) als aktiven Faktor in der Entwicklung der Formen. Helldunkel-Effekte sind denn sehr ausgeprägt in seinem Werk; und, in einer Anzahl früher Bilder, experimentierte Gris mit Lichtflächen in Form einer Reihe diagonaler Bänder.»[89]

Verwendung von Licht, eher als Inhalt oder Thema denn als formales Mittel, ist auch in den *Stilleben: Teekanne und Glas* von 1916 (Nr. 16) und *Stilleben: Der Tabaksbeutel* von 1918 (Nr. 19) zu sehen. Das gesetzmässige Spiel des Lichts ist aber einem abstrahierenden und streng rationalen Prozess unterworfen und wird so zu sorgfältig bestimmten Licht- und Schattenzonen, welche die Raumkontinuität von Gegenständen und Umraum zugleich verunklären und definieren, analysieren und «aus den Angeln heben». Für Gris konzentriert sich zu diesem Zeitpunkt der schöpferische Prozess auf die Spannung zwischen lesbarem Bild-Gegenstand und aus ihm entwickelter eigenständiger Bild-Struktur.[90]

tinuous and actually intersects or "overlaps" with the form of the glass at the right.[87]

A more radical abstraction emerges in Gris' work of 1911–12, as he digests his lessons from Cézanne and gradually absorbs the Cubist idiom emerging in the works of Picasso and Braque. In *Still-life with Cup and Glass*, 1911 (No. 13) the objects are fragmented and float precariously in an ill-defined space consisting of diagonal lines which move from upper left to lower right. The fragmentation of the glass, simultaneously presenting segments of the base of the glass, its stem, the inside point at which the stem meets the vessel, the outside surface of the glass, and the inside surface, as well, betrays Gris' understanding of Analytical Cubism.[88]

One reads the diagonal stripes in this work as shafts of light. That is, this insubstantial element is given aggressive form, which invades and transforms both sold and void in the composition. Cooper writes about Gris' manipulation of light: "Also Gris used light (from a single source) as an active factor for developing forms. Chiaroscuro effects are therefore very marked throughout his work and in a number of his early paintings Gris experimented with planes of light formalized as a succession of diagonal bands."[89]

The use of light, almost as substance or subject rather than distinct formal device, is apparent in *Still-life: Teapot and Glass*, 1916 and *Still-life: The Tobacco Pouch*, 1918 (Nos. 16, 19). However, the pattern of the light is abstracted and severely rationalized, and transformed thence into delicately defined passages of light and dark which at once obscure and define, analyze and eradicate the continuity of the objects and the space around them. There is a crystalline quality to this drawing typical of Gris work in 1916. The tension between subject-object and subject-pattern is the crux of Gris' creative process at this point.[90]

In *Still-life: Teapot and Glass*, one also has a glimpse of the elaborate rhymes (formal metaphors or correspondences with which Gris composed his canvases of this period), between similar shapes or forms which

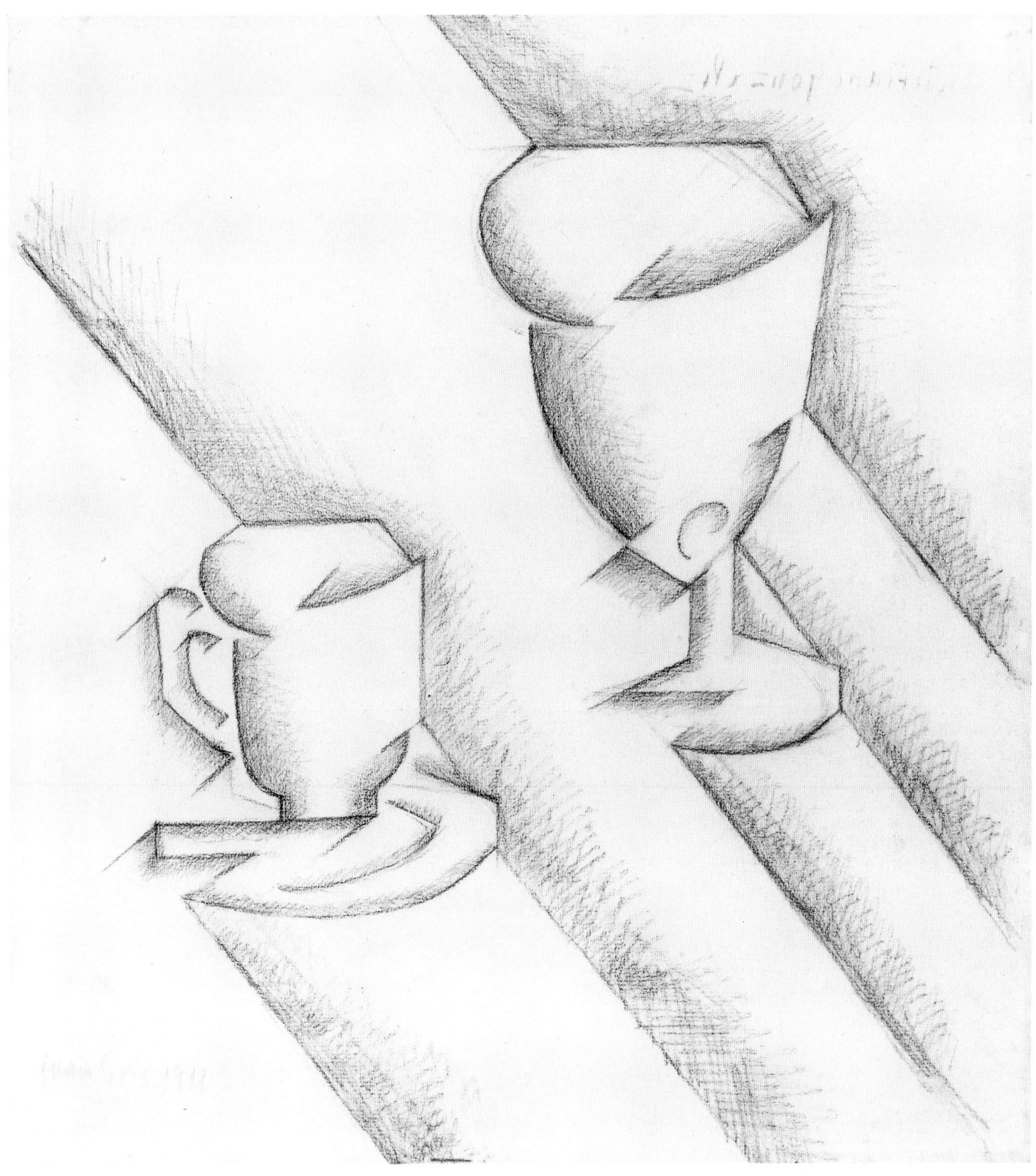

13 JUAN GRIS
(Stilleben mit Tasse und Glas; Still-life with Cup and Glass) 1911

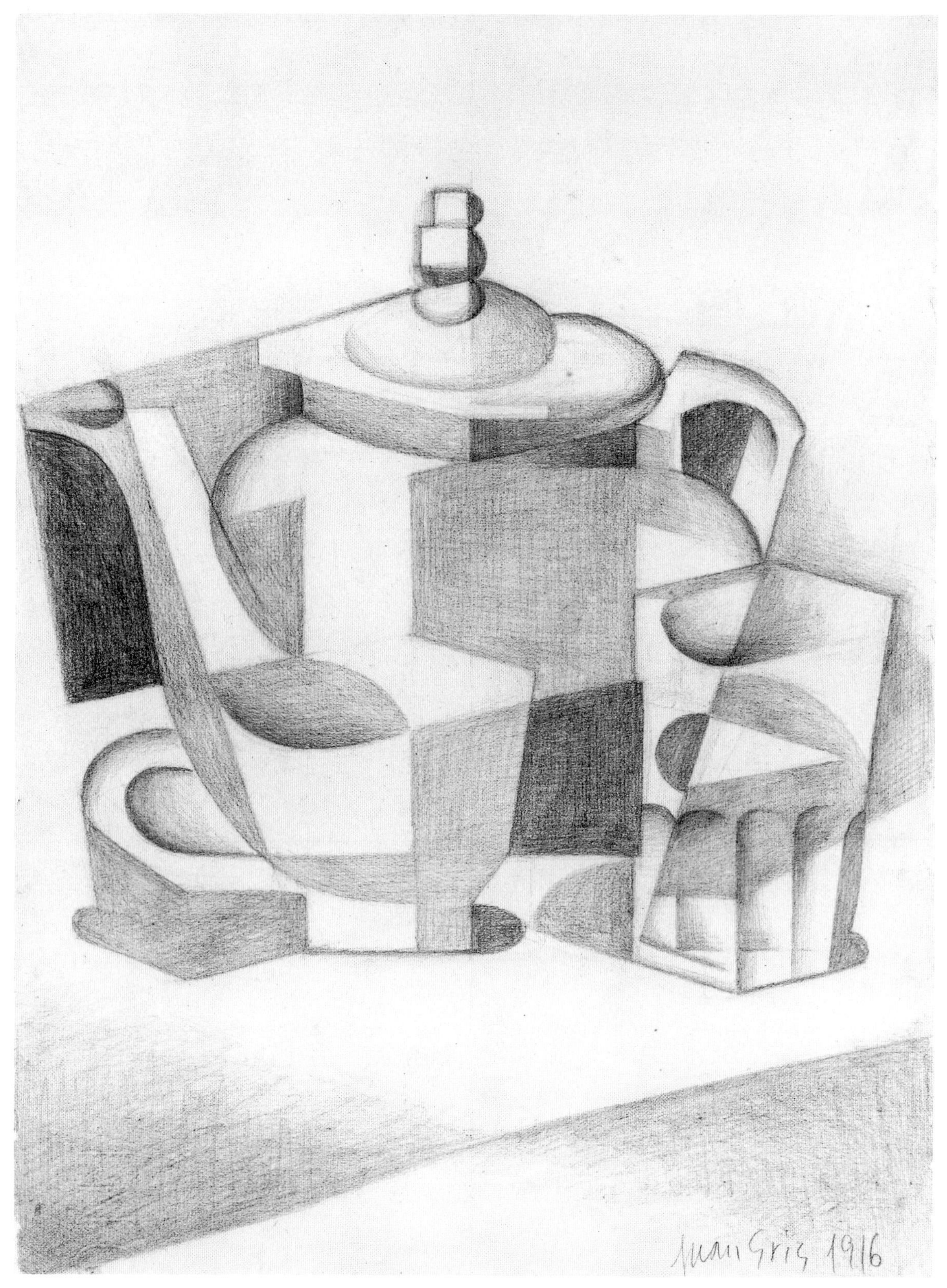

16 JUAN GRIS
(Stilleben: Teekanne und Glas; Still-life: Teapot and Glass) 1916

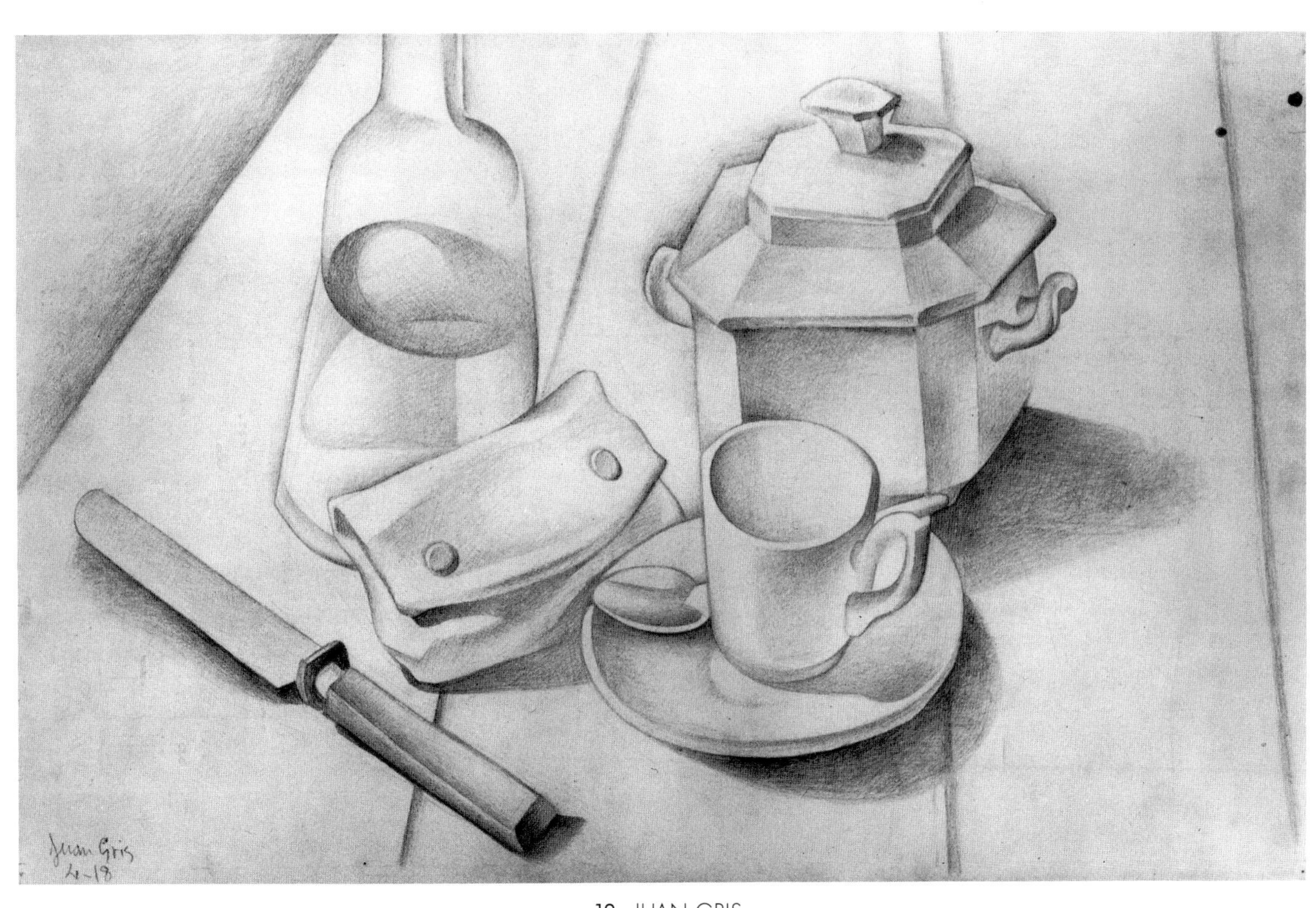

19 JUAN GRIS
(Stilleben: Der Tabaksbeutel; Still-life: The Tobacco Pouch) 1918

Das *Stilleben: Teekanne und Glas* gibt auch Einblick in sorgfältig ausgearbeitete Reime (formale Metaphern oder Korrespondenzen, mit welchen Gris die Kompositionen dieser Zeit schuf), Reime also zwischen ähnlichen Formen, die jedoch verschiedene Bedeutungen und Funktionen haben. Dieses Phänomen, die «‹Reim›-Wirkung», wurde von Cooper schon in einem Artikel von 1936 besprochen.[91] Hier gibt es subtile Entsprechungen zwischen den Ovalformen der Schnabelöffnung der Kanne, ihres Deckels, der innern Verbindung von Schnabel und Gefäss, des Glasfusses und Glasrandes usw.

Im Gegensatz dazu ist das *Stilleben: Der Tabaksbeutel* von 1918 zwar eine vorzügliche Zeichnung, aber doch recht konservativ hinsichtlich der Entwicklung eines kubistischen Idioms bei Gris. Die Gegenstände sind fester, körperlicher, ihre Umrisse nicht von Helldunkel-Strukturen, Formen oder Flächen unterbrochen. Die lineare Artikulation der Tragfläche, die weder eine hintere noch vordere Begrenzung hat (der «Tisch» wird von den Rändern der Komposition oben und unten beschnitten und scheint sich in beiden Richtungen unendlich fortzusetzen), diese lineare Artikulation hat quasi die Funktion von Strahlen – des starken Lichts, das im Bild von oben links herabströmt. Die feingebildeten Gegenstände scheinen beinahe verletzlich in diesem intensiven Lichtbad. Die einzige starke Lichtquelle, die linearen Elemente, welche die Bildfläche durchqueren, und das dramatische Helldunkel erinnern an die oben besprochenen Werke der Jahre 1910–11. Die dramatisch aufwärtsgekippte Horizontlinie, die klare Lichtführung, betont durch lineare Streifung, kommen auch in anderen Werken dieser Periode zur Anwendung.[92]

1912 experimentierte Gris mit Papier collé und Collage, erst zaghaft und vorsichtig, dann aber immer wagemutiger, je wohler er sich fühlte, als er 1913 immer intensiver und 1914 fast ausschliesslich in diesen Techniken, kombiniert mit Ölmalerei, arbeitete. Die Collagetechnik prägte nun die stilistische Entwicklung seiner Bilder. Cooper betont, dass Gris' Verständnis und Anwendung der Collage einen wichtigen und eigenständigen

carry, however, different functions or significances. This phenomenon, "the effect of rhyme", was discussed by Cooper already in a 1936 article.[91] Here there is a subtle correspondence established between the ovals which signify the mouth of the spout, the cover of the pot, the inner conjunction of spout and vessel, the base of the glass, the top of the glass, etc.

In contrast, *Still-life with Tobacco-Pouch*, 1918, is an exquisite drawing but somehow more conservative in terms of Gris' evolution of a Cubist idiom. The objects are more solid, their contours uninterrupted by patterns of light and dark, forms or planes. The linear articulation of the supporting surface, with only an indication of, but no visible near or far edge (the "table" is cropped by the edges of the composition at top and bottom and appears to extend infinitely up and down) functions almost like rays of the intense light which emanates from above-left. The delicately rendered objects seem almost vulnerable to the intense bath of light. The intense single-source light, the linear elements which traverse the picture plane and the dramatic chiaroscuro hearken back to the works from 1910–1911 already discussed. The dramatically upward-tilted horizon line, the intensely directed light, emphasized through linear striations is used in other works of this period.[92]

Gris experimented timidly or conservatively at first in 1912 with papier collé and collage, but gradually grew more comfortable and experimental working more intensely in 1913 and in 1914 almost exclusively with these media combined with oil painting. The technique of collage helped to evolve and transform the subsequent style of his paintings. Cooper stresses that Gris' understanding of and use of collage, distinct from the approaches of Picasso or Braque, constitutes an important and personal contribution to the history of Cubism.[93] In 1949 in *Juan Gris ou Le Goût du Solennel*, Cooper describes the difference in Gris' approach to *papier collé*:

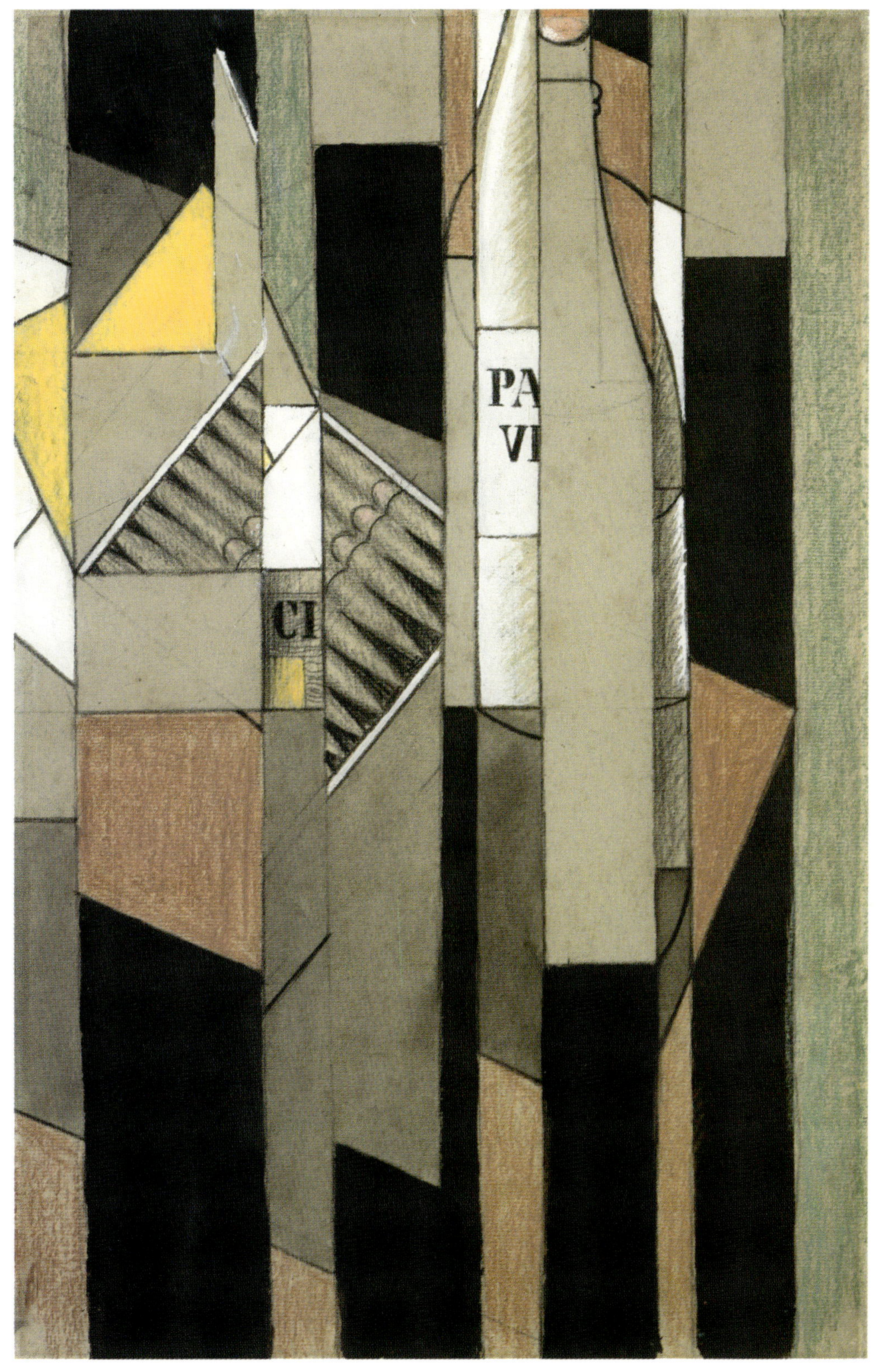

14 JUAN GRIS
(Stilleben mit Flasche und Zigarren; Still-life with Bottle and Cigars) (1912)

Beitrag zur Geschichte des Kubismus darstelle und getrennt von den Versuchen Picassos oder Braques gesehen werden müsse.[93] Den Unterschied beschreibt Cooper im 1949 erschienenen *Juan Gris ou Le Goût du Solennel*:

> *Das heisst, Gris' Papiers waren nur sich selbst; sie waren keine deskriptiven Elemente. Das gedruckte Muster war an sich eine beigefügte Dekoration; indem er frei über diesen farbigen Untergrund hinwegzeichnete, konnte er eine Folge von Ebenen schaffen, die sich vom Hintergrund her nach vorne fortsetzten. Braque und Picasso hingegen brauchten Papiers collés als Mittel, sich an ein reales Element – an eine absolute Wirklichkeitsebene – zu binden, auf die alle anderen strukturell bezogen werden konnten. Gris jedoch baute seine Kompositionen mit farbigen Papieren auf, die dann, im Lauf seiner Arbeit, zu Wirklichkeit wurden.*[94]

Die Gegenstände im *Stilleben mit Flasche und Zigarren* von 1912 (Nr. 14) werden vertikal in Teile zerschnitten, wo sie in verschiedenen zeitlichen und räumlichen Momenten oder Phasen zu existieren scheinen. Die vertikale Struktur vereinheitlicht, obwohl sie die Gegenstände mit kaleidoskopischem Effekt spaltet, die Komposition. In *The Cubist Epoch* schreibt Cooper:

> *Im Frühling 1913 hatte Gris auf sein lineares Gerüst verzichtet und ein neues Kompositionsmittel gefunden, das sich zweifellos von der Technik der Papiers collés herleitete, nämlich ein System von flächigen vertikalen, horizontalen und dreieckigen Formen, die sich überschneiden, aber nicht transparent sind* (Spielkarten und Glas Bier; Landschaft bei Céret). *Diese Flächenformen, die voneinander farblich und auch der Textur nach unterschieden sind, geben, indem sie ihre Plätze vor- oder hintereinander einnehmen, der Komposition ihre räumliche Struktur. Gris stellt nun auf jeder dieser Flächen einen einzelnen Aspekt eines oder mehrerer Gegenstände dar, entweder in ihrer Kompaktheit*

> *That is to say that Gris papiers were there as themselves and not as descriptive elements. The printed pattern was in itself an added decoration, and by drawing freely over this coloured base he could create a succession of planes coming forwards from the background... Now Braque and Picasso used papiers collés as a means of tying themselves down to a real element, to an absolute plane of reality to which all others could be pictorially related. Gris on the other hand built up his composition with coloured papers and they thus became reality as he worked.*[94]

In *Still-life with Bottle and Cigars*, 1912, (No. 14) the objects are segmented by a series of vertical passages. Indeed, they seem to exist in distinct moments or phases within these different vertical areas. The pattern of the vertical elements invests the composition with unity even as it disrupts the objects with this kaleidescopic effect. In *The Cubist Epoch* Cooper writes:

> *By the spring of 1913, Gris had dispensed with his linear framework and had arrived at a new compositional device-deriving undoubtedly from the technique of papiers collés-namely a system of vertical, horizontal and triangular planes which overlap but are not transparent* (Playing Cards and Glass of Beer; Landscape at Céret). *These planes, which are differentiated from each other tonally, and often texturally as well, provide the spatial structure of the composition as they take their places in front of or behind others. On each of them Gris either represents, in its solidity, a single aspect of one or more objects, or else in outline some related aspect. These methods were purely personal or used only by Gris.*[95]

In this work Gris achieves a high degree of textural contrast through the use of densely saturated passages of black water color, thick chalky areas of brilliant white or yellow gouache, loosely applied areas of colored crayon, and pasted papers. This work captures the tension between Gris' compositional brilliance and the

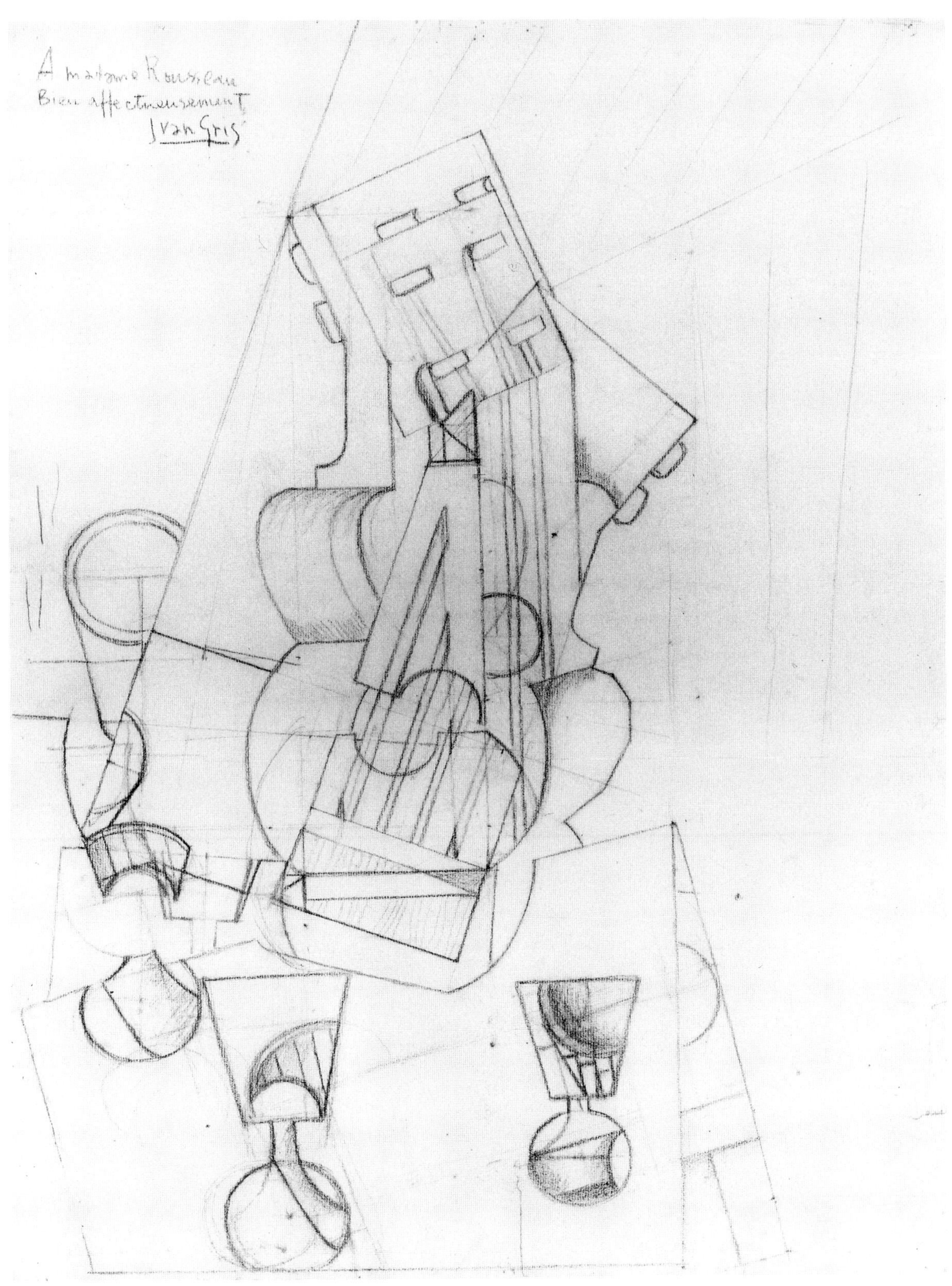

15a JUAN GRIS
(Gitarre; Guitar)

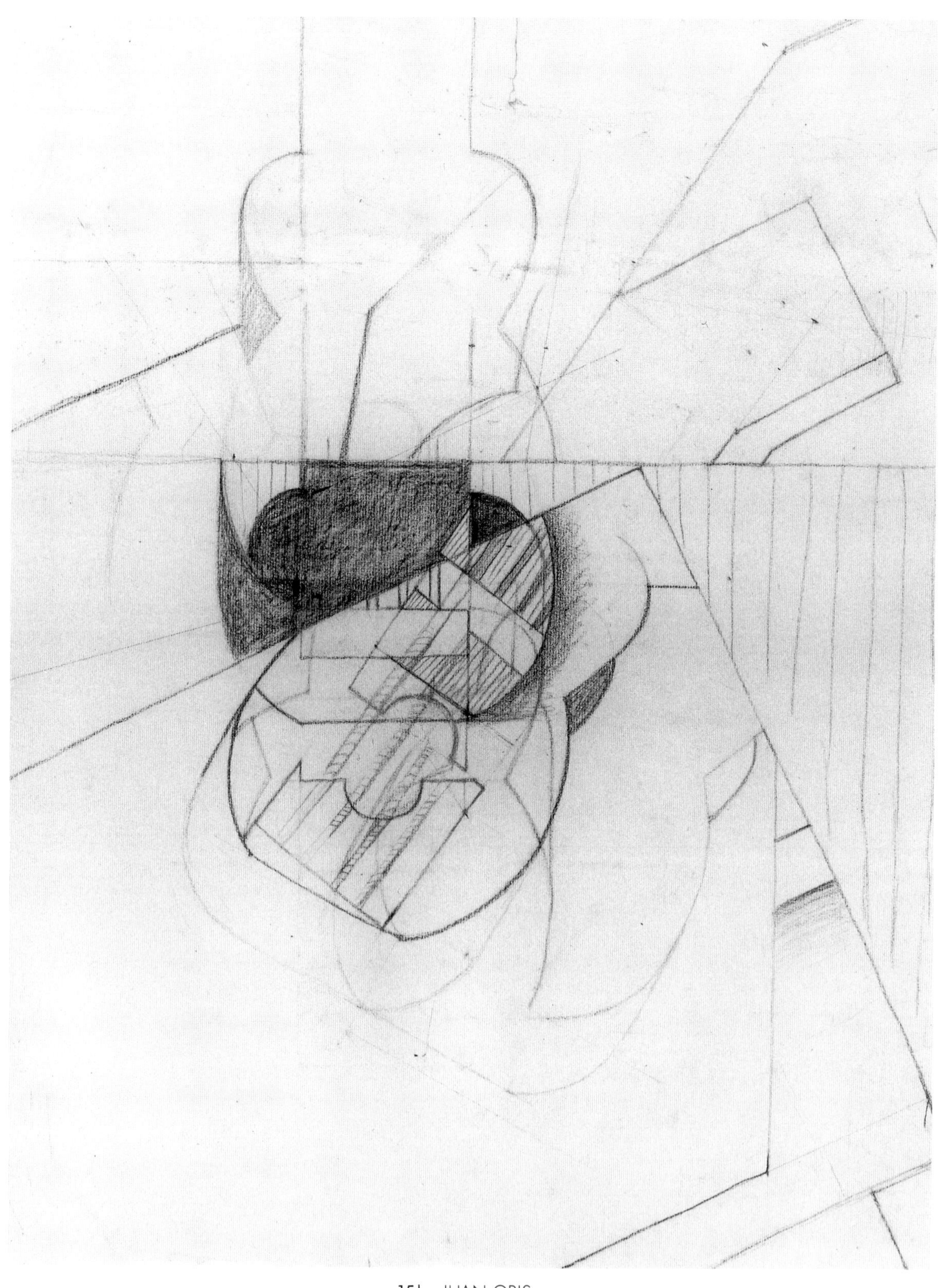

15b JUAN GRIS
(Violine; Violin) (1913)

oder im Umriss, der auf sie verweist. Diese Methoden waren ganz eigenständig von Gris entwickelt und angewendet worden.[95]

In diesem Stilleben erzielt Gris in hohem Masse Texturkontraste durch die Verwendung von dicht mit schwarzer Wasserfarbe gesättigten Partien, dicken kreidigen Gouache-Passagen von leutendem Weiss oder Gelb, von locker mit Ölkreide bemalten Stellen und von geklebten Papieren. Dieses Werk fängt die Spannung zwischen Gris' brillanter Kompositionsweise und der kruden Anti-Beaux-Arts-Qualität der geklebten Papiere ein. Cooper schrieb über Gris' «flächige farbige Architektur»:

Aber im Gegensatz (zu Picasso und Braque) war die Basis für Gris' Komposition eine Konstruktion aus verschiedenfarbigen Elementen, die er seine «flächige farbige Architektur» nannte. Er entwickelte dieses Verfahren, weil er, wie er sagte, es «natürlicher fand, den Gegenstand X in Übereinstimmung mit dem Bild (das er im Kopf hatte) zu bringen als das Bild X in Übereinstimmung mit einem bestimmten Gegenstand». Das heisst, Gris «ging von einer Abstraktion aus, um zu einer wirklichen Tatsache zu gelangen», ein Prozedere, welches seinen frühen kubistischen Bildern charakteristische Strenge verleiht, ihm aber auch erlaubte, sich eines aussergewöhnlichen Farbenreichtums zu bedienen.[96]

Gitarre/Violine und *Stilleben mit Gitarre und Noten* (Nr. 15a, 15b und 20) sind Beispiele für die wichtige Rolle, welche Musikinstrumente in Gris' Œuvre spielen. Die doppelseitige Zeichnung *Gitarre/Violine* steht in direktem Zusammenhang mit *Gitarre und Glas auf einem Tisch*, 1913, Graphit/Aquarell.[97] Die Rückseite der Zeichnung entspricht so genau dem Aquarell, dass sie als vorbereitende Studie angesehen werden kann, in der Gris die komplexe gegenseitige Beziehung der simultanen Front- und Profilansichten klärt. Die dramatische Aufsicht des Tisches, die drei Gläser und die

crude, decidedly anti- beaux arts quality of the pasted papers. Cooper discussed Gris' "flat colored architecture":

But unlike [Picasso and Braque], Gris based his compositions on an arrangement of differently colored elements which he referred to as his "flat, colored architecture." And he adopted this procedure because, he said, he found it "more natural to make subject 'X' coincide with the picture that (he had) in mind than to make picture 'X' coincide with a given subject." That is to say, Gris began "with an abstraction in order to arrive at a true fact," a procedure which gives his early Cubist paintings a characteristic severity but also allowed him to indulge in an exceptional richness of color."[96]

Guitar/Violin and *Still-life with Guitar and Sheet Music* (Nos. 15a, 15b and 20) document the importance of musical instruments in Gris' œuvre. The double sided drawing of *Guitar* and *Violin* relates most directly to *Guitar and Glass on a Table*, 1913, graphite and watercolor.[97] The verso of the drawing relates so exactly to the watercolor, that it can be seen as a preparatory drawing in which Gris resolves the complex interrelationship of the simultaneous frontal and profile views of the instrument. The dramatically upraised table, the three glasses and the striated wall paper are likewise present in drawing and watercolor.

Still-life with Guitar and Sheet Music ca. 1923. was included by Cooper in the 1955 Gris exhibition in Bern.[98] The articulation of the overlapping and intersecting planes with tightly, nervously rendered calligraphic patterns of varying density is also evident in other works of this period.[99]

Only two figural compositions by Gris are included in this exhibition (Nos. 17 and 18). These are two of several works executed by Gris in 1916, copies after black and white repoductions of paintings by Cézanne.[100] Gris returns to the artist who had a profound impact on the evolution of his work between his arrival in Paris in

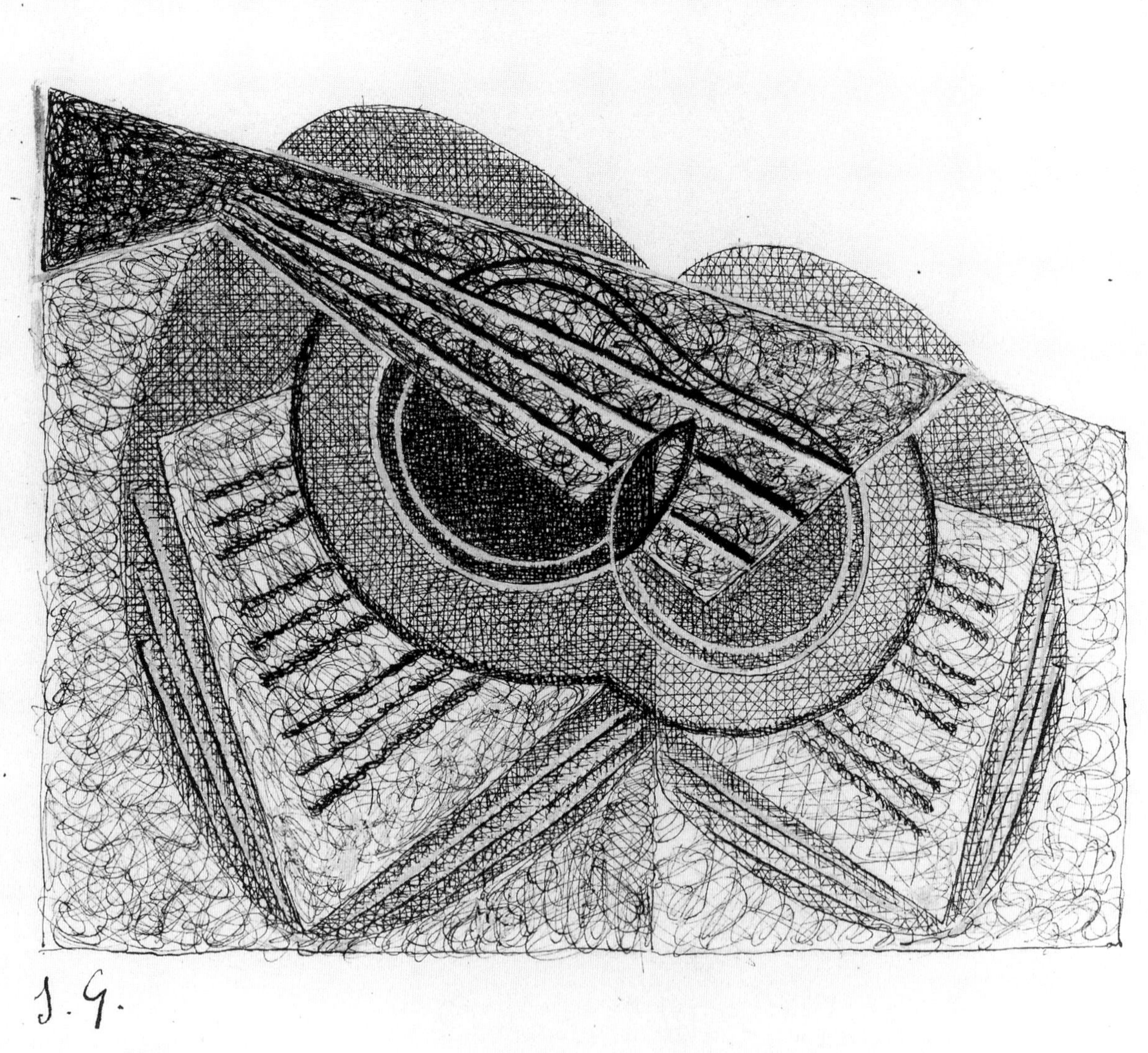

20 JUAN GRIS
(Stilleben mit Gitarre und Noten; Still-life with Guitar and Sheet Music) (1923)

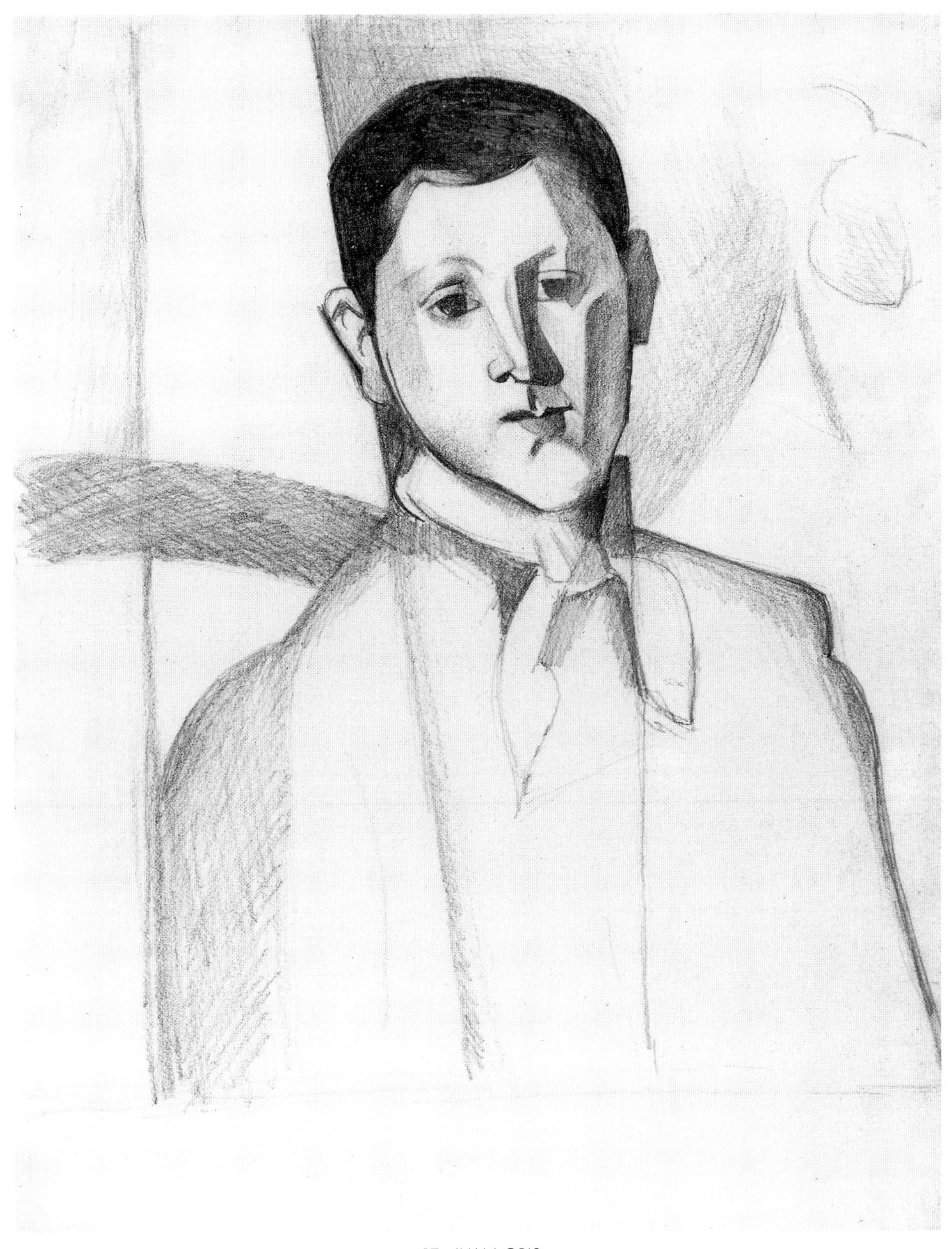

17 JUAN GRIS

(Copie nach Cézanne, «Louis Guillaume»; Copy after Cézanne's "Portrait of Louis Guillaume") (1916)

gestreifte Tapete sind in der Zeichnung wie im Aquarell zu finden.

Stilleben mit Gitarre und Noten, um 1923, nahm Cooper in die Gris-Ausstellung in Bern auf.[98] Die Artikulation der sich überschneidenden und durchdringenden Flächen durch gedrängt und nervös hingesetzte kalligraphische Muster verschiedener Dichte kann auch in anderen Werken aus dieser Zeit beobachtet werden.[99]

In dieser Ausstellung werden nur zwei Figurenkompositionen von Gris gezeigt (Nr. 17 und 18). Es sind zwei von mehreren Kopien nach Schwarzweiss-Reproduktionen von Werken Cézannes, entstanden im Jahr 1916.[100] Gris kehrt zu dem Künstler zurück, der von so grossem Einfluss auf die Entwicklung seines Schaffens zwischen seiner Ankunft 1906 in Paris und 1910–11 war. Die Bleistiftzeichung nach Cézannes *Porträt seiner Frau* hat engen Bezug zu einem Ölbild, das Gris zwei Jahre später, 1918, vollendete.[101] Die andere hier ausgestellte Zeichnung basiert auf Cézannes *Porträt Louis Guillaume*.[102] Gaya-Nuño beschreibt Gris' Interesse an Cézanne in dieser Zeit als «noch tiefere, ja programmatische Besessenheit».[103] Diese Beschäftigung mit Cézanne ist innerhalb eines Zurück-zu-den-alten-Meistern und ihrer Reevaluation zu sehen. Ende 1916, also zur selben Zeit, schuf Gris in Beaulieu-sur-Loches eine Bleistiftzeichnung nach dem Velàsquez-Porträt *Don Gaspar de Guzman* im Rijksmuseum Kröller-Müller in Otterloo[104] und malte eine Version von Corots *Mädchen mit Mandoline* von 1860/5 im Saint Louis Art Museum (Gris' Version befindet sich im Kunstmuseum Basel). Klar ist, dass Gris' genaue Beschäftigung mit Corot auch an seinem ebenfalls 1916 entstandenen *Porträt von Josette* (von Cooper dem Prado, Madrid, geschenkt) abzulesen ist.

Seit seiner ersten Schrift über den Künstler von 1935 hebt Cooper Gris' Rolle als einer der vier Hauptkubisten hervor, betont aber auch seinen eigenständigen Charakter. Er bezeichnet ihn als eher rational oder intellektuell in seiner Einstellung zum Kubismus, «als weniger intuitiven und empirischen Künstler als Braque oder

1906 and 1910–1911. The pencil drawing after Cézanne's portrait of Madame Cézanne clearly relates to an oil which Gris completed two years later in 1918.[101] The other drawing exhibited here is based on Cézanne's *Portrait of Louis Guillaume*.[102] Gaya-Nuño describes Gris' interest in Cézanne at this time as a "deeper and programmatic obsession".[103] This study of Cézanne is part of a more general return to and reevalution of the masters. At the same time, in the latter part of 1916 at Beaulieu-sur-Loches, Gris executed a pencil drawing after the Velasquez portrait of Don Gaspar de Guzman, Rijksmuseum Kröller-Müller, Otterlo[104] and painted a version of Corot's 1860–65, *Girl with a mandolin*, The Saint Louis Art Museum. (Gris' version is in the Kunstmuseum, Basel). It is clear that the lessons which Gris derived from this meticulous examination of Corot informs his *Portrait of Josette*, painted also in 1916 (given by Cooper to the Prado Museum, Madrid).

From his first publication on Gris in 1935, Cooper stressed Gris' role as one of the four major Cubist artists, while also stressing his distinctive character. He characterized Gris as more rational or intellectual in his approach to Cubism, "a less intuitive and empirical artist than Braque or Picasso".[105] He found, however, that Gris never fell into a programmatic approach, but rather, "he knew how to temper science with intuition". There was a "compensatory side of his nature – the lyrical as opposed to the intellectual, the sensuous as opposed to the severe".[106]

81 James Thrall Soby, *Juan Gris*, New York, Museum of Modern Art, 1958, p. 96.

82 Gertrude Stein, "Picasso", p. 13 as quoted by Mark Rosenthal, *Juan Gris*, Berkeley, 1983, p. 142.

83 Cooper, *Juan Gris, catalogue raisonné*, Paris, Berggruen & Cie., 1977, p. xxx. The same phrase "netteté et austérité" was used in the title of Cooper's article on Gris which appeared in *Réalités* April 1977, pp. 52–62].

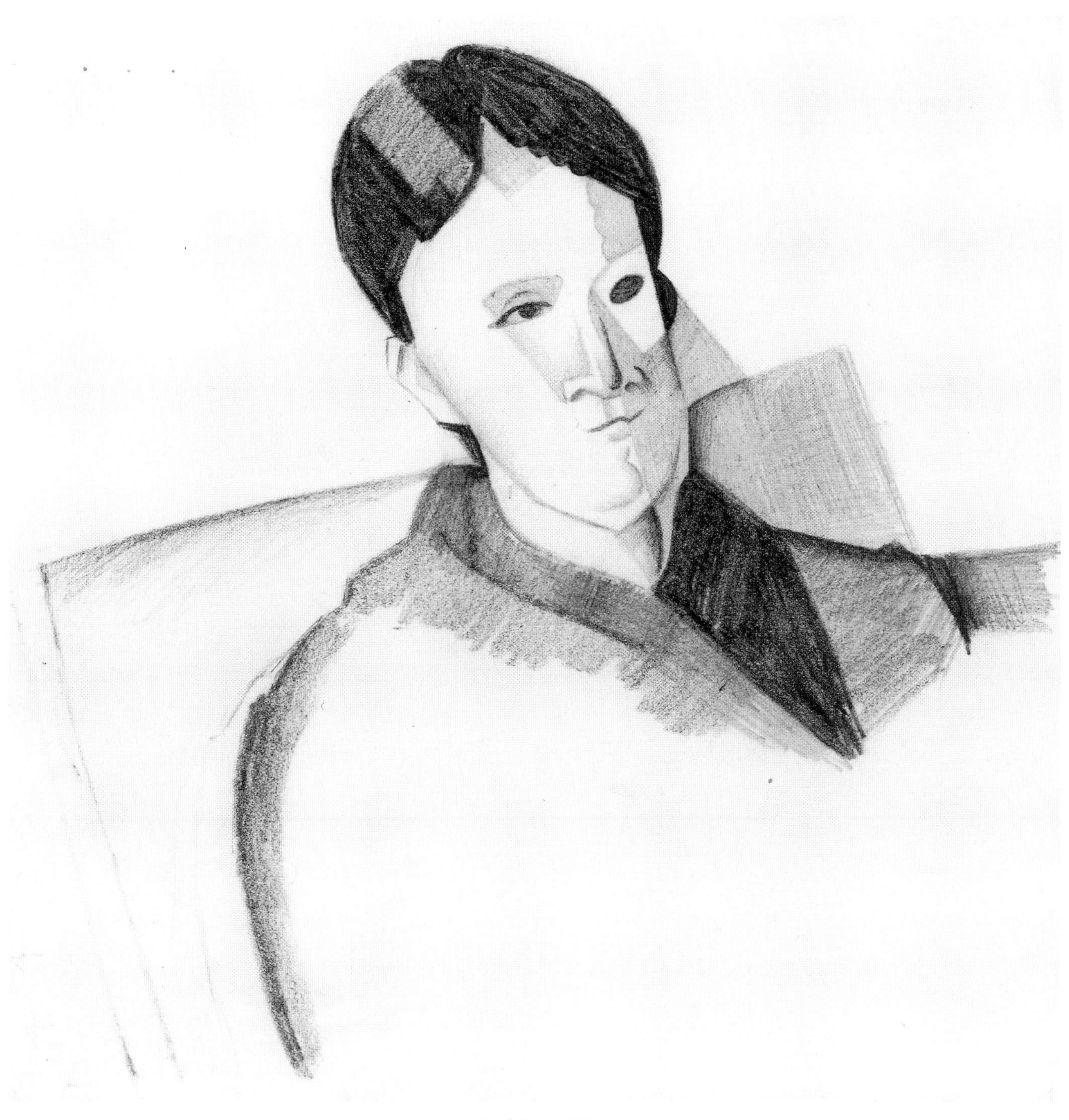

18 JUAN GRIS
(Kopie nach Cézanne, Porträt seiner Frau; Copy after Cézanne's portrait of his wife) (1916)

Picasso».[105] Doch fand er, dass Gris' Haltung nie kategorisch war, vielmehr dass er fruchtbar «Wissenschaft mit Intuition zu verbinden wusste». Da war immer eine «kompensatorische Seite in seinem Wesen – die lyrische im Gegensatz zur intellektuellen, die sinnliche im Gegensatz zur strengen».[106]

81 James Thrall Soby, *Juan Gris*, New York, Museum of Modern Art, 1958, S. 96.

82 Gertrude Stein, «Picasso», S. 13, zitiert nach Mark Rosenthal, *Juan Gris*, Berkeley, 1983, S. 142.

83 Cooper, *Juan Gris, catalogue raisonné*, Paris, Berggruen & Cie, 1977, S. XXX. Dieselben Worte, «Klarheit und Ernst», wurden von Cooper im Titel seines Artikels über Gris verwendet, der in *Réalités*, April 1977, S. 52–62, erschien.

84 ibid., S. xxx–xxxi.

85 Vgl. *Die Eier*, 1911, Öl auf Leinwand (Soby, 1958, New York, S. 15, Schwarzweissabb.) oder *Krug, Flasche und Schale*, 1911 (Gary Tinterow, *Juan Gris*, Madrid, Sala Picasso, 1985, Nr. 109), wo die Störung des Gegenstandskonturs sowie die Stilisierung des Lichts zu deutlichen oder unabhängigen Flächen jedoch extremer ist.

86 Vgl. mit *Flasche und Krug*, 1911, Kohle (Tinterow, 1985, Nr. 106) und auch mit *Stilleben mit Flasche und Trichter*, Bleistift, 1911 (Tinterow, 1985, Nr. 110), ähnlich in der feinfühligen oder suchenden Art des Gegenstandkonturs und in der Zersetzung der Festigkeit dieser Gegenstände durch scharf umrissene Partien von Hell und Dunkel.
N.B. ein weiteres Werk, das die Lampe aufweist: *Die drei Lampen*, 1910–11, Aquarell (Tinterow, 1985, Nr. 105).

87 Diese Cézanneschen Elemente werden noch kühner in andern Werken dieser Periode: zum Beispiel in *Flasche Wein und Wasserkrug*, 1911 (*The Cubist Epoch*, Nr. 107) oder *Stilleben mit Buch*, 1911 (Soby, 1958, S. 141).

88 S. verwandte Werke: *Krug, Fläschchen und Glas*, 1911 (Tinterow, 1985, Nr. 7) und *Flaschen und Messer*, 1912 (Tinterow, 1985, Nr. 9).

89 Cooper, *The Cubist Epoch*, S. 198. Schon 1949, in *Juan Gris ou le goût du solonnel*, Paris und Genf, Albert Skira, 1949, (S. 3, Ms.), erkannte Cooper die wichtige Rolle des Lichts in Gris' Werk, was es

84 *Ibid.*, p. xxx–xxxi.

85 Compare with *The Eggs*, 1911, oil on canvas, (Soby, p. 15 bw) or to *Pitcher, Bottle and Bowl*, 1911, pencil and charcoal, (Gary Tinterow, *Juan Gris*, Madrid, Sala Picasso, 1985, no. 109). In that work, however, the distortion of the contours of the objects, as well as the stylization of light into intrusive or independent areas is more extreme.

86 Compare to *Bottle and Jug*, charcoal, 1911 (Tinterow, 1985, no. 106); Compare as well *Still-life with bottle and funnel*, 1911, pencil (Tinterow, 1985, no. 110) similar in terms of the sensitive or meandering linear quality of the contours of objects and the disruption of the solidity of those objects with sharply delineated passages of light and shadow. Note, as well, another work which includes the lamp: *The Three lamps*, 1910–11, watercolor (Tinterow, 1985, no. 105).

87 These Cézannesque elements become even more audacious in other works of this period: note for example, *Bottle of Wine and Water Jug*, 1911 (*The Cubist Epoch*, no. 107) or *Still-life with Book*, 1911 (Soby, 1958, p. 14).

88 See related works: *Jar, Flask and Glass*, 1911 (Tinterow, 1985, no. 7) and *Bottles and Knife*, 1912 (Tinterow, 1985, no. 9).

89 Cooper, *The Cubist Epoch*, p. 198. Already in 1949, in *Juan Gris, ou Le goût du Solennel*, Paris and Geneva: Skira, 1949 (p. 3 ms.), Cooper recognizes the important role of light in Gris' work, an aspect of his painting which sets it apart from Picasso or Braque. His analysis of Gris' oil painting also focuses on this important compositional element: In regards to *Portrait of the Artist's Mother*, ca. March 1912, oil on canvas (purchased by Cooper from the Galerie de Beaune in 1938) he writes: "Gris has here developed his analytical method of representation by combining full-face and profile views of the head of his mother, by evoking volume through a strong play of light and shadow coupled with emphatically rounded, often hollowed-out forms, and by devising a new structure of broad planes through which the head is related to the space around it" (*The Essential Cubism*, p. 140; see also *Juan Gris, catalogue raisonné*, p. xiv).

90 Gris stated in 1921: "Cézanne va vers l'architecture, moi j'en pars, c'est pourquoi je compose avec des abstraction (couleurs) et j'arrange quand ces couleurs sont devenues des objets, par exemple, je compose avec un blanc et un noir et j'arrange quand ce blanc est devenu un papier et ce noir une ombre; je veux dire que j'arrange le blanc pour le faire devenir un papier et le noir pour le faire devenir une ombre." (as quoted by Cooper, *Juan Gris, catalogue raisonné*, p. xx; see also Cooper, *The Cubist Epoch*, p. 205.)

von Picassos oder Braques absetzt. Seine Analyse von Gris' Ölmalerei konzentriert sich ebenfalls auf dieses wichtige kompositionelle Element: Bezüglich *Porträt der Mutter des Künstlers*, ca. März 1912, Öl auf Leinwand (von Cooper 1938 bei der Galerie de Beaune erworben) schreibt er: «Gris hat hier seine analytische Methode der Darstellung entwickelt, indem er Front- und Profilsicht des Kopfes seiner Mutter kombiniert, Körperlichtkeit durch ein starkes Licht-Schatten-Spiel verbunden mit emphatisch gerundeten, oft ausgehöhlten Formen evoziert und indem er eine neue Struktur von grossen Flächen schafft, durch die der Kopf im umgebenden Raum verankert wird.» (*The Essential Cubism*, S. 140; s. a. *Juan Gris, catalogue raisonné*, S. XIV).

90 1912 äusserte sich Gris so: «Cézanne strebt der Architektur zu, ich gehe von ihr aus, deshalb komponiere ich mit Abstraktionen (Farben), und ich ordne, wenn diese Farben Objekte geworden sind, ich komponiere zum Beispiel mit einem Weiss und einem Schwarz, und ich ordne, wenn dieses Weiss zu einem Papier und das Schwarz zu einem Schatten geworden ist; ich möchte sagen, dass ich das Weiss ordne, um es zu einem Papier und das Schwarz, um es zu einem Schatten werden zu lassen.» (zitiert von Cooper in *Juan Gris, catalogue raisonné*, S. xx; s. a. Cooper, *The Essential Cubism*, S. 205).

91 Cooper, «Juan Gris», *Axis*, Herbst 1936, Nr. 7, S. 9–12. (Vgl. eine verwandte Zeichnung, *Stilleben mit Kaffeemühle*, 1916; Tinterow, 1985, Nr. 139).

92 Vgl. mit *Stilleben mit Salzfässchen*, 1918, Tinterow, 1985, Nr. 154; in diesem Katalog erläutert Ann Temkin, in «Los dibujos de Juan Gris» (S. 312), wie die geheimnisvolle Qualität des Lichts, die Gris in seinen Kohlezeichnungen erreicht, dazu diene, die Banalität des Inhalts oder des Bildgegenstands zu verschleiern.

93 S. Cooper, *Juan Gris, catalogue raisonné*, S. xvii.

94 Cooper, *Juan Gris ou le goût du solennel*, S. 5 (Ms.).

95 Cooper, *The Cubist Epoch*, S. 202; zwei Werke können dazu in Beziehung gesetzt werden: *Stilleben mit Zigarrenkiste*, 1912, Kohle, enthält die gleiche Zigarrenkiste und Schablonenschrift (Tinterow, 1985, Nr. 117); *Rumflasche*, 1913, farbige Ölkreiden und Tusche, verwendet dieselbe vertikale Struktur, welche die Gegenstände in Teile zerschneidet (Tinterow, 1985, Nr. 124).

96. Cooper, ibid., S. 205.

97 In Cooper, *The Essential Cubism*, Nr. 85. S. Ann Temkin, «Los dibujos de Juan Gris», S. 309, wo Gris' vorbereitende Zeichnungen

91 Cooper, "Juan Gris," *Axis*, autumn 1936, no. 7, p. 9–12. (For a related drawing, see Tinterow, 1985, no. 139, *Still-life with Coffee Mill*, 1916).

92 Compare to *Still-life with a Salt Cellar*, 1918 Tinterow, 1985, no. 154; In that catalogue, *Juan Gris*, Ann Temkin, "Los dibujos de Juan Gris" page 312, discusses how the mysterious quality of light which Gris achieves in his charcoal drawings, serves to conceal the banality of his subject matter or imagery.

93 See Cooper, *Juan Gris catalogue raisonné*, p. xvii.

94 Cooper, *Juan Gris ou le goût du Solennel*, (p. 5 ms.).

95 Cooper, *The Cubist Epoch*, p. 202; See related works: *Still-life with Box of Cigars*, 1912, charcoal, which includes the same box of cigars and stenciled letters (in Tinterow, 1985, no. 117); *Bottle of Rum*, 1913, colored crayons and ink, which uses the same structure of vertical planes which dissect the objects (in Tinterow, 1985, no. 124).

96 Cooper, *Ibid.*, p. 205.

97 In Cooper, *The Essential Cubism*, no. 85. See Ann Temkin, "Los dibujos de Juan Gris", p. 309, for discussion of Gris' preparatory drawings of 1913 which mediate between visible theme and finished product. In the watercolor, however, Gris introduces color – pale green stripes in the wall paper, light blue in the glasses, wood grain on the table surface – and most dramatically, penetrating black which functions as a shadow, accentuating and reinforcing the forms.

98 Cooper, *Juan Gris*, Bern, Kunstmuseum, 1955, no. 160.

99 See for example, *Glass and Grapes*, 1923, ink, Galerie Theo, Madrid (Tinterow, 1985, no. 177). Understandably, Gris applied this linear technique by which he achieves variation in rhythm and tone, in engravings to illustrate Tristan Tzara's *Mouchoirs des nuages*. This work might reflect, as well, the impact of the painted reliefs of his friends Laurens and Lipchitz. (See *The Cubist Epoch*, p. 228)

100 Entry number 88 in *The Essential Cubism*, mentions ten such pencil drawings after works by Cézanne. See Tinterow, 1985 no. 133, *Bathers*, 1916, pencil, collection Walter Feilchenfeldt, Zürich; no. 134, Harlequin, 1916 graphite, John Rewald, New York; no. 135, *Harlequin*, 1916, pencil, Musée National d'Art Modern, Centre Georges Pompidou; no. 136, *Self-portrait of Cézanne*, pencil, 1916, Art Institute of Chicago, for examples.

von 1913 zur Sprache kommen, die zwischen angedeutetem Thema und ausgearbeiteter Fassung schwanken. Im Aquarell verwendet Gris hingegen Farben – blassgrüne Streifen für die Tapete, Hellblau für die Gläser, Holzmaserung für die Tischplatte und, sehr dramatisch, tiefes Schwarz für den Schatten, welcher die Formen akzentuiert und verstärkt.

98 Cooper, *Juan Gris,* Kunstmuseum Bern, 1955, Nr. 160.

99 S. z.B. *Glas und Trauben,* 1923, Tusche, Galerie Theo, Madrid (Tinterow, 1985, Nr. 177). Verständlicherweise verwendet Gris diese linearen Techniken, mit denen er rhythmisch und tonlich differenzieren kann, in den Radierungen zu Tristan Tzaras *Mouchoirs des nuages*. Dieses Werk zeigt vielleicht auch den Einfluss der bemalten Reliefs seiner Freunde Laurens und Lipchitz (s. *The Cubist Epoch,* S. 228).

100 Eintrag Nr. 88 in *The Essential Cubism:* erwähnt werden zehn solche Bleistiftzeichnungen nach Werken Cézannes.
S. Tinterow, 1985, Nr. 133 (*Badende,* 1916, Bleistift, Sammlung Walter Feilchenfeldt, Zürich), Nr. 134 (*Harlekin,* 1916, Graphit; John Rewald, New York), Nr. 135 (*Harlekin,* 1916, Bleistift; Musée Nationale d'Art Moderne, Centre Georges Pompidou), Nr. 136 (*Selbstporträt Cézannes,* 1916, Bleistift; The Art Institute of Chicago) als Beispiele.

101 Cézannes *Porträt Mme Cézanne,* 1890, Metropolitan Museum of Art, New York (Venturi, *Cézanne, son art – son œuvre,* Paris: Rosenberg, 1936, Nr. 569), dürfte die Vorlage für die Zeichnung in dieser Ausstellung gewesen sein. Mit dem *Porträt Mme Cézanne,* ca. 1886, The Art Institute of Chicago (Venturi Nr. 572) beschäftigte sich Gris im Hinblick auf das Ölbild, welches in *The Cubist Epoch* zu Nr. 127 abgebildet ist (Tafel 277). Eine weitere Version von Gris, Öl auf Karton, befindet sich in der Sammlung Marie-Laure de Noailles, Paris; s. *Juan Gris,* Paris, Orangerie, 1974, Nr. 72. Eine weitere Bleistiftzeichnung von Gris zu diesem Porträt wurde 1965 in der Galerie Louise Leiris ausgestellt.

102 Venturi Nr. 374.

103 J. A. Gaya-Nuño, *Juan Gris,* New York, Rizzoli, 1986, S. 20.

104 Tinterow, 1985, Nr. 137.

105 Cooper, *The Cubist Epoch,* S. 196.

106 Cooper, "The Temperament of Juan Gris", *Metropolitan Museum of Art Bulletin,* New York, Bd. 29, Nr. 8, April 1971, S. 360. Auch in der Einleitung des Katalogs zur Ausstellung *Juan Gris* 1955 in Bern hebt Cooper dieses ausbalancierte Wesen des Künstlers hervor: «In Juan Gris mischten sich spanische Zähigkeit und Ausdauer mit französischer douceur, und er verband mit dem Temperament eines Ingenieurs und rationaliste das eines caresseurs» (unpaginiert).

101 Cézanne's *Portrait of Madame Cézanne,* 1890, New York, Metropolitan Museum of Art (Lionello Venturi, *Cézanne, son art – son œuvre,* Paris: Rosenberg, 1936, no. 569) may be the model for the drawing in the present exhibition. *Portrait of Madame Cézanne,* ca. 1886, The Art Institute of Chicago, Venturi no. 572 was the work which Gris apparently studied for his oil, illustrated in *The Cubist Epoch,* no. 127, plate 277. There is also another version by Gris, oil on cardboard, in the Collection of Marie-Laure de Noailles, Paris, see *Juan Gris,* Paris, Orangerie, 1974, no. 72. Another Gris pencil drawing for this portrait of Madame Cézanne was also exhibited at Galerie Louise Leiris in 1965.

102 Venturi no. 374.

103 J. A. Gaya-Nuño, *Juan Gris,* New York, Rizzoli, 1986, p. 20.

104 Tinterow, 1985, no. 137.

105 Cooper, *The Cubist Epoch,* p. 196.

106 Cooper, "The Temperament of Juan Gris", *Metropolitan Museum of Art Bulletin,* New York, vol. 29, no. 8, April 1971, p. 360. Also, in the introduction to the 1955 *Juan Gris* exhibition in Bern, Cooper emphasizes the same balance in Gris' artistic personality: "In Juan Gris mischten sich spanische Zähigkeit und Ausdauer mit französischer *douceur,* und er verband dem Temperament eines Ingenieurs das eines *rationaliste* und eines *caresseur.*" [not paginated]

FERNAND LEGER

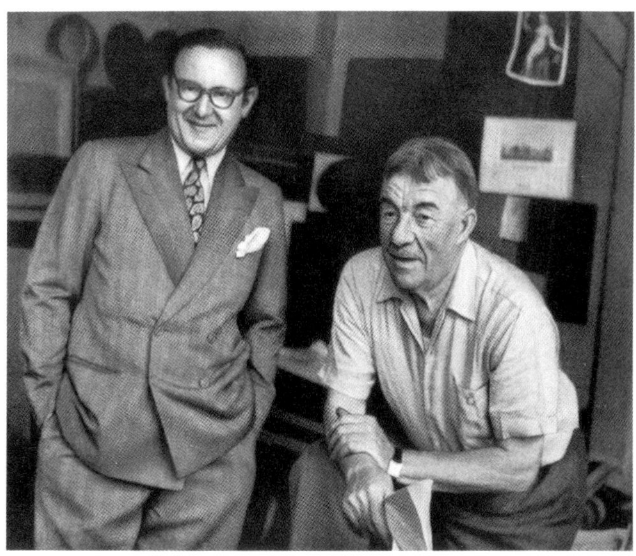

Cooper und Léger, 1949, von *Fernand Léger et le nouvel espace.*

Cooper and Léger, 1949, from *Fernand Léger et le nouvel espace.*

Coopers Widmung in seiner 1949 erschienenen Monographie *Fernand Léger et le nouvel espace* lässt die Herzlichkeit und Tiefe seiner Freundschaft mit dem Künstler erkennen: «Hier, mein lieber Léger, eine Hommage an Dich, Dir in aller Freundschaft gewidmet. Zwanzig Jahre Bewunderung haben mich gelehrt, dass es der erste Schock ist, der zählt.» Und das erste Kapitel des Buches endet mit diesem überschwenglichen Ausdruck seiner Bewunderung für den Künstler:

In Fernand Léger, Bauer aus der Normandie, Bildner von Natur, grüsse ich den Beherrscher der Maschine, den Schöpfer neuartiger Rhythmen und den Malerdichter des Heute. Fernand Léger ist Maler, einfacher Maler, und mir, wie einst Apollinaire, bereiten die Einfachheit und Zuverlässigkeit seines Urteils Freude. Ich liebe diese Kunst, und ich liebe den Menschen, weil er echt ist. Ich liebe seine starken, heftigen oder fröhlichen Farben, ich liebe seine anmutigen, sperrigen oder metallischen Gegenstände. Ich liebe seine Kraft und

The dedication in Cooper's 1949 monograph *Fernand Léger et le nouvel espace*, reveals the warmth and depth of his friendship with the artist: "Voici, mon cher Léger, un hommage que je te dédie en toute amitié. Vingt années d'admiration m'ont appris que c'est le premier choc qui compte." The first chapter of the book concludes with this effusive exclamation of his admiration of the artist:

Je salue en Fernand Léger, paysan normand, plasticien instinctif, le dominateur de la machine, le créateur de rythmes neufs et le peintre-poète de la réalité actuelle. Fernand Léger est peintre, simple peintre, et je me réjouis, à la suite d'Apollinaire, "autant de sa simplicité que de la solidité de son jugement". J'aime cet art et j'aime l'homme, parce qu'il est authentique. J'aime ses couleurs fortes, violentes ou gaies, j'aime ses objets gracieux, raides ou métalliques. J'aime son énergie et son plaisir de vivre, son bouillonnement de sa rudesse. J'aime sa robuste conception de la pein-

seine Lebenslust und das Aufbrausen seiner Derbheit. Ich liebe seine solide Auffassung von Malerei, und ich liebe seine Begeisterung in der Ausführung. Ich stehe zu dir, Fernand Léger.[107]

Zum ersten Mal sah Cooper Bilder von Léger in der Galerie Paul Rosenberg, 1930, in Paris. 1933 war er, anlässlich der Retrospektive des Künstlers im Kunsthaus, in Zürich. Auf Drängen seines Freundes Carl Einstein besuchte er endlich Légers Atelier: «Und so erstieg ich denn im Mai 1933 zum ersten Mal die Wendeltreppe im Haus Nr. 86 an der Rue Notre Dame-des-Champs, die zum Atelier im zweiten Stock führte, wo Fernand Léger seit dreissig Jahren arbeitete.»[108] Die enge Freundschaft dauerte bis zu Légers Tod im Jahre 1955. Oft besuchte der Künstler Argilliers, ja er war, wie ein Brief von Curt Valentin vom 16. April 1952 zeigt, der erste Hausgast im eben renovierten Schloss Castille.[109] 1954 gab Cooper *Die Trapezkünstler* in Auftrag, ein grossformatiges Wandbild für das Treppenhaus des Schlosses.

Coopers Sammlung und auch seine Schriften zeugen von seiner Aufgeschlossenheit für die entscheidenden Momente oder die wichtigsten Phasen in Légers künstlerischem Werdegang: für die frühen, von Cézanne beeinflussten Werke, die ungegenständlichen *Contrastes de formes*, die persönlichen Erfahrungen und das Schaffen während des ersten Weltkriegs, für das Verarbeiten eines puristischen Vokabulars in den zwanziger Jahren und die Integrierung einer populistischen Bildsprache in die Werke der vierziger und fünfziger Jahre.

Eine Reihe von Aktzeichnungen, darunter die Nr. 28, sind Beispiele eines mager dokumentierten Abschnitts der Entwicklung Légers; sie machen den Einfluss von Cézanne deutlich.[110] 1913 sagte Léger: «Cézanne lehrte mich Formen und Körper lieben, und er brachte mich dazu, dass ich mich aufs Zeichnen konzentrierte. Und da wurde mir klar, dass man mit Disziplin und nicht nach Gefühl zeichnen soll».[111] Cooper hatte auch,

ture, et j'aime son élan dans l'exécution. Je suis avec vous, Fernand Léger.[107]

He first encountered Léger's painting in 1930 at the Galerie Paul Rosenberg in Paris. In 1933 he attended the retrospective of the artist's work at the Kunsthaus in Zürich, and upon the urging of his friend Carl Einstein visited Léger's studio. "C'est ainsi qu'au mois de mai 1933 je gravis pour la première fois l'escalier en spirale du numéro 86 de la rue Notre Dame-des-Champs, qui mène au studio du second étage où Fernand Léger travaille depuis trente ans."[108] The strong friendship continued until Léger's death in 1955. Léger was a frequent visitor in Argilliers, in fact, as a letter to Curt Valentin dated 16 April 1952 reveals, Léger was the first house guest at the newly restored Château de Castille.[109] In 1954 Cooper commissioned *The Trapeze Artists*, a large scale mural painting for a stairway landing in the Château de Castille.

Cooper's collection and his writings, as well, demonstrate an appreciation of the essential stages or crucial moments in Léger's artistic development: the early works influenced by Cézanne, the non-figurative *Contrastes de formes*, the personal experiences and artistic output during World War I, the digestion of a Purist vocabulary in the twenties and the embracing of populist imagery in his later works during the forties and fifties.

A series of drawings of nudes, including No. 28, examples of a poorly documented period in Léger's development, reveal the impact of Cézanne.[110] In 1913 Léger said: "Cézanne taught me to love forms and volumes, he made me concentrate on drawing. And then I realized that drawing had to be rigid and in no way sentimental."[111] Cooper has suggested as well the influence of Archipenko in Léger's stylizations.[112]

Cooper links Léger's truly Cubist works, executed between 1910–1912, to the artist's struggle to free himself from the influence of Cézanne and to develop his own style. Léger explains in 1954: "His grip was so strong that in order to free myself I had to go as far as

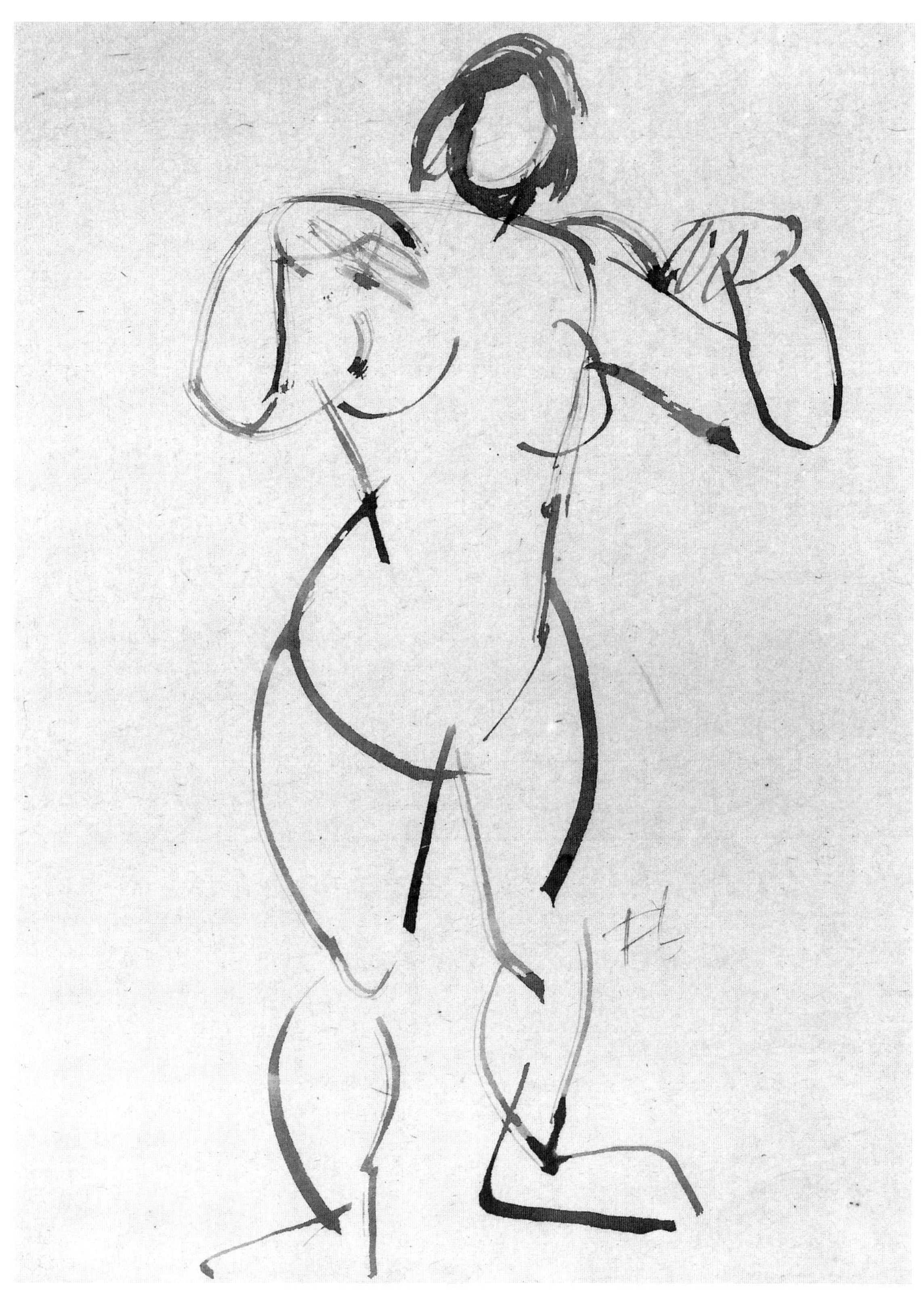

28 FERNAND LEGER
(Stehender Akt; Standing Nude) (1911)

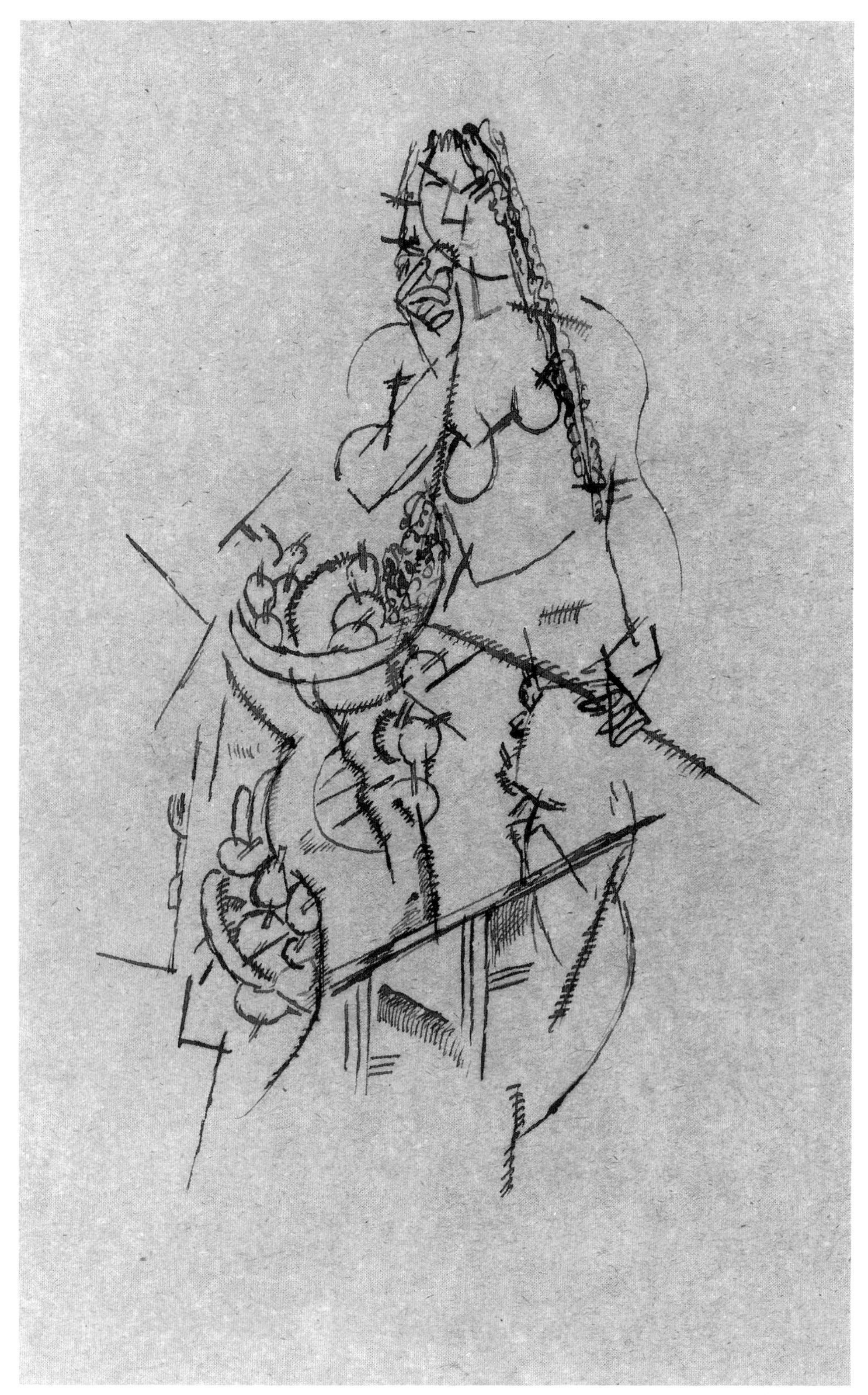

29 FERNAND LEGER
(Studie für eine «Abundantia»; Study for an "Abundance") (1912)

was Légers Stilisierungen betraf, auf den Einfluss von Archipenko hingewiesen.[112]

Für Cooper steht ein Bezug von Légers eigentlichen kubistischen Werken aus den Jahren 1910–12 zum Ringen um Befreiung vom Einfluss Cézannes und um einen eigenen Stil fest. Der Künstler erläuterte 1954: «Seine Macht über mich war so gross, dass ich, um mich davon befreien zu können, bis zur Abstraktion gehen musste. Endlich spürte ich bei «Frau in Blau» und «Bahnübergang», dass ich mich von Cézanne gelöst und mich gleichzeitig weit weg vom impressionistischen Wohllaut bewegt hatte».[113] In seinen *Contrastes de formes* erforscht Léger wagemutig ein rein abstraktes oder nonfiguratives Idiom, ein Formenvokabular oder eine Kompositionsstruktur, wovon, wie Cooper meint, das gesamte spätere Werk durchdrungen ist.

> *Dennoch, in einigen seiner Bilder mit dem Titel* Contrastes de formes, *scheint er sich zu einer ungegenständlichen, zu einer abstrakten Kunst vorgewagt zu haben. Doch dem ist nicht so. Schauen wir sie uns heute mit neuen Augen an, hier, zusammen mit den andern, deren figuratives Anliegen nicht in Zweifel gezogen werden kann! In den Bildern beider Art sind die Formen und die Weise, wie sich der Künstler ihrer bedient, sozusagen identisch. Die Figuren auf der Treppe oder dem Balkon, die Gegenstände auf den Tischen – sie können durchaus gegen die reinen Formen ausgetauscht werden. Und diese Entdeckung zwingt uns zur Erkenntnis, dass diese* Contrastes de formes *wesentlich die grundlegende Syntax einer neuen Bildsprache bilden, welche es Léger in der Folge möglich machte, von seinen Versuchen mit planparalleler Abstraktion zu einer Figuration zu kommen, bereichert von seinem Wissen um Mensch, Maschine und Alltag.*[114]

Nature morte, 1913 (Nr. 30), wird beherrscht von kräftigen Kontrasten zwischen grob aufgetragenen weissen und schwarzen Streifen in Gouache und Öl, welche die «Gegenstände» auf der Tischplatte als in

abstraction. Finally, in *'Woman in Blue'* and *'Railroad Crossing'* I felt I had liberated myself from Cézanne and at the same time I had moved far from the melody of impressionism''.[113] In his *contrastes de formes*, Léger audaciously explores a purely abstract or non-objective idiom, a formal vocabulary or compositional structure which Cooper sees informing all of the later work.

> *Néanmoins dans certains de ses tableaux intitulés* Contrastes de formes *il paraît s'être aventuré dans un art abstrait, un art de non-figuration. Il n'en est rien. Regardons-les aujourd'hui avec un œil frais, ici, parmi d'autres dont le but figuratif ne peut pas être mis en doute. Dans les tableaux des deux genres les formes et la façon dont l'artiste s'en sert sont, pour ainsi dire, identiques. Les figures dans l'escalier ou sur le balcon, les objets sur les tables, sont donc interchangeables avec les formes pures. Et cette décourverte nous oblige à reconnaître que ces* Contrastes de Formes *sont essentiellement la syntaxe à la base d'un nouveau langage pictural qui permettait ensuite à Léger de passer de ses essais sur le plan parallel de l'abstraction à une figuration enrichie par ses expériences de l'homme, de la machine et de la vie quotidienne.*[114]

Nature morte, 1913, (No. 30) is dominated by forceful contrasts between roughly applied stripes of white and black gouache and oil, which produce the effect that the ''objects'' on the table surface are bathed in a dazzling light. Cooper wrote in 1949:

> *Réagissant aussi contre un art purement asservi à la couleur et qui tendait avant tout à rendre des effets de lumière, il entreprit d'explorer les formes. Mais toujours ses formes sont modelées par la lumière, et le sont délibérément et manifestement: en effet, les blancs intenses qui courent le long de ses formes tubulaires, flanqués de traits noirs, verts, rouges ou bleus, lui sont particuliers. Léger a simplifieé et grossi mais jamais analysé ses formes… Des formes simples, des couleurs pures et descriptives, un emploi élémentaire mais significatif du*

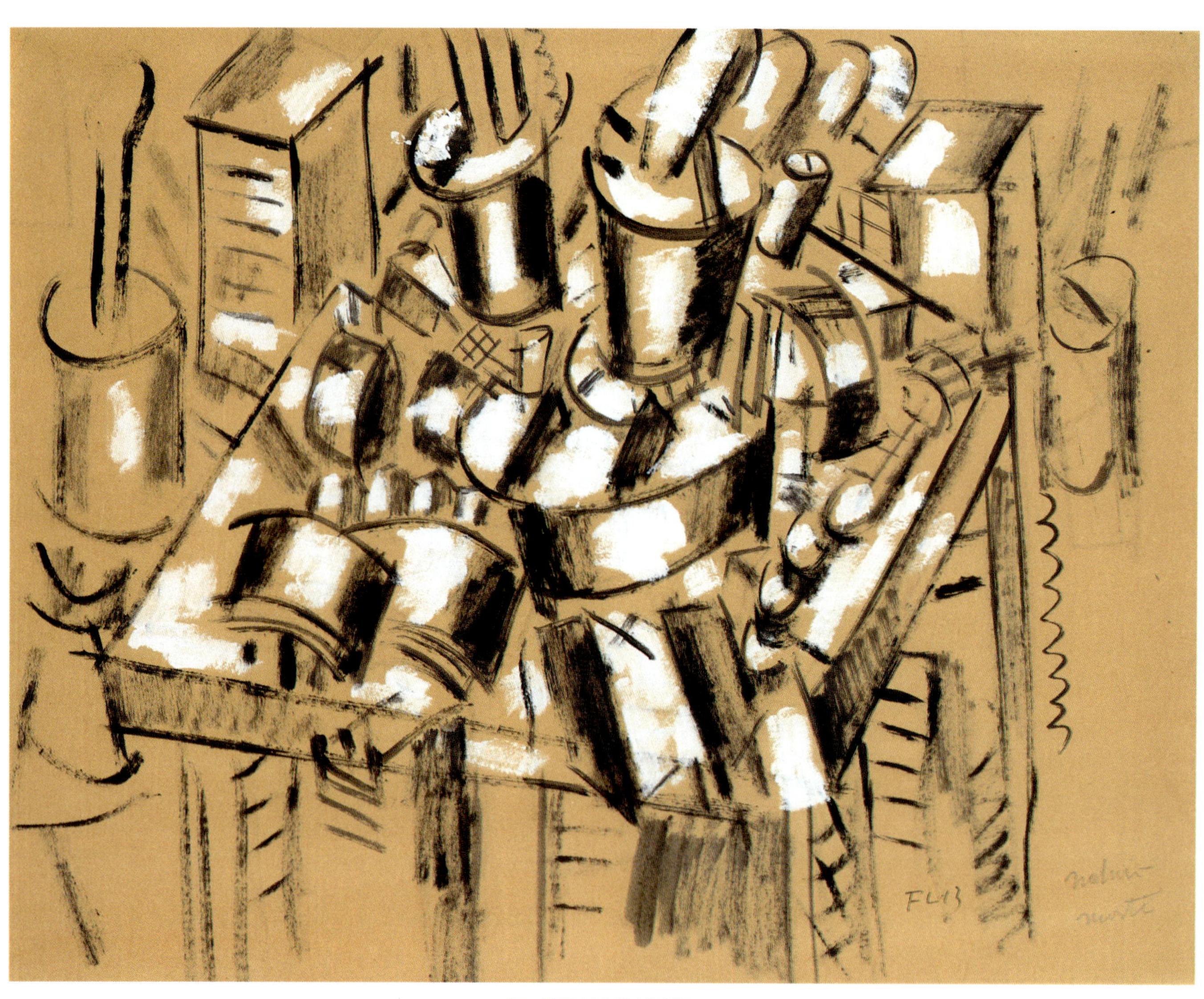

30 FERNAND LEGER
Nature morte (Stilleben; Still-life) 1913

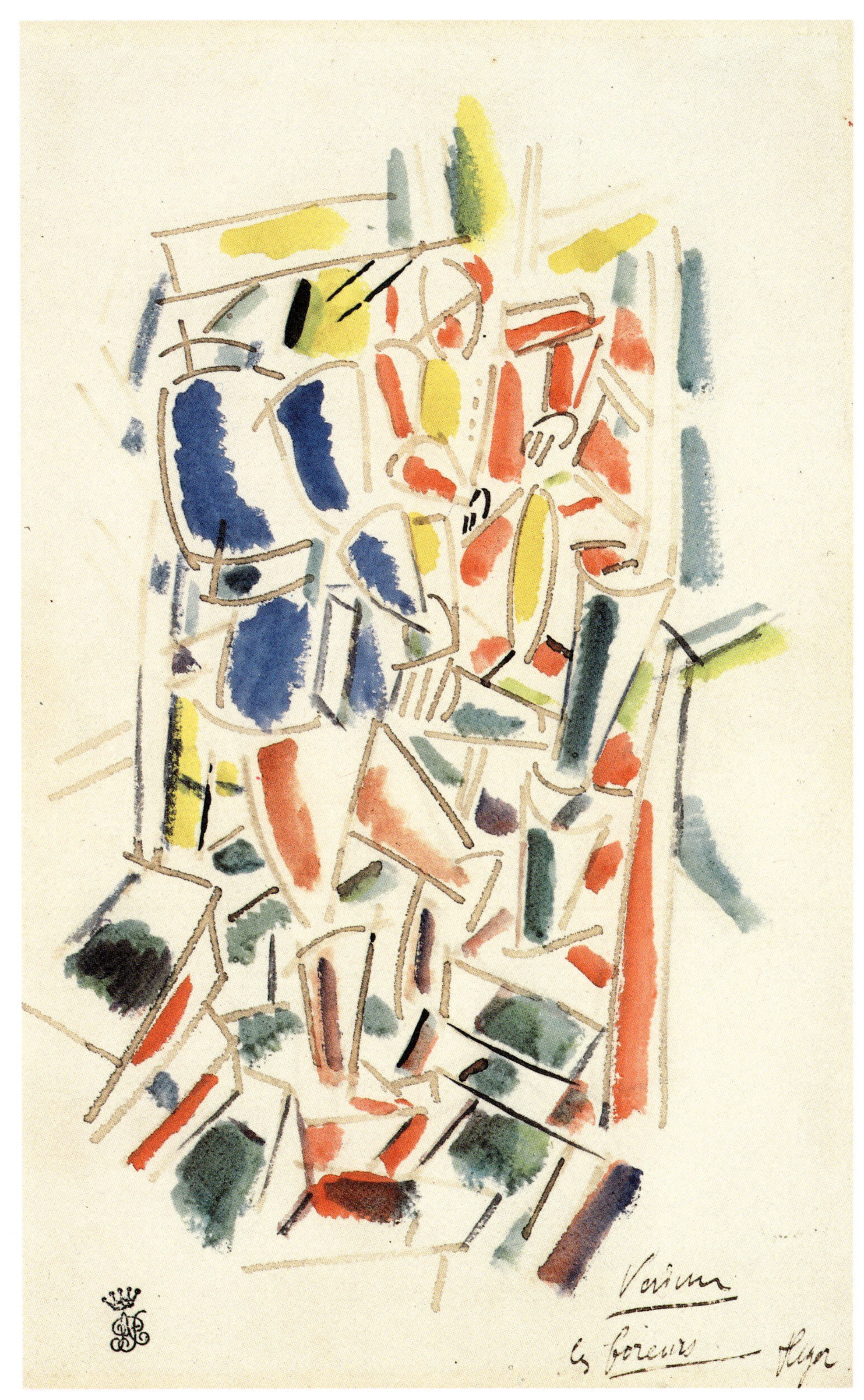

31 FERNAND LEGER
Les Foreurs (Die Sappeure; The Sappers) (1916)

blendendes Licht getaucht erscheinen lassen. Cooper schrieb 1949:

> *Indem er auch auf eine Kunst, die rein der Farbe diente und die vor allem die Wirkung des Lichts wiedergeben wollte, reagierte, machte er sich an die Erforschung der Formen. Aber noch immer werden diese durch das Licht modelliert, und zwar offensichtlich und mit Vorbedacht: ihm eigen ist denn auch das intensive Weiss, welches längs der Röhrenformen verläuft, flankiert von schwarzen, grünen, roten und blauen Strichen. Léger hat die Formen vereinfacht und vergröbert, aber nie analysiert... Einfache Formen, reine deskriptive Farben, eine elementare, aber bedeutsame Anwendung des Helldunkels, das Licht als Mittel zur Verdeutlichung der Form und die Betonung gut definierter Flächen: das sind die Elemente, mit denen Léger von 1910 bis 1916 arbeitete...*[115]

Légers Fronterlebnisse im ersten Weltkrieg machten seinem Liebäugeln mit der Abstraktion ein Ende. In moralischer wie ästhetischer Hinsicht betrachtete er diese Erfahrung als Wendepunkt.

> *Im Krieg erst stand ich mit beiden Beinen auf dem Boden. Innerhalb von zwei Monaten habe ich mehr gelernt als in meinem ganzen bisherigen Leben. Ah! Diese starken Kerle. Auch ich war kräftig, und ich bekam keine Angst. Wir sind Kameraden geworden. Sogar als man mir sagte, ich solle weg von der Front und in Deckung, wollte ich sie doch nicht verlassen. «Ich bleibe», sagte ich. Während die Kerle Karten spielten, blieb ich bei ihnen, betrachtete sie, machte Zeichnungen, Skizzen, wollte sie festhalten. Die Kerle machten mir grossen Eindruck, und ich hatte spontan den Wunsch, sie zu zeichnen. Daraus entstanden später* Die Kartenspieler.[116]

Demgemäss betrachtete Cooper die Kriegsskizzen und Kriegszeichnungen als Schlüssel zum Verständnis des offensichtlichen und tiefen Wandels in Légers Schaffen

> *clair-obscur, la lumière servant à révéler des formes, et l'accent porté sur des plans bien marqués: tels sont les éléments avec lesquels Léger travaille de 1910 à 1916...*[115]

Léger's flirtation with abstraction was dramatically reversed by his experiences at the front during World War I. Léger, of course, acknowledged his war-time experience as a profound moral and aesthetic turning point.

> *C'est à la guerre que j'ai mis les pieds dans le sol... En espace de deux mois j'ai appris plus que dans toute ma vie... Ah! Ces gros gars. J'étais costaud moi aussi et je n'ai pas eu peur. Je suis devenu camarade avec eux. Même-quand on m'a proposé d'aller dans le camouflage loin du front, je n'ai pas voulu les quitter, "Je reste", j'ai dit. Pendant que les gars jouaient aux cartes, je restais à côté d'eux, je les regardais, je faisais des dessins, des croquis, je voulais les saisir. J'étais très impressionné par les gars et le désir de les dessiner m'est venu spontanément. C'est de là que plus tard est sorti* La Partie de Cartes.[116]

Accordingly, Cooper saw Léger's wartime drawings and sketches as the key to understanding the profound change evident in his pre-war and post-war production. "Les dessins de ce volume illustrent... l'evolution spirituelle d'un des plus grands artistes français des temps modernes. Ils ont en plus le grand intérêt d'être le seul lien, et un lien essentiel entre les langages picturaux dont Léger usa avant et après la guerre."[117]

It was Cooper who initiated the project with the war drawings and pursued it with great enthusiasm. (See No. 48, Léger's gouache maquette for the cover of the publication.) He first proposed it to his friend Curt Valentin in 1952. In a letter dated October 6, 1952 Cooper writes:

> *I now have these drawings and watercolor in my possession. There are about 60 drawings in pencil*

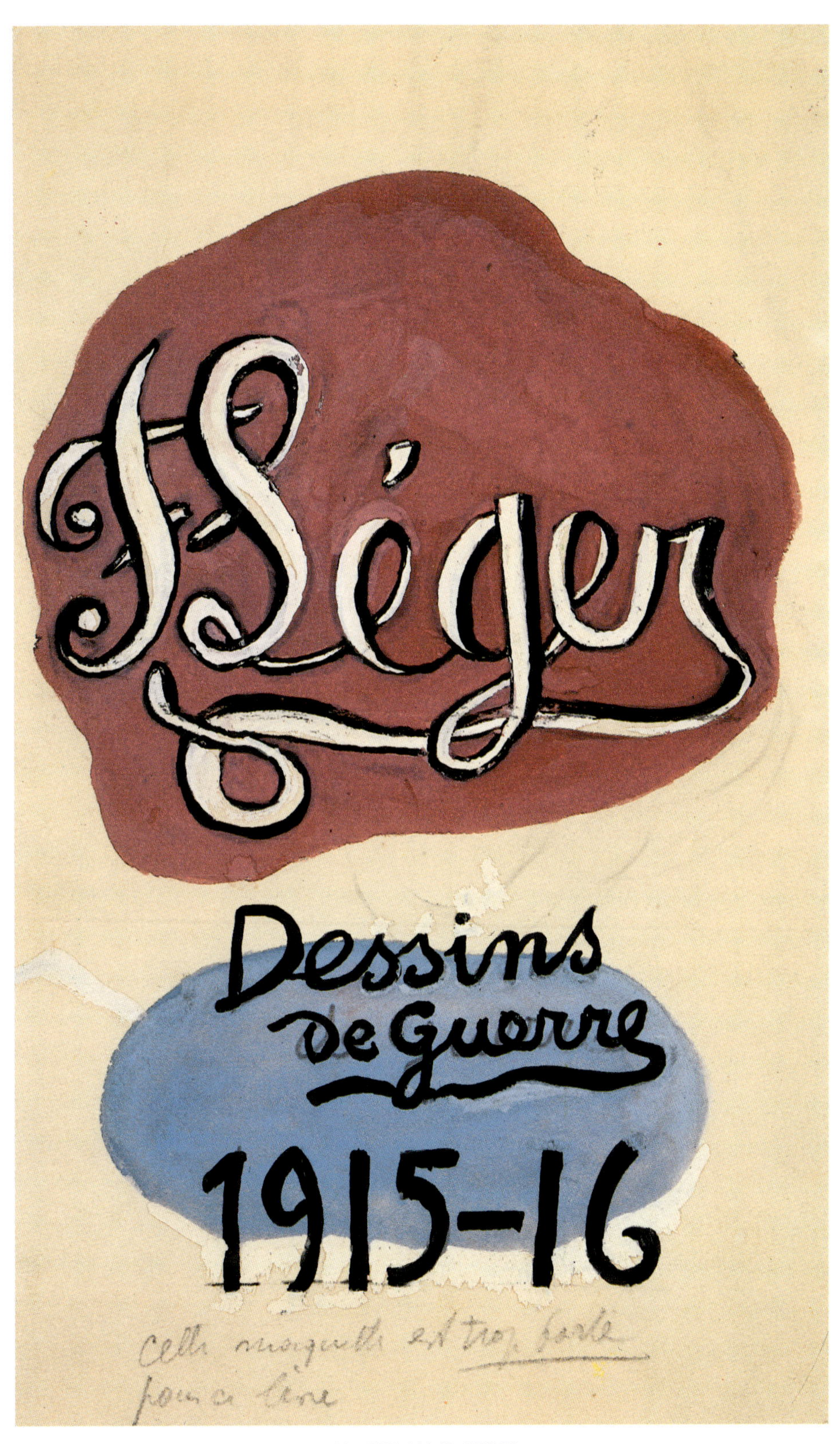

48 FERNAND LEGER
(Maquette für Katalogtitelblatt; Maquette for catalogue cover) (1956)

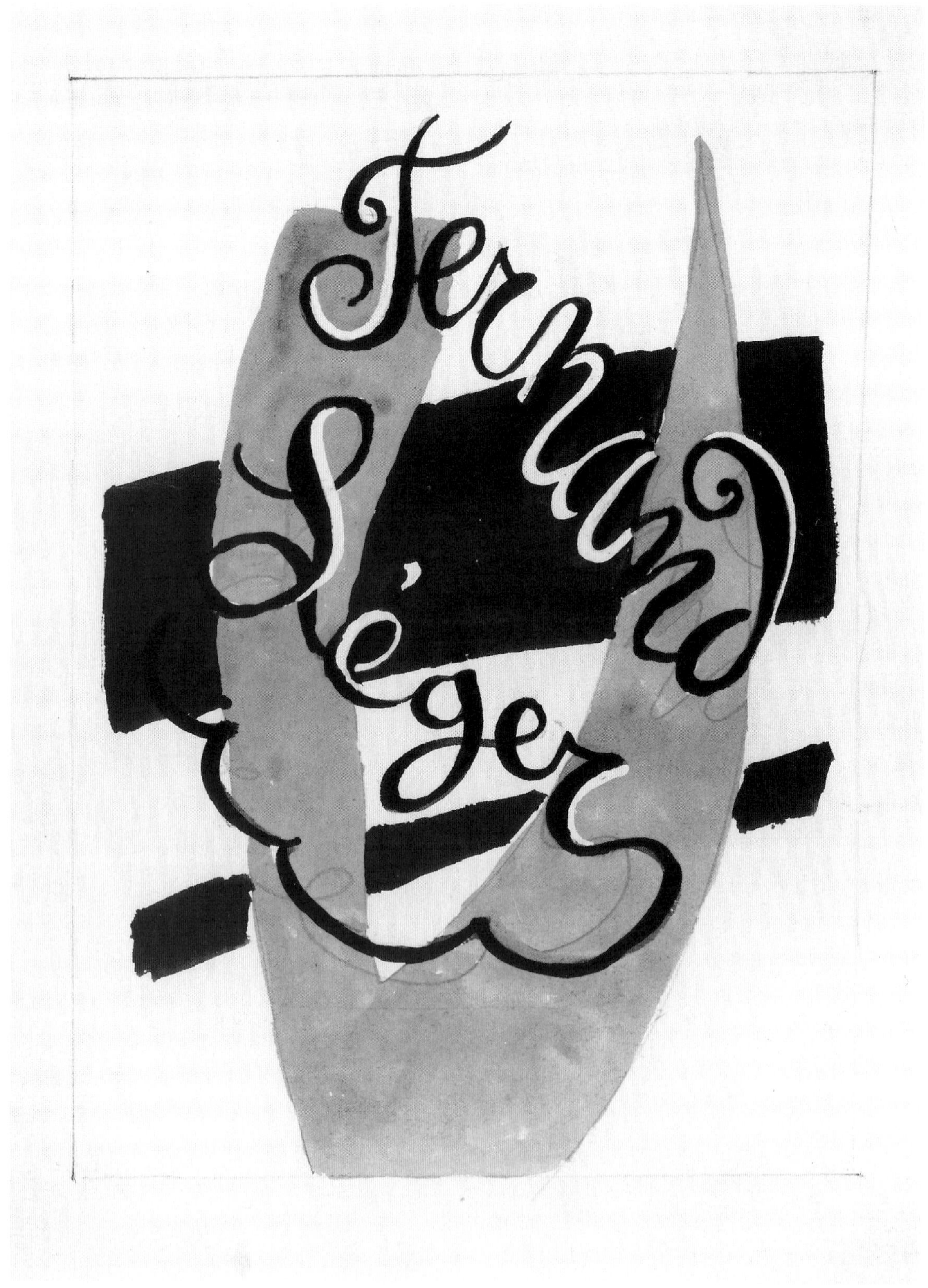

47 FERNAND LEGER
(Maquette für Katalogtitelblatt; Maquette for catalogue cover) (1950)

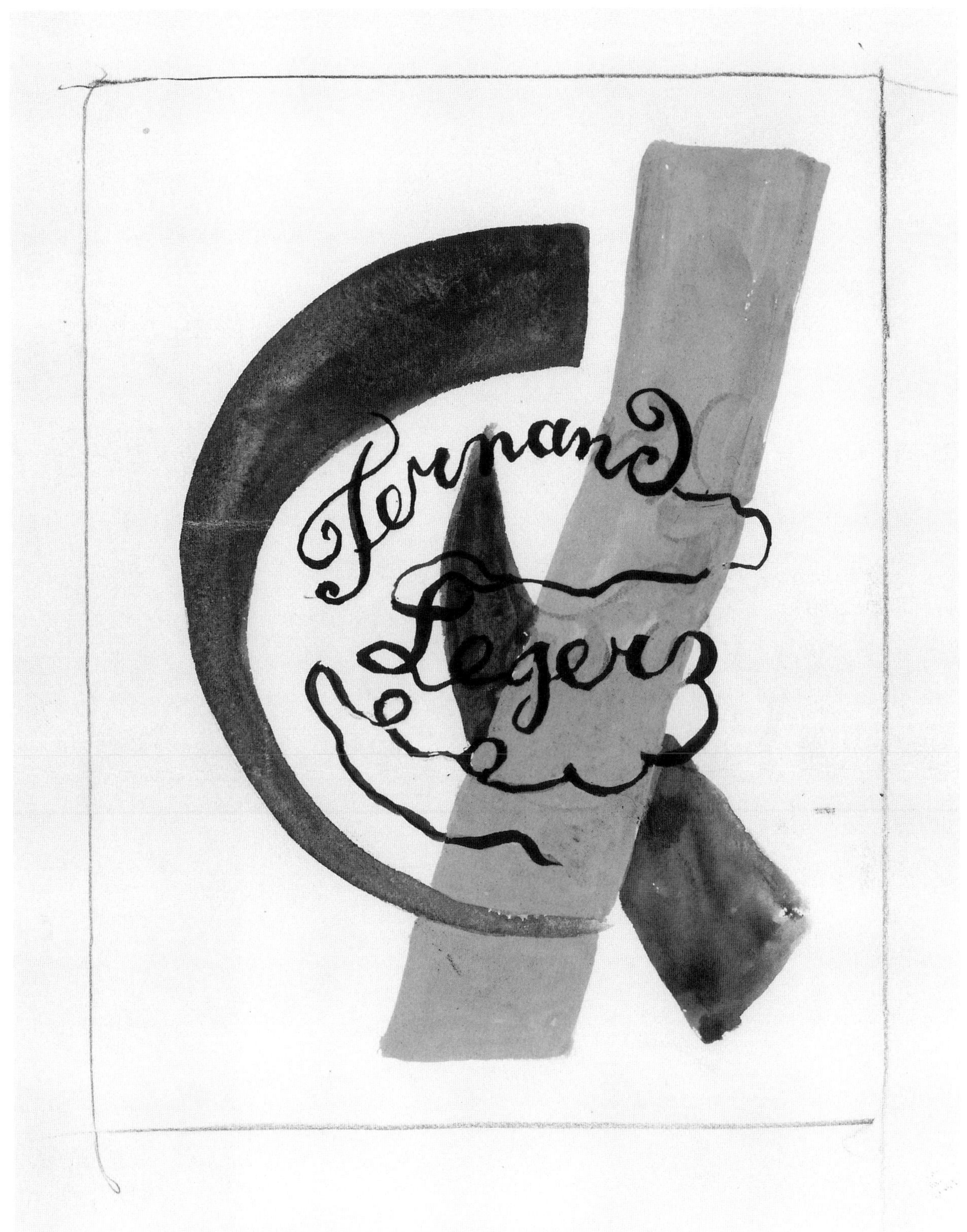

46 FERNAND LEGER
(Maquette für Katalogtitelblatt; Maquette for catalogue cover) (1950)

nach dem Kriege. «Die Zeichnungen in diesem Band illustrieren... die geistige Entwicklung eines der grössten französischen Künstler der Moderne. Sie sind ausserdem von grossem Interesse, weil sie das Bindeglied, und zwar das einzige, darstellen zwischen den Bildsprachen, die Léger vor und nach dem Krieg verwendete.»[117]

Es war Cooper, der die Idee für eine Publikation der Kriegszeichnungen hatte und sie auch mit grossem Enthusiasmus verfolgte (s. Légers Maquette für das Titelblatt, Nr. 48); als erstem unterbreitete er sie 1952 seinem Freund Curt Valentin; in einem Brief vom 6. Oktober schreibt er:

> *Diese Zeichnungen und Aquarelle sind nun in meinem Besitz. Ungefähr sechzig Bleistiftzeichnungen und etwa 60 Aquarelle sind es, erste Skizzen nach dem Leben für* Die Kartenspieler *im Kröller-Müller, Kanonen-Studien, Ansichten vom bombardierten Verdun, Cafés, Häuser usw., Lazarett-Szenen, getarnte Flugzeuge usw. Eine schöne und dichte, aber unbekannte Dokumentation, die zeigt, wie Légers Nachkriegsstil entstand. Ich habe sie eben mit François Lachenal, der übers Wochenende hier war, durchgesehen. Wir – Léger, er und ich – glauben, dass man eine Auswahl von, sagen wir, dreissig, vierzig treffen und in einer Art Album dann zusammenstellen könnte, ähnlich Deinem Cézanne, nur anders 'rum, da es sich ja nicht um ein Skizzenbuch handelt und die meisten Hochformate sind. Sie könnten in derselben Technik reproduziert werden, und zwar von Jacomet. François ist definitiv interessiert, es zu machen, und Léger möchte auch, dass es gemacht wird, durch ihn oder François oder Dich dazu...*[118]

Cooper teilte die Kriegszeichnungen in drei Gruppen: die zwischen Juli 1915 und Januar 1916, d.h. vor der ersten deutschen Offensive am 21. Februar 1916 geschaffenen; die während der Schlacht um Verdun, also während der deutschen Offensive von Februar bis August 1916 entstandenen, und die, welche Léger vor,

> *and ink, and some six watercolors. They are first sketches from life for* The Card Players *in Kröller-Müller, studies of guns, views of shell-blasted Verdun, cafes, houses, etc., scenes in hospital, camouflaged aeroplanes, etc. A very nice and compact documentation, unknown and showing how Léger's post-war style was born. I have just looked through them with François Lachenal who has been here for the weekend. Both Léger, he and myself feel that one could make a selection of say thirty or forty which could be done in a sort of album like your Cézanne, only the other way up since it is not a sketch-book and the majority are uprights. They could be reproduced in the same technique, and done by Jacomet. François is definitely interested in doing them, and Léger is keen that they should be done, by him or by François and yourself in conjunction...*[118]

Cooper organized the wartime drawings into three groups: those executed between July 1915 and January 1916, that is, before the first German offensive of February 21, 1916; those done during the Battle at Verdun during the German offensive of February – August 1916; and those done just before, during or after the French counter offensive of August 24, 1916. *Les Foreurs (The Sappers)* and *Les deux tués (The Two Dead)* (Nos. 31, 32) belong to this third group. The watercolor is consistent with Léger's pre-war style. The two sappers working in a trench are barely discernable amidst the rhythmic contrast of discrete forms highlighted with rough stripes of pure colour. The ink drawing on the post card to Yvonne Dangel, is unusual in the realism of the subject, capturing the brutality of Léger's war experience.[119]

Four oils emerged from this war period: *The Smoker*, summer 1916, *The Sappers*, fall 1916 (never completed), *The Wounded Man*, 1917 and *The Game of Cards*, 1917. *Dessin pour "La Partie de Cartes"*, (No. 33) is a study for the figure at the left of the Kröller-Müller painting. Here Léger reembraces a legible subject mat-

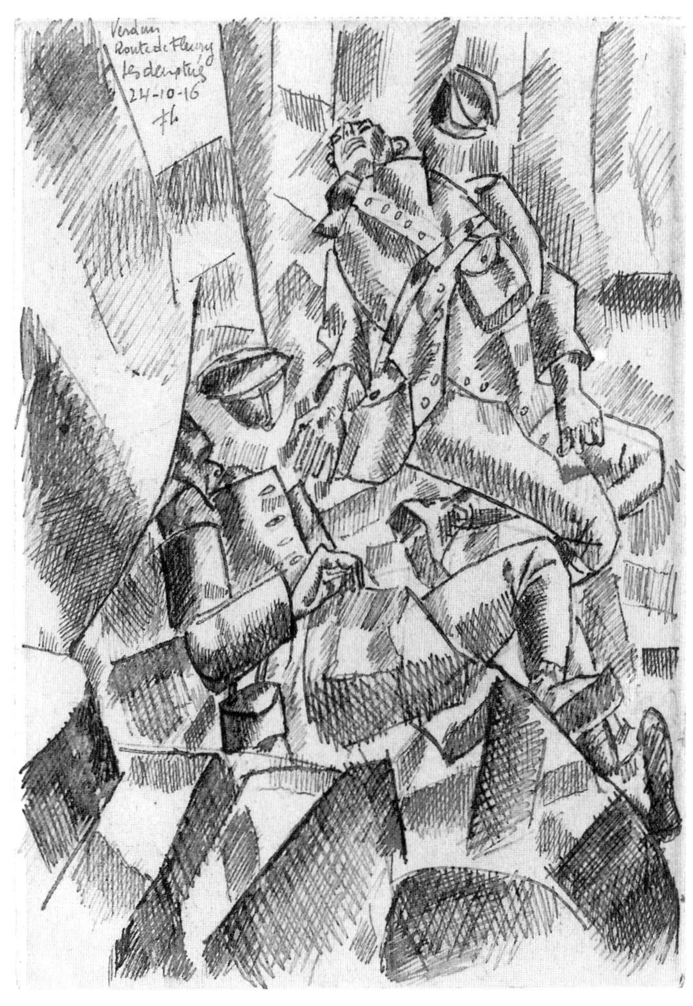

32 FERNAND LEGER
Les deux tués (Die zwei Getöteten; Two Dead) 1916

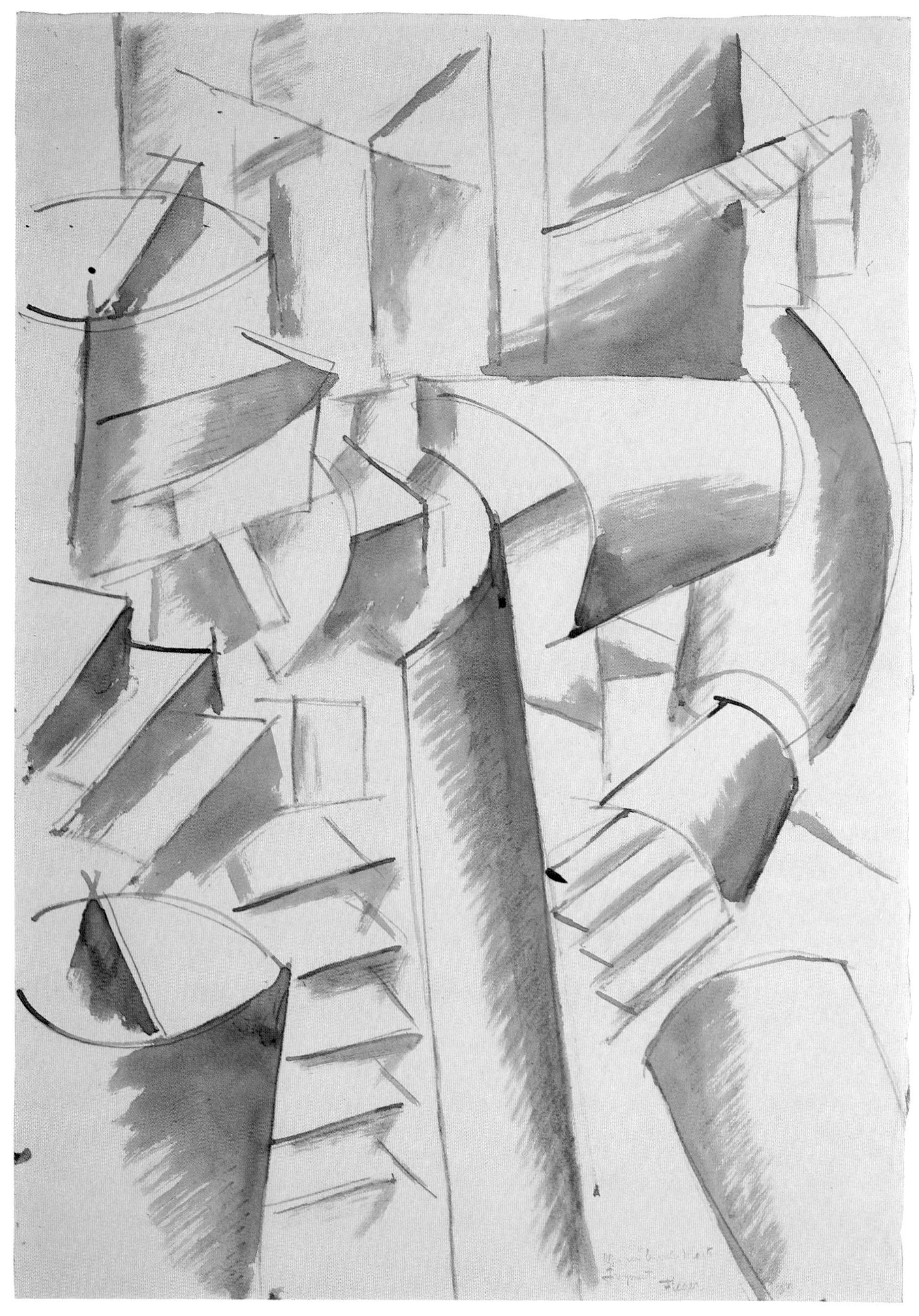

33 FERNAND LEGER
Dessin pour «La Partie de Cartes» (Zeichnung für «Das Kartenspiel»; Drawing for "The Cardplayers") (1916–17)

während und nach der französischen Gegenoffensive vom 24. August 1916 gemacht hatte. *Les Foreurs (Die Sappeure)* und *Les Deux Tués (Die zwei Getöteten)* (Nr. 31 und 32) gehören zur dritten Gruppe. Das erstgenannte, ein Aquarell, ist stilistisch den Vorkriegsjahren zuzuordnen. Die zwei in einem Schützengraben arbeitenden Sappeure sind im rhythmischen Kontrast der einzelnen, durch grobe Striche in ungemischten Farben hervorgehobenen Formen kaum auszumachen. Die Tuschzeichnung *Les Deux Tués* auf der Postkarte an Yvonne Dangel, hingegen, fängt mit ihrem ungewöhnlich realistisch wiedergegebenen Sujet die Brutalität der Kriegserlebnisse von Léger ein.[119]

In der Kriegszeit entstanden auch vier Ölbilder: *Der Raucher*, Sommer 1916, *Die Sappeure*, Herbst 1916 (das Bild wurde nie vollendet), *Der Verwundete*, 1917, und *Die Kartenspieler*, 1917. *Dessin pour La Partie de Cartes (Zeichnung zu den Kartenspielern)* (Nr. 33) ist eine Studie zur Figur links auf dem Kröller-Müller-Bild. Hier arbeitet Léger wieder mit lesbaren Inhalten, die für das nach seiner Rückkehr von der Front, also ab Frühjahr 1917, entstandene Werk charakteristisch sind.[120]

Im Werk *Mann in mechanischer Landschaft* von 1918 (Nr. 34) befinden sich zwei kleine Figuren in einer Welt aus Rädern, Röhren, Säulen, Treppen und Schablonenschrift. Die Art und Weise, wie die menschliche Figur dieser wirbelnden Masse gigantischer mechanischer Formen untergeordnet ist, nimmt die rein (oder fast rein) mechanischen Kompositionen der nächsten Jahre (1918 – 1924) vorweg, wie es *Der Typograph* von 1919 im Philadelphia Museum of Art zeigt, in dem Léger die Dynamik und Kraft der modernen Welt des Menschen feiert.[121] Die *Zwei Figuren* von 1920 (Nr. 35), aus röhrenförmigen Elementen gebaut, sind Teil eines Gefüges aus kompakten gestreiften Scheiben.[122]

Die nächsten zwei Zeichnungen, *Drei Frauen*[123] (Nr. 36) und *Studie für «Mutter und Kind»; drei Figuren in einer Landschaft* (Nr. 37), typisch für Légers Schaffen der zwanziger Jahre, werden durch Ordnung und einen gewissen Klassizismus gekennzeichnet. Es sind

ter, representative of the stylistic change which characterizes his works from early 1917 upon his return from the front.[120]

In *Man in a Mechanical Landscape*, 1918, (No. 34) two diminutive figures exist within an environment of wheels, pipes, columns, stairs, and stenciled letters. The manner in which the human figure is subsumed in a whirling mass of giant mechanistic forms anticipates the more purely mechanistic compositions of the next several years (1918–1924), such as *The Typographer*, 1919 (The Philadelphia Museum of Art), in which Léger celebrates the energy and power of man's modern world.[121] In *Two Figures*, 1920, (No. 35), the tubular figures are part of a circular configuration of striped and solid disks.[122]

The next two drawings, *Three Women*[123] and *Study for "Mother and Child", Three Figures in a Landscape* (Nos. 36, 37), typical of Léger's work during the twenties, are characterized by a certain classicism and order. These drawings are tight works, with the same degree of finish as Léger's paintings. Massive, sculpturesque, severely stylized figures are assembled in complex spaces composed of overlapping and intersecting patterned planes. In *Study for "Mother and Child", Three Figures in a Landscape*, 1922,[124] classically derived nudes are replaced with figures of everyday domesticity, rendered, however, in the same crisp smooth style. The intricate environments in both works, based upon precise penciled grids, combine post-Cubist spatial ambiguities with conflicts in spatial perspective that seem directly inspired by pre-Renaissance models.[125] Moreover, the figures are, at once, inimitably Léger in their awkward, machine-like, sheet-metal stiffness and, yet they draw upon a rich aesthetic tradition of the nude.

In *Two Men in a Stairway*, 1924, (No. 38) the contemporaneity of the two figures is made unmistakable through their clothing and the urban environment which surrounds them. This is one of a series of drawings and paintings executed in August and September 1924, during a month trip in Italy with his dealer Léonce

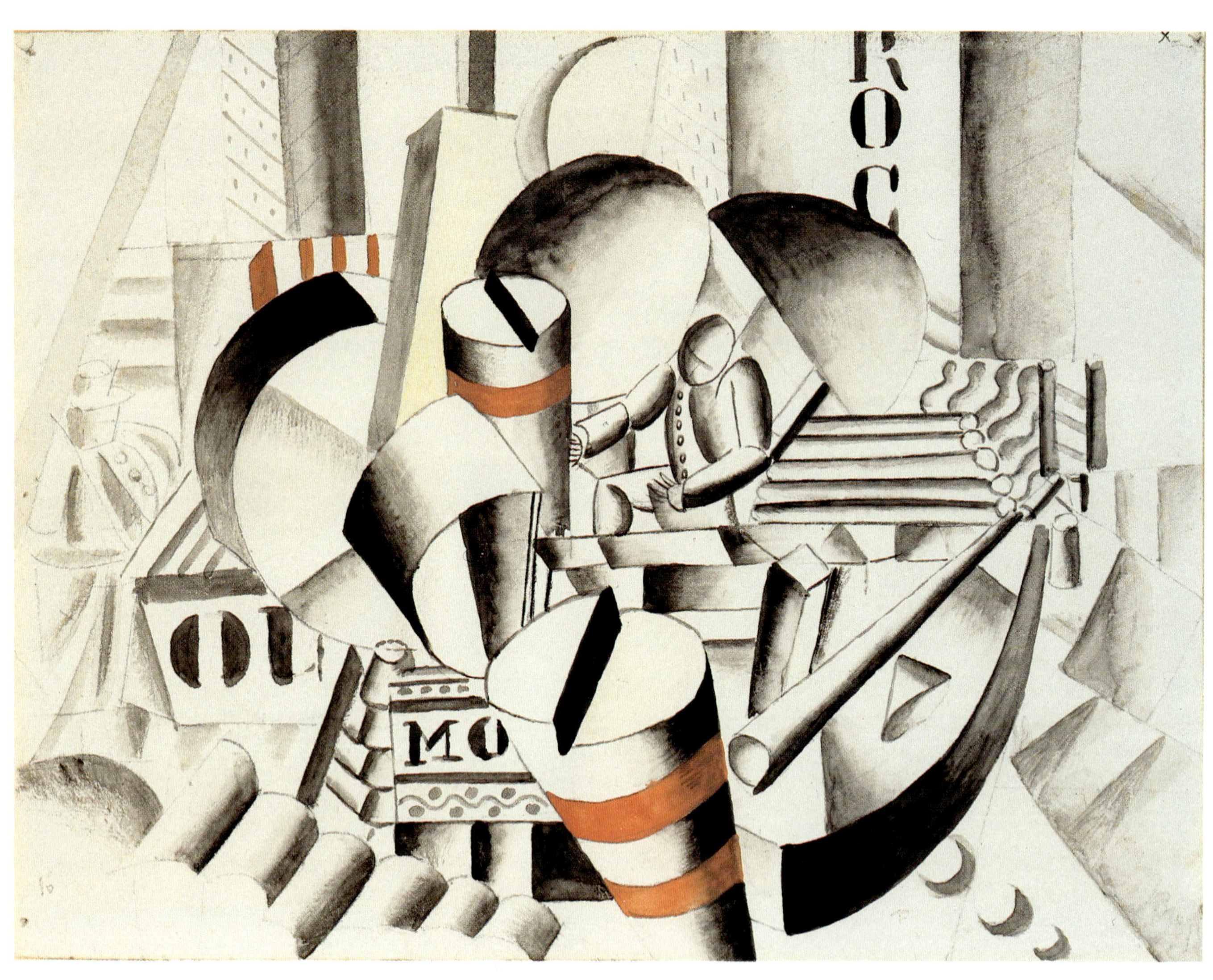

34 FERNAND LEGER
(Mann in mechanischer Landschaft; Man in a Mechanical Landscape) 1918

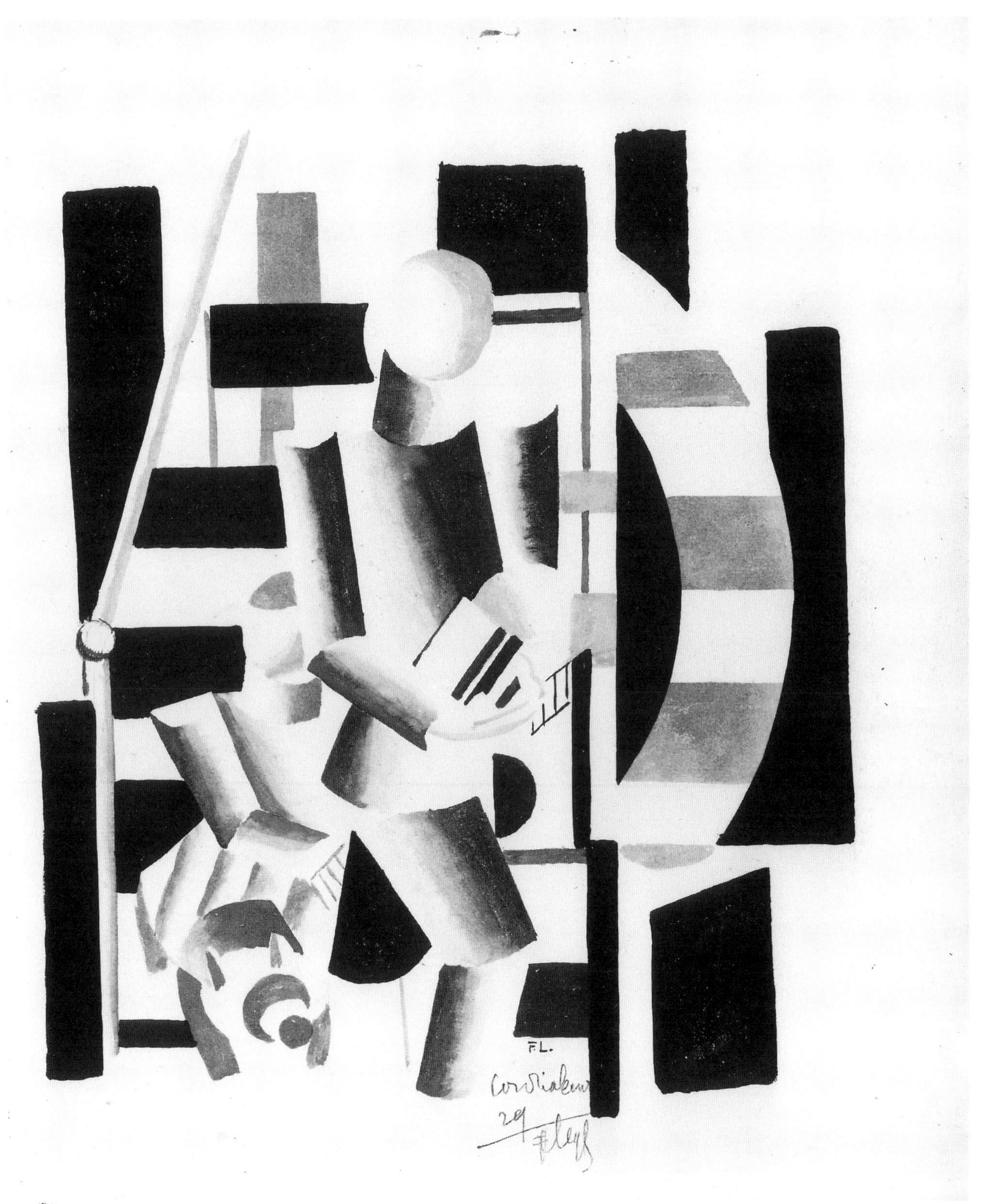

35 FERNAND LEGER
(Zwei Figuren; Two Figures) (1920)

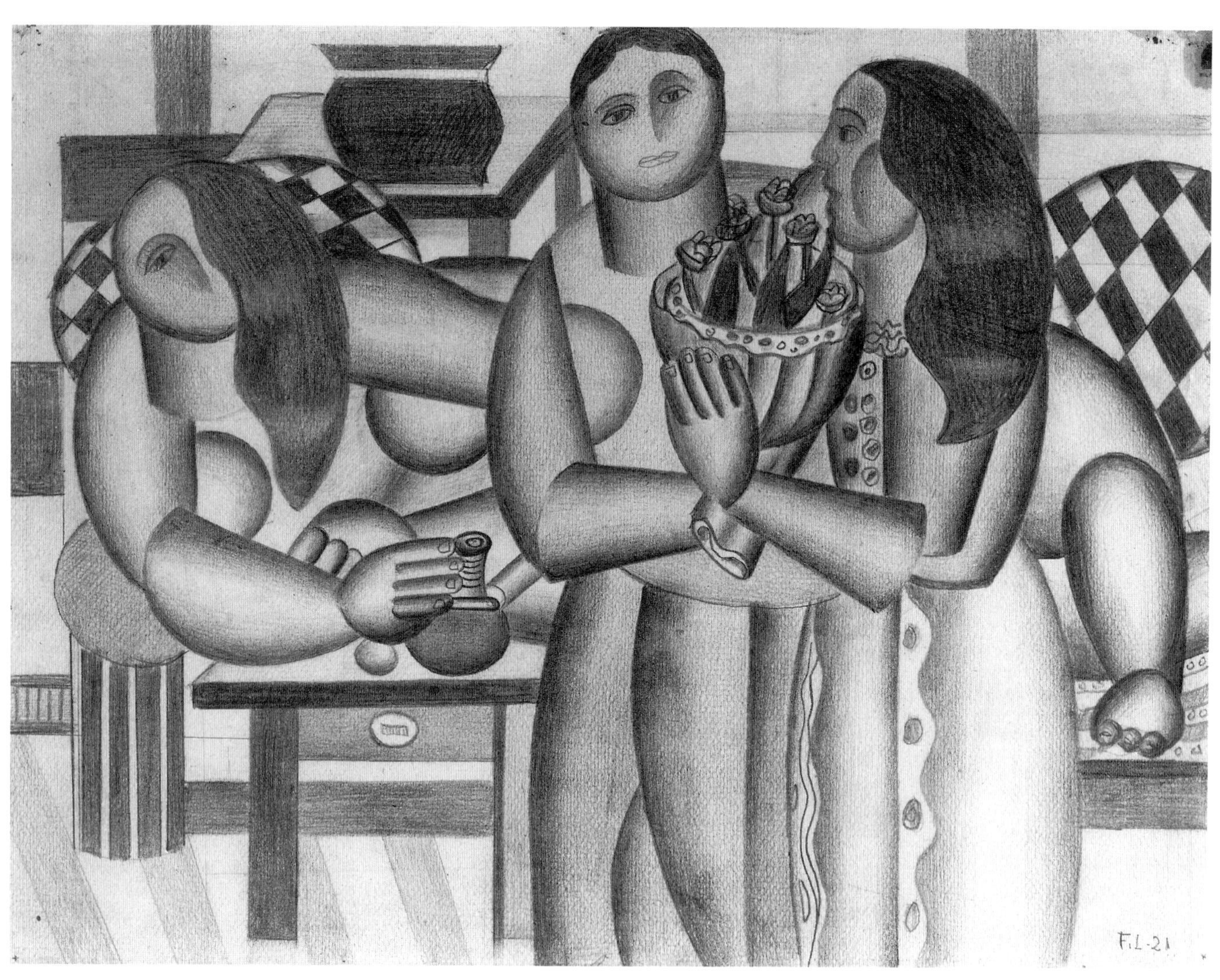

36 FERNAND LEGER
(Drei Frauen; Three Women) 1921

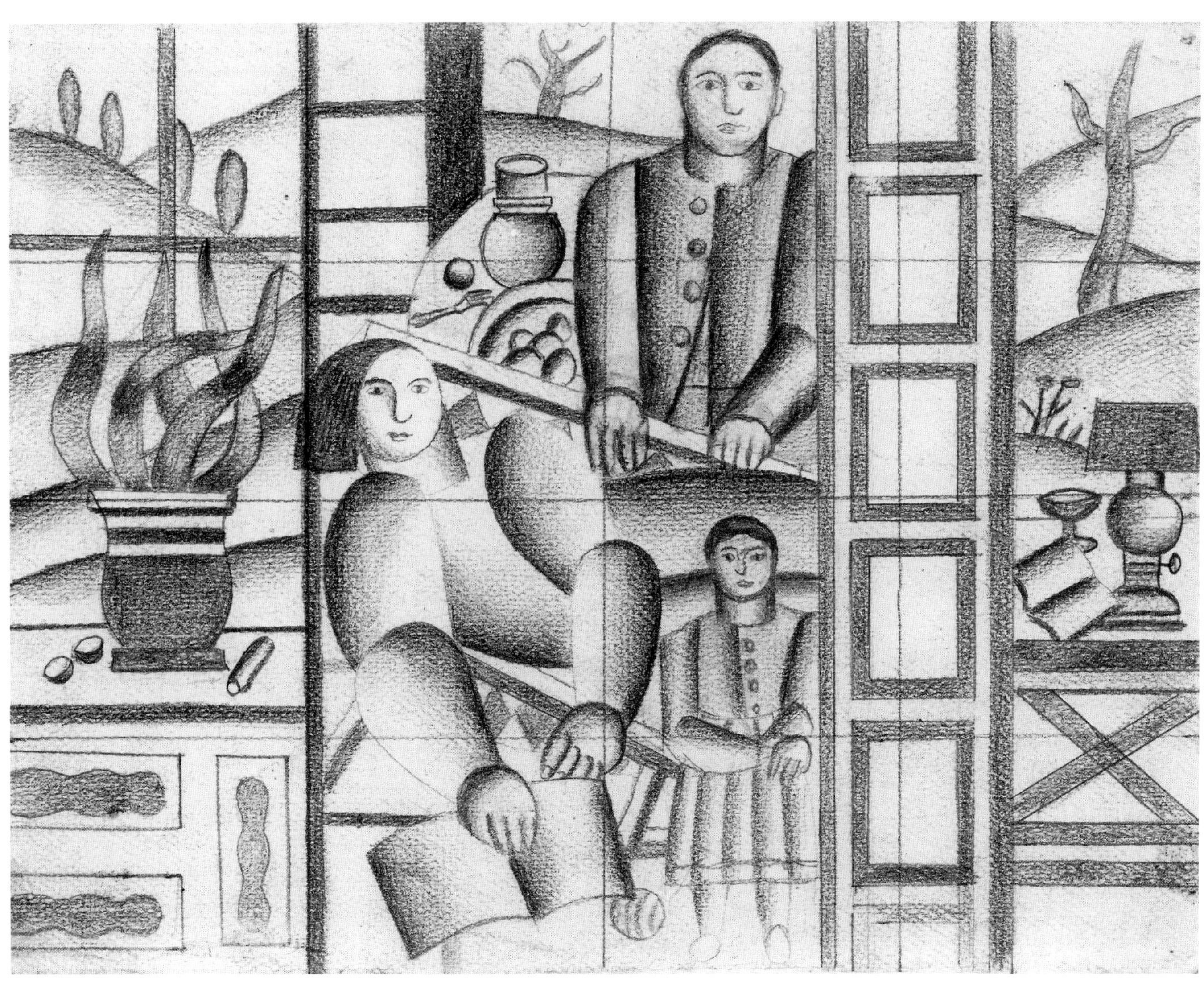

37 FERNAND LEGER

(Studie für «Mutter und Kind»; drei Figuren in einer Landschaft; Study for "Mother and Child"; Three Figures in a Landscape) (1922)

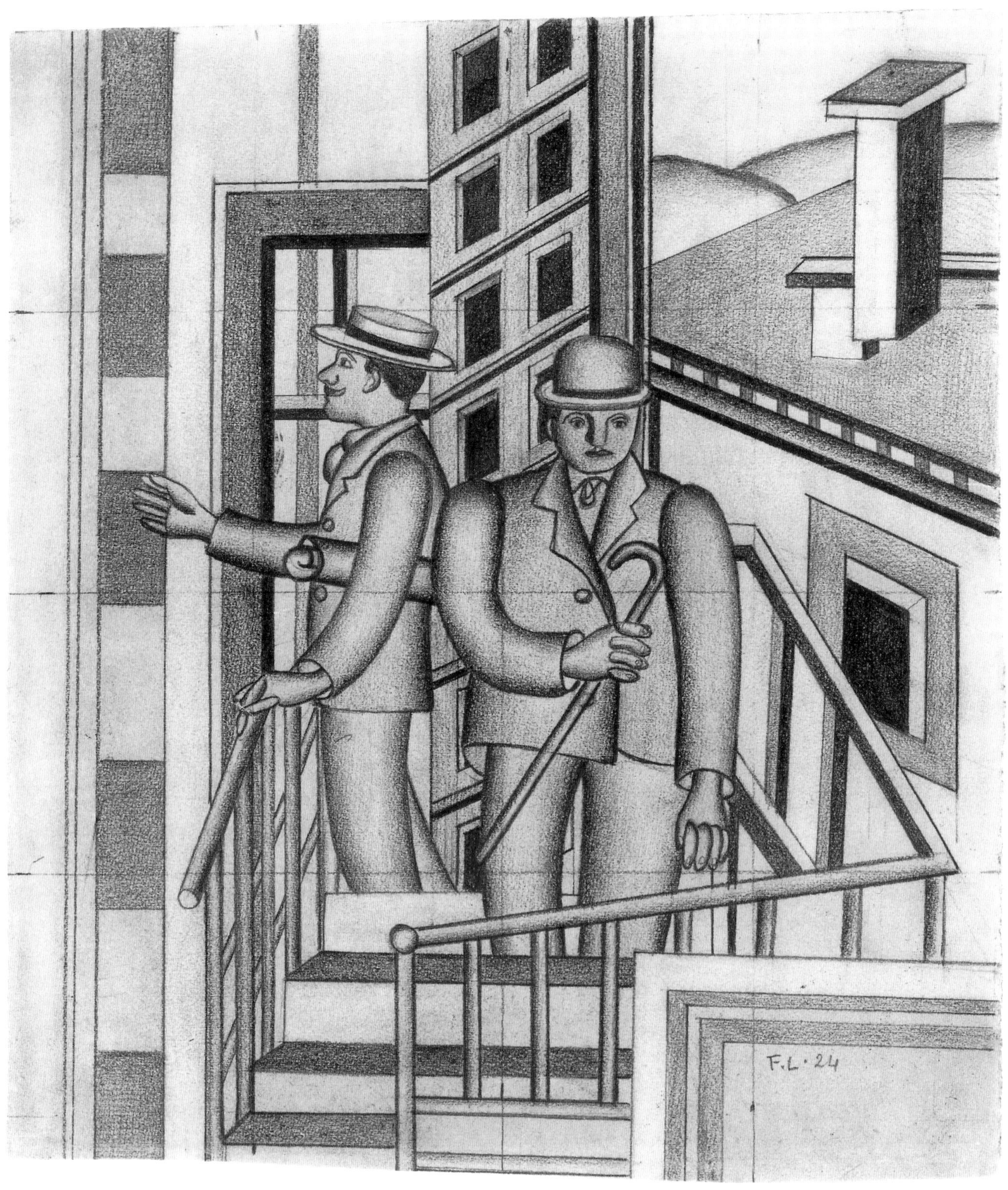

38 FERNAND LEGER
(Zwei Männer auf der Treppe; Two Men in a Stairway) 1924

ganz dichte Werke, in gleich hohem Grade ausgearbeitet wie die Gemälde. Massige, statuarische, strengstilisierte Körper sind zusammengebracht in einem komplexen Raumgefüge aus sich überschneidenden und durchdringenden gemusterten Flächen. In der *Studie für «Mutter und Kind», drei Figuren in einer Landschaft,* von 1922[124], werden die klassisch-inspirierten Akte ersetzt durch Figuren in alltäglich-häuslicher Umgebung; sie werden jedoch im selben präzisen runden Stil wiedergegeben. Die komplizierte Raumsituation beider Werke, verankert in einem genau gezeichneten Raster, vereinigt die räumliche Ambivalenz des Post-Kubismus mit Raumtiefe-Problemen, welche direkt von Proto-Renaissance-Vorbildern hergeleitet scheinen.[125] Zwar sind die Figuren in ihrer ungelenken, maschinenartigen, blechernen Steifheit unverkennbare Légers; und doch stehen sie in der reichen Bildtradition des Akts.

Die *Zwei Männer auf der Treppe* von 1924 (Nr. 38) sind sofort an ihren Kleidern und ihrer städtischen Umgebung als Zeitgenossen zu erkennen. Das Blatt gehört zu einer Reihe von Zeichnungen und Bildern, welche der Künstler im August und September 1924, während einer einmonatigen Reise in Italien mit Léonce Rosenberg, seinem Galeristen, schuf (der übrigens fest zu Léger stand, obwohl seine klassischen Akte allgemein auf deutliche Ablehnung stiessen).[126]

1949 beschreibt Cooper Légers einfache und klare Objekt-Bilder der zwanziger Jahre:

> *Légers Werk dieser fünf Jahre (1919–1924) zeigt, parallel zum Wunsch nach Stabilisierung, ein wachsendes Streben nach Klärung; der Maler konzentriert sich auf die Details, die er vergröbernd vergrössert, und untersucht die Wirkung von Monumentalität. Immer mehr ersetzt der Teil das Ganze; der Blick hört auf zu suchen und ruht auf den grossen Flächen. In den Jahren 1924–1925 ist Léger endlich zu jener statischen und architektonischen Malerei gekommen, die er schon immer zu verfolgen schien.*[127]

Die nächsten Werke, datiert 1924 oder 1925, können als Objekt-Bilder charakterisiert werden; sie sind

Rosenberg (who remained loyal to him despite the marked unpopularity of his classical nudes).[126]

In 1949 Cooper described Léger's simple and clear object-pictures of the twenties:

> *L'œuvre de Léger, au cours de ces cinq années (1919 à 1924), manifeste, parallèlement à un désir de stabilisation, une volonté croissante de clarification; le peintre se concentre sur le grossissement des détails et recherche l'effet monumentale. De plus en plus, le fragment remplace le tout, le regard cesse d'explorer et se fixe sur les gros plans. En 1924–1925, Léger parvient enfin à cet art statique et architectural qu'il semble avoir constamment poursuivi.*[127]

The next several works dating from 1924 or 1925 which may be characterized as object-paintings are infused with the concepts of Purism articulated in the periodical *L'Esprit Nouveau.* The subjects – coffeepot, glass, siphon, pipes, books, checker board – every day, easily recognizeable objects attain an almost symbolic quality through their familiarity. These are the Purist "type-objects", artifacts of efficient mass production. The artist achieves an almost exaggerated focus in the manner in which the object fills the composition and in the excessively precise, naive quality of the depiction. Indeed, the pencil drawings are characterized by an exquisite fineness of execution, the graphite and colored pencils achieving subtle shading and dramatic chiaroscuro.[128] In almost every case these drawings relate to an oil painting: *Study for "Still-life with Bust",* 1924 (No. 41) is a preparatory drawing for an oil in Cooper's Collection[129]; *The Siphon,* 1924 (No. 40) relates to the oil in the collection of Mrs. Arthur C. Rosenberg, Chicago; Though not a preparatory study, *Composition with Pipes,* 1925 (No. 42), does clearly relate to *The Three Pipes,* of the same year, Galerie Louise Leiris, Paris; *Composition with Checker Board,* 1926 (No. 43), may be compared to *The Ball Bearing,* 1925, Kunstmuseum, Basel.[130]

In *Les Gants (The Gloves),* 1933 (No. 44), Léger continues to explore the every day object in close-up,

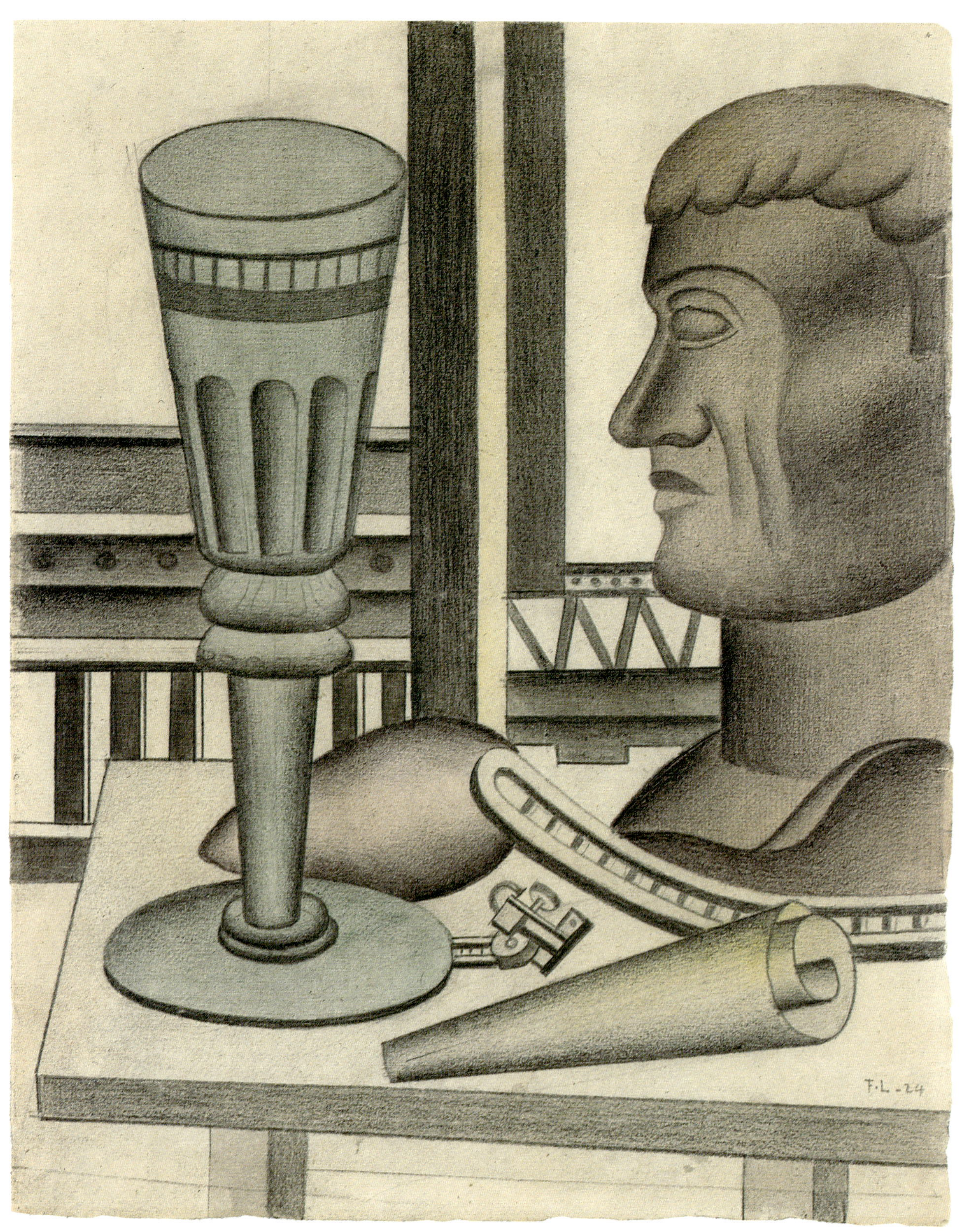

41 FERNAND LEGER
(Studie für «Stilleben mit Büste»; Study for "Still-life with Bust") 1924

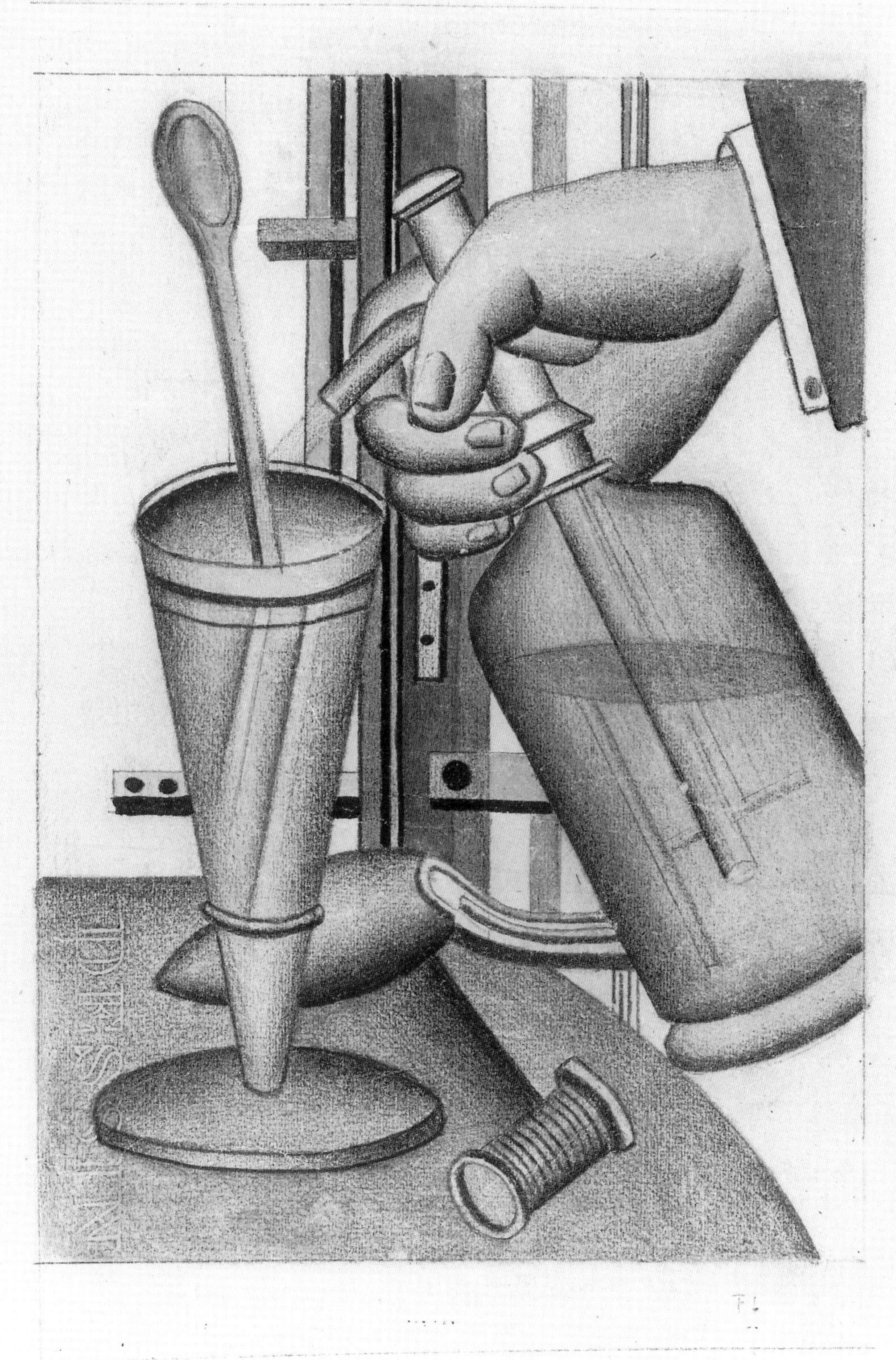

40 FERNAND LEGER
(Die Siphonflasche; The Siphon) (1924)

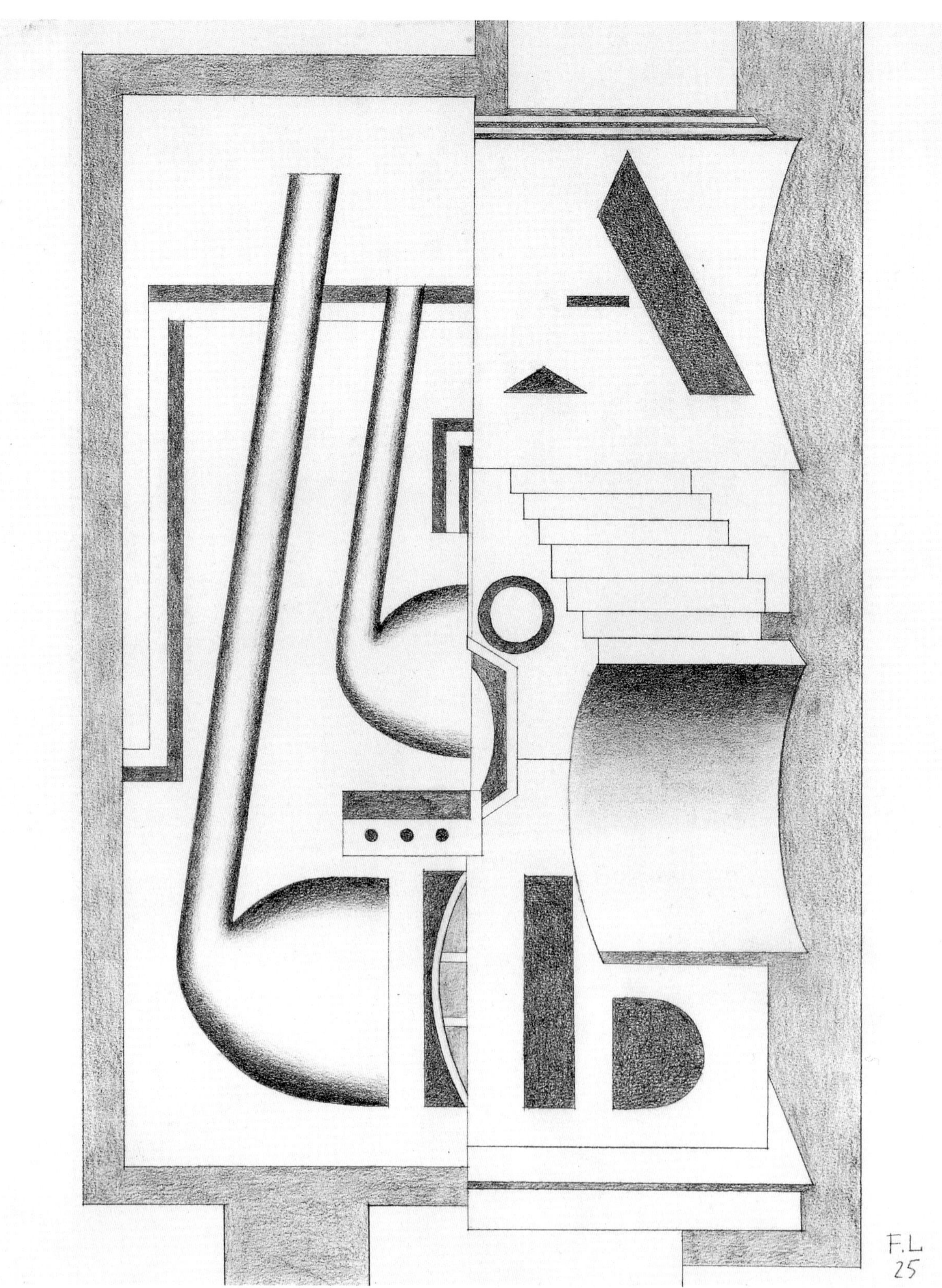

42 FERNAND LEGER
(Komposition mit Pfeifen; Composition with Pipes) 1925

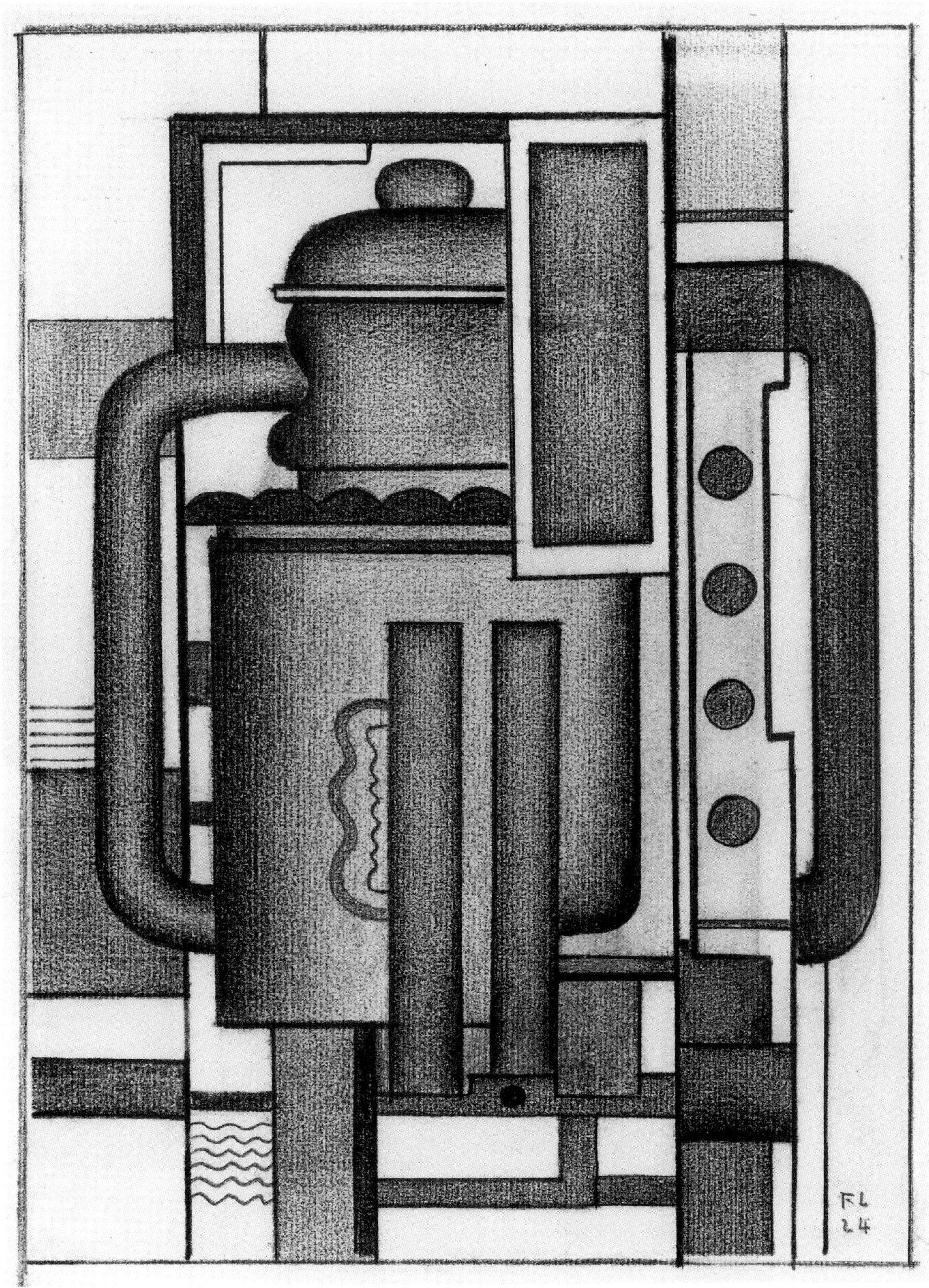

39 FERNAND LEGER
(Stilleben mit Kaffeekanne; Still-life with Coffee-pot) 1924

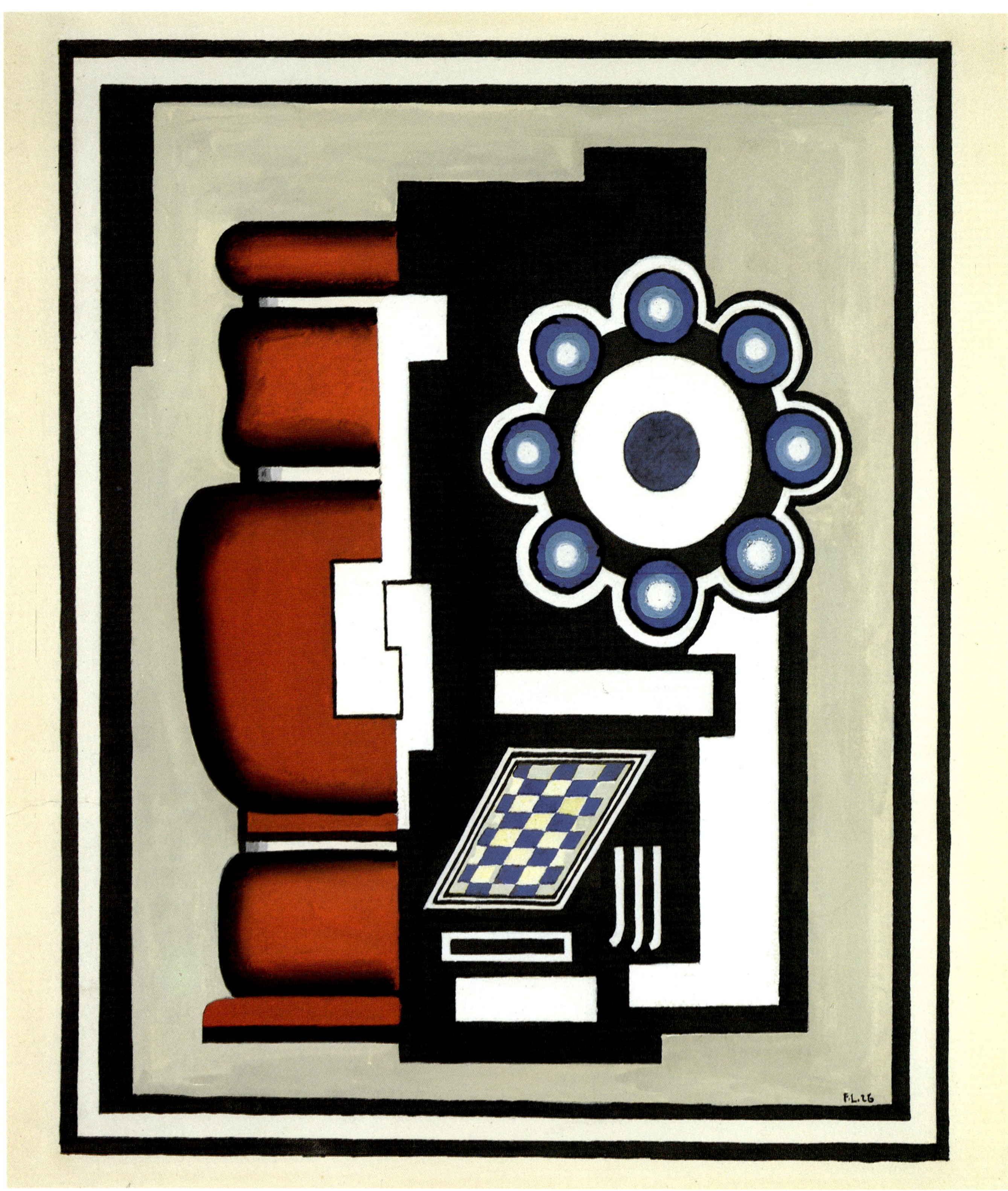

43 FERNAND LEGER
(Komposition mit Damebrett; Composition with Checker Game) 1926

durchdrungen von puristischen Ideen, wie sie in der Zeitschrift *L'Esprit Nouveau* formuliert wurden. Die Sujets – Kaffeekannen, Glas, Siphonflasche, Pfeifen, Bücher, Damebrett –, alltägliche und leichterkennbare Gegenstände (=Objekte), erhalten beinahe symbolische Qualität, gerade wegen ihrer Vertrautheit. Es sind die «Prototypen» des Purismus, moderne Beispiele effizienter Serienproduktion. Der Künstler erzielt eine fast übertrieben konzentrierte Darstellung durch die Weise, wie das Objekt die Komposition dominiert, und durch die fast zu präzise und doch naive Art der Schilderung. Die Bleistiftzeichnungen zeigen denn typischerweise auch eine hohe Präzision der technischen Ausführung; in den mit Graphit und Farbstiften gestalteten Blättern werden feinste Abstufungen und dramatisches Helldunkel erreicht.[128] Fast immer stehen diese Zeichnungen in direktem Zusammenhang mit einem Ölbild: *Studie für «Stilleben mit Büste»*, 1924 (Nr. 41), ist eine vorbereitende Zeichnung für ein Bild in Coopers Sammlung;[129] *Die Siphonflasche*, 1924 (Nr. 40), bezieht sich auf das Gemälde in der Sammlung Mrs. Arthur C. Rosenberg, Chicago; obwohl keine vorbereitende Studie, gehört *Komposition mit Pfeifen*, 1925 (Nr. 42), doch in den Zusammenhang von *Die drei Pfeifen* aus demselben Jahr im Besitz der Galerie Louise Leiris, Paris; *Komposition mit Damebrett*, 1926 (Nr. 43), kann mit dem *Kugellager* von 1925 im Kunstmuseum Basel verglichen werden.[130]

In *Les Gants (Die Handschuhe)* von 1933 (Nr. 44) setzt Léger seine Studien von Alltags-Objekten in Nahsicht und in jedem, auch ausgefallenen Detail fort. Légers visueller Scharfblick hat etwas vom surrealistischen, der verzerrt. Auch sind bei diesen abgenutzten Arbeiterhandschuhen Assoziationen möglich: zu den von der «front populaire» geprägten, sozialistischen Themen, welche im Spätwerk herausragen. Und es gibt einen klaren thematischen Bezug von diesen Handschuhen zum monumentalen Detail der Beine eines Arbeiters von 1951.[131]

Bauarbeiter, Beine (Nr. 45) erweckt durch die Art, wie Körper und Fuss von den Blatträndern beschnitten

excentric detail. There is an edge of surrealistic distortion which accompanies Léger's visual acumen. There is, as well, an associative signficiance to the well-worn workers gloves, which relates to the populist, socialistic themes which emerge prominently in Léger's late works. Indeed, there is a clear thematic relationship between these gloves and the monumental detail of the legs of the construction worker from 1951.[131]

Construction Worker, Legs, 1951 (No. 45), in the manner in which the body and foot are abruptly truncated by the edges of the paper, gives the impression of being a fragment of a large, mural-sized composition. (Note the related work, *Study of Hands*, 1933, ink, Kunstmuseum Basel.) Cooper in his 1949 monograph links the awakening and maturation of Léger's social conscience or awareness with his execution of non-figurative murals for Le Corbusier's Pavillon de l'Esprit Nouveau at the Exposition des Art Décoratifs in Paris in 1925. Indeed, the very title of Cooper's monograph *Fernand Léger ou le nouvel espace* focuses attention on Léger's concepts about mural painting, his desire to destroy the wall, to create an elastic wall, to create "un autre espace". "Nous sommes revenus à la peinture du Moyen Age, avec cette différence que notre peinture n'est plus descriptive mais une création d'un espace nouveau."[132] In 1924 Léger once again, as in 1913, approaches the realm of abstraction.

> *Léger a compris qu'il y avait des possibilités "illimitées" pour un art non-figuratif en tant qu'art mural jouant un role actif et s'accomodant aux volumes d'une architecture, mais que la non-figuration pratiquée en tant que peinture de chevalet n'a plus de sens parce qu'étant suspendu sur le mur, et séparé de celui-ci par un cadre, toute expansion ornementale devient impossible. A deux reprises Léger a été amené à faire une peinture non-figurative, d'abord comme peinture de chevalet, ensuite comme une décoration appliquée."*[133]

The artist's social awareness or humanistic concern forms, therefore, the thematic or conceptual link be-

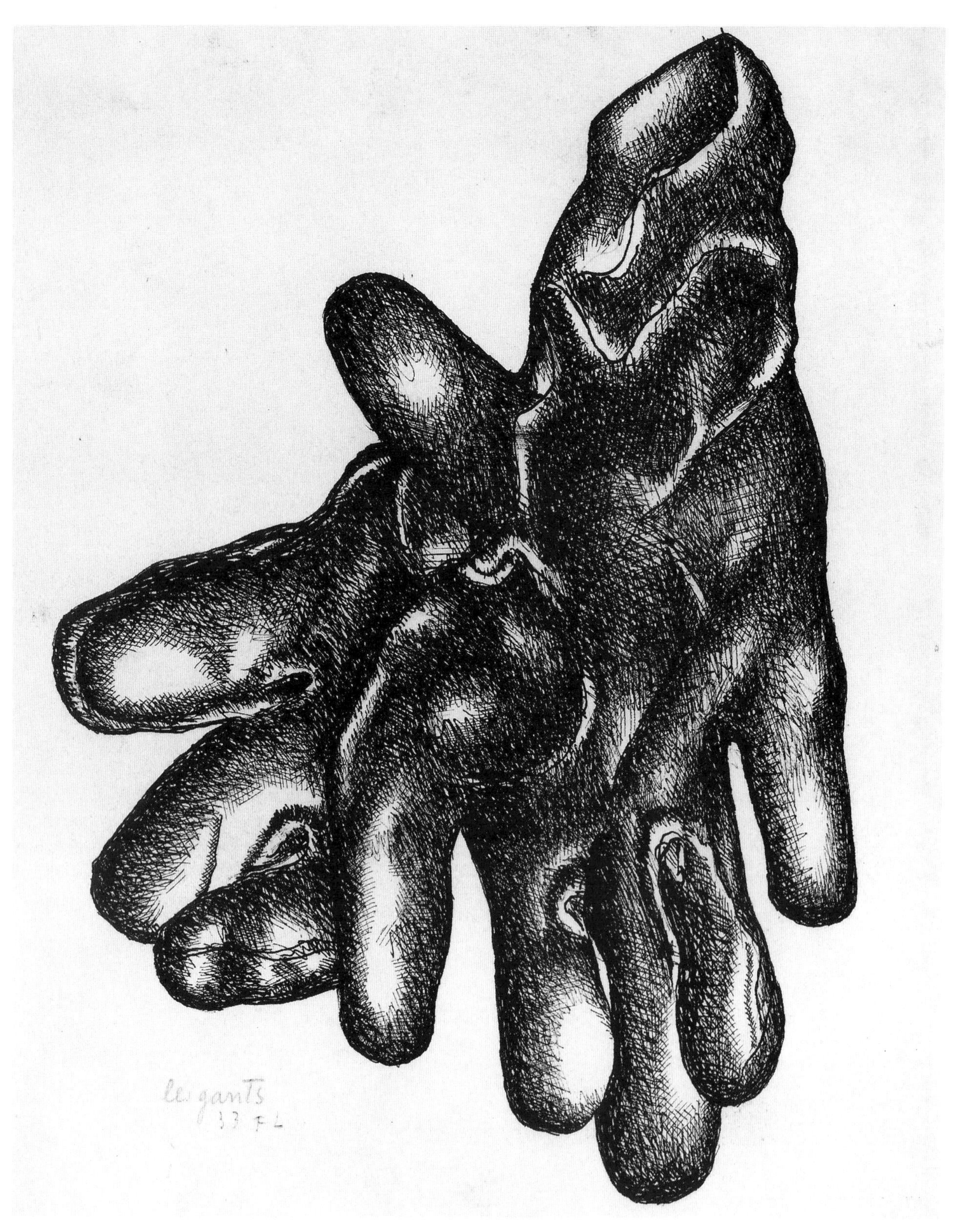

44 FERNAND LEGER
Les gants (Die Handschuhe; Gloves) 1933

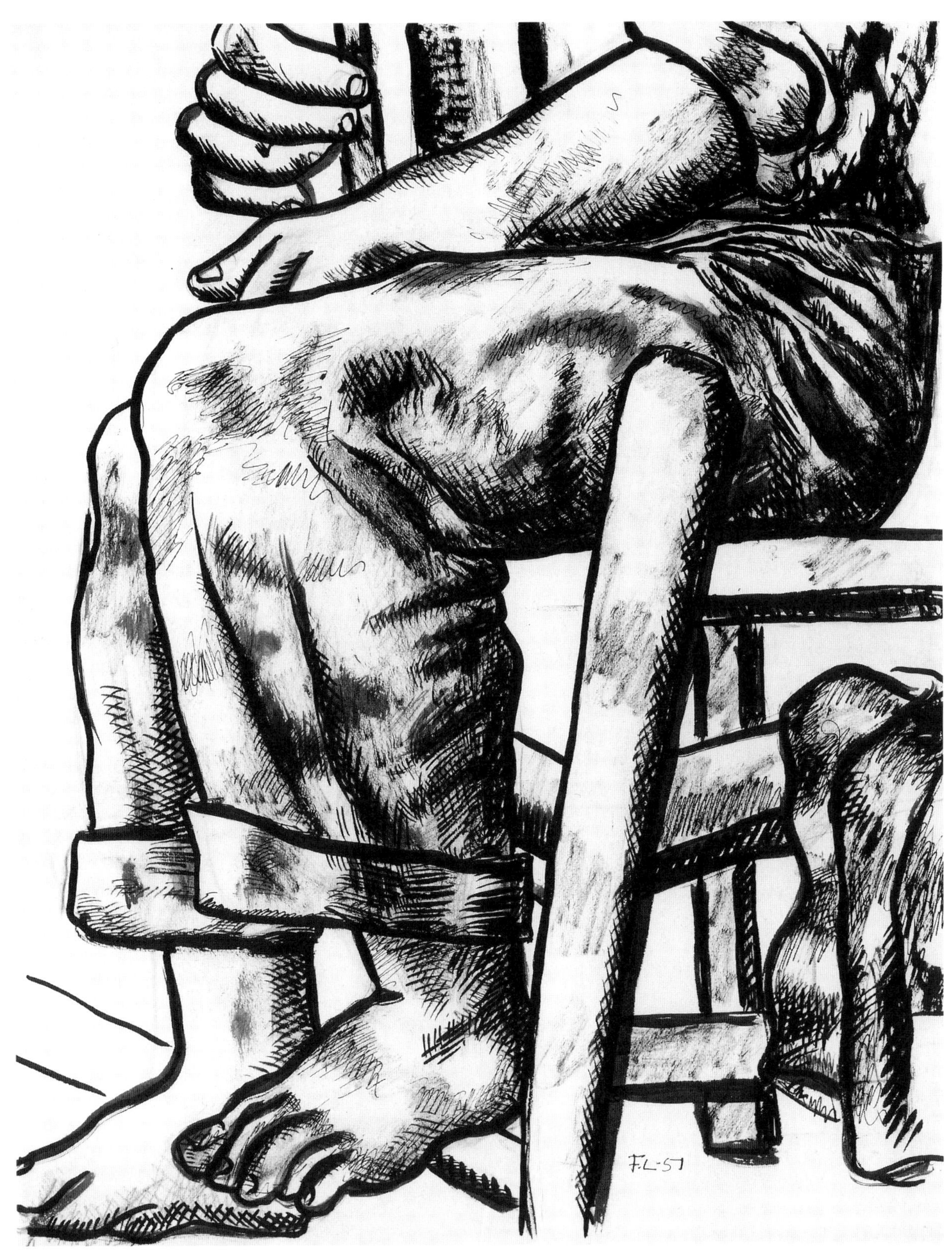

45 FERNAND LEGER
(Bauarbeiter, Beine; Construction worker, Legs) 1951

sind, den Eindruck, Fragment einer grossen Komposition von Wandbildformat zu sein (vgl. das verwandte Blatt *Händestudie*, 1933, Tusche, Kunstmuseum Basel). In seiner Monographie von 1949 verbindet Cooper das Entstehen und Reifen eines sozialen Bewusstseins bei Léger mit der Ausführung seiner ungegenständlichen Wandbilder für Le Corbusiers Pavillon de L'Esprit Nouveau an der Exposition des Arts Décoratifs in Paris 1925. Schon der Titel von Coopers Buch, *Fernand Léger ou le nouvel espace*, weist hin auf Légers Vorstellung von Wandmalerei, auf sein Ziel, die Wand zu zerstören, um so eine elastische Wand, «einen anderen Raum», zu schaffen. «Wir sind wieder zur Malerei des Mittelalters gekommen, mit dem Unterschied, dass unsere Malerei nicht mehr deskriptiv, sondern die Schaffung eines neuen Raums sein will.»[132] Noch einmal nähert sich Léger 1924, wie schon 1913, der Abstraktion.

> *Léger hat begriffen, dass es für eine ungegenständliche Kunst «unbegrenzte» Möglichkeiten gab, doch nur als Wandmalerei, welche eine aktive Rolle spielt und sich in die architektonischen Volumina eingliedert; und dass auf der Staffelei praktizierte Ungegenständlichkeit keinen Sinn hatte, weil ihr – wenn sie an der Wand, und von dieser durch den Rahmen noch getrennt, hängt – jegliche ornamentale Ausdehnung verunmöglicht wird. Zweimal tendierte Léger zur ungegenständlichen Kunst, erst auf der Staffelei, dann in der angewandten Kunst.*[133]

Das soziale oder humanitäre Bewusstsein des Künstlers bildet denn das thematische oder begriffliche Bindeglied zwischen Légers ungegenständlichen Wandbildern von 1925 und seinen letzten Werken, monumentalen Kompositionen, in denen er zur erkennbaren menschlichen Gestalt, zu Arbeitern, Trapezkünstlern, Musikanten und Akrobaten, zurückkehrt.[134]

tween Léger's non-figurative murals of 1925 and his last works, monumental compositions, in which he returns to the recognizeable human form – construction workers, trapeze artists, musicians, acrobats.[134]

107 Cooper, *Fernand Léger et le nouvel espace*, London, Lund Humphries, 1949, pp. 29–30.

108 *Ibid.*, p. 15.

109 See letter to Curt Valentin dated 16 April 1952, Archives, Museum of Modern Art, Library, New York.

110 Cooper, *Fernand Léger et le nouvel espace*, p. 35. Cooper gives this particular drawing a date of 1908. 1910–11 seems more likely. See also Dieter Koepplin, *Kubismus: Zeichnungen und Druckgraphik*, Basel, Kunstmuseum, 1969, entry no. 58 concerning a related ink drawing on brown tissue paper.

111 Quoted by Cooper, *The Cubist Epoch*, p. 86.

112 See p. 46 in Bradley Jordan Nickels, *Fernand Léger*, Indiana University Ph.d., 1966; see as well Peter de Francia, *Fernand Léger*, New Haven and London, Yale University Press, 1983, p. 140 concerning the analogy between Léger's early figural drawings and sculptures by Archipenko whom he got to know in 1905. Peter de Francia, noting the "anti-gracioso" aspect of these quick sketches, the emphasis on structure and counterpoint of forms, appraises their importance in terms of Léger's œuvre generally: "Léger's nudes are the foundation for the whole of his later work, since they established, at a very early stage, one of the priorities which was to become the basis of his pictorial language: that of contrasts."

113 Léger as quoted by Cooper, *The Essential Cubism*, p. 208.

114 Cooper, *Fernand Léger, Contrastes de formes, 1912–15*, Paris, Berggruen, 1952, p. 2.

115 Cooper, *Fernand Léger et le nouvel espace*, p. 45–46.

116 Quoted by Cooper in *Fernand Léger, Dessins de Guerre, 1915–1916*, Paris, Berggruen, 1958 (unpaginated).

117 *Ibid.*, n.p.

107 Cooper, *Fernand Léger et le nouvel espace,* London, Lund Humphries, 1949, S. 29–30.

108 ibid., S. 15.

109 S. Brief an Curt Valentin vom 16. April 1952, Archiv, Museum of Modern Art, Library, New York.

110 Cooper, *Fernand Léger et le nouvel espace,* S. 35. Cooper datiert diese Zeichnung auf 1908. 1910–11 scheint wahrscheinlicher. S. a. Dieter Koepplin, *Kubismus: Zeichnungen und Druckgraphik,* Kunstmuseum Basel, 1969, Eintrag Nr. 58, betreffend eine verwandte Tuschzeichnung auf braunem Seidenpapier.

111 Zitiert von Cooper, *The Cubist Epoch,* S. 86.

112 S. Bradley Jordan Nickels, *Fernand Léger,* Indiana University Ph. D., S. 46; s. a. Peter de Francia, *Fernand Léger,* New Haven and London, Yale University Press, 1983, S. 140, betreffend Analogie zwischen Légers frühen Figurenzeichnungen und den Skulpturen von Archipenko, den Léger 1905 kennenlernte. Peter de Francia, der auf den «anti-gracioso»-Aspekt dieser schnellen Skizzen, die Betonung der Struktur und des Kontrapunkts der Formen hinweist, würdigt ihre Bedeutung in Légers Werk allgemein: «Die Akte bilden die Basis für Légers gesamtes späteres Schaffen, da sie, sehr früh schon, eines der wichtigsten Anliegen seiner Bildsprache formulierten: jenes der Kontraste.»

113 Zitiert von Cooper, *The Essential Cubism,* S. 208.

114 Cooper, *Fernand Léger, Contrastes de formes, 1912–15,* Paris, Berggruen, 1952, S. 2.

115 Cooper, *Fernand Léger et le nouvel espace,* S. 45–46.

116 Zitiert von Cooper, *Fernand Léger, Dessins de Guerre, 1915–16,* Paris, Berggruen, 1958, unpaginiert.

117 ibid., unpaginiert.

118 In einem Brief vom 2. November 1951 (Archiv, Museum of Modern Art, Library, New York) hatte Cooper Valentins Ausgabe des Cézanne-Skizzenbuches gelobt, und, nach einem Brief vom 1. Februar 1952 zu schliessen, schrieb er eine Besprechung für das *Times Literary Supplement.* Nach Valentins Tod 1954 wurde das Projekt offensichtlich von Berggruen weiterverfolgt. Das Thema wird auch noch in vielen späteren Briefen behandelt. Cooper arbeitete direkt mit Léger zusammen und traf sich öfters mit ihm, um das Buch

118 In a letter dated November 2, 1951 in the Archive, Museum of Modern Art Library, New York, Cooper praised Valentin's edition of Cézanne's sketchbook and (according to a letter dated February 1, 1952) wrote a review for the *Times Literary Supplement*; upon Valentin's death in 1954, the project was obviously picked up by Berggruen.
The subject is pursued in subsequent letters, as well. Cooper worked directly with Léger, meeting with him frequently to discuss the book. See for instance, letters of October 18, 1952; December 1952; January 18 and February 5, 1954 to Curt Valentin.

119 See Christopher Green, *Léger and the Avant-garde*, New Haven and London, Yale University Press, 1976, p. 102ff, concerning the similarity of Léger's drawing with the photo of war casualties which appeared on the cover of *Le Miroir,* Sunday, October 8, 1916; see Peter de Francia, *Fernand Léger,* p. 144, concerning this and one other drawing which include direct reference to wartime death.

120 Christopher Green, *Ibid.*, suggests that Léger probably executed this drawing while recuperating in the hospital during the spring of 1917.

121 See the following related works illustrated in Jean Cassou and Jean Leymarie, *Fernand Léger, Drawings and Gouaches*, Greenwich: New York Graphic Society, 1973: no. 50, *Mechanical Forms,* 1917, Private Collection; no. 51, *Mechanical Forms*, 1918, Basel, Öffentliche Kunstsammlung, which relates to no. T7, *Mechanical Elements*, 1918–23, oil, Basel, Kunstmuseum; and no. 52, *Mechanical Elements*, 1918, watercolor, Private Collection, Paris, which relates to T8, *Still-life with Mechanical Elements*, 1918, oil, formerly Collection Maeght.

122 This work may be compared, with *The Stair,* oil on canvas, Rosengart Collection, Lucerne, no. 4, p. 76, *Fernand Léger*, Cologne, Kunsthalle, 1978; see as well no. 69, *Composition with Figure*, watercolor, 1920; no. 66, *Composition with Figures*, 1919, watercolor and wash; no. 73, *Composition with Two Figures*, 1920, watercolor. See also Cassou and Leymarie, no. 66, *Composition with Figure*, 1920, watercolor; no. 68, *Composition with Two Figures*, 1920, watercolor; no. 69, *Composition with Two Figures*, 1920, watercolor; no. 70, *Composition with Figure*, 1920, gouache; no. 71, *Composition with Figure*, 1919, gouache.

123 This drawing relates to *Le Grand Déjeuner*, 1921, New York, Museum of Modern Art or to *Two Women and Still-life*, 1920, Von der Heydt Museum, Wuppertal.

124 *Study for "Mother and Child", Three Figures in a Landscape*, 1922, relates to the oil in the collection of Mr. and Mrs. Alan Emil,

zu besprechen. S. z.B. die Briefe vom 18. Oktober 1952, vom Dezember 1952, vom 18. Januar und 5. Februar 1954 an Curt Valentin.

119 S. Christopher Green, *Léger and the Avant-Garde,* New Haven and London, Yale University Press, 1976, S. 102 ff., betreffend Ähnlichkeit der Léger-Zeichnung mit einer Fotografie von Kriegsopfern, die auf dem Titelblatt von *Le Miroir,* Sonntag, 8. Oktober 1916, erschien; s. Peter de Francia, *Fernand Léger,* S. 144, betreffend diese und eine andere Zeichnung, welche direkten Bezug zu Kriegstod besitzt.

120 Christopher Green, ibid., vertritt die Ansicht, dass Léger wahrscheinlich die Zeichnung ausführte, als er sich im Frühling 1917 im Spital erholte.

121 S. die folgenden verwandten, in Jean Cassou und Jean Leymarie (*Fernand Léger, Drawings and Gouaches,* Greenwich, New York Graphic Society, 1973) abgebildeten Werke: Nr. 50, *Mechanische Formen,* 1917, Privatsammlung, Nr. 51, *Mechanische Formen,* 1918, Kunstmuseum Basel (verwandt mit T7, *Mechanische Elemente,* 1918–23, Öl, Kunstmuseum Basel), und Nr. 52, *Mechanische Elemente,* 1918, Aquarell, Privatsammlung Paris (verwandt mit T8, *Stilleben mit mechanischen Elementen,* 1918, Öl, vormals Sammlung Maeght).

122 Dieses Werk kann verglichen werden mit *Die Treppe,* Öl auf Leinwand, Sammlung Rosengart, Luzern (Nr. 4, S. 76, *Fernand Léger,* Kunsthalle Köln, 1978; s. a. Nr. 69, *Komposition mit Figur,* Aquarell, 1920; Nr. 66. *Komposition mit Figuren,* 1919, Aquarell; Nr. 73, *Komposition mit zwei Figuren,* 1920, Aquarell. S. a. Cassou und Leymarie, *Fernand Léger,* Nr. 66, *Komposition mit Figur,* 1920, Aquarell; Nr. 68, *Komposition mit zwei Figuren,* 1920, Aquarell; Nr. 69, *Komposition mit zwei Figuren,* 1920, Aquarell; Nr. 70, *Komposition mit Figur,* 1920, Gouache; Nr. 71, *Komposition mit Figur,* 1919, Gouache).

123 Diese Zeichnung steht in Bezug zu *Le Grand Déjeuner,* 1921, Museum of Modern Art, New York, oder zu *Zwei Frauen und Stilleben,* 1920, Von der Heydt Museum, Wuppertal.

124 *Studie für «Mutter und Kind»; drei Figuren in einer Landschaft,* 1922, steht in Bezug zum Ölbild in der Sammlung von Mr. and Mrs. Alan Emil, New York (Nr. 36, *Léger and Purist Paris,* The Tate Gallery, 1970; hat auch Bezüge zum Ölbild *La femme et l'enfant,* 1922, Kunstmuseum Basel, und zur Zeichnung mit Datum 1924 im Philadelphia Museum of Art).

125 S. Christopher Green, *Léger and the Avant-Garde,* S. 223 ff.; Green weist auch auf kompositionelle Ähnlichkeiten zu Werken von New York, No. 36, *Léger and Purist Paris,* London, The Tate Gallery, 1970; it relates. as well to the oil, *La femme et l'enfant (Mother and Child),* 1922, in the Kunstmuseum, Basel, and the related drawing (dated 1924) in The Philadelphia Museum of Art.

125 See Christopher Green, *Léger and the Avant-Garde,* p. 223ff; Green also indicates compositional similarities with works by Le Nain, David and Poussin; Bradley Jordan Nickels, *Fernand Léger,* p. 261 states that the grid indicates that Léger had intended to mechanically enlarge the sketch.

126 See the related oil, *The Visitors,* 1925, Collection Mrs. Leigh B. Block, Chicago. Other related drawings include *Figures in the City,* nos. 111, 112, 113, and *In Port,* no. 114 in Cassou and Leymarie; Christopher Green, *Léger and the Avant Garde,* p. 243 and 258ff, sees Léger's depictions of modern man in a city setting as "irrational and pressurized" and deriving ultimately from De Chirico's perspectival distortions. De Chirico was known to Léger and the other Cubists already in 1912–1914. Mark Roskill mentions that Apollinaire and Raynal had written on the Italian metaphysical artist and that pictures by Gris, Léger and De Chirico were includes by André Breton in the first soirée organized for the periodical *Littérature* in January 1920. Roskill, *The Interpretation of Cubism,* Philadelphia, The Art Alliance Press, (London and Toronto, Associated University Presses), 1985, p. 136 and 154–182.

127 Cooper, *Fernand Léger et le nouvel espace,* p. 86.

128 Peter de Francia, *Fernand Léger,* p. 156 refers to "the implacable finality of Léger's graphic language" in these drawings of monumentalized objects, separated through distinct and heavy contours.

129 Cooper, *Fernand Léger et le nouvel espace,* p. 100 illus.

130 Christopher Green sheds light on Léger's choice of subject and mode of depiction through quoting Léger's own explanation of the inspiration of a Campari Advertisement in *Le Matin. (Léger and The Avant-Garde,* p. 270ff.) Green also cites the important impact of *Le Ballet Mécanique* and the Parisian cinematic avant-garde generally in Léger's depiction of simple manufactured objects. (Note Gris' depictions of siphons, for example, *The Siphon,* 1913, oil on canvas, Rose Art Museum, Brandeis University or *The Siphon,* 1916, oil on canvas, Museum Ludwig, Cologne, no. 14 and 32, Rosenthal, *Juan Gris,* 1983, Berkeley.) See *The Siphon,* 1924, oil, Albright Knox Art Gallery, Buffalo, no. 39, Berlin Staatliche Kunsthalle, *F. Léger,* 1980.

131 See a related work, *Les Vieux Gants* in the Kunstmuseum, Basel. See de Francia, *Fernand Léger,* p. 160–163, who aptly com-

Le Nain, David und Poussin hin; Bradley Jordan Nickels, *Fernand Léger*, S. 261, vertritt die Ansicht, Léger habe die Skizze mechanisch vergrössern wollen, liest den Raster also als Quadratur.

126 S. das verwandte Ölbild *Die Besucher*, 1925, Sammlung Mrs. Leigh B. Block, Chicago. Andere verwandte Zeichnungen, in Cassou und Leymarie, *Fernand Léger: Figuren in der Stadt* (Nr. 111, 112, 113) und *Im Hafen* (Nr. 114). Christopher Green, *Léger and the Avant-Garde*, S. 243 und 258 ff., betrachtet Légers Darstellung des modernen Menschen in städtischer Umgebung als «irrational, wie unter Druck» und letztlich als von de Chiricos perspektivischen Verzerrungen hergeleitet. De Chirico war Léger und den andern Kubisten schon 1912–14 bekannt. Mark Roskill erwähnt, dass Apollinaire und Raynal über den italienischen Metaphysiker geschrieben hätten und dass Bilder von ihm, neben solchen von Gris und Léger, von André Breton in die erste für die Zeitschrift *Littérature* organisierte Soirée (Januar 1920) aufgenommen worden seien. S. Roskill, *The Interpretation of Cubism*, Philadelphia, The Art Alliance Press, (London and Toronto, Associated University Presses), 1985, S. 136 und 154–182.

127 Cooper, *Fernand Léger et le nouvel espace*, S. 86.

128 Peter de Francia, *Fernand Léger*, S. 156, spricht von «der unerbittlichen Entschiedenheit von Légers zeichnerischer Sprache», wie man sie in diesen Werken mit monumentalisierten, voneinander durch klare kräftige Konturen getrennten Gegenständen beobachten kann.

129 Cooper, *Fernand Léger et le nouvel espace*, S. 100 (Abb.).

130 Christopher Green wirft Licht auf Légers Themenwahl und Darstellungsweise, indem er den Künstler selbst zitiert, der seine Inspiration durch eine Campari-Reklame in *Le Matin* erläutert (*Léger and the Avant-Garde*, S. 270 ff). Green weist auch auf die grosse Wirkung des *Ballet Mécanique* und der Pariser Filmer-Avantgarde im allgemeinen auf Légers Darstellung gewöhnlicher massenproduzierter Gegenstände hin. N.B. Gris' Darstellung von Siphonflaschen, z.B. *Die Siphonflasche*, 1913, Öl auf Leinwand, Rose Art Museum, Brandeis, University, Waltham, Massachusetts, oder *Die Siphonflasche*, 1916, Öl auf Leinwand, Museum Ludwig, Köln; Nr. 14 und 32, Rosenthal, *Juan Gris*, Berkeley 1983. S. *Die Siphonflasche*, 1924, Öl, Albright Knox Art Gallery, Buffalo (Katalognr. 39, *Fernand Léger*, Staatliche Kunsthalle Berlin 1980).

131 S. das verwandte Werk *Les Vieux Gants*, Kunstmuseum Basel. S. de Francia (*Fernand Léger*, S. 160–163), der treffend Légers Zeichnungen dieser Zeit mit Fotografien von Paul Strand vergleicht. Auch weist er hin auf Légers berühmte, Simone Herman 1931 erzählte

pares Léger's drawings of this period with photographs of Paul Strand. He includes, as well, Léger's famous comment to Simone Herman in 1931 describing his scrutiny of a bit of rag on a speeding train from Chicago to New York.

132 Quoted by Cooper in *Fernand Léger*, Marseille, Musée Cantini, 1966, p. 6 (Ms.).

133 *Ibid.*, p. 7 (Ms.).

134 See Cooper, "La grande parade de Fernand Léger", *l'Oeil*, no. 2, 1955, pp. 13–16.

Geschichte von seiner genauen Untersuchung eines Stücks Lumpen im Schnellzug von Chicago nach New York.

132 Zitiert von Cooper, *Fernand Léger*, Marseille, Musée Cantini, 1966, S. 6 (Ms.).

133. ibid., S. 7 (Ms.).

134 S. Cooper, «La grande parade de Fernand Léger», *l'Oeil*, Nr. 2, 1955, S. 13–16.

PABLO PICASSO

Cooper dürfte Picasso 1932 in Paris getroffen haben, als er sich die Retrospektive in der Galerie Georges Petit ansah – wahrlich, eine wichtige Ausstellung für ihn, erwarb er doch im Lauf der folgenden fünf Jahre mindestens sieben bedeutende Ölbilder.[135]

Einer seiner ersten Käufe, 1933 bei der Arnold Haskell Gallery, London, war *Frauenkopf, Schatulle und Apfel* (Nr. 54). Die Zeichnung vereinigt drei bedeutsame ikonographische Motive in Picassos Schaffen von 1909. In Horta de Ebro porträtierte er häufig Fernande Olivier.[136] Die Schatulle und der Apfel sind oft wiederkehrende Elemente in den Stilleben dieser Zeit, und sie können Picassos immer strengere formalen Analysen im entwicklungsgeschichtlichen Kontext des Frühkubismus aufzeigen.[137]

Cooper may have met Picasso in Paris in 1932 when he saw the retrospective mounted at Galerie Georges Petit. This was indeed an important exhibition for Cooper as he purchased from it at least 7 major oils within the next 5 years.[135]

One of his first purchases was the drawing *Head of a Woman, Casket and Apple* (No. 54), from Arnold Haskell Gallery in London in 1933. The drawing brings together three crucial iconographic features of Picasso's work during 1909. At Horta de Ebro he frequently depicted Fernande Olivier.[136] The box and apple are repeatedly depicted elements in the still lifes of this period, which reveal Picasso's increasingly rigorous formal analysis within the evolution of early Cubism.[137]

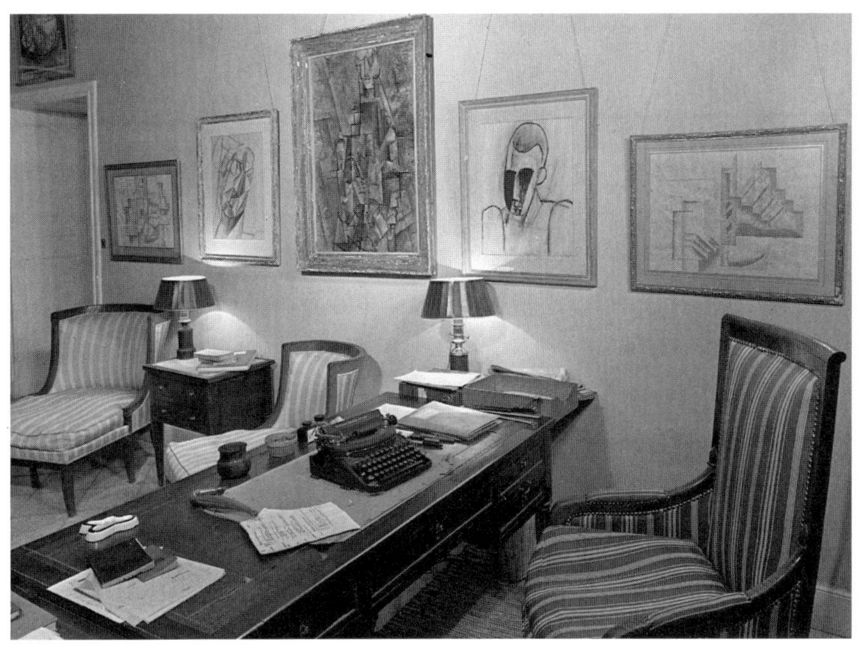

Château de Castille, ca.1955, Werke von Picasso, von links nach rechts: *Grenouille*, 1949; *Eine Flasche "Bass" und Gitarre*, 1912 (No.60); *Kopf*, 1909 (DC41; Z II** 713); *Klarinettist*, 1911 (DC59; Z II* 288); *Männerkopf*, 1908 (No.52); *Eine Flasche "Bass" und Gitarre*, 1912–13 (Z II** 375).

Château de Castille, ca.1955, works by Picasso, left to right: *Grenouille*, 1949; *Bottle of Bass and Guitar*, (No.60); *Head*, 1909 (DC41; Z II** 713); *Clarinetist*, 1911 (DC59; Z II* 288); *Head of a Man*, 1908 (No.52); *Bottle of Bass and Guitar*, 1912–13 (Z II** 375).

Eine von Coopers letzten Erwerbungen – vom November 1963 – war ein weiterer Picasso aus dem Jahr 1909, das *Stilleben: Zuckerdose und Fächer* (Nr. 55), dessen Hauptgegenstände, neben Zuckerdose und Fächer, wieder der Apfel und die Schatulle sind.[138] Dieses Aquarell wurde 1973 zusammen mit einem Bronzekopf von Fernande in der Ausstellung mit dem Titel *Œuvres Cubistes*, einer Darstellung des Kubismus im Jahre 1909, in der Pariser Galerie Berggruen gezeigt. Cooper beschrieb in einer kurzen Einleitung diese Schau als «eine Art idealer Privatsammlung, wie ich sie mir in den Vorkriegsjahren erträumte. Sie erlaubt mir nun, mich in der Phantasie bei einem jener grossen Kunstfreunde, den ich einst kannte, im Kabinett wiederzufinden, das ihm in stillen Stunden zum geniessenden Betrachten einiger seiner rarsten Schätze diente.»[139]

Noch durch ein weiteres Stilleben wurde das für die Bildung des Frühkubismus entscheidende Jahr 1909 vertreten, durch das *Stilleben mit Schokoladenkanne* (Nr. 53) nämlich, das 1953 bei Reid & Lefevre in London erworben wurde. In *The Cubist Epoch* beschreibt Cooper dieses sehr ausgearbeitete Aquarell als Synthese der Einflüsse von Cézanne und Rousseau, welche Picassos Schaffen dieser Zeit bestimmen.[140]

Auch die frühere Entwicklung von Picasso war in Coopers Sammlung gut vertreten, und zwar durch *Stehender weiblicher Akt*, Herbst 1906 (Nr. 50), *Zeichnung für die «Demoiselles d'Avignon»*, Frühling 1907 (Nr. 51), *Drei Akte unter einem Baum*, Winter 1907, und *Männerkopf*, Ende 1908 (Nr. 52).[141] Die in diese Ausstellung aufgenommenen *Stehender weiblicher Akt* und *Männerkopf* vermitteln einen Sinn für das Monumentale. Der stehende Akt ist eine imposant aufragende Figur, deren Grösse das Blatt buchstäblich nicht fassen kann. Die fliessenden Bänder und hingepeitschten Schraffen der schwarzen Tusche lassen die Umrisse des stämmigen Körpers klar hervortreten. Die aggressive physische Präsenz der Figur wird durch rote und braune Sepia-Kleckse noch verstärkt.[142] Cooper gab als Faksimile ein katalanisches Skizzenbuch heraus; es stammte vom Sommer 1906, den Picasso und Fernande Olivier im

One of Cooper's last purchases, in November 1983, was another 1909 Picasso, *Still-life: Sugar Bowl and Fan* (No. 55) which once again features the apple and casket along with fan and covered sugar bowl.[138] This watercolor, along with a bronze *Head of Fernande* were included in a 1973 exhibition at Galerie Berggruen in Paris entitled *Oeuvres Cubistes,* to represent Cubism of 1909. Cooper wrote a short introduction describing this exhibit as "une sorte de collection particulière idéale telle que je la concevais dans les années d'avant-guerre. Elle me permet donc de me retrouver en imagination chez un de ces grands amateurs que j'ai connu jadis, dans le cabinet réservé pour sa contemplation et sa jouissance personnelle, aux heures creuses, de quelques-uns de ses trésors les plus rares."[139]

This crucial formative year in early Cubism, 1909, was furthermore represented by yet another still life, *Still-life with Chocolate Pot,* (No. 53) purchased in 1953 from Reid and Lefevre in London. In *The Cubist Epoch* this highly finished watercolor is described as a synthesis of the influences of Cézanne and Rousseau which dominate Picasso's work during that period.[140]

The earlier development within Picasso's work was also well represented in Cooper's collection: *Standing Female Nude,* fall 1906 (No. 50); *Drawing for the "Demoiselles d'Avignon",* spring 1907 (No. 51a); *Three Nudes under a Tree,* winter 1907; and *Head of a Man,* late 1908 (No. 52).[141] *Standing Female Nude* and *Head of a Man,* included in this exhibition, convey a sense of monumentality. The standing nude is a towering figure whose height is quite literally not contained within the field of the composition. The fluid ribbons and slashing hatched lines of black ink define the contours of the chunky limbs of the body. The aggressive physicality of the figure is reinforced with blotches of red and brown sepia gouache.[142] Cooper edited a facsimile edition of a Catalan notebook, originating from the summer of 1906 which Picasso and Fernande Olivier spent in Gosol in the Iberian peninsula. He discerns a marked change in Picasso's style: "La manière

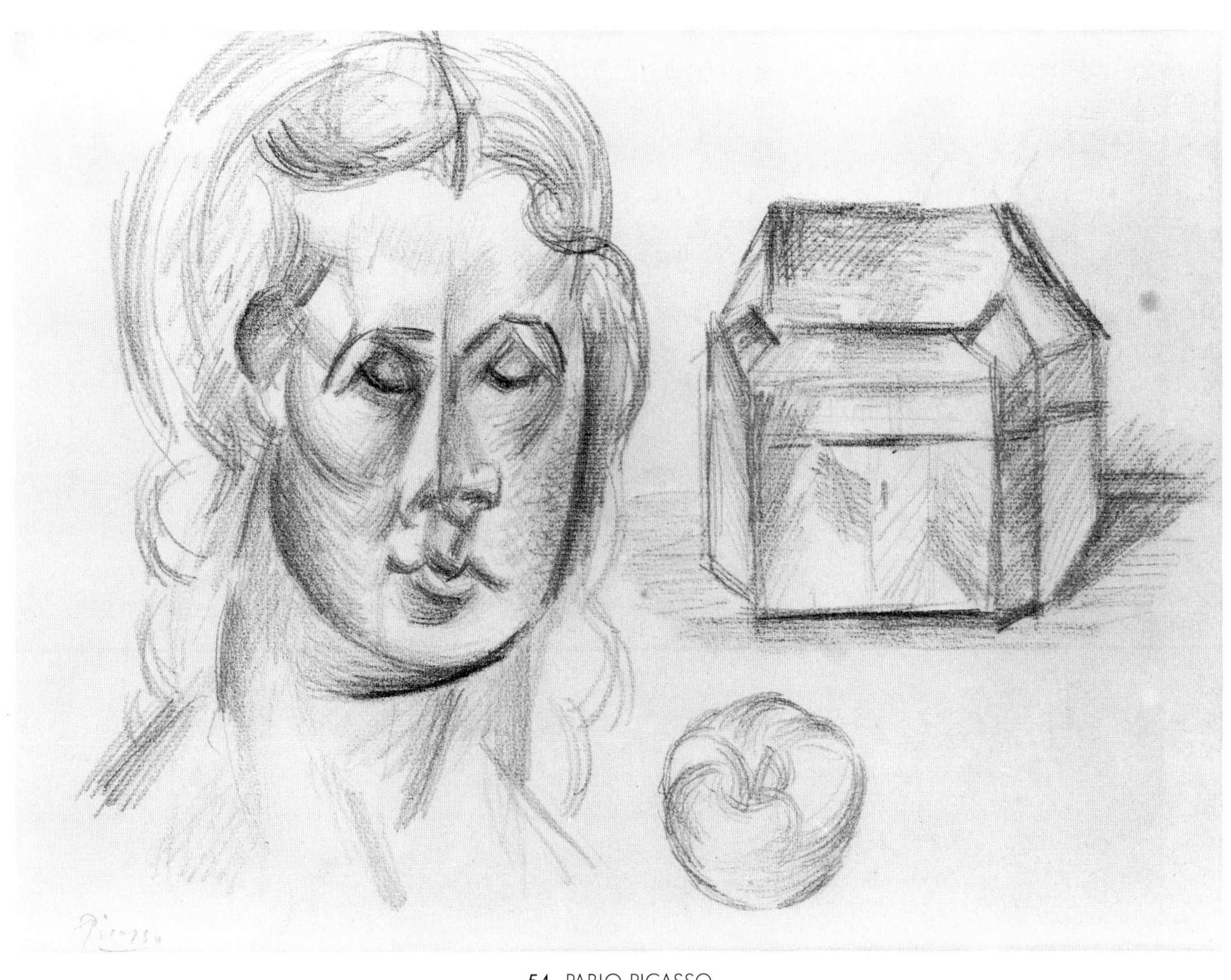

54 PABLO PICASSO
(Frauenkopf, Schatulle und Apfel; Head of a Woman, Casket and Apple) (1909)

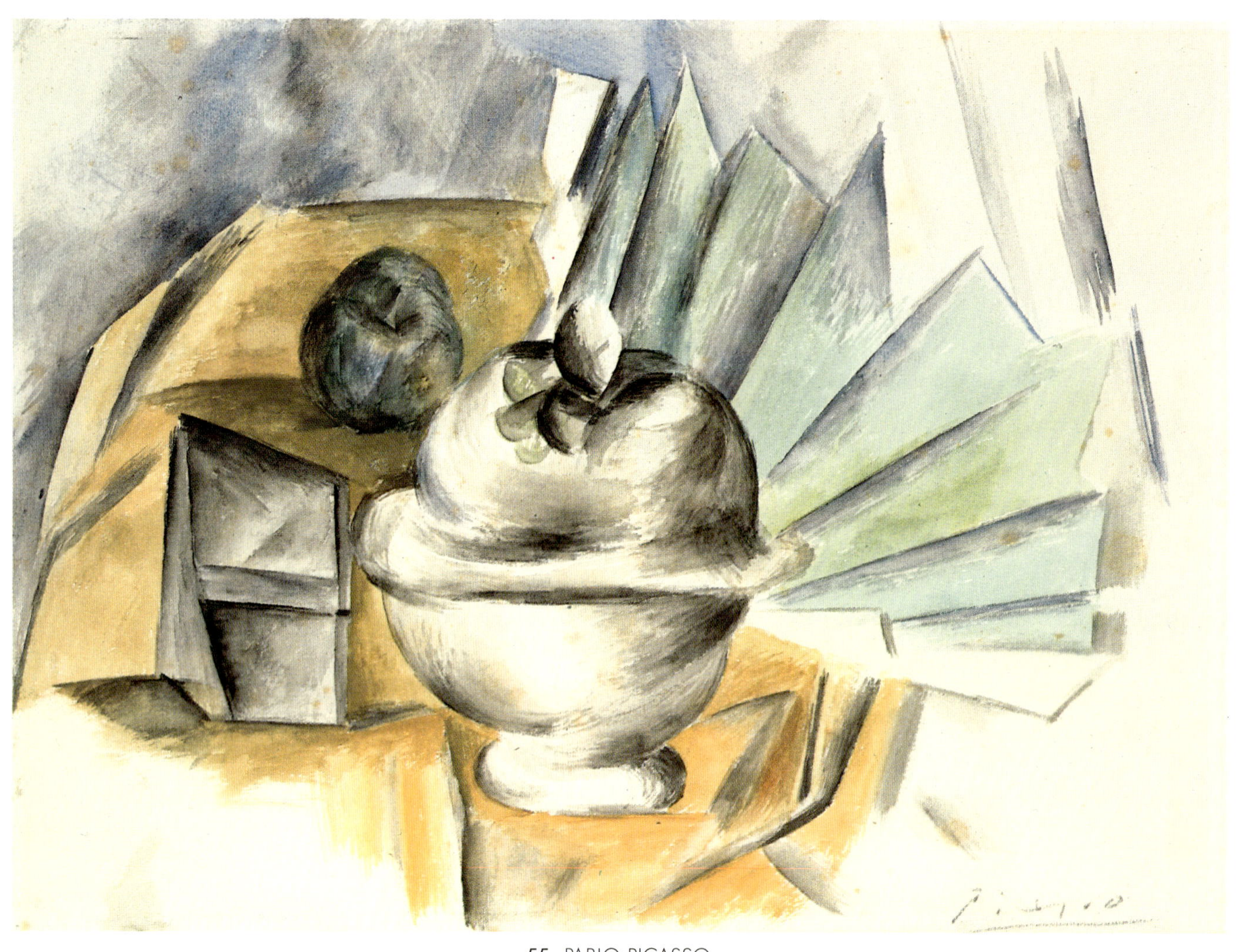

55 PABLO PICASSO
(Stilleben: Zuckerdose und Fächer; Still-life: Sugar Bowl and Fan) (1909–1910)

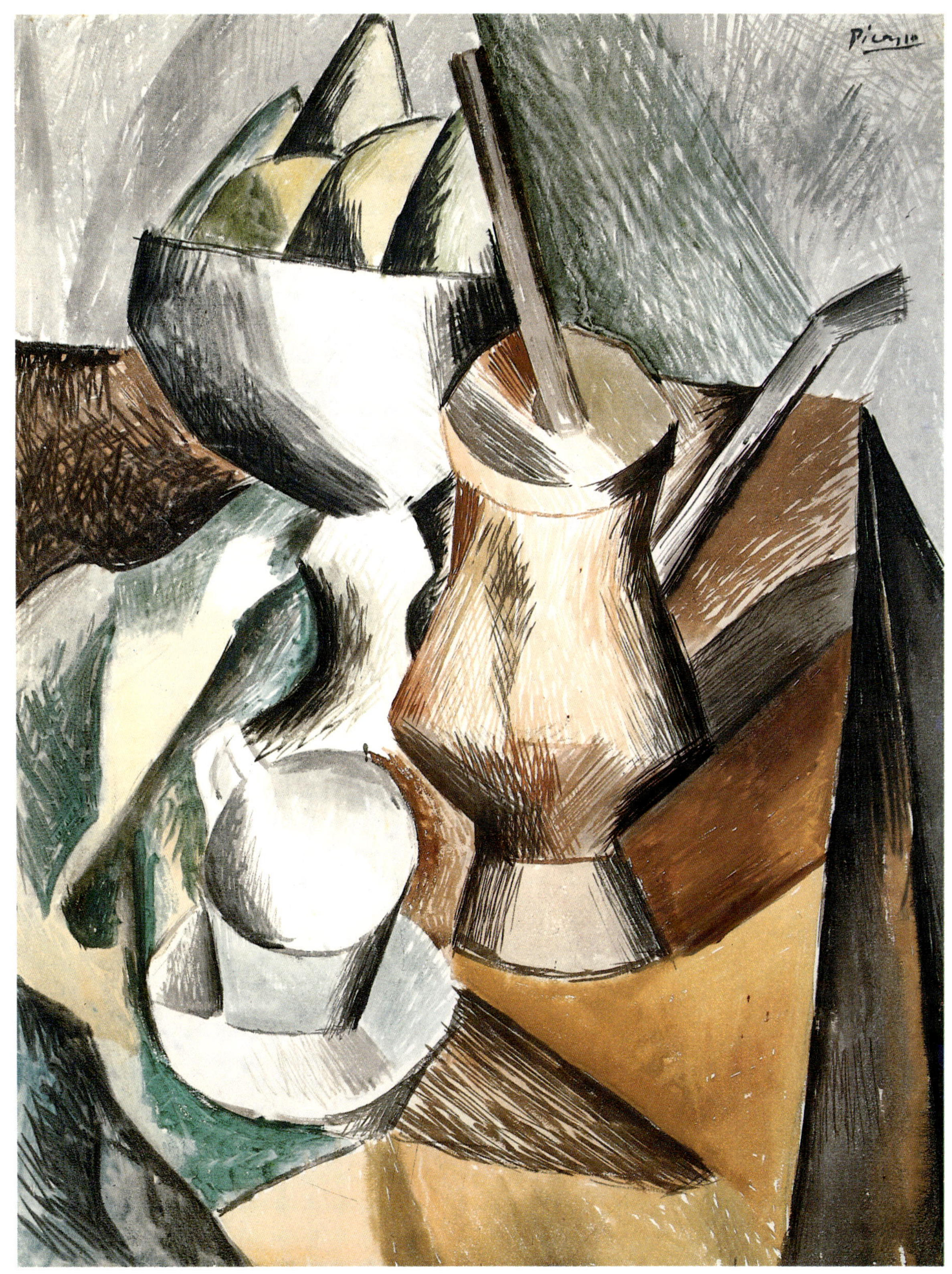

53 PABLO PICASSO
(Stilleben mit Schokoladenkanne; Still-life with Chocolate Pot) (early 1909)

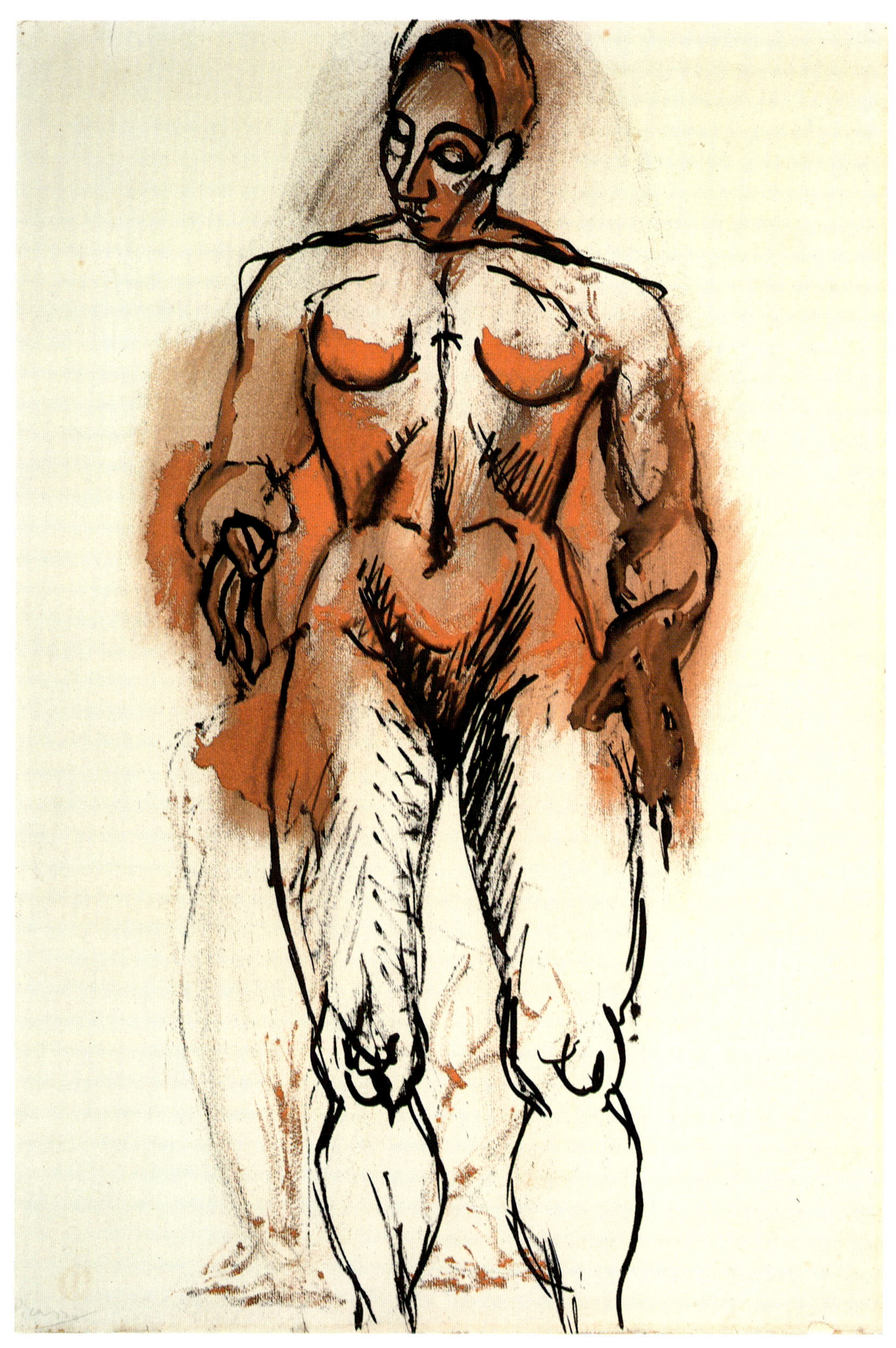

50 PABLO PICASSO
(Stehender weiblicher Akt; Standing Female Nude) (1906–07)

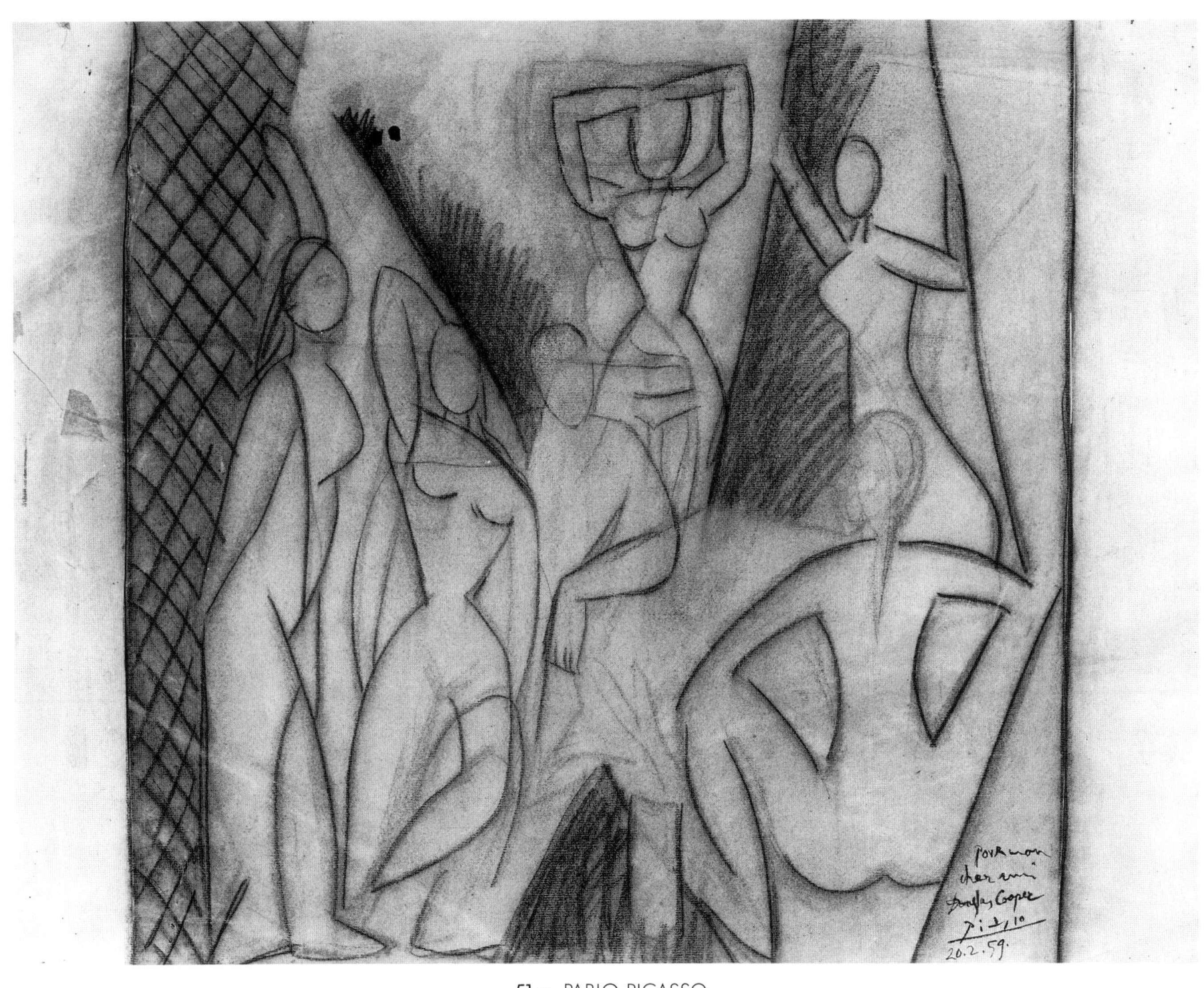

51 a PABLO PICASSO
(Zeichnung für die «Demoiselles d'Avignon»; Study for ''Les Demoiselles d'Avignon'') (Spring 1907)

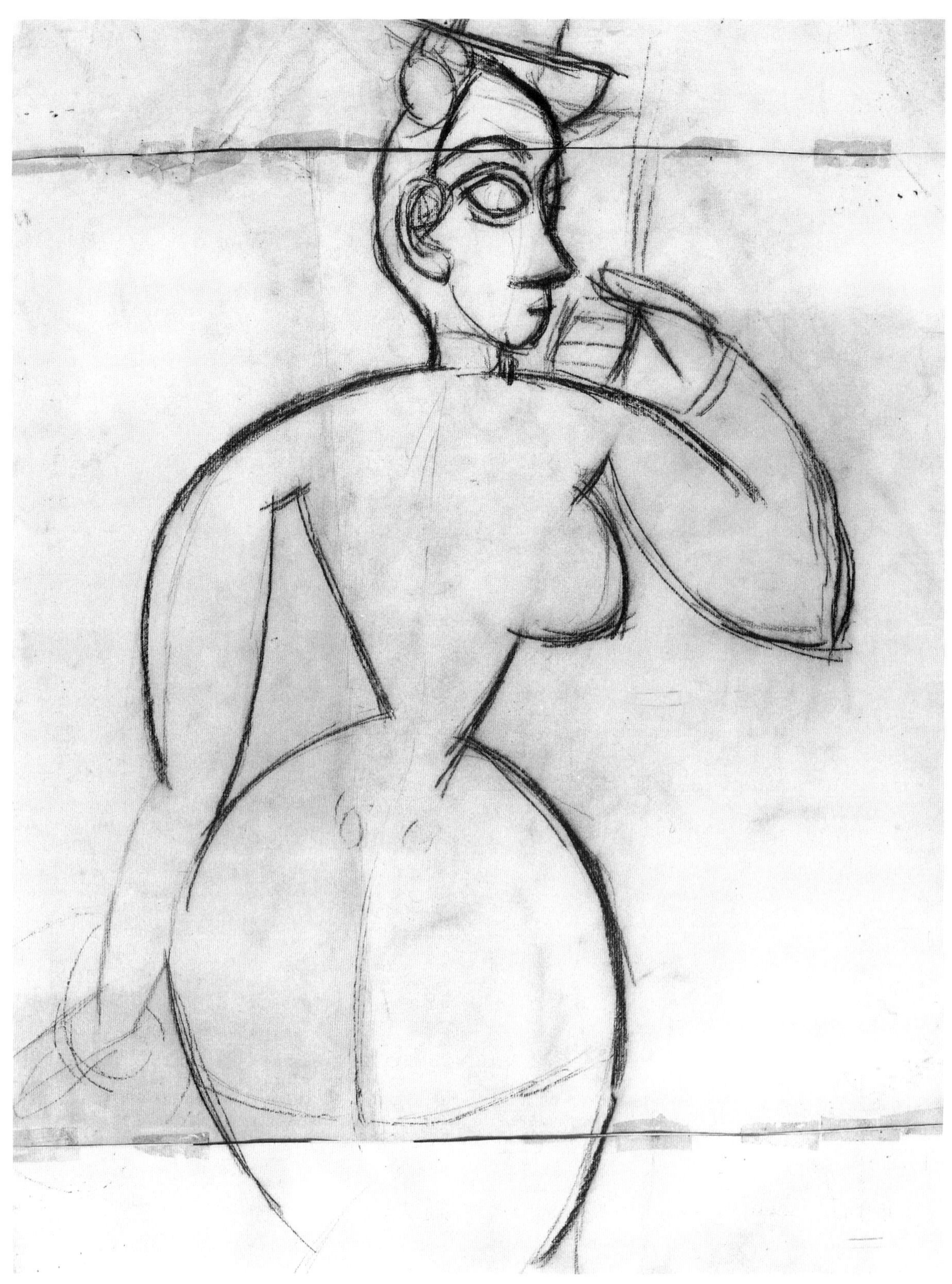

51 b PABLO PICASSO
(Amazone; Amazone, Woman in Riding Habit) (Spring 1907)

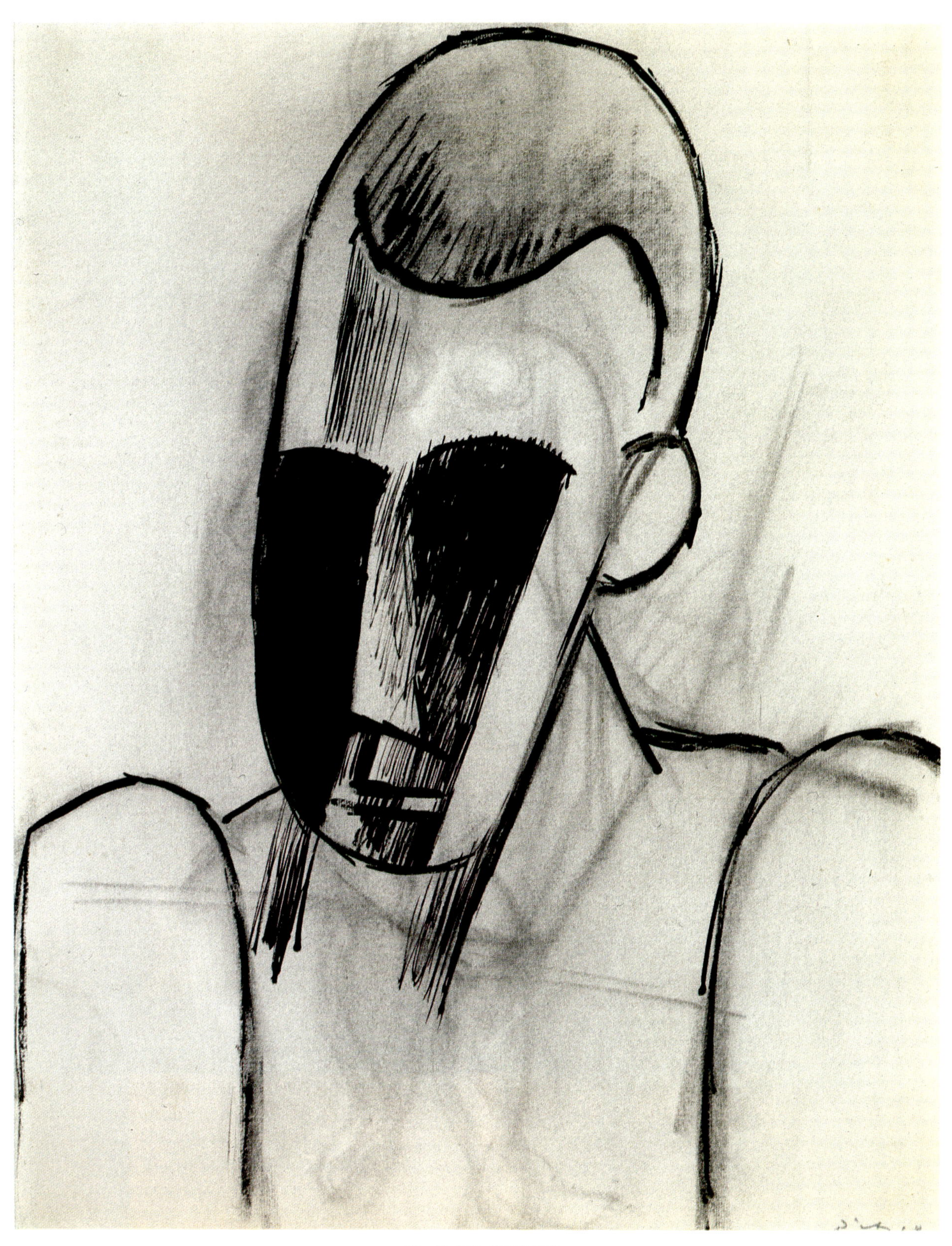

52 PABLO PICASSO
(Männerkopf; Head of a Man) (late 1908)

spanischen Gosol verbrachten. Cooper stellt einen deutlichen Stilwandel fest: «Die anmutige und elegante klassische Manier, typisch für ihn während des ersten Halbjahres 1906, wird rasch ersetzt durch einen strengeren Stil...»[143] Im fast genau zwei Jahre älteren *Männerkopf* wird der Körper der Figur ebenfalls radikal von den Blatträndern beschnitten; die Schultern sind eingezogen, als ob sie auf diesen engen Raum reagierten, was einen verblüffenden Eindruck von Monumentalität hervorruft. Die Stilisierung des Gesichts, beherrscht durch zwei mächtige Hiebe von sattem Schwarz, welche die Augen decken und dann abwärts verlaufen, leitet sich zweifellos von primitiver Kunst her, an welcher Picasso so grosses Interesse zeigte.

«Die heroischen Jahre des Kubismus» 1910–1912, wie Cooper sie nannte, waren vertreten durch *Der Klarinettist*, 1911, *Stehende Frau*, 1911–12 (Nr. 56), *Stilleben mit toten Vögeln*, 1912, *Stilleben mit Tisch und Birnenschale*, 1912 (Nr. 58), *Komposition mit Violine*, 1912 (Nr. 59), *Eine Flasche «Bass» und Gitarre*, 1912–13 (Nr. 60), und auch durch graphische Blätter, darunter *Stilleben mit Marc-Flasche*, 1912 (Nr. 57).

Die Figur im Blatt *Stehende Frau* wird evoziert durch eine komplizierte Montage einzelner Flächen von verschiedener Textur und Dichte, die entlang einer vertikalen Achse erregt zusammenlaufen und so Veränderungen des Kontraposts suggerieren.[144] Die Artikulation der Flächen durch Kreuzschraffur oder kurze parallele Federstriche verschiedener Dichte hat ihre Entsprechung in den kleinen einzeln hingesetzten Pinselstrichen, welche für Picassos Bilder dieser Periode charakteristisch sind.[145]

Die übrigen Werke dieser Zeit, 1911–13, sind alles Stilleben. Die Radierung *Stilleben mit Marc-Flasche* entstand 1911 im Auftrag von Daniel Henry Kahnweiler und war offenbar als Pendant zu Braques *Stilleben mit Gin-Flasche auf einem Tisch (FOX)* (Nr. 3) gedacht. Ähnlich, durch hartes lineares Konturieren der Form, wird auch das *Stilleben mit Tisch und Birnenschale* charakterisiert. Schattierung, in der Radierung auf ein blosses Minimum reduziert, fehlt in der Kohlezeichnung völlig. Die

classique, élégante et suave, qui a été la sienne pendant la première moitié de l'année 1906 – est rapidement détrônée par un style plus sévère..."[143] In *Head of a Man*, dating from almost precisely two years later, the body of the figure is also radically cropped by the edges of the paper, the shoulders are drawn inward as though in reaction to this cramped space, creating therefore a striking impression of monumentality. The stylization of the face, dominated by two great blades of penetrating black which cover and descend from the eyes, is undoubtedly inspired by primitive art in which Picasso was so interested.

What Cooper termed "the heroic years of Cubism", 1910–1912, was represented by *The Clarinet Player*, 1911, *Standing Woman*, 1911–12 (No. 56), *Still-life with Dead Birds*, 1912, *Still-life with Table and Dish of Pears*, 1912 (No. 58), *Composition with Violin*, 1912 (No. 59), *Bottle of Bass and Guitar*, 1912–13 (No. 60) and also prints including *Still-life with Bottle of Marc*, 1912 (No. 57).

In *Standing Woman*, the figure is evoked through an intricate assemblage of distinct planes of varying texture and density, which converge in fluttering masses along a vertical axis, suggesting the contrapostal shifts of the figure. [144] The articulation of the planes with cross hatching or short parallel pen strokes of various densities, is paralleled by the small individual brushstrokes which characterize Picasso's paintings of this period.[145]

The other works from this period, all still-lifes, date from 1911 through 1913. The etching *Still life with a Bottle of Marc*, was executed in 1911 upon a commission from D.-H. Kahnweiler, and conceived apparently as a pendant to the print by Braque, *Still-life with a Bottle of Gin on a Table (Fox) (No. 3)*. *Still-life with Table and Dish of Pears*, 1912, is similarly characterized by a stark linear outlining of form. Shading, reduced to a bare minimum in the etching, is deleted entirely in the charcoal drawing. The phantom outlines of the pears (they are drawn in heavy lead pencil rather than charcoal), the distinctive profile of the bottle, the knob on the

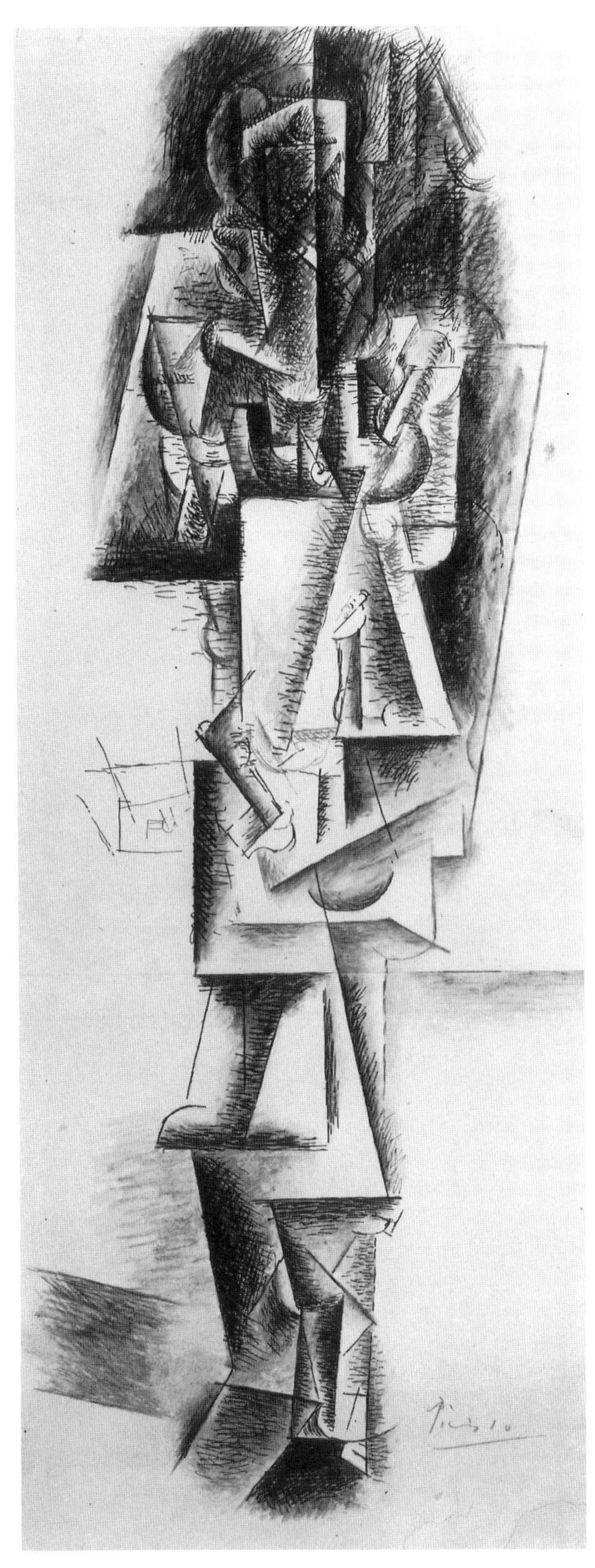

56 PABLO PICASSO
(Stehende Frau; Standing Woman) (1911–1912)

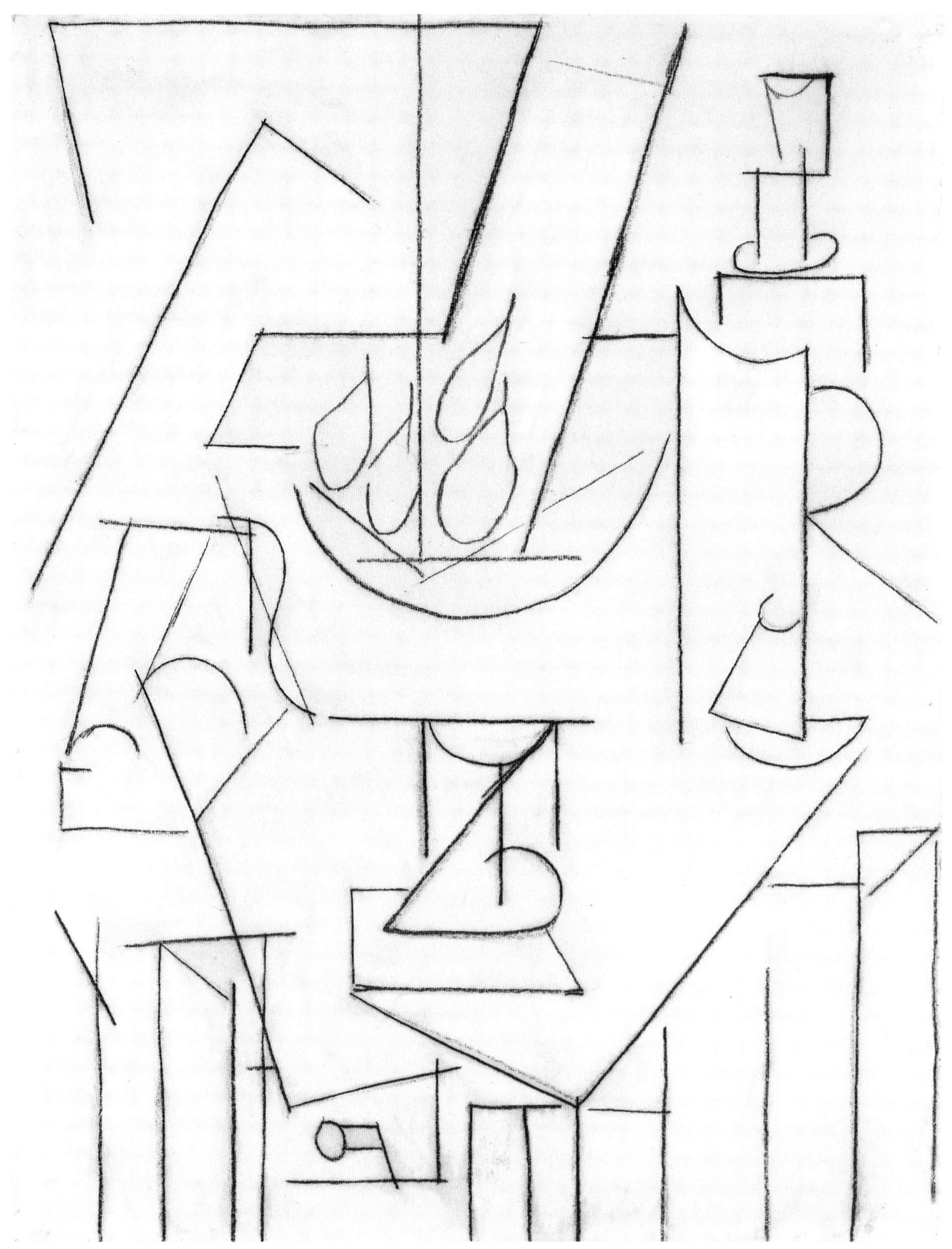

58 PABLO PICASSO
(Stilleben mit Tisch und Birnenschale; Still-life with Table and Dish of Pears) (1912)

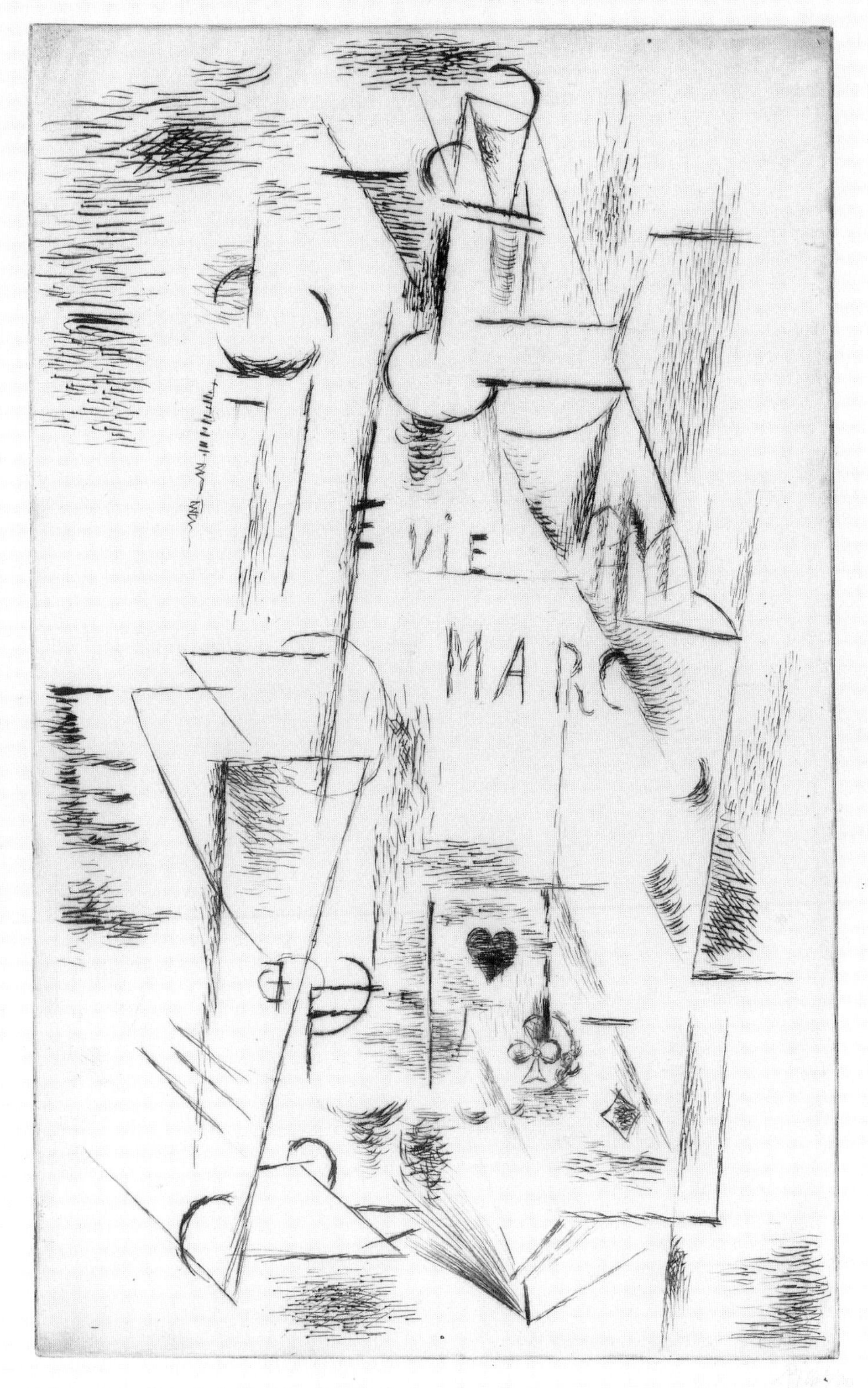

57 PABLO PICASSO
(Stilleben mit Marc-Flasche; Still-life with Bottle of Marc) (1912)

gespenstischen Umrisse der Birnen (nicht mit Kohle, sondern mit dickem Bleistift gezeichnet), das klare Profil der Flasche, der Knauf der Tischschublade: das alles schafft – wie die Buchstaben, die Flaschenform, die Farben der Karten in der Radierung – eine gewisse Klarheit und «Lesbarkeit».

In *Komposition mit Violine* wird eine ähnlich karge Kohlezeichnung kontrastiert mit einem aufgeklebten Zeitungspapier; eine säulenartige Form im Zentrum ist durch leichte Schattierung und eine tiefschwarze Rechtecksform artikuliert; sie bilden den «Körper» des Instruments. Das Werk muss nach dem 7. Dezember 1912 entstanden sein, da einigen Artikeln der Zeitung dieses Datum vorgesetzt ist. Vorherrschendes Thema des Zeitungsausschnitts ist die Friedenskonferenz in London, die 1912 begann und im Mai 1913 mit dem Abschluss des ersten Balkankriegs zu Ende ging. Zu sehen ist dieses Papier collé auf einer Photographie von Picassos Atelier am Boulevard Raspail, die Ende 1912 gemacht wurde.[146] John Richardson erinnert sich an den Kauf dieses Blattes in den fünfziger Jahren als an ein festliches Ereignis, da das Blatt nun mit dem schon 1946 erworbenen Papier collé *Fruchtschale und Glas* von Braque sozusagen ein Paar bildete.[147] Wie schon oben zur Sprache kam, war die Frage der «Erfindung» der Papier-collé-Technik durch Braque ein Hauptthema in Coopers Schriften; sie war auch wesentlich dafür verantwortlich, wie er die Chronologie des Kubismus verstand. In diesem Zusammenhang ist bemerkenswert, dass Cooper 1959 in seinem Katalog für das Musée Cantini in Marseille Picasso als Schöpfer der ersten Collage (*Stilleben mit Stuhlgeflecht*) anerkannte, die er richtig auf Frühling 1912 datierte.[148]

Das farbige Pastell *Eine Flasche «Bass» und Gitarre* mit seinen sich überschneidenden Flächen und seinen gestuften Formen wird in *The Essential Cubism* in Beziehung gebracht mit den ersten Papiers collés des Künstlers und deshalb auch auf Herbst 1912 datiert. Die leuchtenden Farben lassen sich mit jenen der in Sorgues im Sommer oder Frühherbst 1912 entstandenen Werke vergleichen.[149] Tatsächlich zeigt dieses Blatt eine

drawer of the gueridon provide, – like the lettering, the form of the bottle, the symbols on the cards in the etching, – a degree of clarity or "readability".

In *Composition with Violin,* a similarly minimal charcoal drawing is contrasted with a passage of pasted paper. A central column is articulated with light shading and a densely blackened rectangle which form the "body" of the instrument. This work must date from after the 7th of December 1912, as several articles in the newspaper begin with leaders with that date. The dominant subject of the newspaper segment is the peace conference which took place in London beginning in December 1912 and concluding in May 1913, ending the first Balkan war. This *papier collé* is evident in a photograph of Picasso's Boulevard Raspail studio, dated late 1912.[146] John Richardson remembers the purchase of this *papier collé* in the 1950s as a great celebratory event, forming, as it were, a pair with the Braque papier-collé *Fruit-dish and Glass* purchased already in 1946.[147] As discussed earlier, the issue of Braque's "invention" of the *papier collé* technique figured prominently in Cooper's writings on Braque, determining a great deal about his understanding of the chronology of Cubism. It is worth noting in this context, that in his 1959 catalogue for the Musée Cantini in Marseille, Cooper had credited Picasso with the first collage *(Still-life with chair caning)* and had properly dated the work to spring 1912.[148]

In *The Essential Cubism,* the colorful pastel, *Bottle of Bass and Guitar,* with its overlapping planes and stepped form, is related to the artist's first *papiers collés* and hence dated autumn 1912. The bright colors do evoke comparison with works from the summer or early autumn of 1912, done at Sorgues.[149] Indeed, this work is characterized by an aggressive palette of acid colors and an intricately complex assemblage of overlapping planes and segments. The entire composition is anchored by the dark stenciled letters of the beer bottle label at center. The thrice repeated sets of four grey lines (mere phantoms, produced by black ink applied to the reverse of the sheet) to the left of the composition,

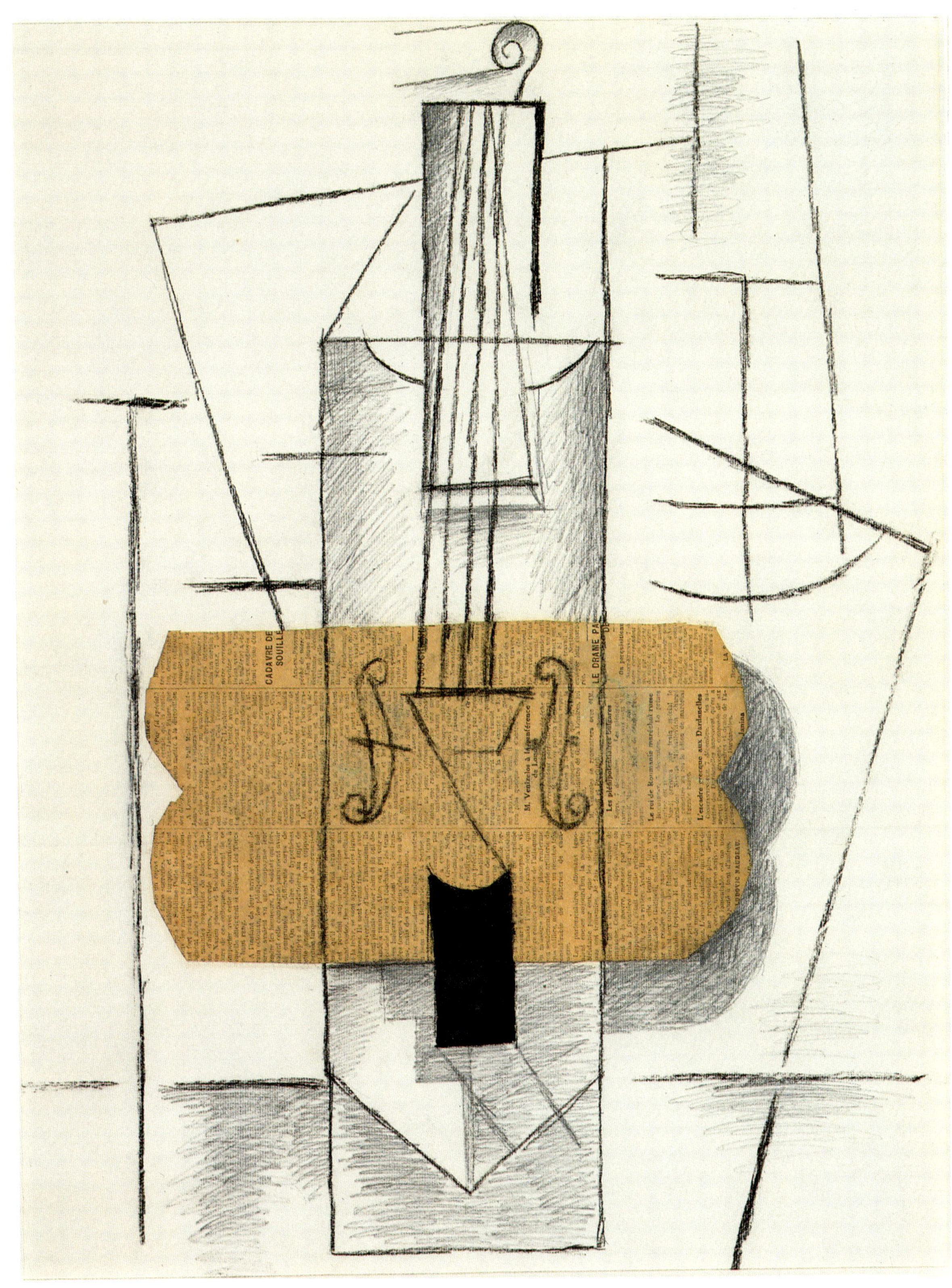

59 PABLO PICASSO
(Komposition mit Violine; Composition with Violin) (1912)

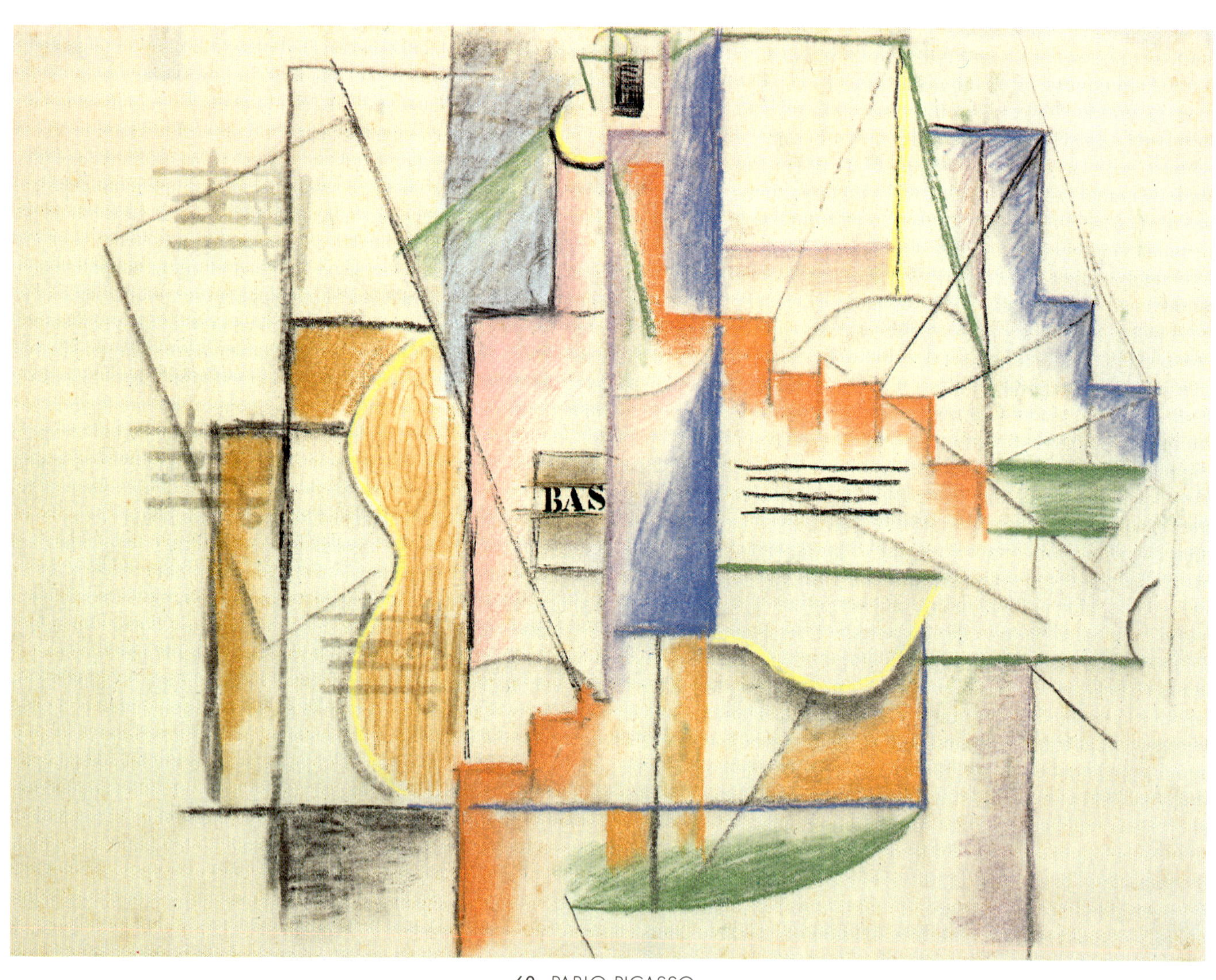

60 PABLO PICASSO
(Eine Flasche «Bass» und Gitarre; Bottle of ''Bass'' and Guitar) (1912–13)

aggressive Palette ätzender Farben; weiter kennzeichnet es ein vertracktes Gefüge sich überschneidender Flächen und Segmente. Die ganze Komposition wird verankert von der schwarzen Schablonenschrift auf der Bierflaschenetikette im Zentrum. Die dreimal repetierten Gruppen von vier grauen Linien links (die mit schwarzer Tusche eigentlich auf der Rückseite des Blatts angebracht sind, aber durchscheinen) erinnern an Gitarrensaiten oder Notenlinien.

Diese Ausstellung enthält mehrere Werke von Picasso aus dem Jahr 1914: *Stilleben: Glas und eine Flasche «Bass», Stilleben mit Pfirsichen und Spielkarten, Bärtiger Mann, Gitarre spielend* und *Der Kartenspieler* (Nr. 61, 62, 64 und 63).[150] Die im Frühling 1914 entstandene Collage beinhaltet ein Zusammenspiel von Farbe und Textur. Das Glas links wird von einer mit weisser Gouache dicht bemalten Fläche gebildet, die Bierflasche rechts von einem Stück Grün und der Schablonenschrift «BASS». Die sprudelnde Flüssigkeit ist sogar angedeutet durch konfetti-artige Tüpfchen in Rosa und Mauve.[151]

Stilleben mit Pfirsichen und Spielkarten, Bärtiger Mann, Gitarre spielend und *Der Kartenspieler* entstanden alle im Sommer 1914, den Picasso mit seiner Geliebten Eva Gouel in Avignon verbrachte. Komposition wie Thema verraten Picassos erneute Auseinandersetzung mit Cézanne und ein konzentriertes Studium seines Werks. Das Stilleben, so an Cézannesche Kompositionen erinnernd, spricht aber doch die neue Sprache des synthetischen Kubismus. Die Gegenstände und die farbigen und getüpfelten Partien scheinen so getrennt voneinander wie die Teile eines Papier collé.

Der Kartenspieler kann in Beziehung gebracht werden mit Cézannes *Der Raucher*, 1890–92, in der Ermitage, Leningrad, *Der Raucher*, 1890–92, im Puschkin Museum, Moskau, und, weniger direkt, mit *Knabe mit Schädel*, 1892–94, in der Barnes Foundation, Merion, Pennsylvania. Picassos Figur scheint recht eigentlich eine Mischung all dieser Figuren mit dem Mann ganz links auf Cézannes Bild *Die Kartenspieler*, 1890–92, im Metropolitan Museum of Art, New York, zu sein. Tatevoke once again the strings of the guitar, as well as lines of musical notation.

This exhibit includes several works by Picasso dating from 1914: *Still-life: Glass and Bottle of Bass, Still-life with Peaches and Playing Cards, Bearded Man Playing a Guitar,* and *The Card Player* (Nos. 61, 62, 64 and 63).[150] The collage, dating from the spring of 1914, involves an interplay of color and texture. The glass to the left, is formed of an area of dense white gouache; the bottle of ale, to the right, by a passage of green, as well as by the stenciled letters "BASS". The effervescent liquid is suggested, even, by the confetti-like stippling of pink and mauve.[151]

Still-life with Peaches and Playing Cards, Bearded Man Playing a Guitar, and *The Card Player,* all date from the summer of 1914 which Picasso spent in Avignon with his mistress Eva Gouel. In composition and subject matter, they demonstrate the renewal of Picasso's dialogue with and focused study of Cézanne. The still-life, so reminiscent of compositions by Cézanne, is transformed by a Synthetic Cubist idiom. The objects and passages of stippled color seem detached from one another like elements of a *papier collé*.

The Card Player may be related to Cézanne's *The Smoker,* 1890–92, The Hermitage, Leningrad; *The Smoker,* 1890–92, Pushkin Museum of Fine Arts, Moscow; and less directly to *Boy with a Skull*, 1892–94, The Barnes Foundation, Merion, Pa. Picasso's figure, in fact, suggests an amalgam of these figures with the left most man in Cézanne's *The Card Players,* 1890–92, The Metropolitan Museum of Art, New York. This drawing is in fact one of a large group of related drawings of seated men executed in 1914, characterized by varying degrees of stylization or abstraction. In this drawing one notes, for instance, the distortion of the arm, elongated into a rubbery limb, detached somewhat from the body of the figure.[152]

In *Bearded Man Playing a Guitar* there is a marked contrast between the naturalistic treatment of the face of the guitar player and the extreme Cubist stylization of his body.[153] In *Still-life with Peaches and Playing*

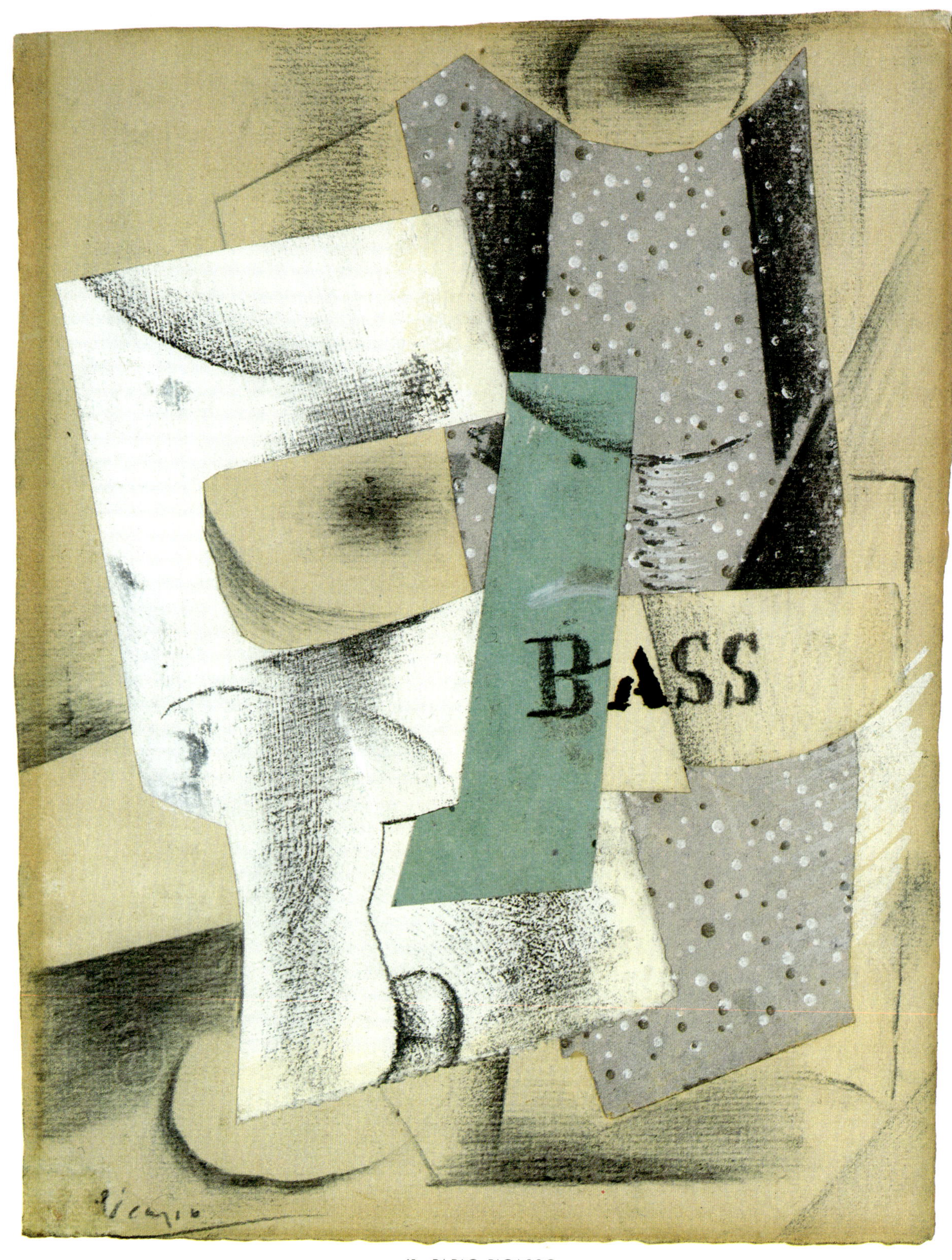

61 PABLO PICASSO
(Stilleben: Glas und eine Flasche «Bass»; Still-life: Glass and Bottle of "Bass") (1914)

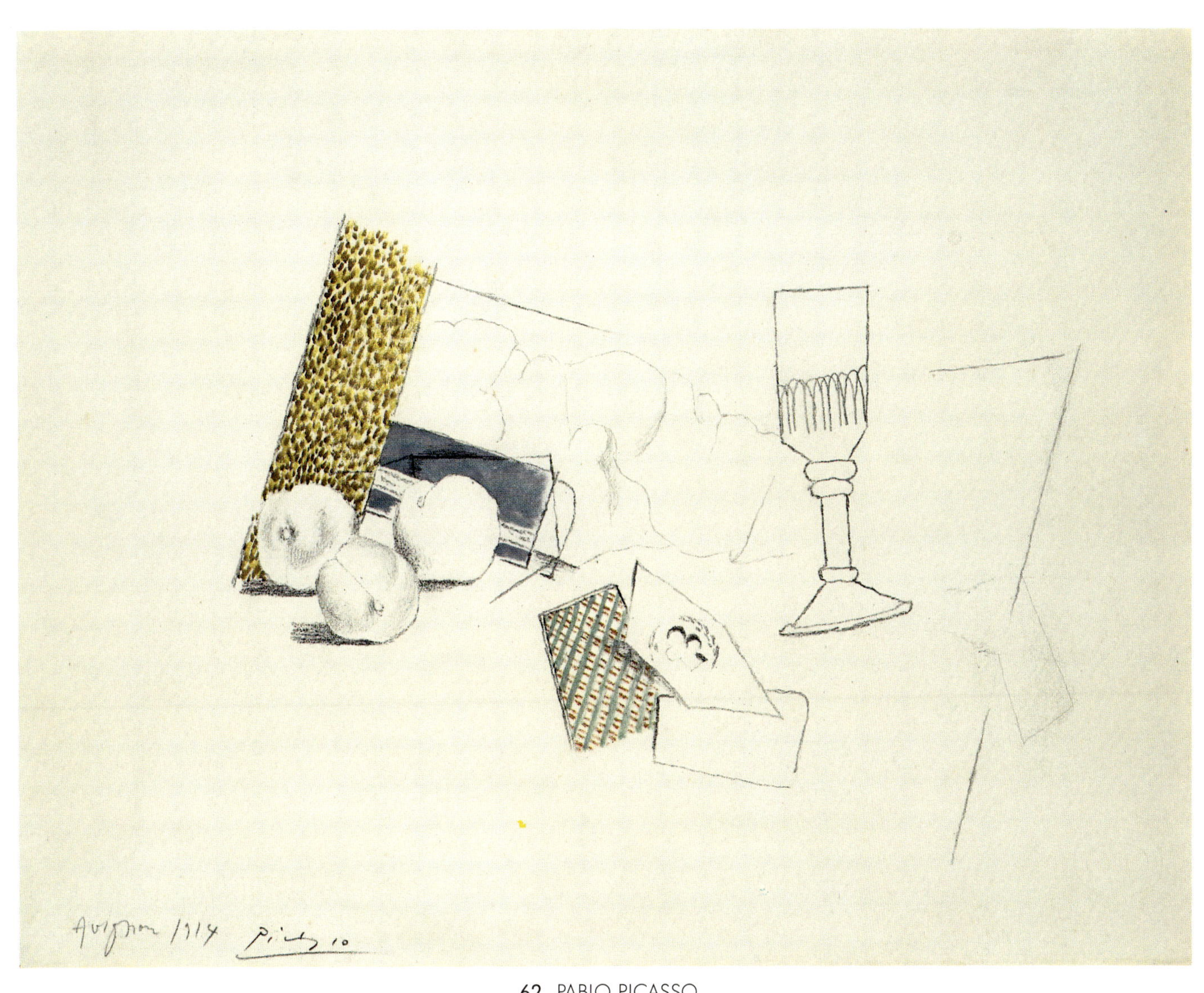

62 PABLO PICASSO
(Stilleben mit Pfirsichen und Spielkarten; Still-life with Peaches and Playing Cards) 1914

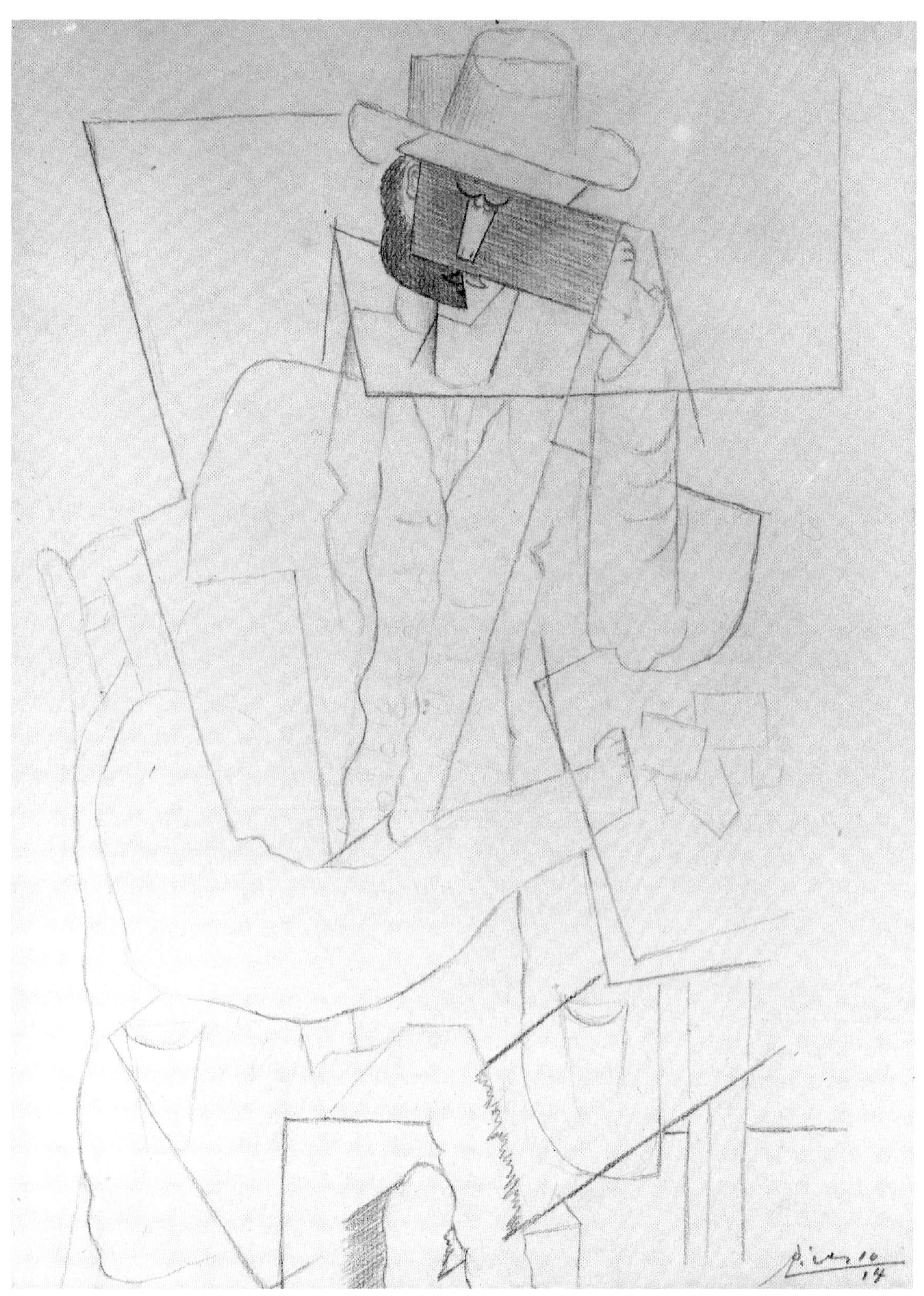

63 PABLO PICASSO
(Der Kartenspieler; The Card Player) 1914

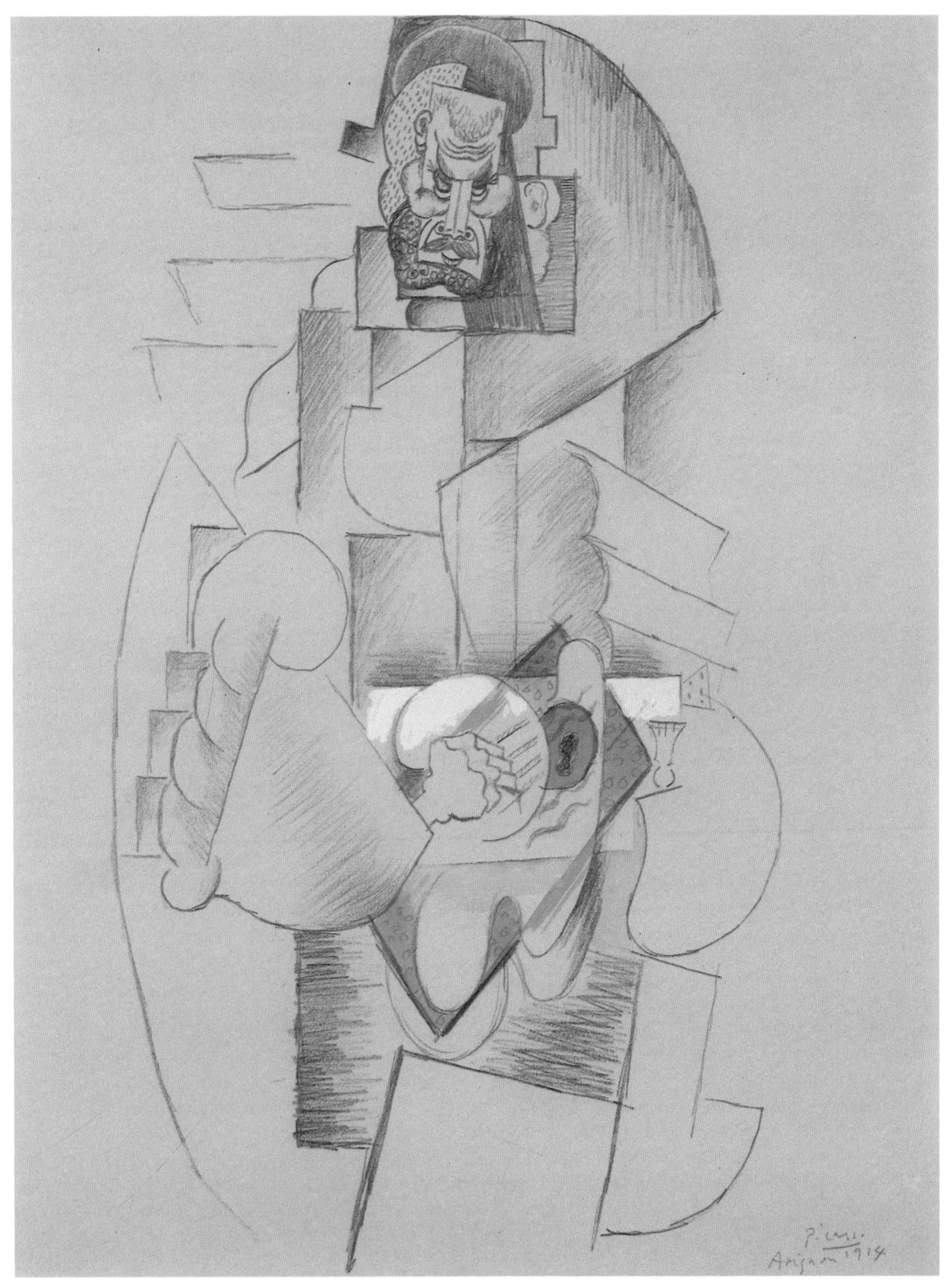

64 PABLO PICASSO
(Bärtiger Mann, Gitarre spielend; Bearded Man Playing a Guitar) 1914

sächlich gehört das Blatt hier zu einer grossen Gruppe verwandter Zeichnungen, die 1914 entstanden sind, sitzende Männer zum Thema haben und unterschiedliche Grade von Stilisierung oder Abstraktion aufweisen. Auf dieser Zeichnung bemerkt man, zum Beispiel, die Verformung des Arms zu einem sich in die Länge ziehenden gummi-artigen Glied, das vom Körper der Figur etwas getrennt ist.[152]

Bärtiger Mann, Gitarre spielend weist einen deutlichen Kontrast zwischen dem relativ realistisch gestalteten Kopf des Gitarrespielers und der extremen kubistischen Stilisierung seines Körpers auf.[153] Im *Stilleben mit Pfirsichen und Spielkarten* besteht eine Spannung zwischen den sanft modellierten Pfirsichen links und den groben, kaum nuancierten Umrissen des Glases rechts.[154] Cooper hat sich denn auch zum Zusammenspiel von realistischen Details mit einer Stilisierung im Sinne des synthetischen Kubismus, wie es die Werke Picassos und Braques aus den Jahren 1913–14 aufweisen, geäussert.[155]

In Coopers 1967 erschienener umfassender Studie *Picasso, Theatre* waren *Frau und Harlekin* von 1915–16 und *Pierrot und Harlekin* von 1920 abgebildet (Nr. 65 und 71). Diese Werke spiegeln, wie auch der *Pierrot* von 1918 (Nr. 70)[156], Picassos starkes Interesse am Theater und an dessen Tradition. Die Figur des Harlekin hatte gewissermassen immer die Funktion eines Alter ego. Einer der vielen Faktoren, die Picassos Entscheid, mit Cocteau 1917 an *Parade* mitzuarbeiten, beeinflussten, war seine erneute Beschäftigung mit der Figur des Harlekins.[157] Nach seiner Arbeit für Diaghilew und nachdem er sich während eines Italienaufenthalts für die Commedia dell'arte begeistert hatte, spielten Harlekin, Pulcinella und die melancholische Figur des Pierrot, die oft zusammen beim Ständchen, beim Spiel auf der Bühne oder mit Instrumenten gesehen sind, eine noch grössere Rolle in Picassos Schaffen. Das Blatt *Pierrot und Harlekin* ist typisch für eine Serie von Gouachen mit Commedia dell'arte-Szenen, welche 1920 in Juan-les-Pins entstand. Cooper kommentiert eine Anzahl

Cards, there is a tension between the softly modelled peaches to the left and the crudely unnuanced profile of the glass to the right.[154] Indeed, Cooper has remarked on the interplay between Synthetic Cubist stylization and naturalistic details in the works of both Picasso and Braque in 1913–1914.[155]

Cooper's copious study, *Picasso Théâtre,* which appeared in 1967, included as illustrations, *Woman and Harlequin,* 1915–16 (No. 65) and *Pierrot and Harlequin,* 1920 (No. 71). These works, as well as *Pierrot* (No. 70)[156] reflect Picasso's intense interest in the tradition of the theater. The figure of the harlequin had always functioned as a type of alter ego. Among the many factors which influenced Picasso's decision to agree to Cocteau's proposal to collaborate on *Parade* in 1917 was his renewed preoccupation with the figure of the harlequin.[157] Subsequent to his involvement with Diaghilev, and inspired by his viewings of *Commedia dell'Arte* performances in Italy, the melancholy figure of Pierrot, as well as Harlequin and Pulcinella, play an even more important role in his work, often depicted together, serenading, performing, playing instruments. *Pierrot and Harlequin* is typical of a series of gouaches depicting *Commedia dell'Arte* subjects which Picasso depicted at Juan les Pins in 1920. Cooper comments on the series of works which followed the designs for *Pulcinella* in 1920:

> *Il est encore plus fascinant de suivre les post-scriptum à Pulcinella qui, pour la plupart, prennent la forme d'une suite de petites gouaches très colorées exécutées dans un style cubiste synthétique. Quelques-unes nous montrent Polichinelle, une guitare à la main, saluant devant le rideau, alors que d'autres, dans lesquelles Pierrot et Arlequin apparaissent ensemble, assis à une table ou jouant de leurs instruments de musique, sont d'une plus grande importance parce qu'elles sont un maillon conduisant directement à ces deux chefs-d'œuvre du cubisme synthétique, les deux versions des Trois Musiciens (1921).*[158]

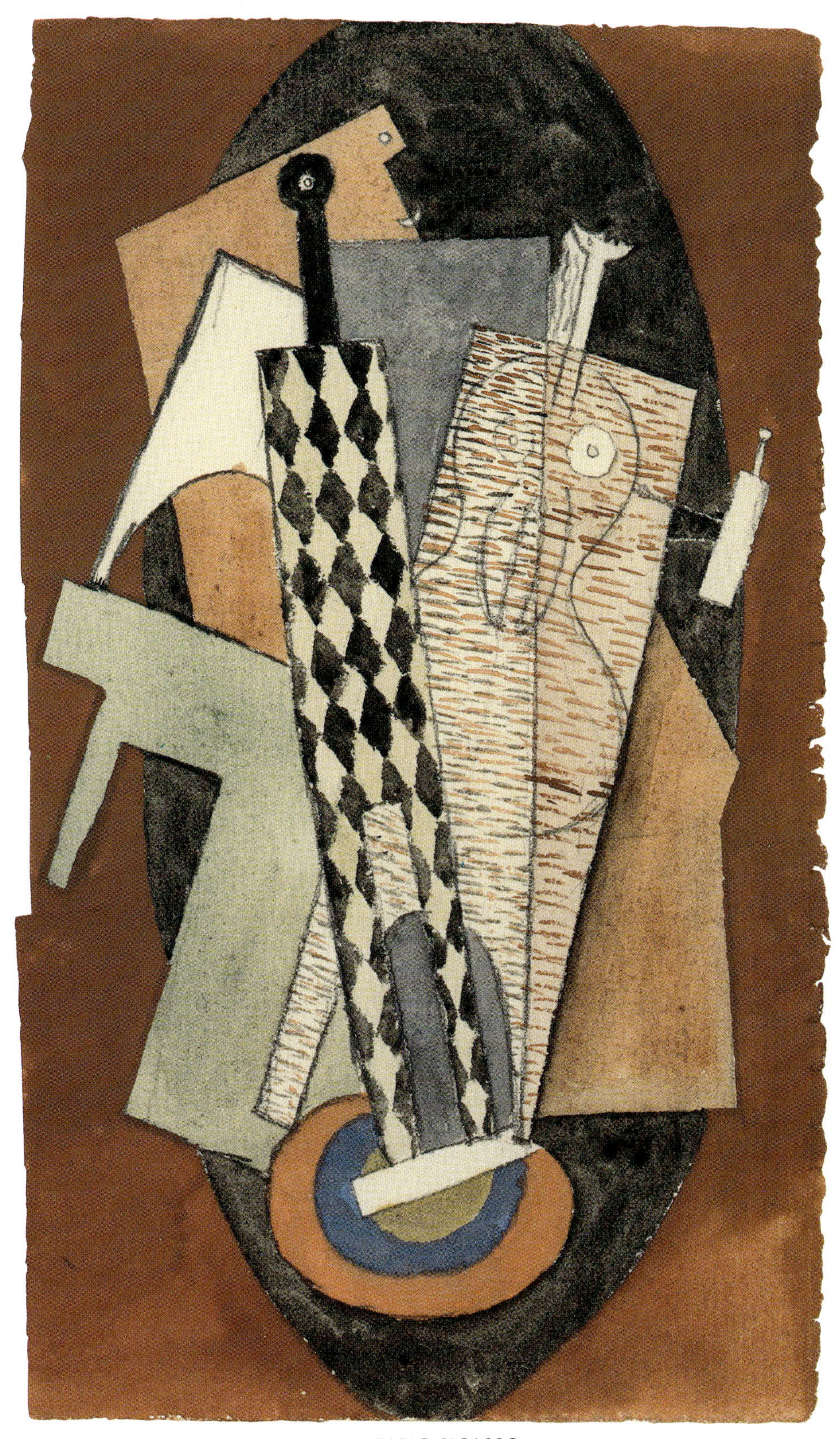

65 PABLO PICASSO
(Frau und Harlekin; Woman and Harlequin) 1915

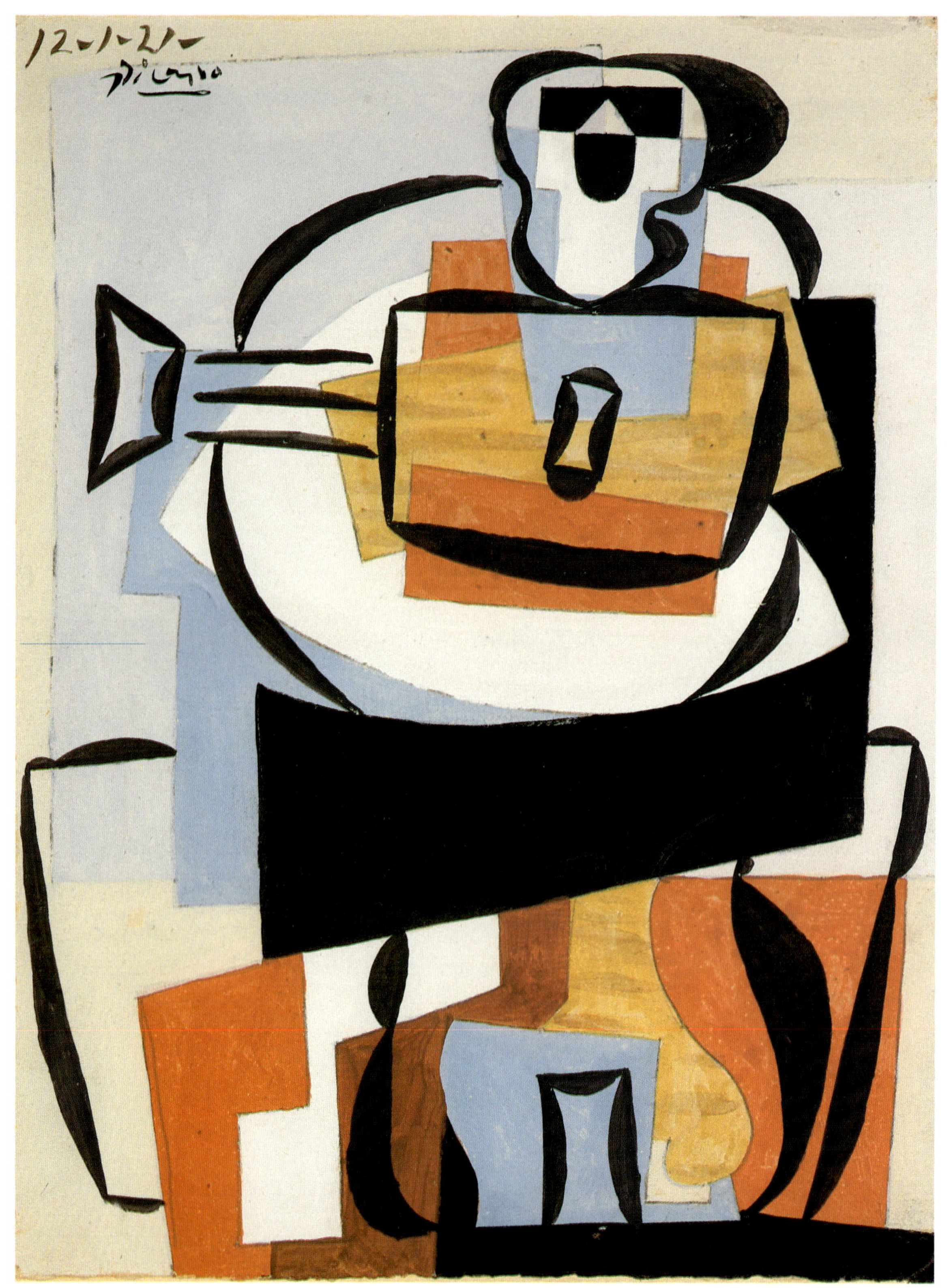

73 PABLO PICASSO
(Stilleben mit Mandoline auf einem Tisch; Still-life with Mandolin on a Guéridon) 1921

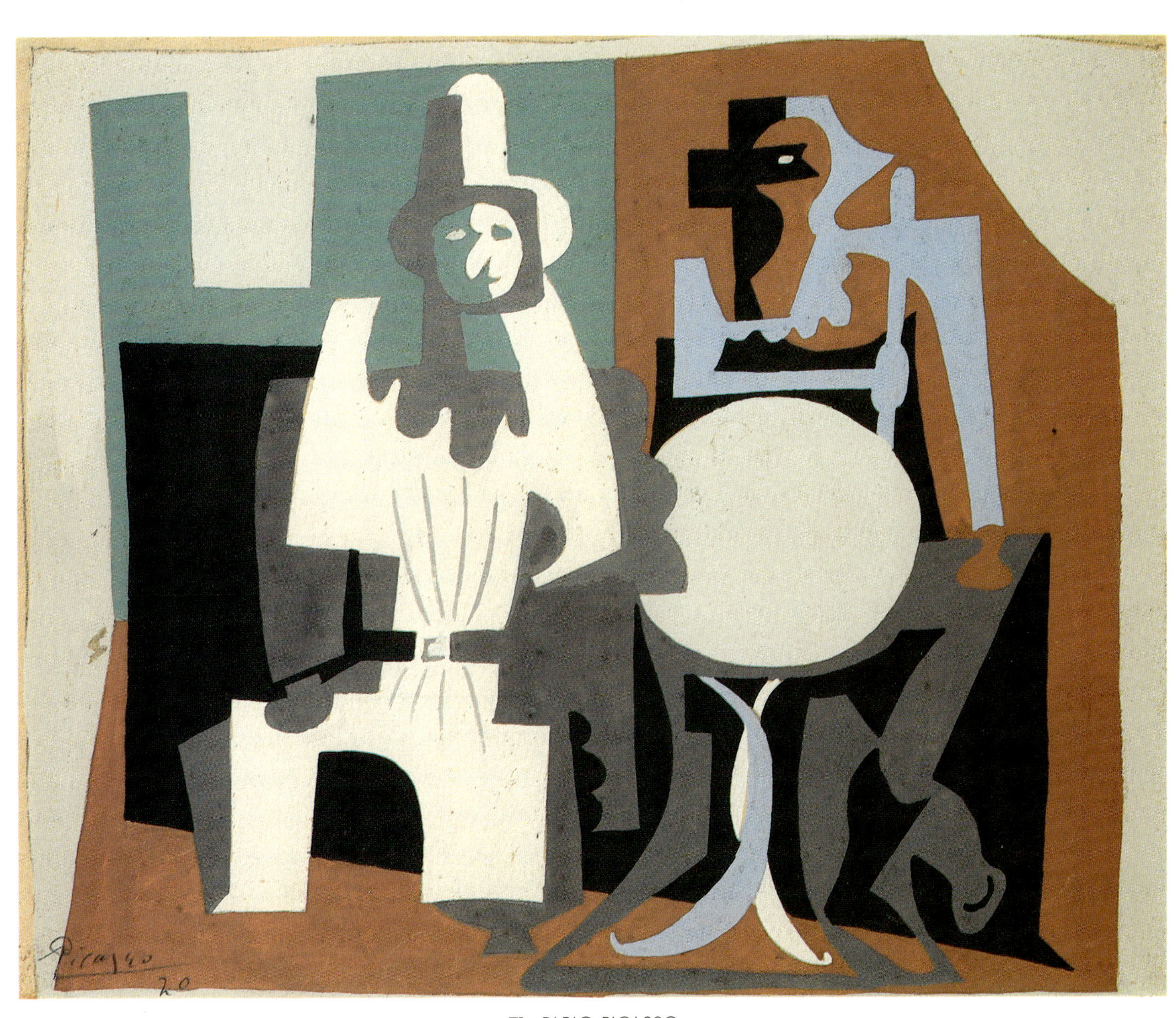

71 PABLO PICASSO
(Pierrot und Harlekin; Pierrot and Harlequin) 1920

Werke, die Picasso nach den Bühnenbildern und Kostümentwürfen zu *Pulcinella*, 1920, schuf:

> *Noch faszinierender ist es zu verfolgen, was nach Pulcinella entstand: es war vor allem eine Serie von sehr farbigen kleinformatigen Gouachen im Stil des synthetischen Kubismus. Einige zeigen uns Pulcinella, die Gitarre in der Hand, sich vor dem Vorhang verbeugend; wichtiger sind hingegen andere, auf denen Pierrot und Harlekin zusammen erscheinen, an einem Tisch sitzen oder ihre Musikinstrumente spielen, denn sie bilden das direkte Bindeglied zu jenen Hauptwerken des synthetischen Kubismus, wie sie die zwei Versionen der Drei Musiker (1921) darstellen.*[158]

Kompositionell besteht ein enger Zusammenhang zwischen *Frau und Harlekin* und dem *Harlekin*[159] im Museum of Modern Art in New York, jenem monumentalen Werk, das eine Schlüsselstellung in Picassos Entwicklung eines synthetisch-kubistischen Idioms einnimmt. Beiden gemeinsam sind Details wie das Rautenmuster des Harlekinkostüms und die periskop-artige Stilisierung von Kopf und Hals sowie die allgemeine Kompositionstechnik des Schichtens flacher Spielkarten-Formen in raumloser Umgebung. Ebenfalls exemplarisch für Picassos synthetischen Kubismus ist das *Stilleben mit Mandoline auf einem Tisch* (Nr. 73). Farbflächen in Aquarell und Gouache und breite kalligraphische Bänder in schwarzer Gouache ahmen die flächigen Elemente des Papier collé nach.

Eine verblüffende Stil-Divergenz kennzeichnet Picassos Werk gegen 1910 und in den zwanziger Jahren.[160] In der Bleistiftzeichnung des *Pierrot* verwendet Picasso wieder realistische Mittel und zeichnet, wie es scheint, gleichzeitig in zwei verschiedenen linearen Stilen. Das Gesicht ist stark gearbeitet, die Rückseite des Blattes zeigt denn auch die tiefen Spuren des Stifts. Dieses Pierrotgesicht besitzt übrigens spezifische Porträtqualität.[161] Im Gegensatz zum Kopf sind der Körper der Figur, die ineinandergelegten Hände und besonders die Falten des Gewands in viel weicherem fliessendem Duktus ausgeführt.

Compositionally, *Woman and Harlequin* relates to the *Harlequin*[159], in the Museum of Modern Art, New York, that monumental work which marks a turning point in Picasso's evolution of a Synthetic Cubist idiom. They share details such as the lozenge shaped decoration of the harlequin's costume, the periscope stylization of that figure's head and neck, as well as the more general compositional technique of layering of flat playing card forms in a spaceless environment. *Still-life with Mandolin on a Gueridon* (No. 73) is also exemplary of Picasso's Synthetic Cubism. Flat color planes of watercolor and gouache, and broad calligraphic ribbons of black gouache imitate the flat elements of *papier collé*.

An extraordinary divergence in styles characterizes Picasso's work during the late teens and twenties.[160] In the pencil drawing of *Pierrot,* Picasso turns to naturalism, juxtaposing, it seems, two different linear styles. The face is heavily worked, the reverse of the paper deeply grooved with the action of the pencil. This Pierrot's face, in fact, has the specific quality of a portrait.[161] In contrast, the figure's body, his clasped hands and especially the folds of his garments are indicated with a less intense, more fluid line.

Cooper comments upon a number of drawings executed between 1919–1920 which indicate a dialogue with Ingres. They are characterized by a pure linearity.

> *Il était aussi, semble-t-il, ému par des souvenirs d'Ingres qui avaient présidé si longtemps sur les jeunes artistes de l'Académie Française à la Villa Médici. Dans de nombreux tableaux et dessins exécutés par Picasso entre 1917 et 1919 – les premiers portraits d'Olga, des auto-portraits et de nombreuses compositions – nous sentons à travers le langage linéaire pur, la régularité des formes et les contours bien définis, un désir évident de mettre ses capacités à l'épreuve dans une rivalité amicale avec Ingres.*[162]

Cooper indicates, as well, the role of Picasso's exposure to Michelangelo and classical art in con-

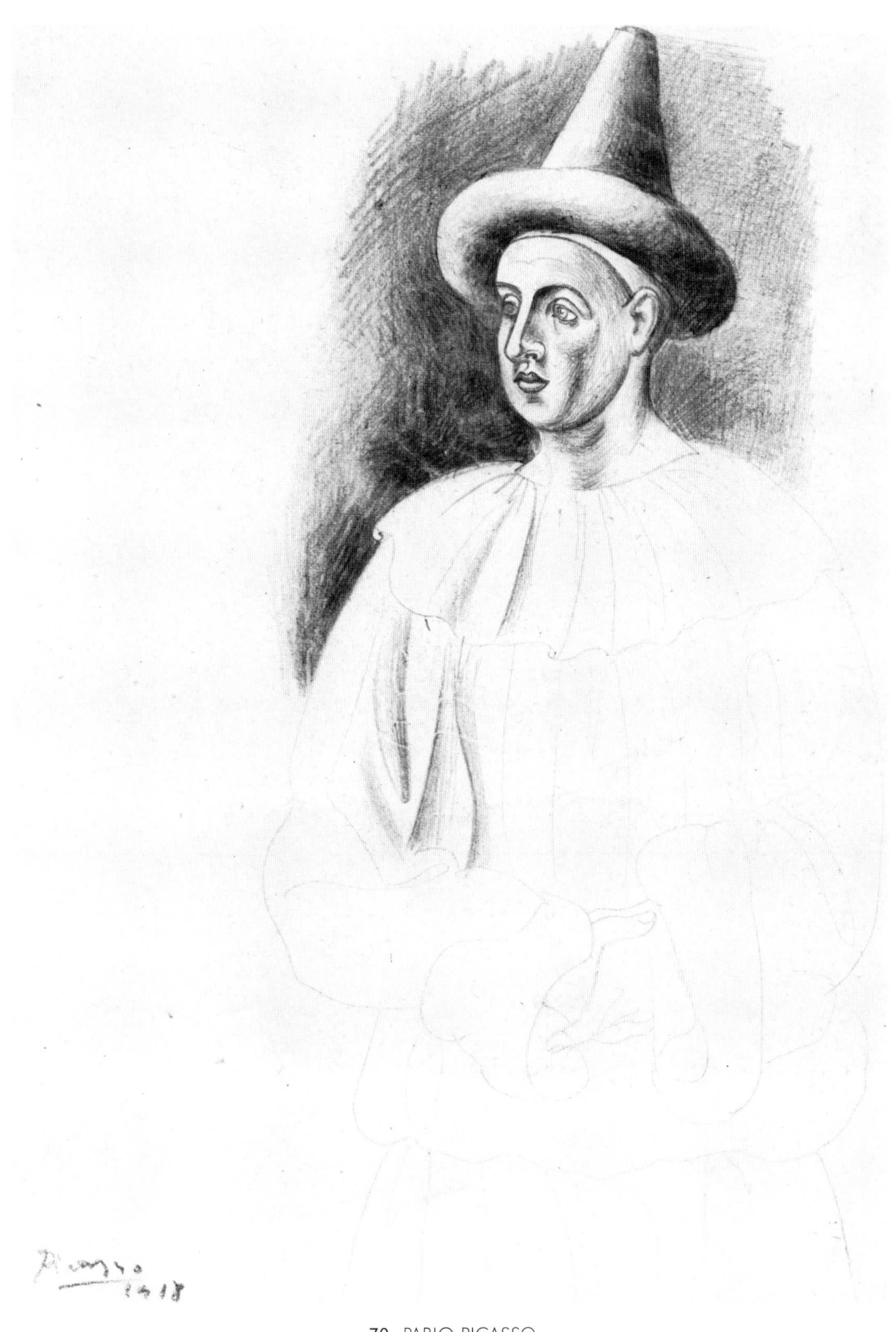

70 PABLO PICASSO
(Pierrot) 1918

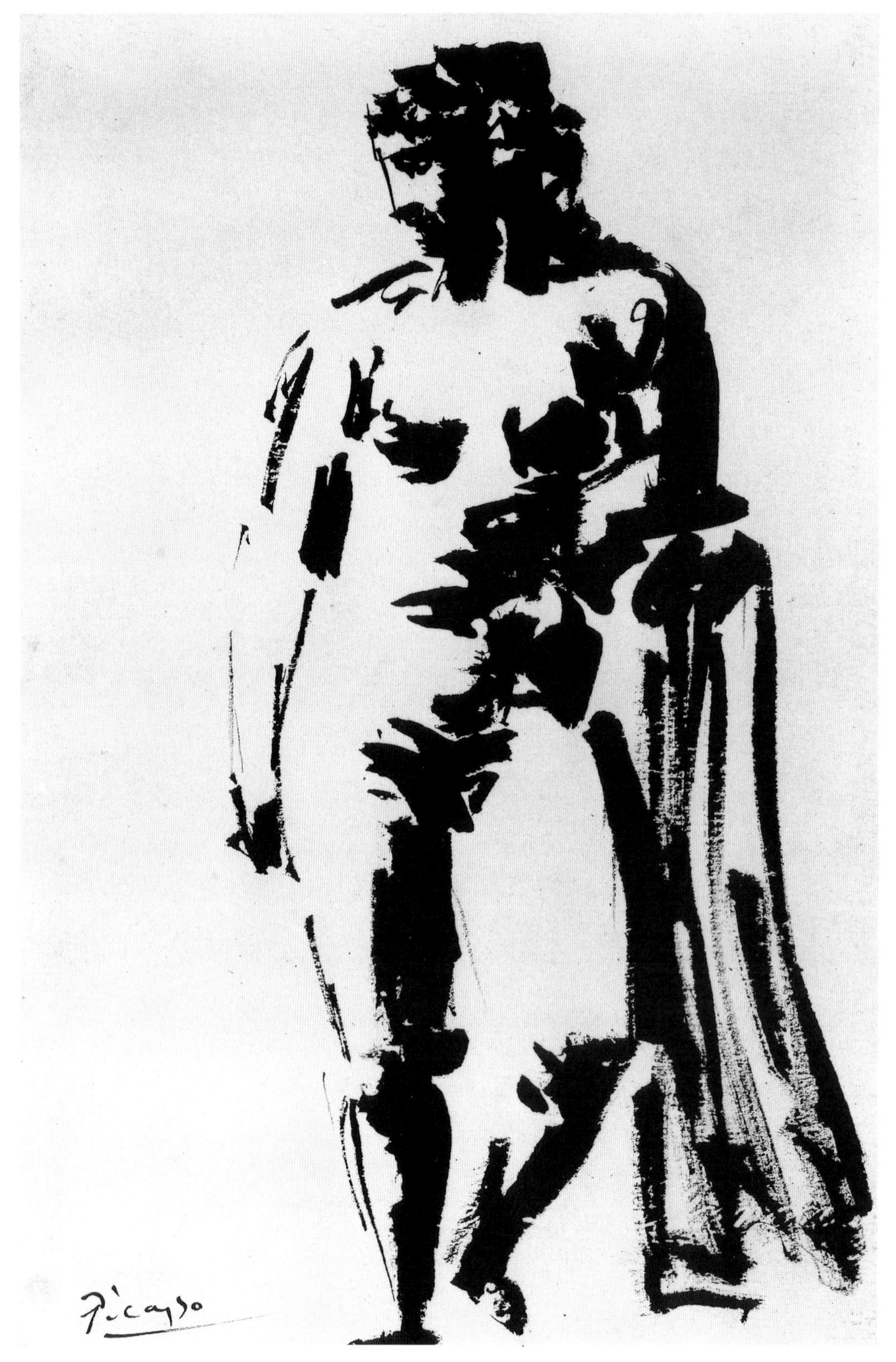

72 PABLO PICASSO
(Stehender weiblicher Akt mit Faltenwurf; Standing Female Nude with Drapery) (1920)

Cooper kommentiert eine Anzahl 1919–20 entstandener Zeichnungen, die einen Dialog mit Ingres verraten; ihr Kennzeichen ist die reine Linearität.

> *Es scheint, dass er auch berührt war von Erinnerungen an Ingres, unter dessen Direktion so viele Stipendiaten der Académie Française in der Villa Medici waren. In zahlreichen Bildern und Zeichnungen der Jahre 1917–1919 – den ersten Porträts von Olga, den Selbstporträts und den übrigen Arbeiten – spüren wir in der Sprache strenger Linearität, in der Regelmässigkeit der Formen und im exakt definierten Kontur ein offensichtliches Verlangen, zum Beweis seiner Fähigkeiten in freundschaftlichen Wettbewerb mit Ingres zu treten.*[162]

Cooper weist auch darauf hin, dass eine Beschäftigung mit Michelangelo und klassischer Kunst überhaupt Picasso zu «neuer geistiger Grösse, zu einer Reinheit des Stils und zu einem ungekünstelten Realismus»[163] gebracht habe. Das Sujet wie seine bündige Formulierung im Blatt *Stehender weiblicher Akt mit Faltenwurf* (Nr. 72) mögen typisch sein für solches Zusammenkommen von Einflüssen.

Ingres wirkt wohl auch noch in der delikaten Porträtzeichnung von Eugenia Errazuriz von 1918 (Nr. 69) nach, welche Cooper in *Pour Eugenia, Une suite de 24 dessins inédits, exécutés en 1918* aufgenommen hat.[164] Diese Publikation, in der er das Thema Theater in Picassos Werk verfolgte, war vielleicht die Verwirklichung eines Projekts, das Cooper schon um 1953 ins Auge fasste. Am 10. April dieses Jahres schrieb er an Curt Valentin, er wolle sich mit Picasso verabreden, um ein «sehr schönes Skizzenbuch» abzuholen. Später erwähnt Cooper, wieder in einem – undatierten – Brief an Valentin, ein paar «herrliche Skizzenbücher von 1918–20, voller Ballettänzerinnen und ähnlichem, was sich sehr gut [für eine Publikation] eignen würde, weil sie nicht zu gross sind. In einigen hat es auch kubistische Zeichnungen und solche der Blauen Periode.»[165]

Cooper erläutert die wichtige Rolle, welche Eugenia Errazuriz in Picassos Leben im Zeitraum von 1917 bis tributing to "une nouvelle grandeur de conception, une pureté stylistique, et un naturalisme sans affectation."[163] The subject, as well as the stylistic concision of *Standing Female Nude with Drapery* (No. 72) may be exemplary of this confluence of influences.

The impact of Ingres is perhaps evident in the delicate portrait drawing of Madame Eugenia Errazuriz, 1918 (No. 69). This drawing was included in Cooper's *Pour Eugenia, Une suite de 24 dessins inédits exécutées en 1918.*[164] In this publication, Cooper pursued the theme of the theater in Picasso's work. This may have been the fulfillment of a project that Cooper envisioned as early as 1953. On April 10, 1953 he wrote to Curt Valentin about making a date with Picasso to go fetch a "really fine notebook" ... Subsequently, in an undated letter to Valentin, Cooper talks of some "lovely sketchbooks of 1918–20 full of ballet dancers and the like which would do perfectly because they are not too big. There are some which have Blue period and Cubist drawings in them as well."[165]

Cooper explains the important role which Mme. Errazuriz played in Picasso's life from 1917 through 1920, pulling him from his bohemian existence into glamorous society. In particular, Cooper stresses the importance of this new circle of acquaintances in terms of his introduction to the prestigious dealer Paul Rosenberg. Picasso made Errazuriz' acquaintance in June 1917 in Madrid through Diaghilev whom she had known since 1912. This drawing and the others published in 1976 commemorate the three-month long honey moon which Picasso and Olga Koklova spent together at Mme. Errazuriz's Villa la Mimoseraie in Biarritz. According to Picasso, the drawings which were given to Mme. Errazuriz as a gift upon Picasso's departure in September 1918, formed three identifiable groups: scenes from the theater and circus; bathers; and caricatures. Picasso also decorated a room in her villa with neo-classical scenes.[166]

In 1957, Cooper wrote a brief, friendly introduction for an exhibition at Galerie Berggruen in Paris, *Dora Maar, paysages.* Cooper owned a few small water-

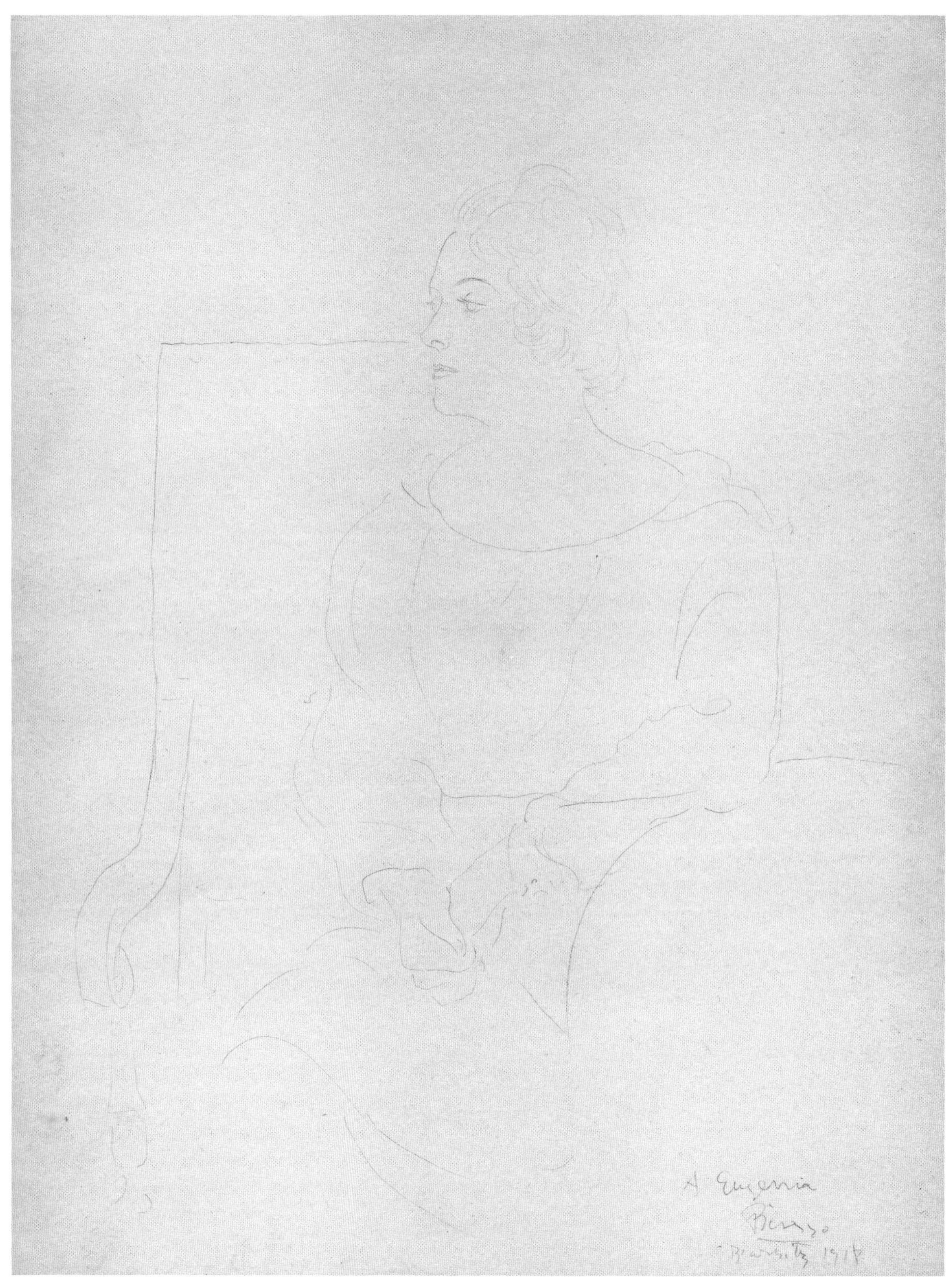

69 PABLO PICASSO
(Porträt Madame Eugenia Errazuriz; Portrait of Mme Eugenia Errazuriz) 1918

1920 spielte, indem sie ihn aus seiner Bohémien-Existenz heraus- und in die grosse Gesellschaft brachte. Cooper betont die Bedeutung dieser neuen Kreise insofern, als Picasso dadurch mit dem renommierten Kunsthändler Paul Rosenberg in Kontakt kam. Der Künstler traf Eugenia Errazuriz im Juni 1917 in Madrid durch die Vermittlung von Diaghilew, den diese schon seit 1912 kannte. Die Zeichnung hier, wie auch die übrigen 1976 publizierten, erinnern an die drei Monate dauernden Flitterwochen, die Picasso und Olga Koklova in La Mimoseraie, der Errazuriz-Villa in Biaritz, verbrachten. Nach Picasso bildeten die Zeichnungen, die er bei seiner Abreise im September 1918 der Gastgeberin schenkte, drei Gruppen: Theater- und Zirkusszenen, Badende und Karikaturen. Picasso schmückte auch einen Raum ihrer Villa mit neoklassizistischen Szenen aus.[166]

1957 schrieb Cooper eine kurze und wohlwollende Einführung zur Ausstellung *Dora Maar, paysages* in der Galerie Berggruen, Paris. Er besass auch einige kleine Aquarelle von ihr. Dora Maar war Picassos Geliebte in den dreissiger Jahren. *Knabe mit Eislutscher* (Nr. 74) entstand am 23. Juli 1938; diesen Sommer verbrachte Picasso mit Dora Maar sowie Paul und Nusch Eluard in Mougins bei Cannes. Dem frischen Bild des Knaben, der an einem Eis lutscht, entspricht der spontane Duktus der Kohlezeichnung. Porträts von Dora Maar und andere Versionen des Eiscreme-Themas machen einen gewichtigen Teil von Picassos Schaffen in diesem Sommer aus.[167]

Die nächste Gruppe von Zeichnungen, *Liegender weiblicher Akt* vom 24. Dezember 1961, *Achilles* vom 28. Oktober 1962, *Reiter* vom 1. November 1962 sowie die drei Zeichnungen nach Manets *Déjeuner sur l'Herbe* mit den Daten 14., 16. Juni und 1. August 1962 (Nr. 75, 79, 80, 76, 77 und 78) sind wichtige Dokumente zweier grosser Projekte, die Cooper sich in den sechziger Jahren vorgenommen hatte: die Gestaltung der Loggia-Wand im Garten von Schloss Castille mit den eben genannten Zeichnungen (der letzten ausgenommen) und seine grosse Studie über Picassos zahl-

colors by Dora Maar, who had been Picasso's mistress in the 1930s. *Boy with a popsicle,* dates from July 23, 1938, (No. 74) during Picasso's summer in Mougins in the hills near Cannes, with Dora Maar and Paul and Nusch Eluard. Here the fresh image of the boy eating an ice cream on a stick is matched by the spontaneity of Picasso's charcoal technique. Portraits of Dora Maar or other versions of the ice cream theme, figure significantly in Picasso's output from this summer.[167]

The next group of drawings, *Reclining Female Nude,* 24 December 1961; *Achilles,* 28 October, 1962; *Cavalier,* 1 November 1962; and the three drawings after Manet's *Déjeuner sur l'Herbe,* dated 14th June 1962, the 16th June 1962, and the 1st of August 1962 (Nos. 75, 79, 80, 76, 77, 78) are important documents of two major projects undertaken by Cooper in the sixties: the loggia wall in the garden at the Château de Castille decorated with these same works by Picasso (All except the last drawing listed here were included on this wall); and his major study of Picasso's many (27 paintings, 150 drawings and related prints) variations on Manet's *Déjeuner sur l'Herbe,* Paris, Editions cercle d'art, 1962.[168]

Five of the drawings included in this exhibition were reproduced in enlarged format on Cooper's loggia wall at the Château de Castille. They were executed by means of sandblasting on reinforced concrete imbedded with grey and black pebbles, a technique termed *Betograve* developed by the Nowegian architect, Erling Viksjö in the early 1950s, and explored by the artist Carl Nesjar. This technique had been used in 1961 to produce a frieze by Picasso with subjects from Catalan folklore on the facade (as well as some smaller interior panels) of the College of Catalan Architects in Barcelona. On May 4, 1962 Picasso responded to Cooper's enthusiasm about the friezes in Barcelona by proposing that the garden wall at the Château de Castille in Argilliers be decorated in the same manner. The wall and adjacent garden structure were rebuilt by the Norwegian architect, Leif Johannessen. On November 25, 1962, Picasso and Cooper lunched

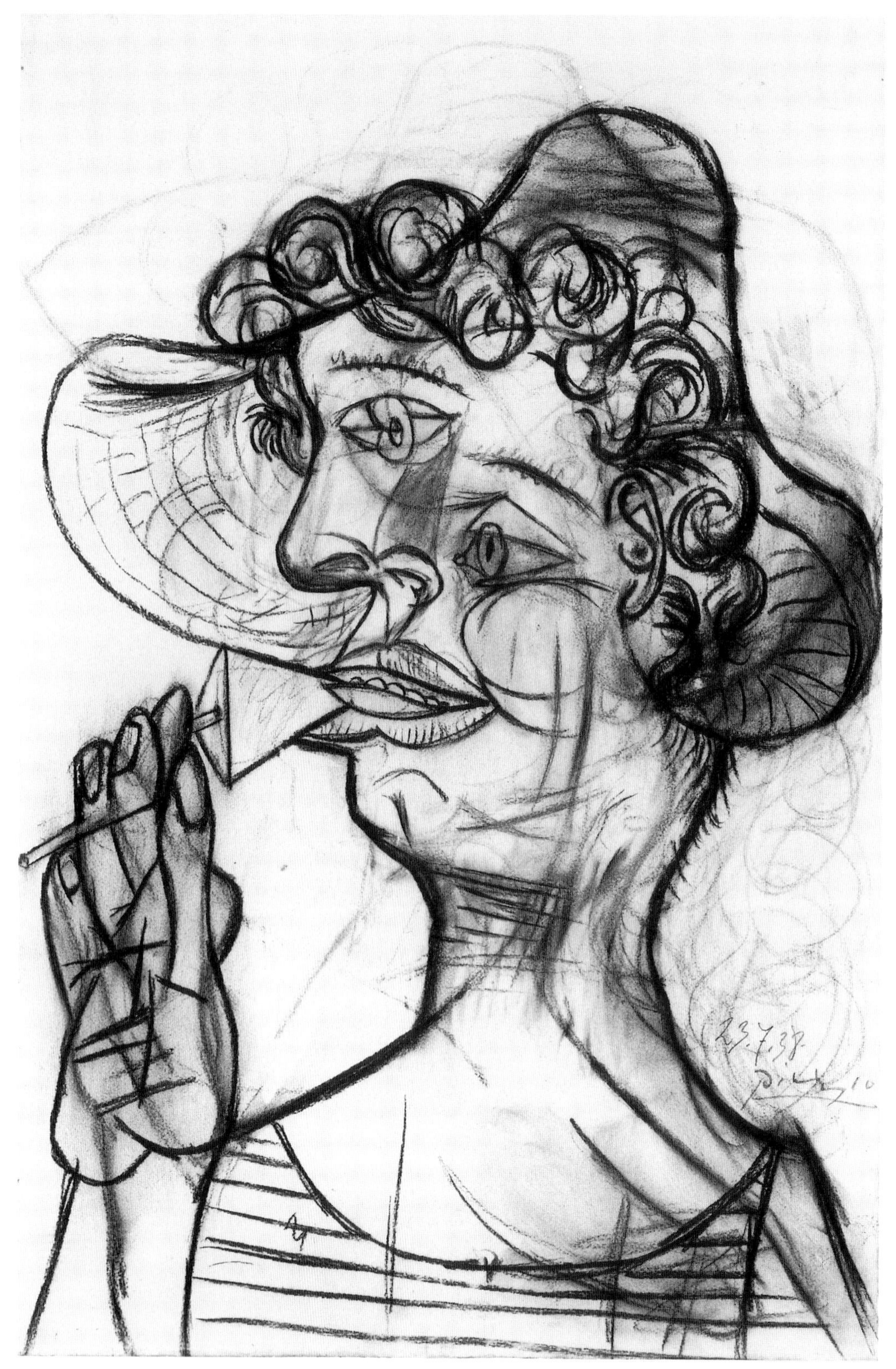

74 PABLO PICASSO
(Knabe mit Eis-Lutscher; Boy with a Popsicle) 1938

reiche, 27 Bilder, 150 Zeichnungen und Graphik umfassende Variationen zu Manets *Déjeuner sur l'Herbe*, erschienen 1962 in den Editions cercle d'art, Paris.[168]

Fünf dieser Zeichnungen, die auch in dieser Ausstellung zu sehen sind, wurden in vergrössertem Massstab mittels Sandstrahlgebläse und Eisenbeton, in den graue und schwarze Kiesel eingelassen waren, auf die Loggia-Wand gebracht, in einer *Betograve* genannten Technik, die vom norwegischen Architekten Erling Viksjø in den fünfziger Jahren entwickelt und vom

together at Nôtre Dame de Vie at Mougins and chose the drawings from the notebooks, with the artist favoring bold black and white, horizontal, compositions which would be elegantly accomodated to the structure of the wall and the *Betograve* technique. The project was completed by April 1963, and inaugurated with a fête attended by Picasso and Jacqueline on August 25, 1963, at which time Picasso dedicated the five original drawings as well as inscribed a page in Cooper's illustrated record on the making of the wall at

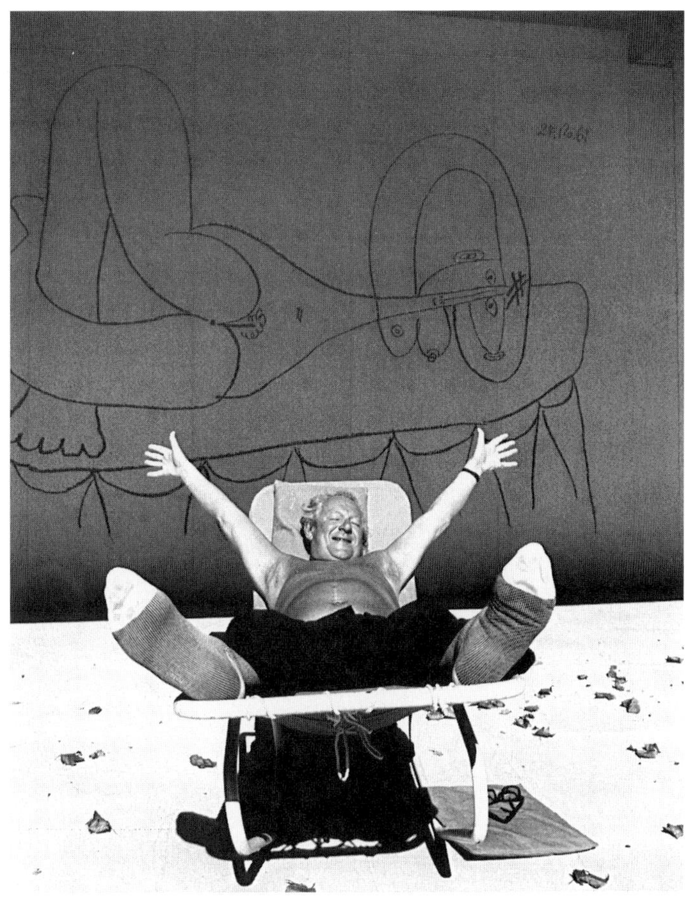

Château de Castille, nach 1963, Cooper vor der Loggia-Wand, welche mit Picasso's *Liegendem weiblichen Akt* dekoriert ist (No.75).

Château de Castille, after 1963, Cooper before loggia wall, decorated with Picasso's *Reclining female nude* (No.75).

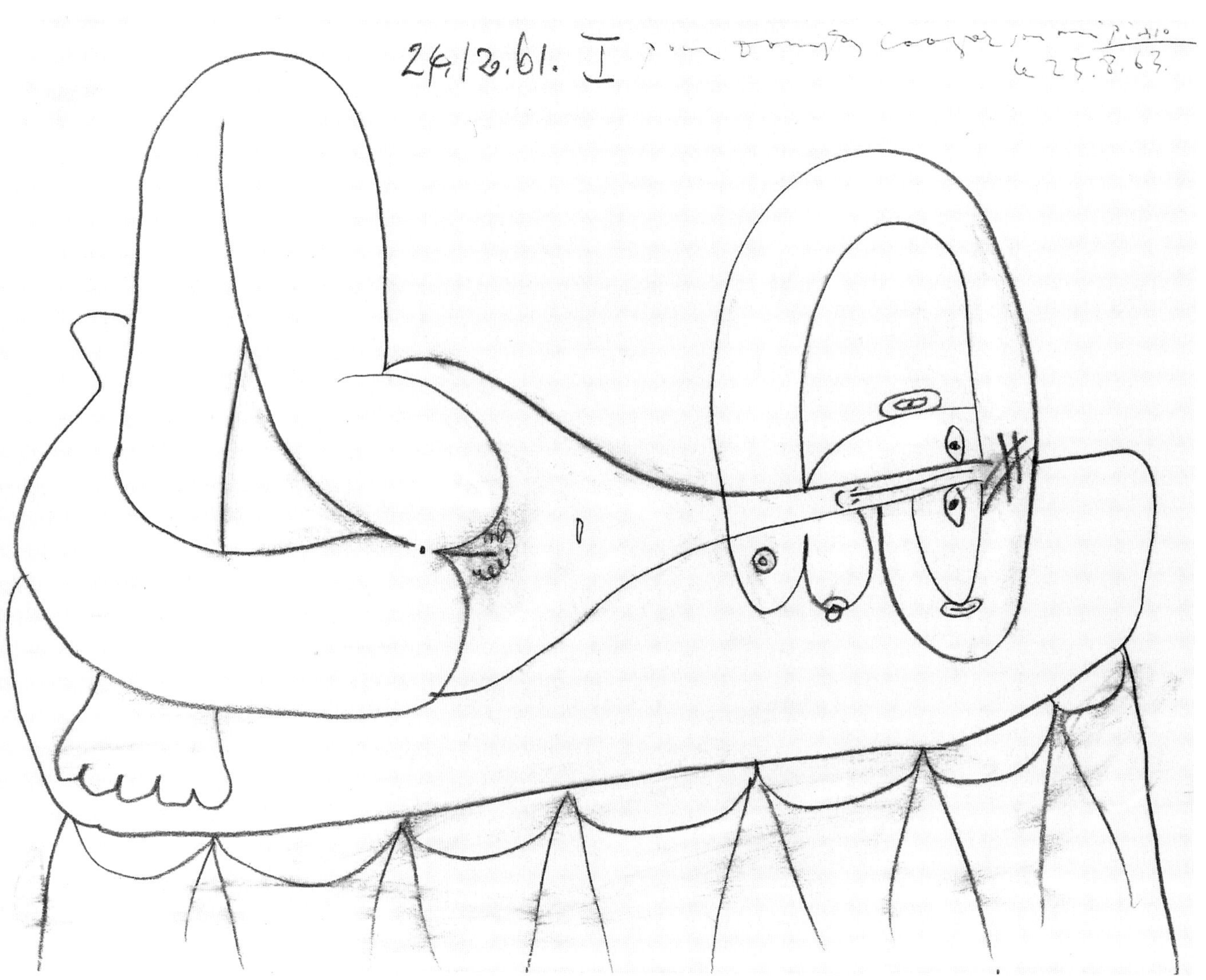

75 PABLO PICASSO
(Liegender weiblicher Akt; Reclining Female Nude) 1961

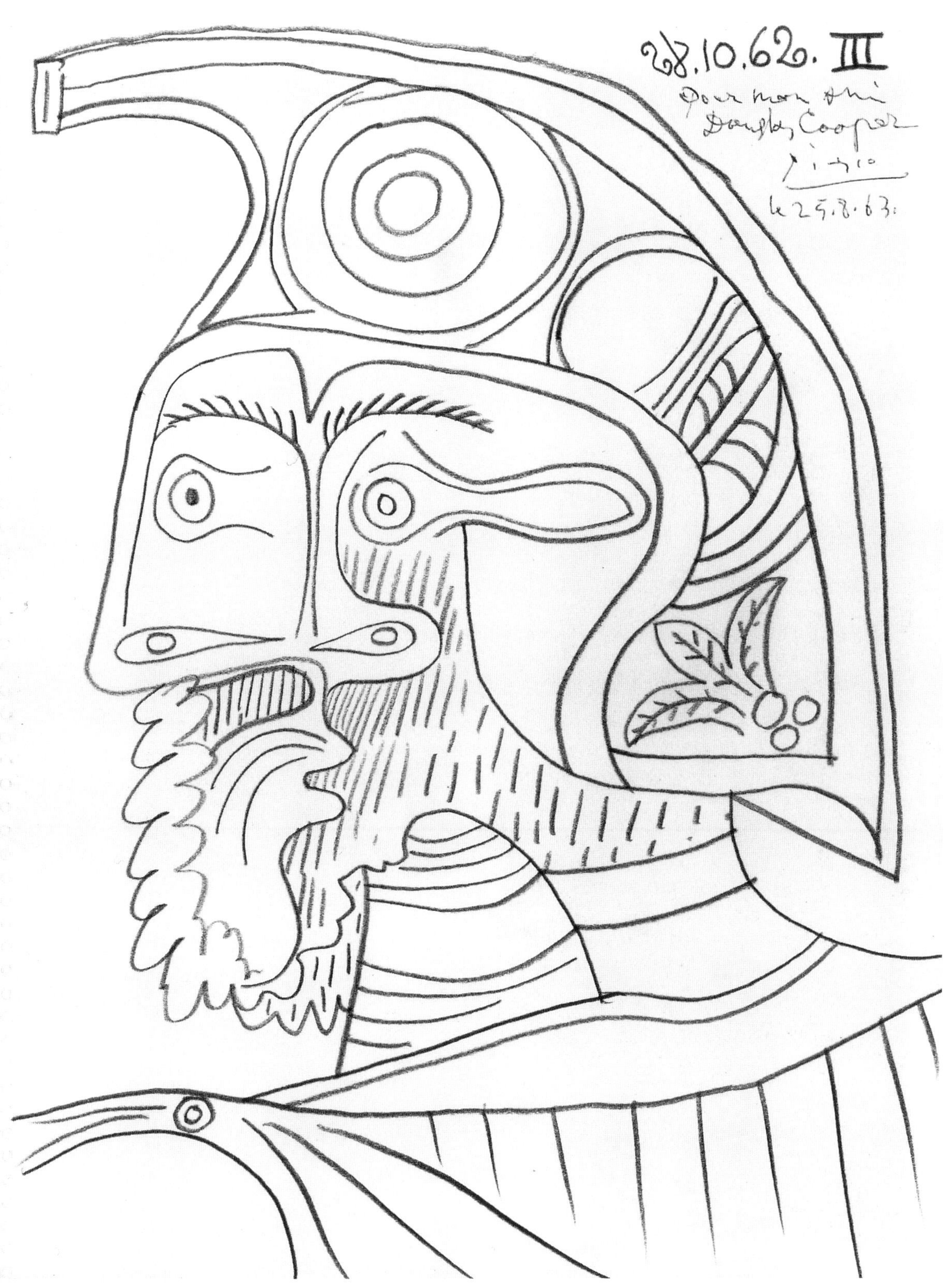

79 PABLO PICASSO
(Achilles) 1962

Künstler Carl Nesjar erstmals angewendet wurde. Zum Einsatz war sie schon in Picassos Fries mit Themen aus dem katalanischen Volkstum auf der Fassade (wie auch auf kleineren Innenwandteilen) des Colegio de arquitectos de Cataluña in Barcelona gekommen. Die Antwort Picassos auf Coopers Begeisterung über diesen Fries war der Vorschlag vom 4. Mai 1962, die Loggia-Wand auf Schloss Castille in derselben Art zu gestalten. Die Wand, wie auch die benachbarten Gartenbauten, wurden daraufhin vom norwegischen Architekten Leif Johannessen neu errichtet. Nach einem Mittagessen am 25. November 1962 in Picassos Haus Notre Dame de Vie in Mougins wählten die beiden die Zeichnungen aus den Skizzenbüchern aus, wobei der Künstler den kühnen schwarz-weissen und querformatigen Kompositionen den Vorzug gab, da sie sich am besten für die Art der Wand und die *Betograve*-Technik eignen würden. Das ganze Unternehmen fand im April 1963 seinen Abschluss. Anlässlich der festlichen Einweihung des Werks am 25. August, an der Picasso und Jacqueline anwesend waren, widmete der Künstler Cooper die Originale der fünf Zeichnungen und trug sich ein in Coopers Dokumentation über die Entstehungs- und Baugeschichte der Wand. Cooper betrachtete dieses Projekt sehr ernsthaft als Beitrag an das kulturelle Erbe Frankreichs, ja Europas. Er war natürlich begeistert von der Möglichkeit, so eng mit Picasso zusammenarbeiten zu können, und vermochte nie, seine Gefühle zu verbergen, wenn er über dieses Erlebnis schrieb: «Ich weiss, dass er auf dem Gebiet der Kunst ein schöpferisches Genie war – zweifellos das einzige wahre Genie (das Wort ist so missbraucht worden, dass es fast keine Bedeutung mehr hat) des 20. Jahrhunderts –, aber auch, was persönliche Beziehungen angeht, erkannte ich deutlicher als je zuvor, dass Picasso nicht nur ein grosser Mensch, sondern auch ein höchst zuverlässiger und aufmerksamer Freund war. Nichts liess er ausser acht, wenn es um sein Werk ging; er dachte auch an die kleinen Details. Er versuchte nie, Schwierigkeiten zu machen, stellte nie zu hohe Forderungen und munterte stets alle auf.»[169]

Castille. Cooper clearly took this project very seriously as a contribution to France's and Europe's cultural heritage. He was, understandably enthusiastic about this opportunity to work so closely with Picasso and wrote about the experience with great emotion: "I know that, on the plane of art, he was an inventive genius – undoubtedly, the only *true* genius (the word is now so much abused that it has virtually lost all significance) of the 20th century – but, on the plane of personal relationships, I came to realize, even more intensely than before, that Picasso was not only a great human being, but also a most reliable and considerate friend. There was no aspect of a problem which he failed to consider when his own work was involved; he even thought about small details. He never tried to create difficulties, his demands were never excessive and he always gave encouragement."[169]

Cooper found in the Déjeuner variations, many of the most important themes which preoccupied Picasso over decades. He organized the works into four major groups: country outing, baignade, night time excursion and classical idyll. Clearly, however, two of the drawings included in the wall at Castille, *Achilles* and *Cavalier,* are not part of the Déjeuner series, but rather, belong to one of two notebooks devoted to another of Picasso's great variations, this time the *Rape of the Sabines* after Poussin and David.[170] In fact, the conjunction of the two series on the wall, is not at all curious, in that Picasso's notebooks from 1962 reveal his exploration of both themes. The third Déjeuner sketch included in this exhibit (No. 78, which was not included on the wall in Castille) perhaps reveals the merging of the two themes, as the pacific idyll is transformed by violence and rape.[171]

It is more than a little tragic, that subsequent to this interaction, which testifies so clearly to Cooper's role as collector, scholar and collaborative friend of the artist, that this relationship should drastically deteriorate. Cooper felt that subsequent realizations of Picasso's sculptures in *Betograve* technique did not reveal the same creative involvement on Picasso's part,

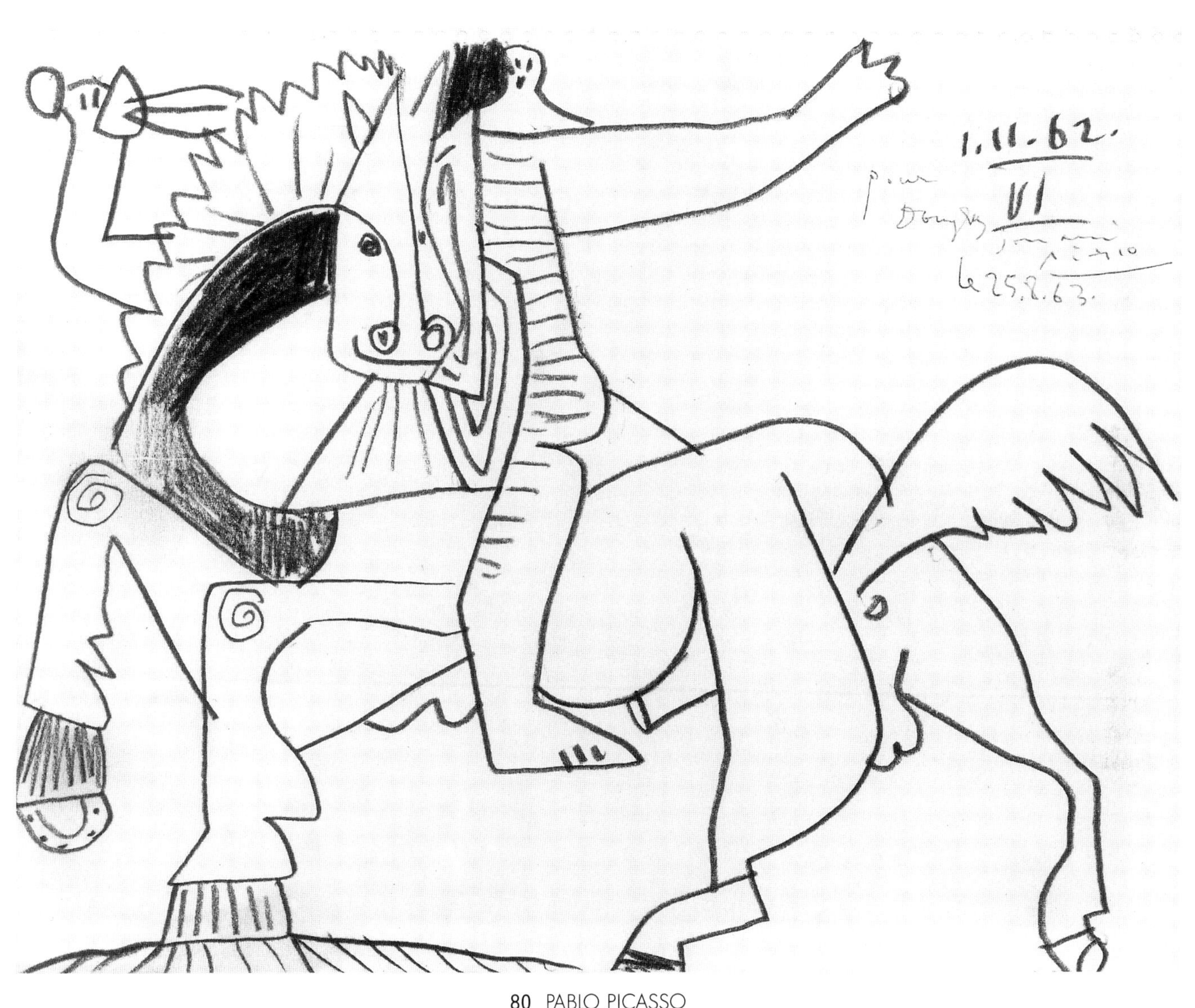

80 PABLO PICASSO
(Reiter; Cavalier) 1962

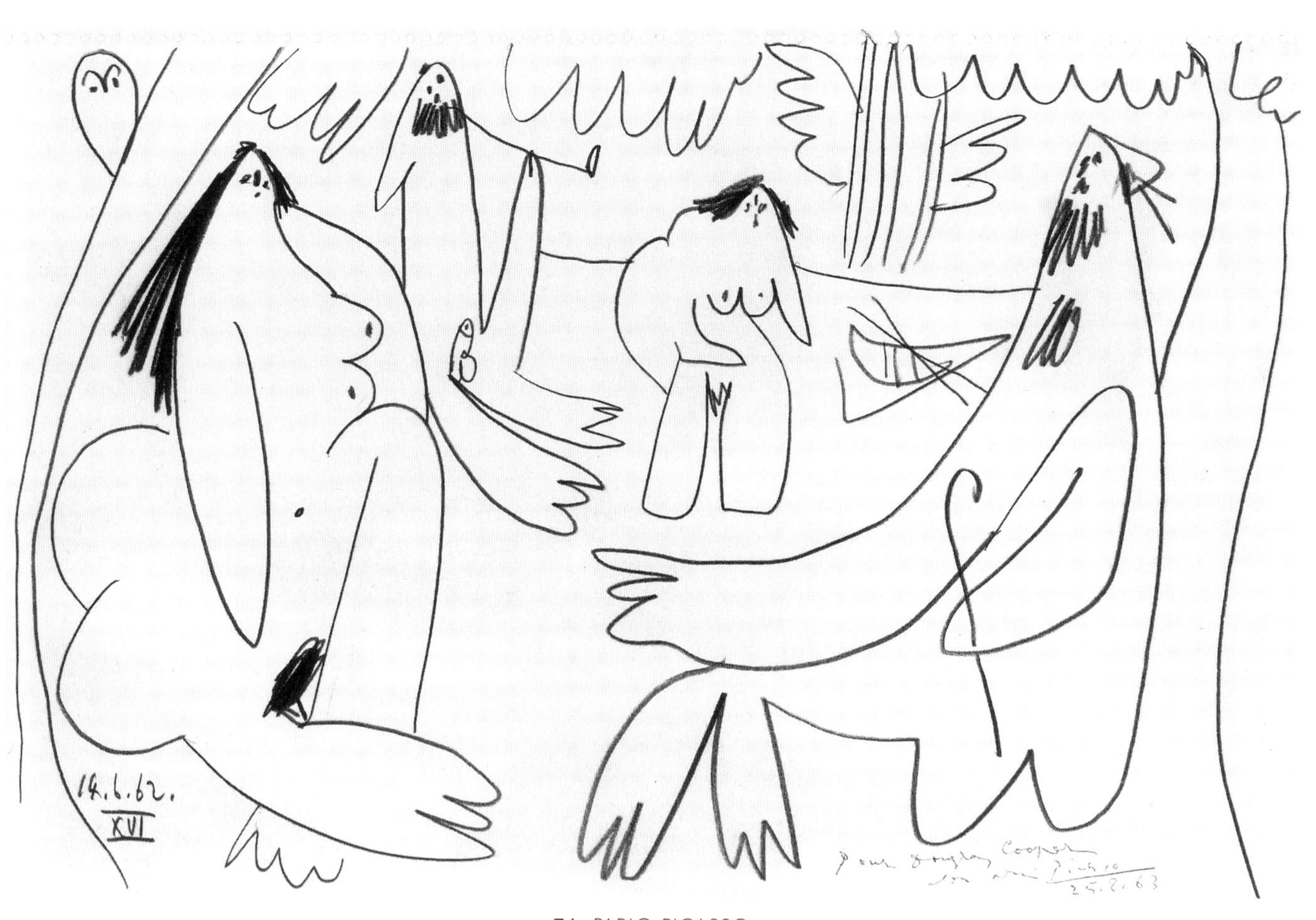

76 PABLO PICASSO
(Zeichnung für «Déjeuner sur l'herbe»; Study for "Déjeuner sur l'herbe") 1962

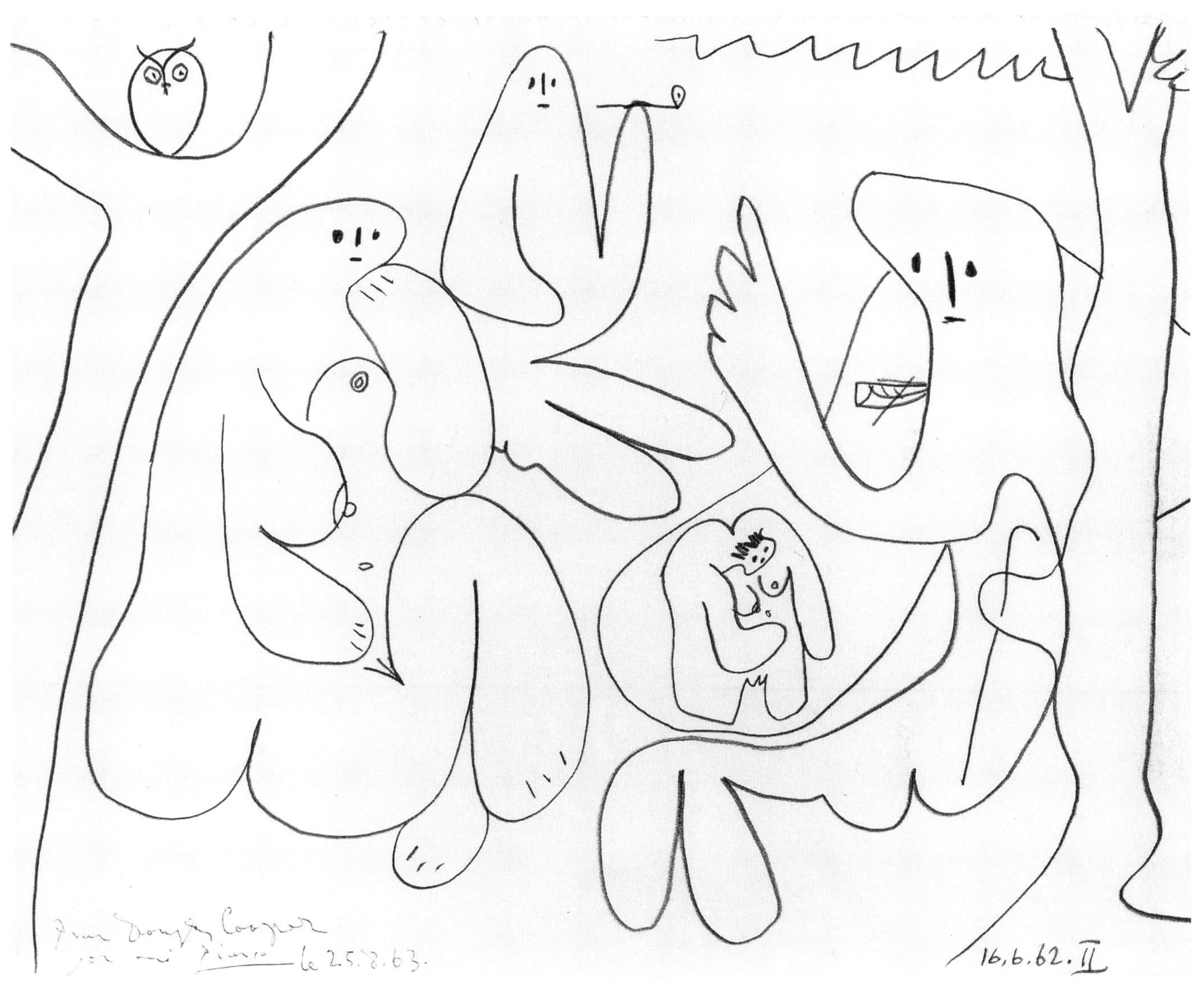

77 PABLO PICASSO
(Zeichnung für «Déjeuner sur l'herbe»; Study for "Déjeuner sur l'herbe") 1962

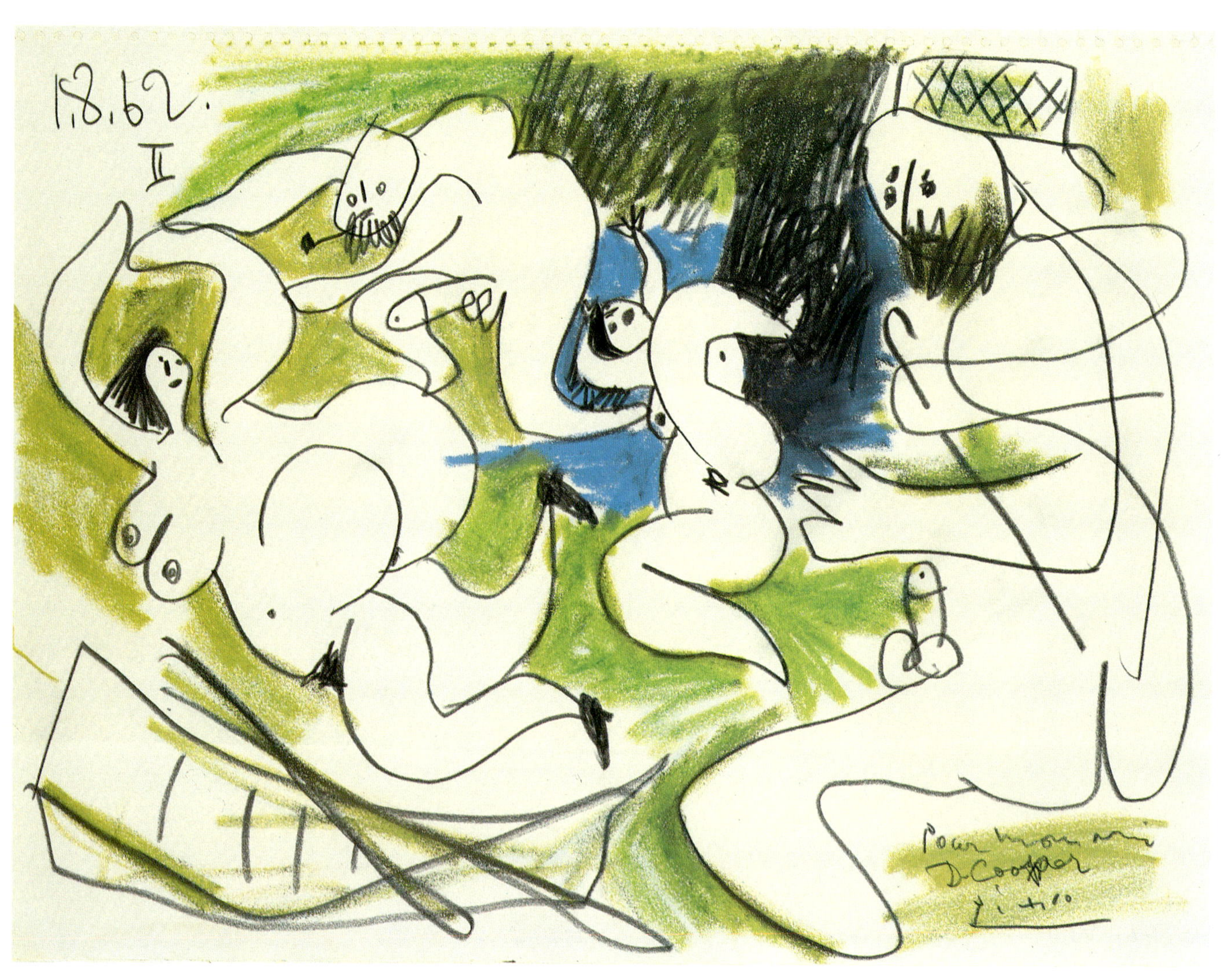

78 PABLO PICASSO
(Zeichnung für «Déjeuner sur l'herbe»; Study for "Déjeuner sur l'herbe") 1962

Cooper fand in den *Déjeuner*-Variationen viele der wichtigsten Motive und Themen, die Picasso über Jahrzehnte hinweg beschäftigten. Er fasste die Werke in vier Hauptgruppen zusammen: Landpartie, Baignade, Nachtausflug und Klassisches Idyll. Natürlich gehören zwei der Zeichnungen für die Wand auf Castille, *Achilles* und *Reiter*, nicht zur *Déjeuner*-Serie, sondern stammen aus einem der zwei Skizzenbücher, in denen noch ein grosses Variationen-Werk von Picasso erdacht wurde: der *Raub der Sabinerinnen* nach Poussin und David.[170] Die Verbindung der zwei Serien auf der Wand ist nicht so abwegig, da in Picassos Skizzenbüchern von 1962 eine Beschäftigung mit beiden Themen ersichtlich ist. Die dritte *Déjeuner*-Skizze in dieser Ausstellung (Nr. 78), welche nicht für die Wand verwendet wurde, zeigt vielleicht die Verschmelzung beider Themen: die Verwandlung des friedlichen Idylls durch Gewalt und Vergewaltigung.[171]

Eher tragisch mutet an, dass sich nach diesem Kontakt, der von Cooper, dem Sammler, Gelehrten und kollaborativen Freund des Künstlers so schönes Zeugnis ablegt, diese Beziehung drastisch verschlechtern sollte. Cooper glaubte, dass in nun folgenden Arbeiten in der *Betograve*-Technik weder dasselbe künstlerische Engagement bei Picasso noch ein vergleichbares Empfindungsvermögen bei Nesjar, der für die technische Seite des Unternehmens zuständig gewesen war, zu sehen sei. Doch die Verschlechterung ihrer Beziehung hatte längst nicht nur damit zu tun. Offenbar gab es auch Spannungen zwischen Cooper und Jacqueline. John Richardson weist auf ein spezifisches Ereignis hin, bei dem Cooper, der Picasso gewöhnlich während der Arbeit im Atelier besuchen durfte, den Künstler so weit brachte, dass er ihm die Tür wies. Wie nah Cooper diese Entfremdung ging, wird klar in seinem besonders boshaften Kommentar zur Ausstellung des Spätwerks 1973 im Palais des Papes in Avignon – bekanntlich nach Picassos Tod: «Ich glaube, ich darf den Anspruch erheben, mich zu den ernsthaften Bewunderern von Picassos Werk zählen und es also beurteilen zu können. Auch habe ich mir die Bilder lange angesehen. Kurz, es sind

nor a similar level of sensibility on the part of Nesjar. However, the disintegration of their relationship was played out in a more general arena. There was, apparently, tension between Jacqueline and Cooper. John Richardson points to a specific incident, in which Cooper, unusually allowed to visit the studio while Picasso worked, antagonized him to the point of being ejected. The depth of Cooper's alienation is clear in a particularly vicious commentary on the exhibition of late work at the Palais des Papes in Avignon in 1973, (after Picasso's death): "J'ai les titres, je crois, pour pouvoir me compter parmi les admirateurs sérieux de l'œuvre de Picasso et de pouvoir la juger. Aussi, ai-je longuement regardé les tableaux. Or ceux-ci sont des gribouillages incohérents exécutés par un vieillard frénétique dans l'antichambre de la mort. Voilà ce qu'il fallait dire."[172]

Picasso's dialogue with Manet and Poussin is amplified, or gains another participant, so to speak, as the wall at Castille becomes later, part of David Hockney's interaction with Picasso. Hockney's *Three Chairs with a section of a Picasso Mural* is based on photographs taken at Castille during a visit in March 1970.[173] The wall at Castille becomes, then, an instrument of Hockney's extended dialogue with Picasso. His sketch, *Portrait of Douglas Cooper, 29 March 1974* (No. 22), documents not only his enthusiastic perception of late Picasso, but also his friendship with Cooper.

135 In his 1949 monograph, *F. Léger ou le nouvel espace*, (p. 14) Cooper acknowledges the impact of that exhibition.
Among the works in the exhibition at Georges Petit subsequently purchased by Cooper were: *Three Nudes under a Tree*, 1907 (Z, II*, 53) purchased from Reber in 1937; *Nude Women in an Armchair*, winter 1909 (Z, II*, 174) purchased from Reber in 1937; *Clarinet Player*, 1911–12 (Z, II*, 288) purchased from Reber in 1937; *Still-life with Dead Birds*, 1912 (Z, II*, 339) purchased from Alfred Flechtheim in 1935; *The Student*, 1917–18 (Z, III, 104) purchased from Pierre Matisee in 1937; *Still-life with Guitar, Grapes and Bottle*, 1922–23, purchased from Reber in 1937; *Still-life with Guitar and Fruitdish*, 1932 (Z, VII, 375) purchased from Paul Rosenberg in 1935.

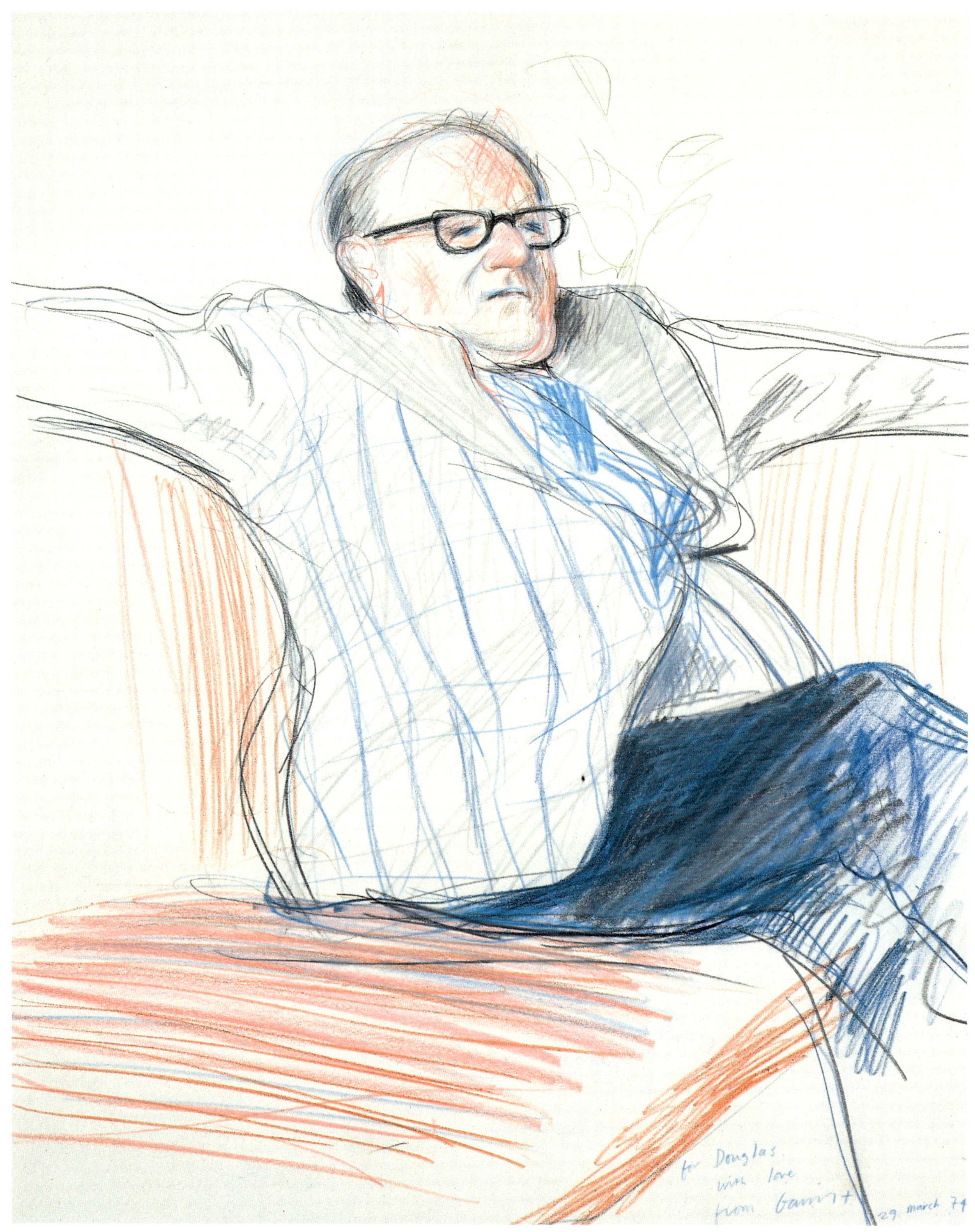

22 DAVID HOCKNEY
(Porträt Douglas Cooper; Portrait of Douglas Cooper) 1974

zusammenhangslose Schmierereien eines rasenden Greises im Vorzimmer des Todes. Das musste einmal gesagt sein.»[172]

Picassos Dialog mit Manet und Poussin wird erweitert oder erhält sozusagen einen neuen Gesprächspartner, als die Wand auf Schloss Castille für David Hockney Anlass zu einer Beschäftigung mit Picasso wird. Seine *Drei Stühle mit einem Stück Picassowandbild* basieren auf 1970 vor Ort gemachten Photographien. Die Wand wird Mittel einer langen Auseinandersetzung Hockneys mit Picasso. Des Künstlers Skizze *Porträt von Douglas Cooper* vom 29. März 1974 (Nr. 22) ist Dokument seiner Freundschaft mit Cooper.

135 Cooper weiss um die grosse Wirkung, welche diese Ausstellung auf ihn hatte (s. seine Monografie *Fernand Léger ou le nouvel espace*, S. 14).
Unter den bei Georges Petit ausgestellten und später von Cooper erworbenen Werken waren: *Drei Akte unter einem Baum,* 1907 (Z, II*, 53), 1937 von Reber erworben; *Akt in einem Lehnstuhl,* Winter 1909 (Z, II*, 174), 1937 von Reber erworben; *Der Klarinettist,* 1911–12 (Z Bd. II*, Nr. 288), 1937 von Reber erworben; *Stilleben mit toten Vögeln,* 1912 (Z, II*, 339), 1935 von Alfred Flechtheim erworben; *Der Student,* 1917–18 (Z, III, 104), 1937 von Pierre Matisse erworben; *Stilleben mit Gitarre, Trauben und Flasche,* 1922–23, 1937 von Reber erworben; *Fruchtschale und Gitarre,* 1932 (Z, VII, 375), 1935 von Paul Rosenberg erworben.

136 Als spätere Varianten könnten angesehen werden: *Zwei Köpfe,* Öl auf Leinwand, *Frau mit Birnen,* Öl auf Leinwand, und *Kopf,* Gouache (alle im Museum of Modern Art, New York; alle 1909). 1937 kaufte Cooper zwei grosse Figurenbilder, die ebenfalls Fernande Olivier darstellen: *Sitzende Frau* (Z, II*, 176; von Earl Horter, Philadelphia) und *Akt in einem Lehnstuhl* (von Georges Reber, Lausanne).

137 z.B. *Schatulle, Tasse und Apfel,* Tusche (Z, II*, 180), etwas später in diesem Jahr entstanden (ebenfalls im Museum of Modern Art, New York) oder *Apfel,* Frühjahr 1910, Gips, Musée Picasso, Paris (Z, II**, 718, 719).

138 Anscheinend wollte Cooper zuerst ein Aquarell von Cézanne kaufen, fand aber den Preis zu hoch. Er wählte dann dieses Aquarell, das er noch besser fand – «ein Cézanne von Picasso» (der

136 *Two Heads* oil on canvas, *Woman with Pears*, oil on canvas (Z, II*, 170) and *Head*, gouache, all dated 1909, and all in the Museum of Modern Art, New York, could, for instance, be considered later variants of this series. In 1937 Cooper purchased two major figural paintings of 1909; *Seated Woman* (Z, II*, 176; from Earl Horter in Philadelphia) and *Nude Woman in an Armchair,* (Z, II*, 174; from Georges Reber in Lausanne) which similarly portray Fernande Olivier.

137 See for instance: *Casket, Cup and Apple*, an ink wash from later that year (Z, II*, 180; also in the Museum of Modern Art, New York) or the plaster *Apple*, from early 1910 (Z, II**, 718, 719, Musée Picasso, Paris.)

138 Cooper apparently initially intended to purchase a watercolor by Cézanne but found its price too high. He "settled" for this watercolor which he considered even better – "a Cézanne by Picasso". (As reported to the author by William McCarty – Cooper, April 1987.) Cézanne, *Crâne sur une draperie*, watercolor and pencil, was sold the previous day in New York, at Christies on November 15, 1983, in a sale of Impressionist and Modern Painting and Sculpture from the Collection of Paul Mellon.

139 *Oeuvres Cubistes*, Paris, Berggruen & Cie., 1973, p. 2.

140 Cooper, *The Essential Cubism*, p. 324.

141 *Three Nudes under a Tree: Z, II*, 53.*

142 See Tinterow, *Master Drawings of Picasso*, Cambridge, Fogg Art Museum, 1981, entry no. 24 concerning a similar drawing in the Fogg Art Museum. John Richardson, in *Picasso Aquarelle und Gouachen*, Basel, Holbein Verlag, 1956, no. 7, discusses Picasso's interest in Gauguin and El Greco, but especially the impact of Iberian statuary.

143 Cooper, *Carnet Catalan*, Paris, Berggruen & Cie., 1958, p. 9

144 This drawing may be compared to the *Standing Female Nude* in the Metropolitan Museum of Art, Z II*, 208, variously dated, autumn 1910 (Tinterow, *Master Drawings of Picasso*, 1981, no. 37) or summer 1910 (William Rubin, *Pablo Picasso, A Retrospective*, New York, Museum of Modern Art, 1980, p. 141). Another related drawing is *Standing Woman*, 1911, Z, XXVIII, 38. See also, *L'Arlésienne*, summer 1912, Z, II*, 337.

145 See for instance, *The Accordionist*, summer 1911, The Solomon R. Guggenheim Museum, Z II*, 277.

Schreibenden mitgeteilt von William McCarty-Cooper im April 1987).
Am 15. November 1983 wurde Cézannes *Schädel auf einem Tuch,* Aquarell/Bleistift, bei Christie's in New York auf einer Auktion moderner Malerei und Skulptur aus der Sammlung Paul Mellon verkauft.

139 *Oeuvres Cubistes,* Paris, Berggruen, 1973, S. 2.

140 Cooper, *The Essential Cubism,* S. 324.

141 *Drei Akte unter einem Baum:* Z, II*, 53.

142 S. Gary Tinterow, *Master Drawings of Picasso,* Cambridge, Fogg Art Museum, 1981, Eintrag Nr. 24, betreffend eine ähnliche Zeichnung im Fogg Art Museum. John Richardson, in *Picasso/Aquarelle und Gouachen,* Basel, Holbein Verlag, 1956, Nr. 7, äussert sich zu Picassos Interesse an Gauguin und El Greco und besonders zum Einfluss von iberischer Skulptur.

143 Cooper, *Carnet Catalan,* Paris, Berggruen, 1958, S. 9.

144 Diese Zeichnung kann mit dem *Stehenden weiblichen Akt* im Metropolitan Museum of Art verglichen werden (Z, II*, 208), der verschieden datiert wird: Herbst 1910 (Tinterow, *Master Drawings of Picasso,* 1981, Nr. 37) oder Sommer 1910 (William Rubin, *Pablo Picasso, A Retrospective,* New York, Museum of Modern Art, 1980, S. 141). Eine weitere verwandte Zeichnung ist *Stehende Frau,* 1911 (Z, XXVIII, 38). S. a. *L'Arlésienne,* Sommer 1912 (Z, II*, 337).

145 S. z.B. *Der Akkordeonspieler,* Sommer 1911, The Solomon R. Guggenheim Museum, New York (Z, II*, 277).

146 Abgebildet in: Daix und Rosselet, *Le Cubisme de Picasso,* Neuchâtel 1979, S. 358, Illustr. 242, sowie in Rubin, *Picasso,* 1980, S. 151.

147 Cooper hatte von Earl Horter, Philadelphia, ein Papier collé von 1913 und eine Bleistiftzeichnung *Stilleben,* nebst einer *Sitzenden Frau,* Öl, von 1909 erworben. Dieses dürfte, wie es scheint, 1957 an Berggruen verkauft oder mit ihm getauscht worden sein, damit das hier besprochene Werk erworben werden konnte.

148 Cooper, *Picasso,* Marseille, Musée Cantini, 1959, Katalognr. 22.

149 S. z.B. *Gitarre* (Z, II*, 357). S. a. Tinterow (*Master Drawings of Picasso,* 1981, Nr. 45) mit einer Datierung dieses Werks auf Frühjahr 1913.

146 It is included in a photo of Picasso's Boulevard Raspail Studio in late 1912, reproduced by Daix and Rosselet, p. 358, illus. 242, *Le Cubisme de Picasso,* Neuchâtel, 1979 and Rubin, *Picasso,* 1980, p.151.

147 Cooper had purchased a 1913 papier collé and pencil drawing *Still-life* from the Philadelphia collector, Earl Horter, along with *Seated Woman,* oil 1909. This, it seems, may have been sold or traded to Berggruen in 1957 in order to obtain the work presently under discussion.

148 Cooper, *Picasso,* Marseille, Musée Cantini, 1959 catalogue no. 22.

149 See for instance: *Guitar,* Z II*, 357. See also Tinterow, *Master Drawings of Picasso,* 1981, no. 45, who attributes a date of early 1913 to the present work.

150 Cooper was, according to John Richardson, obsessed with obtaining a 1914 "pointillist, Ma Jolie" still-life. He did apparently purchase at one point, a painting which had been removed from a plaster wall. The surface had, however, been badly retouched and the plaster chipped away during transit, prompting Picasso to disavow the work as any longer his own. Cooper apparently subsequently tried to resell the work.

151 See William Rubin's discussion of *Pipe, Glass, Bottle of Rum,* March 1914, pasted paper, pencil, gesso on cardboard, *Picasso, in the Collection of the Museum of Modern Art,* New York, Museum of Modern Art, 1972, pp. 92 and 212. Rubin notes that the "gessoed white ground of the field ...has been treated in some areas as simulated collage".

152 One may compare, for instance, the stylization of *The Card Player* with the delicate naturalism of *Seated Man,* in the Collection of the Fogg Art Museum (Fig. 20, in Tinterow, *Master Drawings of Picasso,* 1981). See as well a similar seated figure in *The Painter and his Model,* (no. 48 in *Musée Picasso Paris,* New York, Abrams, 1986). In this regard, see also entry concerning *Man with a Melon Hat,* in William Rubin, *Picasso,* 1972, p. 93 and 213.

153 One might compare the curved line which defines the left edge of the *Bearded Man playing a Guitar* and the arcs which define his sleeve, with the concentric circular pattern to the left of *Harlequin Playing a Guitar,* 1915–16, no. 68, p. 215, William Rubin, *Picasso,* 1972.

This work has been variously titled over the years: by Boeck in 1955 as *L'homme masqué à la palette;* in the 1979 Bielefeld catalogue as

150 Nach John Richardson war Cooper von der Idee besessen, ein «Ma Jolie»-Stilleben von 1914 zu besitzen. (Anscheinend erwarb er einmal eine Malerei, die von einer verputzten Wand abgelöst worden war. Die Oberfläche war aber stark nachgebessert worden, und da auch der Gips auf dem Transport abgebröckelt war, wollte sie Picasso nicht mehr als sein Werk anerkennen. Anscheinend versuchte es Cooper später weiterzuverkaufen).

151 S. William Rubin über *Pfeife, Glas, Rumflasche,* März 1914, geklebtes Papier, Bleistift, Kreidegrund auf Karton, in *Picasso in the Collection of the Museum of Modern Art,* New York, Museum of Modern Art, 1972, S. 92 und 212. Rubin bemerkt, dass die «weisse Kreidegrundfläche ... an einigen Stellen als simulierte Collage behandelt wurde».

152 Man kann z.B. die Stilisierung des *Kartenspielers* mit dem feinen Realismus von *Sitzender Mann* im Fogg Art Museum vergleichen (Tafel 20 in Tinterow, *Master Drawings of Picasso,* 1981).
S. a. eine ähnliche sitzende Figur in *Der Maler und sein Modell* (Nr. 48 in *Musée Picasso Paris,* New York, Abrams, 1986). In diesem Zusammenhang s. a. den Eintrag betreffend *Mann mit Melone* bei William Rubin, *Picasso,* 1972, S. 93 und 213.

153 Man könnte die gebogene Linie, die den linken Rand von *Bärtiger Mann, Gitarre spielend* und die Bögen, welche den Ärmel definieren, mit dem konzentrischen Kreismuster links auf dem Bild *Harlekin, Gitarre spielend,* 1915–16, vergleichen (Nr. 68 in William Rubin, *Picasso,* 1972, S. 215).
Dem Werk wurden über die Jahre hinweg verschiedene Titel gegeben, so von Boeck 1955 *Maskierter Mann mit Palette,* im Katalog von Bielefeld 1979 *Bärtiger Mann* und von Daix und Rosselet 1979 *Mann, Gitarre spielend.*

154 S. die verwandte Zeichnung *Gläser und Flasche,* ebenfalls vom Sommer 1914, Nr. 172 in Cooper, *The Essential Cubism.*

155 Cooper, *The Cubist Epoch,* S. 194.

156 Vgl. mit *Pierrot,* Collection of the Fogg Art Museum, Nr. 285 (Z, III, 126) in Cooper, *Picasso, Theatre,* Paris, Editions cercle d'art, 1967.

157 ibid., S. 16.

158 ibid., S. 48. S. a. Eintrag Nr. 178, *The Essential Cubism.*

159 Z, II*, 555.

160 S. William Rubin (*Picasso,* 1972, S. 103), der sich zum Wechsel eines Nacheinander in der stilistischen Entwicklung zum Nebeneinander der Stile in der Nachkriegszeit äussert.

Bärtiger Mann; and by Daix and Rosselet in 1979 as *Homme jouant de la guitare.*

154 See related drawing also from summer 1914, *Glasses and Bottle,* no. 172 in Cooper, *The Essential Cubism.*

155 Cooper, *The Cubist Epoch,* p. 194.

156 Compare with *Pierrot,* Collection of The Fogg Art Museum no. 285 (Z, III, 126) in Cooper, *Picasso, Théâtre,* Paris, Editions cercle d'art, 1967.

157 *Ibid.,* p. 16.

158 *Ibid.,* p. 48. See also entry no. 178, *The Essential Cubism.*

159 Z II** 555.

160 See William Rubin, *Picasso,* 1972, p. 103, who discusses the change from sequential stylistic development to simultaneous exploration of many styles in the post war period.

161 It is most probably only coincidental that this Pierrot resembles somewhat portraits of D.-H. Kahnweiler. (See for example, Juan Gris' pencil drawing of Kahnweiler dating from 1921, no. 117, in J.A. Gaya-Nuño, *Juan Gris;* or the photograph taken by Picasso in 1912, reproduced in *L'Oeil,* no. 1, January 1955 in "Du Temps que les cubistes étaient jeunes... un entretien au magnétophone avec D.-H. Kahnweiler".)

162 Cooper, *Picasso Théâtre,* p. 30.

163 *Ibid.,* p. 31.

164 Cooper, *Pour Eugenia, Une suite de 24 dessins inédits exécutés en 1918,* Paris, Berggruen, 1976, fig. no. 1.

Cooper also treated the subjects of Madame Errazuriz, Picasso's fascination with theater, especially the Commedia dell'arte, as well as his renewed interest in Ingres, in an unpublished essay "Turmoil and Self-Assertion: Picasso in the 1920s" (presently in the Getty Study Center Archives) which examines that decade as pivotal in Picasso's subsequent development. This formed the subject, as well, of a lecture he presented in March 1981 at the University of Berkeley Art Museum.

165 Letters in Archive, The Museum of Modern Art, Library, New York.

161 Es ist höchst wahrscheinlich blosser Zufall, dass dieser *Pierrot* Porträts von Daniel-Henry Kahnweiler ähnelt (s. z.B. Juan Gris' Bleistiftzeichnung von Kahnweiler von 1921, Nr. 117 in J. A. Gaya-Nuño, *Juan Gris,* oder die 1912 von Picasso gemachte Fotografie, abgebildet in *l'Oeil,* Nr. 1, Januar 1955 zu «Über die Zeit, als die Kubisten noch jung waren ... ein Tonbandgespräch mit D.-H. Kahnweiler»).

162 Cooper, *Picasso, Theatre,* S. 30.

163 ibid., S. 31.

164 Cooper, *Pour Eugenia, Une suite de 24 dessins inédites executés en 1918,* Paris, Berggruen, 1976, Tafel 1.
Eugenia Errazuriz, Picassos Begeisterung für das Theater, speziell für die Commedia dell'arte, sowie seine erneute Beschäftigung mit Ingres waren auch Themen in Coopers unpubliziertem Aufsatz "Turmoil and Self-Assertion: Picasso in the 1920s" (heute im Archiv des Getty Study Center), der sich mit dem für Picassos spätere Entwicklung wegweisenden Jahrzehnt befasst. Demselben Thema gewidmet ist ein Vortrag, den Cooper im März 1981 im University of Berkeley Art Museum hielt.

165 Briefe im Archiv, Museum of Modern Art, Library, New York.

166 Die Nr. 19 des Buches ist *Le récital de piano – une caricature de Jean Cocteau.*
S. John Richardson, «Eugenia Errazuriz», *House and Garden,* April 1987, wo noch mehr Einzelheiten aus Mme Errazuriz' Leben zu erfahren sind. Richardson erklärt, dass sie Picasso zum ersten Mal 1915–16 durch Cocteau getroffen habe.

Cooper besass zwei Cocteau-Zeichnungen: *Portrait de Picasso,* 1917, Bleistift auf Papier, erworben bei Sotheby, London, am 13. Juni 1967 (Lot Nr. 128), und *Selbstporträt,* 1926, Tusche, Geschenk von Cocteau vom Mai 1933.

N.B. auch Coopers Übersetzung, im Jahr 1975, von Geneviève Laportes *Sunshine at Midnight: Memories of Picasso and Cocteau,* London, Weidenfeld and Nicholson.

167 S. William Rubin, *Picasso,* 1972, S. 232, betreffend Figur von Dora Maar in *Nachtfischen bei Antibes,* August 1939, wo Picasso dieses Thema wieder aufnahm.

168 S. a. (Ms.) «80 degrés à l'ombre: un déjeuner transformé en baignade», für eine Spezialnummer von *Le Patriote* vom 25. Oktober 1961 (publiziert in Nizza). Cooper schrieb auch eine Einführung für den Katalog zu einer Ausstellung in der Galerie Louise Leiris, 6. Juni–13. Juli 1962, welche den Déjeuner-Serien gewidmet war;

166 No. 19 in the book is *Le récital de piano – une caricature de Jean Cocteau.*

See John Richardson, "Eugenia Errazuriz," *House and Garden,* April 1987, which includes even more details of Mme Errazuriz's life. Richardson states that she first met Picasso in 1915–16 through Cocteau.

Cooper owned two drawings by Cocteau: *Portrait de Picasso,* 1917, pencil on paper, purchased at Sothebys, London, June 13, 1967, lot no. 128 and *Self-portrait,* 1926, ink, from Cocteau in May 1933.

Note as well Cooper's 1975 translation of Genevieve Laporte's *Sunshine at Midnight: Memories of Picasso and Cocteau,* London, Weidenfeld and Nicholson.

167 See William Rubin, *Picasso,* 1972, p. 232, concerning figure of Dora Maar in *Night Fishing at Antibes,* August 1939, in which Picasso takes up this theme again.

168 See as well (Ms.): "80 degrés à l'ombre – un déjeuner transformé en baignade", contributed to a special number of *Le Patriote,* 25 October 1961 (published in Nice). Cooper also wrote an introduction for a catalogue accompanying an exhibition at the Galerie Louise Leiris, 6 juin – 13 July 1962 devoted to the Dejeuner series. "Manet, Giorgione, Picasso" appeared in *Les Lettres Françaises,* no. 930, June 7–13, 1962.

169 Cooper, "Working with Picasso – The Story of the Wall of Castille," unpublished essay, p. 152ff, in a group of essays, *Negative Takes and Positive Pleasures,* in The Getty Center for the History of Art and the Humanities, Los Angeles.

170 See Gert Schiff, "The *Sabines* Sketchbook," in *Je suis le cahier, The Notebooks of Picasso,* New York, The Pace Gallery, 1986, pp. 179–189.

171 See John Richardson, "Picasso's Sketchbooks, Genius at Work," *Vanity Fair,* May 1986, pp. 74–93.

172 Cooper, [Letter to the editor], *Connaissance des arts,* vol. 257, July 1973, p. 23.

173 See Marco Livingstone, *David Hockney,* New York, Holt, Rinehart and Winston, 1981, p. 133, illus. 136.

My thanks to Gert Schiff for allowing me to read his contribution to the catalogue for the Hockney retrospective planned for 1988 by the Los Angeles County Museum of Art, "A Moving Focus: David Hockney's Dialogue with Picasso".

«Manet, Giorgione, Picasso» erschien auch in *Les Lettres Françaises,* Nr. 930, 7.–13. Juni 1962.

169 Cooper, "Working with Picasso – The Story of the Wall of Castille", unpublizierter Aufsatz (S. 152 ff.) aus einer Gruppe unpublizierter Aufsätze, betitelt *Negative takes and positive pleasures,* The Getty Center for the History of Art and the Humanities, Los Angeles.

170 S. Gert Schiff, "The *Sabines* Sketchbook", in *Je suis le cahier, The Notebooks of Picasso,* New York, The Pace Gallery, 1986, S. 179–189.

171 S. John Richardson, "Picasso's Sketchbooks, Genius at Work", *Vanity Fair,* Mai 1986, S. 74–93.

172 Cooper, Leserbrief an *Connaissances des arts,* Juli 1973, S. 23.

173 S. Marco Livingston, *David Hockney,* New York, Holt, Rinehart and Winston, 1981, S. 133, Abb. 136.
Mein Dank geht an Gert Schiff, der mit gestattete, seinen Beitrag für den Katalog der vom Los Angeles County Museum of Art für 1988 geplanten Hockney-Retrospektive, "A Moving Focus: David Hockney's Dialogue with Picasso", zu lesen.

PICASSOS HEIMLICHE LIEBE
PICASSO'S SECRET LOVE

Trotz allem, was schon über Picassos Leben geschrieben wurde, gibt es in unserem Wissen noch immer ansehnliche Lücken. Gewisse Dinge wollte der Künstler im dunkeln lassen, andre liess er nicht ungern dem Vergessen anheimfallen, und oft kam es darauf hinaus, dass er – wie viele bedeutende Menschen vor ihm – seine eigenen Legenden glaubte. Eine Episode, die er zu vergessen vorzog, war sein feuriges Liebesverhältnis mit Gaby Lespinasse. Ausser der kurzen Erwähnung einer geheimnisvollen «Madame L» von Pierre Daix ist uns nichts von diesem entzückenden Mädchen überliefert, das Picasso sogar vor seinen engsten Freunden, nicht zuletzt vor Gertrude Stein und Alice Toklas, geheimhielt. Man lese – in Steins geschwätziger *Autobiography of Alice B. Toklas* – den Bericht über ihren Besuch 1916 bei Picasso, in dessen Häuschen im elenden Pariser Vorort Montrouge, nach. Sie fanden ihn zwar in aufgeräumter Stimmung vor, doch identifizieren konnten sie nur folgende zwei Mädchen: «Paquerette, ein sehr nettes Mädchen, [und] Irene, eine überaus reizende Frau, die vom Land kam und frei sein wollte...»

Despite all that has been written about Picasso, there are still vast gaps in our knowledge of his life. Certain things the artist chose to keep dark, others he contrived to forget, and like many great men he came to believe his own legends. One episode he chose to forget was his passionate love affair in 1915–16 with an unknown Parisienne, Gaby Lespinasse. Apart from a brief mention by Pierre Daix of a mysterious "Madame L," nothing has been recorded of this ravishing girl whom Picasso kept a secret from even his closest friends, not least Gertrude Stein and Alice Toklas. Witness their account (in the former's gossipy *The Autobiography of Alice B. Toklas*) of a visit in 1916 to Picasso's little house in that dismal Parisian suburb Montrouge. They found him very cheerful, but the only girl friends they identify are "Paquerette a girl who was very nice [and] Irene a very lovely woman who came from the mountains and wanted to be free...."

Why no mention of Gaby Lespinasse, his principal love of this period? Because nobody – not even Stein or Toklas – had been vouchsafed a glimpse of her. Picasso was often secretive and jealous where his mistresses

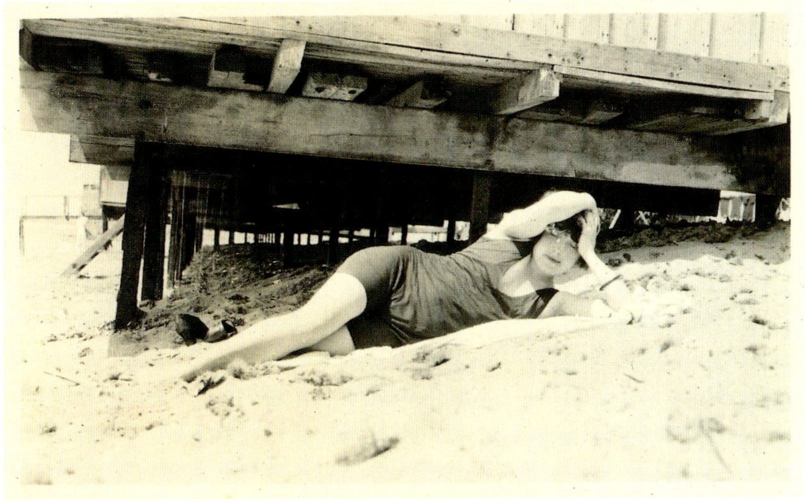

Anonyme Photographie/Anonymous photograph, *Gaby Lespinasse*, ca. 1915–16, Collection William McCarty-Cooper.

Warum keine Erwähnung von Gaby Lespinasse, der grossen Liebe dieser Zeit? Weil auch keinem – nicht mal Stein oder Toklas – gestattet wurde, auch nur einen Blick auf sie zu werfen. Der eifersüchtige Picasso war ja, was seine Geliebten betraf, ein Heimlichtuer; ebenfalls hatte er die Pascha-Allüre, sie zu verstecken – besonders vor potentiellen Räubern und neugierigen Frauen. Doch gab es da noch andere und sehr gute Gründe, die Romanze geheimzuhalten: Gaby war anscheinend schon liiert mit dem gebürtigen Amerikaner Herbert Lespinasse, einem Kupferstecher und Dichter, den sie schliesslich heiraten sollte (zumindest hatte sie seinen Namen angenommen). Leider ist auch noch die unrühmliche Tatsache zu beachten, dass die Liebschaft etwa im Herbst 1915 anfing, zu einem Zeitpunkt also, da der Künstler untröstlich darüber schien, dass Tuberkulose langsam, aber sicher seine damalige Geliebte, die zarte hübsche Eva Gouel, hinwegraffte (Picasso änderte übrigens symbolisch ihren Namen Marcelle zu Eva, «der ersten Frau», wie er sagte, und so natürlich implizierte, dass er der erste Mann war). Allerdings war er nur zu bereit, getröstet zu werden. Seit seine jüngere Schwester Conchita vor zwanzig Jahren an Diphtherie gestorben war, hatte Picasso (Schuld-)Probleme mit Sterblichkeit und Tod; um also den Mut aufbringen zu können, Evas Hand zu halten – was er denn pflichtbewusst auch täglich tat in einer Klinik in Auteuil auf der andern Seite von Paris, wo sie dahinschwand –, brauchte er jemanden, der auch seine Hand hielt. Nicht zu vergessen, dass Schuld für Picasso auch ein Aphrodisiakum war. Also liess er sich ein auf eine Liebesaffäre

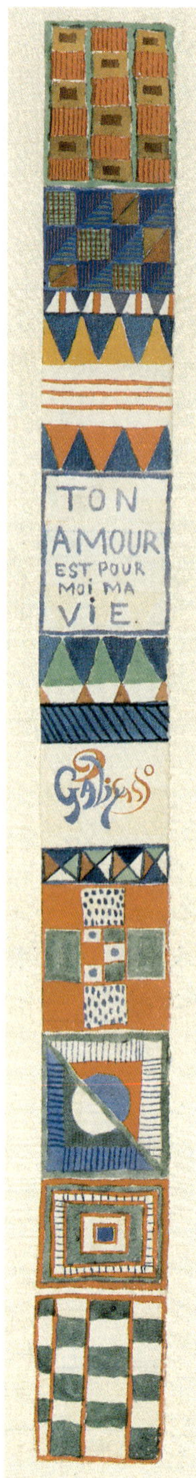

68 PABLO PICASSO

Ton amour est pour moi ma vie (1916)

were concerned, and he had a pasha's tendency to lock them away, above all from predatory men and nosy women. There were other excellent reasons for keeping this romance secret: Gaby, it seems, was already involved with the American-born engraver and poet Herbert Lespinasse, whom she would eventually marry; at least she had adopted his name. We also have to bear in mind the discreditable fact that the romance began sometime in the fall of 1915, when the artist was supposedly inconsolable because tuberculosis was about to carry off his current mistress, the frail and beautiful Eva Gouel. (Picasso had symbolically changed her name from Marcelle to Eva, "the first woman," he said, thus implying that he was the first man.) In fact he was all too ready to be consoled. Ever since his younger sister. Conchita, had died of diptheria twenty years earlier. Picasso had suffered from a guilty fear of disease and mortality, and in order to generate the courage to hold Eva's hand, as he dutifully did every day while she faded away in a clinic the other side of Paris at Auteuil, he needed someone to hold *his* hand. Bear in mind, too, that for Picasso guilt acted as an aphrodisiac. And so he embarked on a passionate affair with a girl who was as gentle and sweet and vulnerable as the one who was dying and, significantly, very similar in looks.

Where and how Picasso met Gaby we do not know. Was she perhaps a friend of Eva? This is very possible. They were much the same age, and although Gaby is said to have come from a good family and to have had private means, they frequented the same

mit einem Mädchen, das so lieb und nett und verletzlich wie die Sterbende war – und ihr natürlich ähnlich sah.

Wo und wie Picasso Gaby kennenlernte, wissen wir nicht. War sie etwa eine Freundin von Eva? Sehr wohl möglich. Die beiden waren fast gleichaltrig und, obwohl Gaby anscheinend aus guter Familie kam und auch etwas über private Mittel verfügte, verkehrten doch beide in der Bohème. Das einzige, was wir sicher wissen, ist, dass Gabrielle Depeyre 1888 in Paris geboren wurde und dass sie somit 27 Jahre alt war, als sie Picasso traf. Nach den vielen Porträts und den Photographien, die Picasso von ihr machte, zu urteilen, war Gaby eine grosse Schönheit, besonders im Profil, das ihren luftigen Pony, ihre grossen seelenvollen Augen und ihre exquisite Stupsnase zur Geltung brachte. Eines dieser unbekümmerten, katzenartigen Mädchen, denk ich mir, wie sie Colette erfand. Den weitschweifigen

bohemian milieu. All we know for certain is that Gabrielle Depeyre was born in Paris in 1888 and was thus 27 when she met the artist. To judge by photographs Picasso took and many portraits he did of her, Gaby was a great beauty, particularly in profile, with her fluffy fringe, big soulful eyes, and exquisite upturned nose. One of those laid-back catlike girls dreamed up by Colette, I imagine. And to judge by the lengthy and loving inscriptions on most of the pictures he gave her, the artist developed an obsessive passion for Gaby. In the four years of his relationship with Eva he had never executed a likeness of her ("I love her very much," he told his dealer, "and will write her name on my pictures" – hence the words *Jolie Eva. J'aime Eva,* or *Ma Jolie* on so many Cubist compositions), but he now did portrait after portrait of Gaby. Indeed he wooed her with art – witness the drawings and watercolors illus-

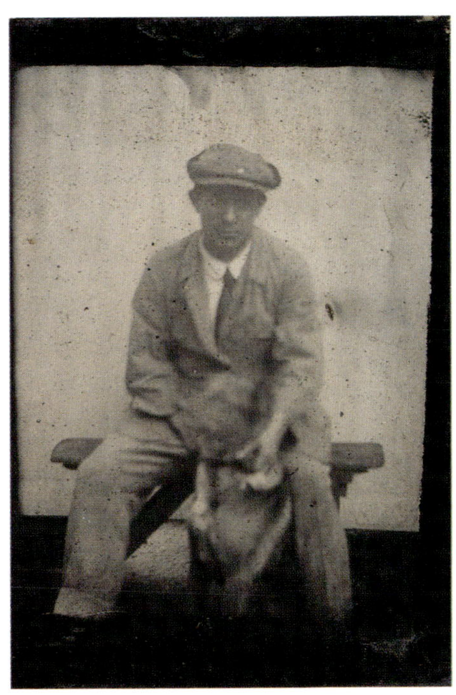

Anonyme Photographie/Anonymous photograph, *Picasso,* ca. 1915–16, Collection William McCarty-Cooper.

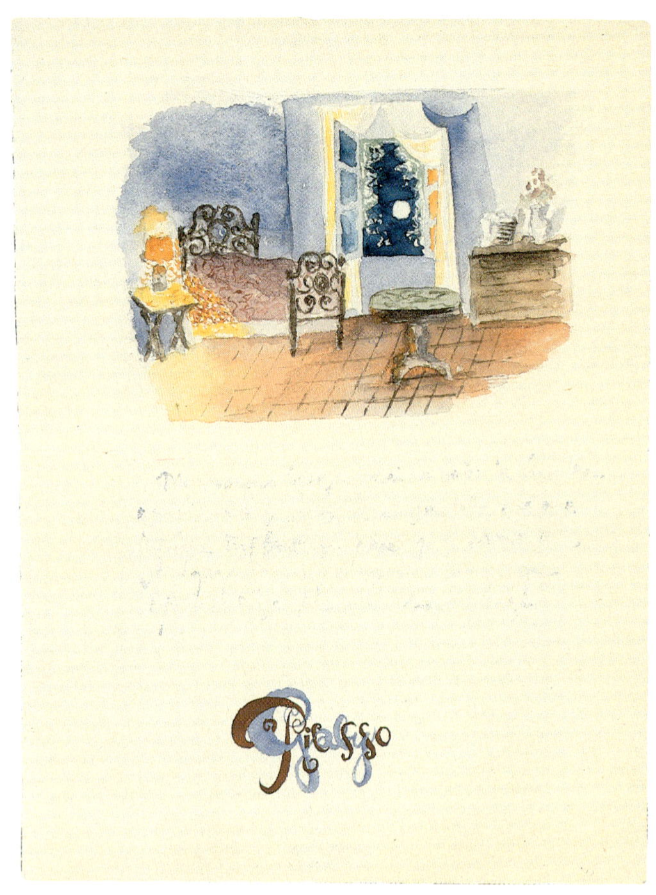

67 a PABLO PICASSO
(Einen Brief mit provenzalischem Intérieur, Schlafzimmer; Letter with Provençal Interior, Bedroom) (1916)

und zärtlichen Widmungen auf den meisten Bildern, die er ihr schenkte, nach zu urteilen, wurde der Künstler von seiner Leidenschaft für Gaby richtiggehend besessen. Während der vier Jahre ihrer Beziehung hatte Picasso Eva nie porträtiert («Ich liebe sie sehr», erzählte er seinem Händler, «und werde ihren Namen auf meine Bilder schreiben» – daher die Worte *Jolie Eva, J'aime Eva* oder *Ma Jolie* auf so vielen kubistischen Kompositionen), doch nun malte er ein Bild von Gaby nach dem andern, ja er warb regelrecht mit seiner Kunst um sie, wie man an den hier abgebildeten Zeichnungen sehen

trated in these pages, not to speak of the love letters in the margins. How sad that some forty years after they were executed the recipient should have erased the adoring and, if I know the artist, erotic messages before putting the drawings (Z, XXIX, 191, 193, 194, 195) on the market. In several cases the last words – *tout mon cœur* (with all my heart) – and the artist's signature are all that remain.

Fortunately the less compromising inscriptions on two of the three watercolor interiors have survived. For

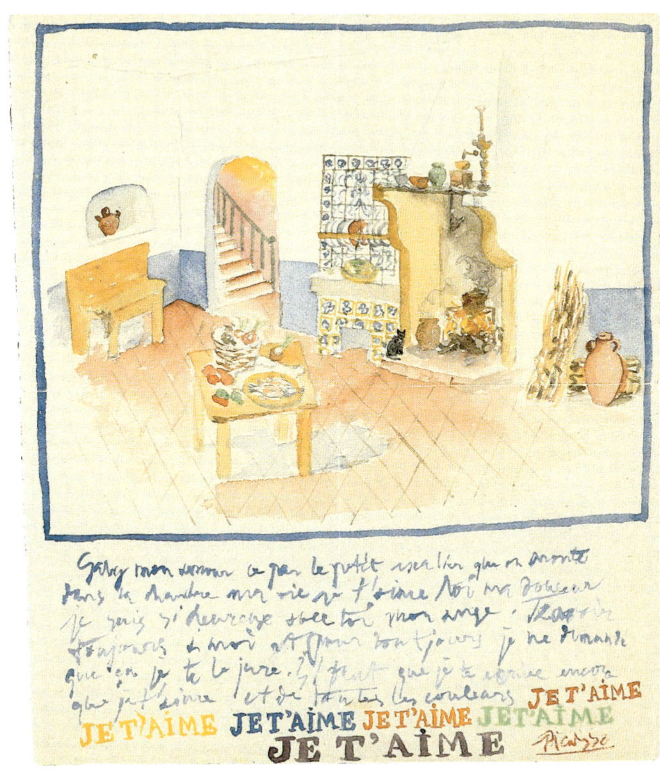

67 b PABLO PICASSO
(Einen Brief mit provenzalischem Intérieur, Die Küche; Letter with Provençal Interior, Kitchen) (1916)

kann, von den Liebesbriefen auf den Rändern ganz zu schweigen. Wie traurig, dass, etwa vierzig Jahre nachdem sie entstanden waren, die Empfängerin die schwärmerischen und, wie ich den Künstler kenne, erotischen Botschaften tilgen sollte, bevor sie die Zeichnungen dem Markt überliess (Z, XXIX, 191, 193, 194, 195). In einigen Fällen sind die letzten Worte – *de tout mon cœur* – und des Künstlers Unterschrift alles, was geblieben ist.

Glücklicherweise sind die weniger kompromittierenden Passagen auf zweien der drei Aquarelle mit Inte-

instance, the unpunctuated one in blue watercolor on *The Provençal Dining Room* (No 67c), reads as follows: "...Gaby my love my angel I love you my darling and I think only of you I don't want you to be sad To take your mind off things look at the little dining room I will be so happy with you... you know how much I love you... Till tomorrow my love it is very late at night with all my heart Picasso." Given the desperate efforts Gaby has made to delete the message beneath *The Moonlit Bedroom* (No 67a), this must have been erotic. But the one below *The Provençal Kitchen* (No 67b) is still legible. It

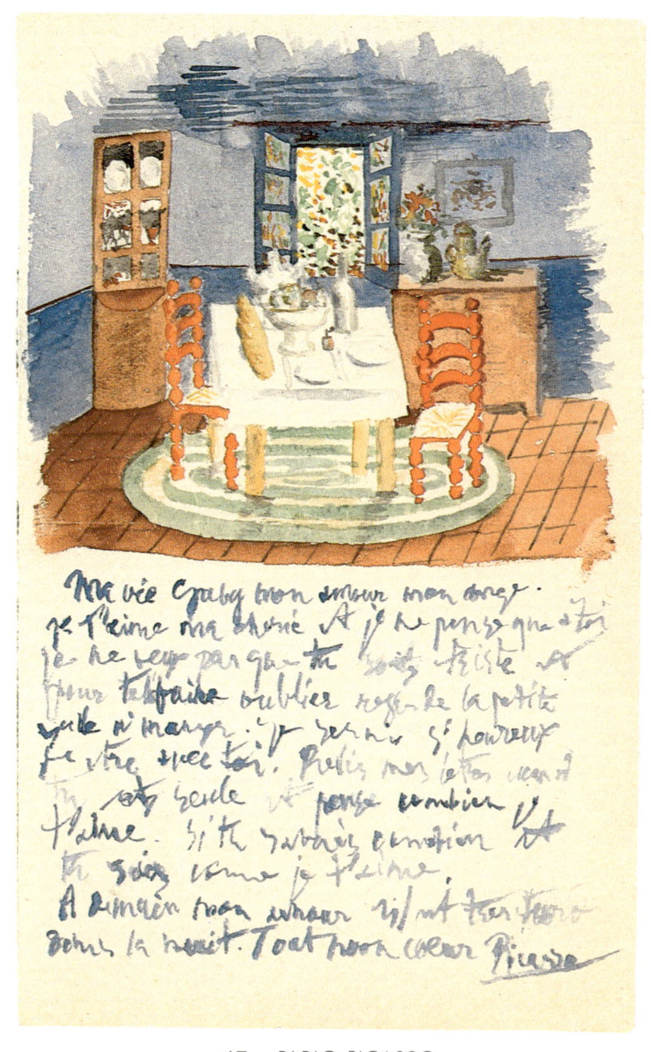

67 c PABLO PICASSO

(Einen Brief mit provenzalischem Intérieur, Das Esszimmer; Letter with Provençal Interior, Dining Room) (1916)

rieurs erhalten. Die interpunktionslose blaue auf dem Blatt *Das provenzalische Esszimmer* (Nr. 67c) liest sich zum Beispiel so: «... Gaby meine Liebe mein Engel ich liebe dich mein Liebling und ich denke nur an dich ich will nicht dass du traurig bist Um dich abzulenken schau dir das kleine Esszimmer an ich werde so glücklich sein bei dir... du weisst wie sehr ich dich liebe... Bis morgen meine Liebe es ist sehr spät in der Nacht *Tout mon cœur Picasso.*» Angesichts der verzweifelten Versuche von Gaby, das Geschriebene unter dem *Schlafzimmer bei Mondlicht* (Nr. 67a) wegzubekommen, ist es wohl von erotischer Natur gewesen. Jenes unter der *Provenzalischen Küche* (Nr. 67b) aber ist noch lesbar; typisch schliesst hier Picasso mit *Je t'aime de toutes les couleurs*, wobei die sechs *JE T'AIME* in sechs verschiedenen Farben erscheinen. Für eine solche Idee muss man eben kindisch, phantasievoll und verliebt bis über beide Ohren sein – wie Picasso. Noch etwas Merkwürdiges

has a characteristically Picassian ending: *Je t'aime de toutes les couleurs*, with the words *Je t'aime* reiterated in six different colors. Only Picasso would have had the childishness, imagination, and infatuation to think up this conceit. Another quaint device that recurs in these works is his name entwined with hers – calligraphic lovemaking.

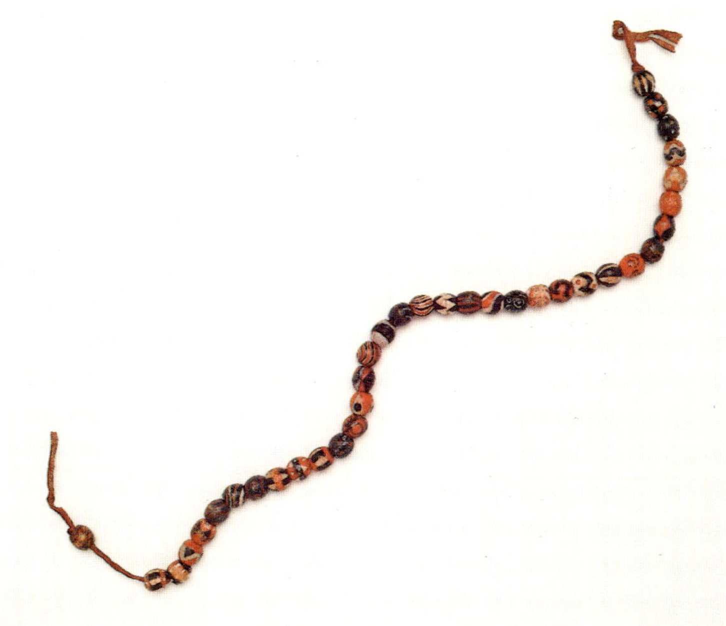

Pablo Picasso, *Bemalte Halskette aus Holzkugeln bestehend/Painted wooden bead necklace,* ca. 1915–16, Collection William McCarty-Cooper.

Besides painting these interiors and contriving a charming necklace out of wooden beads, each one decorated with a different geometric motif, Picasso gave Gaby a whimsical collection of mini-masterpieces: three oval Cubist still lifes and an allegorical portrait of her with a putto hovering overhead. What delicacy and ingenuity – none of them is bigger than a cameo – yet what authority and originality they have. These miniatures (each has a different declaration of love on the back) were framed together, with photographs of Gaby and Picasso, around a central decorative

taucht wiederholt auf: Ihre miteinander verschlungenen Namen – kalligraphisches Liebesspiel.

Nicht nur malte Picasso diese Interieurs und ersann eine hübsche Halskette aus Holzkugeln, die alle mit geometrischen Mustern verziert waren, er schenkte Gaby auch eine wunderliche Sammlung von Mini-Meisterwerken: drei ovale kubistische Stilleben und ein allegorisches Porträt mit einem schwebenden Putto über Gabys Kopf. Welche Zartheit und Geschicklichkeit – kein Bildchen ist grösser als eine Kamee –; und doch: welche Kraft und Eigenart sie besitzen! Diese Miniaturen, die, eigentlich für ein Medaillon geschaffen, alle auf der Rückseite verschiedene Liebeserklärungen tragen, wurden zusammen mit einer Photographie von Gaby und einer von Picasso um ein zentrales Emblem gruppiert (und so gerahmt), das wieder verkündet *Je t'aime*. Nach Pierre Daix *(Picasso créateur,* Paris, 1987) gab der Künstler ihr ebenso ein Gemälde einer Pfingstrose, datiert 1901 und ausgestellt in Picassos erster Ausstellung in Paris.

Das Erstaunlichste aber für den Biographen ist das kleine, nun unter der «Komposition» angebrachte Stück Papier, auf dem neben dem Datum 22. Februar 1916 in Picassos Handschrift zu lesen steht *J'ai demandé ta main au Bon Dieu* (Ich bat den lieben Gott um deine Hand.). Erstaunlich deshalb, weil der Künstler bis anhin keinerlei Interesse an Heirat gezeigt hatte, nicht einmal mit Eva, der «ersten Frau», die lediglich ein paar Monate vorher gestorben war. Und erstaunlich auch deshalb, weil Picasso immer seinen Glauben verleugnet hat, ein Verleugnen, dem dieses kleine innige Gebet für alle Zeit widerspricht. Und auch aufschlussreich, weil, ziemlich genau ein Jahr später, Picasso in Rom eine von Diaghilews russischen Ballerinen, Olga Koklova, belagerte. Hatte er bei Gaby den kürzeren gezogen, war er nun fest entschlossen, bei Olga zu gewinnen – einer Neurotikerin von eiserner Tugend, die den vernarrten Picasso (um den Preis eines Rings für Sex) in die Ehe-Falle lockte. Inzwischen heiratete Gaby (am 23. April 1917) Herbert Lespinasse, und zwar in

emblem that announces once again *Je t'aime*. According to Pierre Daix (*Picasso créateur,* Paris, 1987) the artist also gave her a painting of a single peonie, which dates from 1901 and was exhibited in Picasso's first Paris show.

But to the biographer the most astonishing element is the scrap of paper, dated February 22, 1916, that is now mounted at the bottom of the frame and inscribed in Picasso's writing, *J'ai demandé ta main au Bon Dieu* (I have asked the good God for your hand). Astonishing because the artist had hitherto shown no interest in marriage, not even to Eva, the "first woman," dead a mere couple of months earlier. Astonishing, too, because Picasso always denied his faith, a denial that this heartfelt little prayer once and for all contradicts. And illuminating because almost exactly a year later Picasso left for Rome, where he immediately laid siege to one of Diaghilev's Russian ballerinas, Olga Koklova. Having failed with Gaby, he was determined to succeed with Olga, a neurotic woman of iron virtue who trapped the besotted Picasso into marriage by making a wedding ring the price of sex. Meanwhile (April 23, 1917) Gaby married Herbert Lespinasse at Saint-Tropez, where he had been one of the earliest settlers.

Not the least of the mysteries raised by Gaby's little treasure trove is the whereabouts of the rooms depicted in these watercolors – rooms that evidently had very special memories for the artist, given the tenderness that imbues them. The Provençal rusticity could hardly be less Parisian, nor does it correspond to the look of either of Picasso's Parisian abodes in 1916: the studio on the rue Schoelcher or the little house at Montrouge. The tiled floor (*tomettes de Marseille*, if I am not wrong), the earthenware pots, the rush chairs, the Provençal *bahuts* (chests), the bundle of *sarment de vigne* (faggots made of vine prunings), and the open fireplace with the cooking pot on the hob would indicate the midi, the south of France. The Mediterranean, one feels, is not too far away, and one can almost smell the lavender and rosemary outside the window. True, there is no

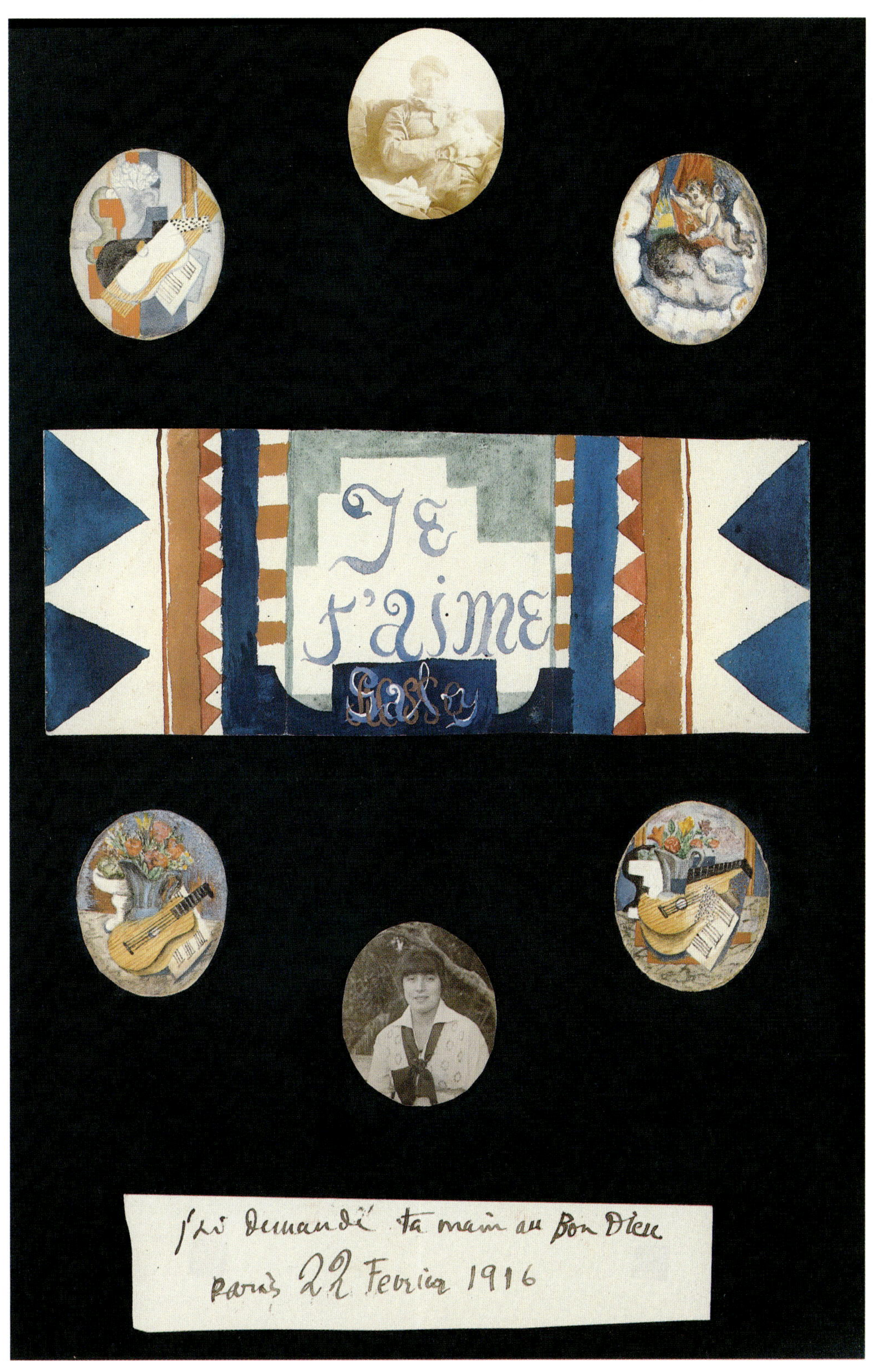

66 PABLO PICASSO
Je t'aime Gaby 1916

Saint-Tropez, wo er sich als einer der ersten Fremden niedergelassen hatte.

Nicht das geringste Geheimnis, das Gabys kleinen Schatz umgibt, ist, wo die in den Aquarellen gezeigten Zimmer denn zu finden seien – Zimmer von offensichtlich besonderer Bedeutung für den Künstler, spürt man doch die Zärtlichkeit, die sie erfüllt. Die provenzalische Rustikalität könnte nicht unpariserischer sein; auch keine der Bleiben Picassos in Paris 1916 – weder das Atelier an der Rue Schoelcher noch das Häuschen in Montrouge – wiesen Ähnlichkeit auf. Der Plattenboden (*tomettes de Marseille*, wenn ich nicht irre), die Stühle mit Binsengeflecht, die provenzalischen *bahuts* (Kommoden), die Rebenreis-(*sarment de vigne*)-Bündel und der Kamin mit dem Kochtopf auf dem Rost – alles deutet auf den Midi, auf Südfrankreich. Man fühlt, dass das Mittelmeer nicht mehr weit weg ist, ja man kann beinahe den Lavendel und den Rosmarin vor dem Fenster riechen. Gut, es gibt keinen Beleg in der Literatur für Picassos Abwesenheit von Paris 1916, doch wäre es nicht mehr als glaubhaft, wenn er die (vom Tod Evas erfüllte) Hauptstadt mit dem Süden vertauscht hätte, wo er doch schon oft den Frühling oder Sommer verbrachte und noch verbringen würde? Man bedenke auch, dass Picasso 1916 nicht nur vom Schatten der Krankheit und des Todes verfolgt war, sondern auch vom Krieg, der vor Paris stand. Dieses Frühlingsidyll muss eine willkommene Abwechslung vom Gemetzel in Verdun gewesen sein.

Im Süden wäre für Picasso eine dreifache Auswahl auf der Hand gelegen: Sorgues (gerade vor Avignon), wo er und Braque 1913 und 1914 zusammen ein Haus teilten und wohin Braque bald zurückkehren sollte, um eine Kriegswunde ausheilen zu lassen; Céret, ein pittoreskes Städtchen am Fusse der Pyrenäen, wo er 1911 und 1912 ein paar Monate verbrachte und immer noch einige alte Freunde hatte, und Saint-Tropez, ein noch unverdorbenes Fischerdorf, bevorzugt von wenigen wählerischen Malern und Schriftstellern. Picasso war noch nie in Saint-Tropez, aber Gaby hatte Kontakte da. Ich neige zur Ansicht, dass Picasso Sorgues und Céret

record in the literature of the artist's leaving Paris in the course of 1916, but isn't it only too likely he would have abandoned the death-haunted capital for a spring or summer vacation in the south, as he had done in the past and would do again and again in the future? Remember, too, that in 1916 Picasso was not only haunted by the shadow of Eva's illness and death but also by the war, which had come within earshot of Paris. This spring idyll must have provided a welcome escape from the carnage of Verdun.

Picasso would have had three obvious choices in the south: Sorgues (just outside Avignon), where he and Braque had shared a house in 1913 and 1914 and where Braque would soon return to convalesce from a war wound: Céret, a picturesque town in the foothills of the Pyrenees where he spent some months in 1911 and 1912 and had a number of old friends; and Saint-Tropez, still an unspoiled fishing village favored by a few discriminating painters and writers. Picasso had never as yet been to Saint-Tropez, but Gaby had local contacts. I am inclined to think that Picasso would have avoided Sorgues and Céret – both had associations with previous mistresses – and gone somewhere he was not known. Saint-Tropez, which he often used in later life as a hideaway for amorous escapades, would have been the perfect place. My hunch is to some extent confirmed by a drawing of Gaby (Z, VI, 1277), one of several that Picasso kept for himself (Z, VI, 1278, 1279, 1280, 1282), a nude in a garden against a typically Saint-Tropez background of hills and cypresses and Roman-tiled roofs; also by the oval blue-and-white rug in the dining room, very like one of the rag mats called *tapis de Cogolin*, which are still made in the village of that name behind Saint-Tropez.

If Saint-Tropez was indeed the setting for this idyll, we can identify the house with reasonable certainty, thanks to exhaustive researches made by Billy Klüver, the historian of Montparnasse. According to Klüver, Lespinasse was one of the original discoverers of Saint-Tropez and owned a little house on the baie des Canoubiers off which he anchored a fishing boat. Sur-

eher vermeiden wollte, da beide mit verflossenen Geliebten verbunden waren, und lieber wohin ging, wo man ihn nicht kannte. Saint-Tropez, das ihm später des öftern als Versteck für seine erotischen Eskapaden diente, wäre also der ideale Ort gewesen. Meine

vivors of the period have told Klüver how this gifted engraver kept open house for artists such as Pascin and the Swede Nils von Dardel and, of course, their wives and mistresses, who liked nothing better than to "live the natural life" on the shores of the Mediterranean. In

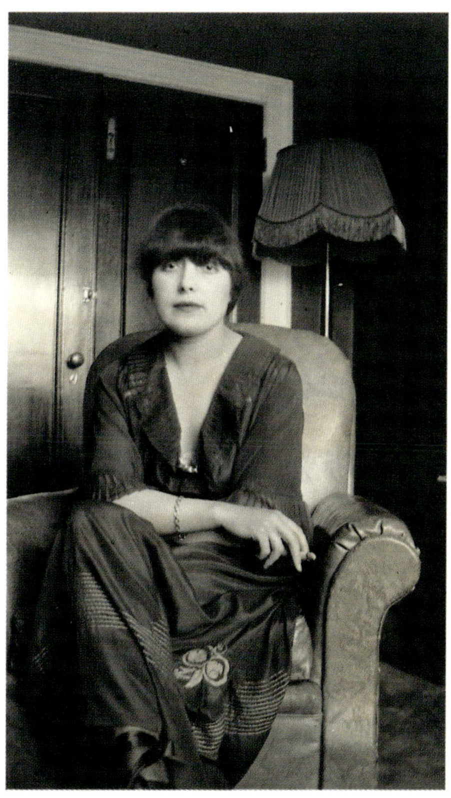

Anonyme Photographie/Anonymous photograph, *Gaby Lespinasse,* ca. 1915–16, Collection William McCarty-Cooper.

Annahme erweist sich in gewissem Masse als begründet durch eine Zeichnung von Gaby (Z, VI, 1277) – eine von mehreren, die Picasso für sich behielt (Z, VI, 1278, 1279, 1280, 1282) – als Akt in einem Garten vor typischem Saint-Tropez-Hintergrund mit Hügeln und Zypressen und römischen Ziegeldächern; übrigens auch durch die blauen und weissen Kreise des Teppichs im Esszimmer, der sehr jenen *tapis de Cogolin* ähnelt, die man immer noch im Dorf gleichen Namens bei Saint-Tropez herstellt.

the morning, shots from Lespinasse's pistol would awaken the guests, who would be obliged to go out and forage for water and firewood. Judging by nude photographs (circa 1925) of Pascin and the famous Kiki of Montparnasse, life on Lespinasse's terrace was liberated, to say the least. Promiscuity was taken for granted, above all by the host. Under the circumstances what more likely than that Gaby should have had the use of this love nest with or without Lespinasse's sanction?

Wenn wir also Saint-Tropez als Schauplatz der Idylle ansehen, können wir auch – dank den ausgiebigen Nachforschungen von Billy Klüver, dem Historiker von Montparnasse – mit angemessener Gewissheit das Haus identifizieren. Nach Klüver war Lespinasse einer der ursprünglichen Entdecker von Saint-Tropez, wo er an der Bucht, genannt des Canoubiers, ein Häuschen besass und wo auch sein Fischerboot vor Anker lag. Überlebende aus dieser Zeit erzählten Klüver, dass dieser begabte Kupferstecher ein offenes Haus hielt für Künstler wie Pascin oder den Schweden Nils von Dardel und natürlich auch für ihre Frauen und Freundinnen, die nichts lieber mochten als das «natürliche Leben» an den

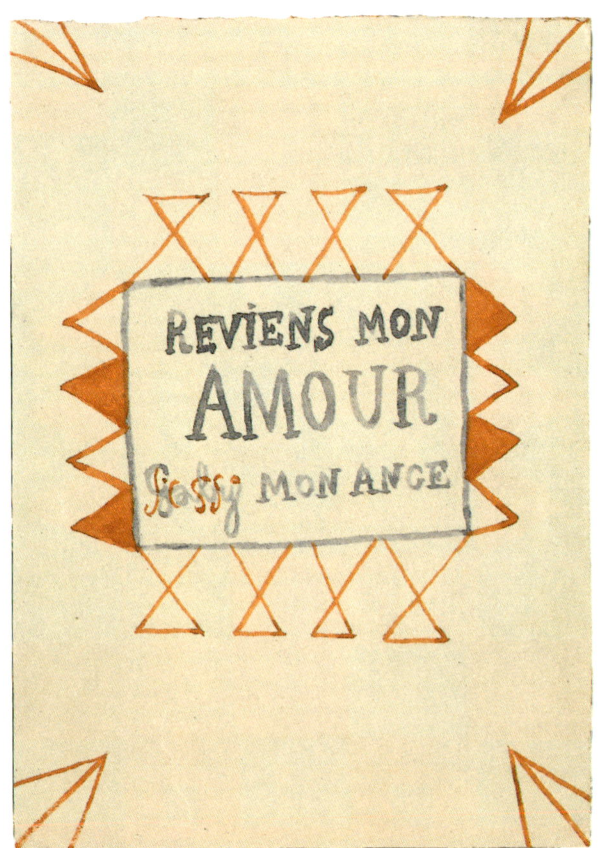

Pablo Picasso, *Zeichnung für/Drawing for Gaby Lespinasse*, ca. 1915–16, Collection William McCarty-Cooper.

If Picasso kept this relationship dark, is it so surprising, given that it ended in his rejection? Far more shameful for an Andalusian than betraying a dying woman. It was only when Gaby finally put some of her portraits on the market in the late fifties that the love story came to light. In connection with some research I was doing at the time, I tried to track Gaby down. Failing to do so, I asked Picasso about the portraits: he was clearly delighted at seeing them but irritated at being reminded of an episode he had chosen to forget. Some time after the deaths of Gaby, about 1970, and her husband, Herbert, in 1972, a niece, who was heir to the estate, decided to sell what was left, the cream of

Küsten des Mittelmeers. Am Morgen weckten jeweils Schüsse aus Lespinasses Pistole die Gäste, die dann Holz und Wasser holen gehen mussten. Den Nacktphotos – ungefähr von 1925 – nach zu schliessen, die Pascin und die berühmte Kiki von Montparnasse zeigen, führte man auf Lespinasses Terrasse ein wahrlich freies Leben. Promiskuität war selbstverständlich, vor allem für den Gastgeber. Was wäre unter den Umständen wahrscheinlicher gewesen, als dass Gaby dieses Liebesnest mit oder ohne Erlaubnis benützte?

Ist es nicht erklärlich, dass Picasso, besonders da er ja abgewiesen wurde, dieses Verhältnis im dunkeln beliess? Für einen Andalusier eben eine viel grössere Schande als eine Sterbende betrügen. Und wirklich, nicht bevor Gaby in den späten fünfziger Jahren ein paar ihrer Porträts auf den Markt brachte, kam die Liebesgeschichte ans Licht. Im Zusammenhang mit meiner damaligen Forschungsarbeit versuchte ich, Gaby auf die Spur zu kommen. Da es mir nicht gelang, fragte ich Picasso, was es mit den Porträts auf sich habe. Er war offensichtlich erfreut, sie wiederzusehen, aber auch unangenehm berührt, da er an etwas erinnert wurde, was er eigentlich hatte vergessen wollen. Einige Zeit nach Gabys Tod (ungefähr 1970) und dem Tod von Herbert (1972) entschloss sich eine Nichte, Erbin des Nachlasses, zu verkaufen, was noch da war – und es waren die Glanzstücke. Weil diese aber weder belegt noch typisch waren und weil auch der Künstler nicht mehr da war, der sie hätte authentisieren können, war ein Verkauf gar nicht leicht.

Schliesslich konsultierte der Pariser Händler Daniel Malingue den Picasso-Experten und -sammler David Cooper, der die Bedeutung der Stücke erkannte. Er kaufte die kleine Sammlung, inklusive Heirats- und Todesurkunden, und behielt sie zeitlebens und eifersüchtig bewacht in seiner Wohnung in Monte-Carlo auf. Weder wurde sie jemals publiziert noch ausgestellt, obwohl Cooper seine Freunde immer des Gegenteils versicherte. Doch tat er's nie. Er war auf keine Art und Weise willig, der Genugtuung und des Machtgefühls zu entsagen, ein kleines, aber wichtiges Teilchen

the crop as it turned out. Since the material was unrecorded and untypical and the artist was no longer around to provide authentication, it was not easy to sell.

In the end the Parisian dealer Daniel Malingue consulted Douglas Cooper, the Picasso expert and collector who recognized the significance of the items. Cooper bought the little collection, complete with marriage and death certificates, and for the rest of his life kept it jealously guarded in his Monte Carlo apartment, unpublished and unexhibited.

Cooper always assured his friends that he intended to publish his Gaby Lespinasse material. However, he never did. He was not, in the last resort, prepared to forego the gratification, the sense of power that he derived from owning a small but vital piece of the Picasso puzzle – a piece without which the story of the artist's life could never be properly told. Cooper thus avoided coming to grips with the problems that his treasure trove posed. In some ways this was a pity, because nobody was better placed to assemble and interpret the material than he. For my part, I am grateful that in effect he left the task to me. So far as I can discover, Gaby was fascinated but daunted by the charismatic genius who had fallen for her. In the circumstances the ravishing girl found herself caught between two fires. Fearful of being destroyed like most of the other women in the artist's life, on the sacrificial altar of his genius, she wisely settled for a free and easy life in the company of a lesser light, her husband, Herbert, and his gang of friends, who were always ready to sacrifice work to pleasure.

Gaby's independence explains Picasso's desperate cajolery – for instance, the decorative but insistent summons that Gaby return to him (from his rival Herbert?): *Reviens mon amour... mon ange.* It would also explain certain stylistic anomalies: for instance, the way he sweetened and scaled down his vision and style in order to accommodate the taste of a girl who would have been immune to the subtleties of Synthetic Cubism. Hence the deceptive innocence of these love tokens: deceptive in that nothing could be more disin-

des Puzzles Picasso zu besitzen – ein Teilchen, ohne das seine Lebensgeschichte nicht vollständig erzählt werden kann. Und so vermied Cooper auch die Probleme, die sein kleiner Schatz eigentlich stellte. Das war zwar schade, denn wer wäre geeigneter gewesen, das Material zusammenzubringen und zu interpretieren? Aber ich bin ihm natürlich dankbar, dass er die Aufgabe quasi mir überliess. So wie ich die Sache bisher überblicke, war Gaby fasziniert, aber auch eingeschüchtert, vom charismatischen Genie, das ihr verfallen war. Und das entzückende Mädchen fühlte sich zwischen Feuer und Flamme hin- und hergerissen. Sie war weise genug zu befürchten, auf dem Altar des Genies geopfert zu werden (wie das den meisten andern Frauen in Picassos Leben geschah), und zog so das freie leichte Leben mit einem kleineren Licht, ihrem Mann Herbert, und dessen Freunden, die stets bereit waren, die Arbeit dem Vergnügen zu opfern, vor.

Gabys Unabhängigkeit erklärt Picassos verzweifelte Überredungskünste, die sich zum Beispiel als dekorative, aber doch beharrliche Aufforderung äusserten, zu ihm zurückzukehren (und den Rivalen Herbert zu verlassen): *Reviens mon amour... mon ange.*

Dies würde auch gewisse stilistische Ungereimtheiten erklären: zum Beispiel wie er Sicht und Stil verniedlichte, nur um sich dem Geschmack eines Mädchens, das mit den Subtilitäten des synthetischen Kubismus gar nichts hätte anfangen können, anzupassen. Daher auch die täuschende Unschuld dieser Liebeszeichen: täuschend in der unübertrefflich hinterlistigen Art, wie Picasso seine Ingresschen Fähigkeiten hinter dem künstlichen Nebel anscheinend naiver Zeichnung verbirgt. Zu guter Letzt aber versagten Picassos Aufmarsch der Unschuld wie seine Rhetorik: er und Gaby gingen getrennte Wege. Doch als historisches Dokument ist diese Romanze von Bedeutung, deckt sie doch nicht nur ein fehlendes Glied in der «Ehen»-Kette des Künstlers auf, sondern zeigt ihn selbst als einen, der wehrlos und leidenschaftlich und zutiefst verliebt für einmal einem hübschen Mädchen ausgeliefert war – und nicht umgekehrt.

genuous than the way Picasso dissembles his Ingresque skills behind a smoke screen of seemingly simplistic drawing. In the long run Picasso's parade of innocence, like his cajolery, failed to work: both parties went their separate ways. But for the record this romance is historically significant because it reveals a missing link in the artist's marital career and because it also reveals Picasso with his guard down, passionately, abjectly in love, for once at the mercy of a pretty girl instead of the other way around.

KATALOG
CATALOGUE

Bemerkung:
Der Katalog ist alphabetisch nach den Künstlern und chronologisch nach den Entstehungsdaten geordnet. Der vom Künstler gegebene Titel (direkt auf das Werk geschrieben) ist zuerst, und in seiner ursprünglichen Sprache, angegeben. In Klammern folgen dann die deutsche und englische Übersetzung dieses Titels oder desjenigen Titels, unter dem das Werk normalerweise bekannt ist. Ähnlich dazu sind alle Daten, welche nicht durch den Künstler auf das Werk geschrieben wurden, in Klammern. Die Grössen sind in Zentimeter angegeben; Höhe vor Breite. Die Stellen der Beschriftungen und Unterschriften des Künstlers sind mit den folgenden Abkürzungen angegeben: u = unten; o = oben; l = links; r = rechts; m = Mitte. Eine Auswahl von Ausstellungs- und Literaturhinweisen wird ebenfalls angegeben. Sämtliche Informationen, welche nicht verifiziert werden konnten, sind mit einem (?) versehen.

Note:
The catalogue is organized alphabetically by artist and chronologically by date. The artist's title, (that is, one inscribed directly on the work) is given first and in the original language. In parentheses follow German and English translations of that title or of the title by which the work is usually known. Similarly, all dates not inscribed by artist on work are given in parentheses. Dimensions are given in centimeters; Height precedes width. The location of the artist's inscriptions and signatures are indicated with the following abbreviations: l = lower; u = upper; l = left; r = right; m = middle. Selected exhibitions and references are provided. Any entries or information which could not be entirely verified are followed by a (?).

GEORGES BRAQUE

1

(Stehender Akt; Standing Nude) (1907)

Tusche auf Papier/Ink on paper
30.9×20 cm.

Signiert in Tusche u.l./Initialed in ink l.r.: *GB.*

Doppelseitiges Bild mit Tuschenskizze auf Rückseite./ Double-faced image with ink sketches on reverse.
Mit Bleistift geschrieben auf Rückseite u.r./Inscribed in pencil l.r. verso: *5 traits*

Herkunft/Provenance: Galerie Kahnweiler, Paris(?); Collection André Lhote, Paris; purchased by Marlborough Fine Art, London, 1955; purchased by Cooper 10 October, 1955.

The Douglas Cooper Collection
(Owned by Churchglade Ltd.)

Literatur/Literature: Nicole Worms de Romilly and Jean Laude, *Braque – Le Cubisme 1907–1914,* Paris, Maeght, 1982, illus. no. 4, p. 62; William Rubin, "Cézannisme and the Beginnings of Cubism", *Cézanne: The Late Work,* New York, Museum of Modern Art, 1977, pp. 170–172.

2

(Stehender Akt; Standing Nude) (1907)

Radierung/Etching
Plate: 27.8×19.6 cm.; Blatt
Sheet: 48.9×32.4 cm.

Mit Bleistift numeriert und signiert auf dem Rand/ Numbered and signed in pencil below plate, u.l./l.l.: *22/25;* u.r./l.r.: *G. Braque*

Probeabzüge, 1907–08. In 1953 macht Maeght eine Edizion (Auflage 55: 25 auf Auvergne Papier; 30 auf Rives Papier.)/ A few trial proofs pulled in 1907–08. In 1953 Maeght Editeur, Paris, produced an edition of 55 prints: : twenty-five on Auvergne paper, thirty on Rives paper.

Herkunft/Provenance: Sold by Galerie Maeght, Paris, 1961; date and source of acquisition by Cooper undetermined.

The Douglas Cooper Collection
(Owned by Churchglade Ltd.)

Literatur/Literature: Edwin Engelberts, *Georges Braque, Catalogue de l'œuvre graphique originale.* Geneva, Galerie Rauch, 1958, p. 11, no. 1, bw p. 12, smaller bw p. 35; Marco Valsecchi, *L'opera completa di Braque,* Milan, Rizzoli, 1977, no G1 bw illus; William Rubin, "Cézannisme and the Beginnings of Cubism", *Cézanne – The Late Work,* New York, Museum of Modern Art, 1977, p. 170 illus; Dora Vallier, *Braque. L'Œuvre gravé,* Paris, Flammarion, 1982, 1, p. 16 illus; Nicole Worms de Romilly and Jean Laude, *George Braque, Le Cubisme, 1907–1914,* Paris, Maeght, 1982, p. 42, fig. A; Douglas Cooper and Gary Tinterow, *The Essential Cubism,* London, The Tate Gallery, 1983, no. 49, pp. 126–127, illus.

3

(Stilleben mit Gin-Flasche auf einem Tisch [FOX]; Still-life with Bottle of Gin on a Table [FOX]) (1911)

Radierung mit Kaltnadel auf Arches Papier/ Etching with drypoint on Arches paper
Plate: 54.7×37.7 cm; Blatt
Sheet: 65.3×50.3 cm.

Signiert in Bleistift u.r. auf dem Rand/ Signed l.r. outside of plate in pencil.
G. Braque

Herkunft/Provenance: printed in edition of 100 by Kahnweiler, Paris, 1912; obtained by Cooper at undetermined date.

The Douglas Cooper Collection
(Owned by Churchglade Ltd.)

Literatur/Literature: Edwin Engelberts, *Georges Braque – Catalogue de l'œuvre graphique original*, Geneva, Galerie Rauch, 1958, p. 11, no. 5; John Richardson, *Georges Braque*, Milano and Vienna and Würzburg, Silvana Edizione and Verlag Andreas Zettner, 1960, bw plate 9; Marco Valsecchi, *L'Opera completa di Braque*, Milan, Rizzoli, 1971, no. G5 bw illus; Douglas Cooper, *The Cubist Epoch*, London and New York, Phaidon, 1970, bw plate 38, p. 52; Dora Vallier, *L'œuvre gravé de Braque*, Paris, Flammarion, 1982, no. 6, illus; Nicole Worms de Romilly and Jean Laude, *Braque, le Cubisme, 1907–1914*, Paris, Maeght, 1982, illus. J p. 58; Douglas Cooper and Gary Tinterow, *The Essential Cubism*, London, The Tate Gallery, 1983, no. 52, pp. 128–129.

4

(Stilleben mit Würfel; Still-life with Dice) (Summer 1912)

Kohle auf Papier/Charcoal on paper
25×32.5 cm

Mit Bleistift signiert auf Rückseite u.r./ Signed in pencil, on reverse, l.r.:
G. Braque

Herkunft/Provenance: the artist to Galerie Kahnweiler, Paris, 1912 (label on verso of sheet: no. 879; photo no. 51); probably sequestered Kahnweiler stock, 1914–23; probably sold in an unidentified lot in one of the Kahnweiler sales, 1921–3; André Lhote, Paris, by 1923; Lhote estate, 1955; Marlborough Fine Art (London), Ltd., 1955; purchased by Cooper, 10 October, 1955.

The Douglas Cooper Collection
(Owned by Churchglade Ltd.)

Ausstellungen/Exhibitions: London, The Tate Gallery, *The Essential Cubism*, 1983, no. 47 illus.

Literatur/Literature: John Richardson, *Georges Braque*, Würzbürg-Wien, A. Zettner, 1960, bw repr. no. 13; Nicole Worms de Romilly and Jean Laude, *Braque, le Cubism 1907–1914*, Paris, Maeght, 1982, no. 130, illus.

5

(Fruchtschale und Glas; Fruit-dish and Glass) (September 1912)

Kohle und bedrucktes Papier auf Papier geklebt/Charcoal and printed paper pasted on paper
62.8×45.7 cm

Mit Bleistift signiert u.r./
Signed in pencil l.r.: *G. Braque*

Herkunft/Provenance: the artist to Galerie Kahnweiler, Paris (photo no. 1083), 1912 until before 1914; Wilhelm Uhde, Paris, before 1914; sequestered Uhde collection, 1914–21; Uhde sale, Hôtel Drouot, Paris, 30 May 1921, lot 69, sold for 200 frs. to Léonce Rosenberg; Galerie de l'Effort Moderne (L. Rosenberg), Paris, 1921–?; André Breton, Paris, by the mid-1920s; Mme. Simone Breton (later Simone Collinet), Paris, until 1946; purchased by Cooper in 1946 (Collection archival records contradict information in *The Essential Cubism* indicating instead purchase from Mme. Charlet in 1947).

Private Collection.

Ausstellungen/Exhibitions: Basel, Kunsthalle, *Braque*, April 9–May 14, 1933, no. 60, bw illus (catalogue Carl Einstein); Edinburgh, The Edinburgh International Festival and London, The Tate Gallery, *An Exhibition of Paintings by Georges Braque* (arranged by the Arts Council of Great Britain in association with the Edinburgh Festival Society), August 18–September 15, 1956 and September 28–November 11, 1956, no. 33, repr. 21a; Cincinnati, The Cincinnati Arts Center, Chicago, The Arts Club, and Minneapolis, The Walker Art Center, *Hommage to Georges Braque*, September 22–October 22, 1962, November 6–December 6, 1962 and December 20, 1962–January 20, 1963 respectively, repr; Munich, Haus der Kunst, *Georges Braque*, October 18–December 15, 1963, no. 37, repr. p. 33 (catalogue D. Cooper); Paris, Orangerie des Tuileries, *Georges Braque*, October 16, 1973–January 14, 1974, no. 46 repr. p. 90, not exhibited

(catalogue J. Leymarie); Paris, Galeries Nationales du Grand Palais, *Jean Paulhan à travers ses peintres*, February 1 – April 15, 1974, repr. pl 3, not in exhibition; Paris, Centre Georges Pompidou, Musée Nationale d'Art Moderne, *Georges Braque, les papiers collés*, June 17 – September 27, 1982, no. 1, reproduced color p. 67; Washington, The National Gallery of Art, *Georges Braque, The papiers-collés*, 1982, no. 1, bw repr. p. 88, including Douglas Cooper, "Braque as Innovator: The First Papiers-Collés", pp. 7–11; London, The Tate Gallery, *The Essential Cubism*, 1983, no. 25.

Literatur/Literature: Maurice Raynal, *Georges Braque*, Rome, Valori plastici, 1921, repr. cover; Maurice Raynal, *Georges Braque*, Rome, Valori Plastici, 1924, rep. 26; Carl Einstein, *Die Kunst des 20. Jahrhunderts, Propyläen Kunstgeschichte*, Berlin, Im Propyläen Verlag, 1928, repr. p. 301; Georges Isarlov, *Georges Braque*, Paris, Jose Corti, 1932, no. 144, p. 18; Carl Einstein, *Georges Braque*, Paris, Editions Chroniques du Jour, 1934, repr. XVIII; Henry Hope, *Georges Braque*, New York, Museum of Modern Art, 1949, repr. p. 54; Maurice Raynal et al, *De Picasso au Surréalisme*, Genève, Skira, 1950, p. 62, color illus; Michel Seuphor, *L'Art abstrait, ses origines, ses premiers maîtres*, Paris, 1950, repr. p. 130; Maurice Raynal, *Peinture moderne*, Geneva, Skira, 1953, repr. color p. 177; Herta Wescher, «Les collages cubistes», *Art d'aujourd'hui*, 3–4, série 4, may – june 1953, repr. p. 34; Maurice Gieure, *Braque – Dessins*, Paris, Pierre Tisné, 1955, repr. p. 4; John Richardson, «Au Château des Cubistes», *L'Œil*, no. 4, April 15, 1955, p. 21; Clement Greenberg, "The Pasted Paper Revolution," *Art News*, Sept. 1958, p. 48, repr. p. 46; John Golding, *Cubism: A History and an Analysis, 1907–1914*, New York, Harper and Row, 1959, p. 103; John Russell, *Georges Braque*, London, Phaidon, 1959, p. 18; Robert Rosenblum, *Cubism and Twentieth Century Art*, New York, Abrams, 1960, no. 37; John Richardson, *Georges Braque*, Milan, Vienna and Würzburg, Verlag Andreas Zettner, 1960, p. 15 bw illus; Jean Leymarie, *Braque*, Genève, Skira, 1961, p. 54 color illus, pps. 54–60; "Homage to Georges Braque," *Art International*, VI/9, Nov. 1962 repr. p. 42; Pierre Cabanne, *L'Epopée du Cubisme*, Paris, La Table Ronde, 1963, p. 182; Edward F. Fry, *Cubism*, London and New York, Thames and Hudson, 1966, repr. p. 38; François Mathey, «La trinité cubiste, Braque, Picasso, Gris», *L'arte moderna 4*, Milan, 1968, repr. p. 158; Edwin Mullins, *Braque*, London, Thames and Hudson, 1968, repr. pl. 50; Herta Wescher, *Die Collage – Geschichte eines Künstlerischen Ausdrucksmittels*, Cologne, Dumont Schanberg, 1968, No. 14, bw illus p. 22; Raymond Cogniat, *Braque* in *Les maîtres de la peinture moderne*, Paris Flammarion, 1970, repr. p. 72; Douglas Cooper, *The Cubist Epoch*, London, Phaidon, 1970, p. 185; Paul Waldo Schwartz, *Cubism*, London, Phaidon, 1971, p. 98, repr. p. 99; Marco Valsecchi, *L'Opera completa di Georges Braque*, Milan, Rizzoli, 1971, no. 87, repr; Eddie Wolfram, *History of Collage*, London, Studio Vista, 1975, p. 16, repr. p. 17; Winthrop Judkins, *Fluctuant Representation in Synthetic Cubism: Picasso, Braque, Gris, 1910–1920, New York and London, Garland Press, 1976, repr. p. 443; Pierre Daix and Joan Rosselet, Le cubisme de Picasso, 1907–1916*, Neuchâtel, Ides et Calendes, 1979, pp. 111–114; Nicole Worms de Romilly and Jean Laude, *Braque: Cubism, 1907–14 Paris, (Maeght Catalogue), 1982, no. 150 repr.*

6

(Stilleben mit Gitarre auf einem Tisch; Still-life with Guitar on a Table) (1917)

Tusche auf Papier (mit Bleistift)/
Ink on paper (with pencil)
19.1×27.8 cm

U.r. mit brauner Tusche/ l.r. in brown ink: *G.B.*

Herkunft/Provenance: Redfern Gallery, London; purchased by Cooper in 1944. (Or purchased St. Georges Gallery, London, December 1946, in exchange for a Léger drawing).

The Douglas Cooper Collection
(Owned by Churchglade Ltd.)

Ausstellungen/Exhibitions: London, The Tate Gallery, *The Essential Cubism, 1983, no. 48.*

Literatur/Literature: Nord-Sud, revue littéraire, no. 13, March 1918, illus; David Henry Kahnweiler, *Der Weg der Kubismus*, Munich, Delphin Verlag, 1920, 37; John Richardson, *Georges Braque*, Milan and Vienna and Würzbürg, Verlag Andreas Zettner, 1960, bw repr. plate 19; Dora Vallier, *Braque, L'Œuvre gravé*, Paris, Flammarion, 1982, p. 300 illus.

7

(Stilleben: Fruchtschale und Zeitung; Still-life: Fruit-dish and Newspaper) (1919)

Tusche und Bleistift auf Papier/
Ink and pencil on paper
19.5×27 cm

In Tusche u.r./In ink l.r.: *G.B.*

Herkunft/Provenance: purchased by Cooper from Redfern Gallery, London, in 1943.

The Douglas Cooper Collection
(Owned by Churchglade Ltd.)

Literatur/Literature: *Nord-Sud, revue littéraire*, no. 13, March 1918; Daniel Henry Kahnweiler, *Der Weg der Kubismus*, Munich, Delphin Verlag, 1920, 43; Marco Valsecchi, *L'opera completa di Braque*, Milan, Rizzoli, 1971, no. D4 bw illus; Dora Vallier, *Braque, L'œuvre gravé*, Paris, Flammarion, 1982, p. 300, illus.

8

(Feuervogel; Fire Bird) (ca.1954)

Oel und Kohle auf Papier auf Platte geklebt/Oil and charcoal on paper pasted to panel
27.7×48.9 cm

Mit Kohle signiert u.l./
Signed in charcoal l.l.: G. Braque

Herkunft/Provenance: Gift from the artist to John Richardson and Douglas Cooper ca.1955.

Collection John Richardson.

9

(Maquette für Katalog, Ausstellung Tate Gallery; Maquette for Catalogue, Tate Gallery Exhibition) (1956)

Gouache, geklebtes Papier und Tusche auf Papier auf Karton geklebt/Gouache, pasted paper and ink on paper pasted to cardboard
24.2×18.8 cm

Herkunft/Provenance: Gift from the artist, 13 May, 1956.

The Douglas Cooper Collection
(Owned by Churchglade Ltd.)

Cover of catalogue, *George Braque*, London, The Tate Gallery, 1956, curated by Cooper.

JUAN GRIS

10

(Stilleben mit Krug; Still-life with Pitcher)
1910

Kohle auf Papier (mit kleinen Tupfen weisser Kreide oder Gouache?)/ Charcoal on paper (with small touches of white chalk or gouache?)
48×31.3 cm

Inschrift und Datum auf Rückseite o.l. mit schwarzer Tusche (Signatur des Künstlers?)/Inscription and date verso u.l. in black ink (artist's signature?): *Victoriano Gonzalez/ 1910*.

Herkunft/Provenance: Georges Gonzalez Gris; Galerie Louise Leiris, Paris; purchased by Cooper 17 February, 1966.

The Douglas Cooper Collection
(Owned by Churchglade Ltd.)

Ausstellungen/Exhibitions: Paris, Galerie Louise Leiris, *Juan Gris, dessins et gouaches, 1910–1927*, 1965, no. 9, p. 9 illus.

11

(Stilleben mit Petrollampe; Still-life with Oil Lamp) (1911)

Kohle auf Papier/Charcoal on paper
47.9×31.5 cm

Herkunft/Provenance: Georges Gonzales Gris; Galerie Louise Leiris, Paris; purchased by Cooper 17 February, 1966.

The Douglas Cooper Collection
(Owned by Churchglade Ltd.)

Ausstellungen/Exhibitions: Paris, Galerie Louise Leiris, *Juan Gris, dessins et*

gouaches, 1910–1927, 1965, no. 6 p. 13; Bielefeld, Kunsthalle, *Zeichnungen und Collagen des Kubismus, Picasso. Braque. Gris, March 11 – April 29, 1979, no. 176*.*

12

(Stilleben: Suppenschüssel und Glas; Still-life: Soup Terrine and Glass) (1911)

Bleistift auf Papier/Pencil on paper 26.8×20 cm

Signatur und Widmung mit Bleistift u.l./Signed and inscribed l.l. in pencil: *A mon cher ami/Maurice Raynal./Juan Gris.*

Herkunft/Provenance: Inscription indicates work was gift to Raynal; date and source of acquisition by Cooper undetermined.

The Douglas Cooper Collection (Owned by Churchglade Ltd.)

13

(Stilleben mit Tasse und Glas; Still-life with Cup and Glass) 1911

Bleistift auf Papier/Pencil on paper 35.7×32 cm

Mit Bleistift signiert und datiert u.l./ Signed in pencil l.l.: *Juan Gris 1911.* (Zusätzlich, geschrieben mit braun-goldener Tusche auf Rückseite o.l.)/ (In addition, inscribed verso u.l. in brown-gold ink): *Victoriano Gonzalez*

Herkunft/Provenance: Galerie Kahnweiler (Inscribed verso u.r. in pencil: *No. 6242/1911/juan gris*); Jacques Zoubaloff; purchased by Cooper at Zoubaloff sale, Hotel Drouot, Paris, November 1935, no. 36 in catalogue.

The Douglas Cooper Collection (Owned by Churchglade Ltd.)

Ausstellungen/Exhibitions: Bern, Kunstmuseum, *Juan Gris,* 1955, no. 122; Bielefeld, Kunsthalle, *Zeichnungen und Collagen des Kubismus. Picasso. Braque. Gris,* March 11 – April 29, 1979, no. 184*; Berkeley, University Art Museum, University of California, and Washington, D.C., The National Gallery of Art, and New York, The Solomon R. Guggenheim Museum of Art, *Juan Gris,* 1983, no. 85.

Literatur/Literature: Daniel Henry Kahnweiler (translation by D. Cooper), *Juan Gris – His Life, His Work,* New York: Curt Valentin, 1947, no. 39, p. 101, bw illus.

14

(Stilleben mit Flasche und Zigarren; Still-life with Bottle and Cigars) (1912)

Kohle, Farbstift oder Kreide, Gouache und Tusche mit geklebtes Papier auf grauem Papier/Charcoal, colored pencil or oil crayon, gouache and ink with pasted paper on grey paper 47.5×31 cm

Herkunft/Provenance: Galerie Kahnweiler, Paris (label on reverse no. 1206, photo no. 240); Vente Kahnweiler; Galerie Simon (9073), Paris; sold, Ronald Fleming, London, 1926; purchased by Cooper from Fleming in 1939.

The Douglas Cooper Collection (Owned by Churchglade Ltd.)

15 a, b

(Gitarre; Guitar) Rückseite/verso: *(Violine; Violin)* (1913)

Bleistift auf Papier/Pencil on paper 65×50 cm

Signatur und Widmung auf Vorderseite o.l./ Signed and inscribed u.l. recto: *A Madame Rousseau/Bien affectueusement/Juan Gris;* Signiert auf Rückseite u.r./ Signed l.r. verso: *Juan Gris*

Herkunft/Provenance: the artist to Madame Rij Rousseau, Paris; Galerie Berggruen, Paris, ca.1955; purchased by Cooper in 1955.

Jasper Johns.

Ausstellungen/Exhibitions: London, The Tate Gallery, *The Essential Cubism,* no. 83, pp. 184–185 illus.

16

(Stilleben: Teekanne und Glas; Still-life: Teapot and Glass) 1916

Bleistift auf Papier/Pencil on paper 39.1×28 cm

Mit Bleistift signiert und datiert u.r./ Signed and dated l.r. in pencil: *Juan Gris 1916.*

Herkunft/Provenance: Purchased by Cooper from Jeanne Bucher, Paris, February 1938.

The Douglas Cooper Collection (Owned by Churchglade Ltd.)

Ausstellungen/Exhibitions: Bern, Kunstmuseum, *Juan Gris,* 1955, no. 134.

17

(Copie nach Cézanne, «Louis Guillaume»; Copy after Cézanne's "Portrait of Louis Guillaume") (1916)

Bleistift auf Papier/Pencil on paper
35.5×27.2 cm

Herkunft/Provenance: Georges Gonzalez Gris; Galerie Louise Leiris, Paris; purchased by Cooper 17th February, 1966.

The Douglas Cooper Collection
(Owned by Churchglade Ltd.)

Ausstellungen/Exhibitions: Paris, Galerie Louise Leiris, *Juan Gris: Dessins et gouaches. 1910–1927*, June 17–July 17, 1965, forward by D.H. Kahnweiler, no. 27, illus p. 32 left; Baden-Baden, Staatliche Kunsthalle, *Juan Gris*, July 20–September 28, 1974, z20 bw illus.

18

(Kopie nach Cézanne, Porträt seiner Frau; Copy after Cézanne's portrait of his wife) (1916)

Bleistift auf Papier/Pencil on paper
22.3×21.7 cm

Herkunft/Provenance: Georges Gonzalez Gris; Galerie Louise Leiris, Paris; purchased by Cooper 17 February 1966.

The Douglas Cooper Collection
(Owned by Churchglade Ltd.)

Ausstellungen/Exhibitions: Paris, Galerie Louise Leiris, *Juan Gris, dessins et gouaches, 1910–1927*, 1965, no. 23, p. 29.

Literatur/Literature: Douglas Cooper, *Juan Gris*, Paris, Berggruen, 1977, no. 257c, p. 28, bw illus p. 29 (see also 257b and 257).

19

(Stilleben: Der Tabaksbeutel; Still-life: The Tobacco Pouch) 1918

Bleistift auf Papier/Pencil on paper
31.8×47.6 cm

Mit Bleistift signiert und datiert u.l./ Signed and dated in pencil l.l.:
Juan Gris/ 4–18

Herkunft/Provenance: Purchased by Douglas Cooper from Jeanne Bucher, February 1938.

Private Collection.

Ausstellungen/Exhibitions: Lowestoft Art Centre, *Exhibition of Contemporary Paintings from the Private Collection of Douglas Cooper*, January 1951 (?); Bern, Kunstmuseum, *Juan Gris*, October 29, 1955–January 2, 1956, no. 141; Baden-Baden, Staatliche Kunsthalle, *Juan Gris*, July 20–September 29, 1974, bw illus no. Z31a, listed as cat. no. Z30a.

Literatur/Literature: Daniel-Henry Kahnweiler (trans. D. Cooper) *Juan Gris- His Life and Work*, New York, Curt Valentin, 1947, p. 3, no. 3, bw illus.

20

(Stilleben mit Gitarre und Noten; Still-life with Guitar and Sheet Music) (1923)

Tusche gehöht mit weisser Gouache auf Papier/Ink with highlights of white gouache on paper
24×30.8 cm

Mit Tusche signiert u.l./ Signed in ink l.l.: *J. G.*; Mit Bleistift u.r./l.r. in pencil: *Juan Gris*; Mit Bleistift u.l./l.l. in pencil: *1513*.

Herkunft/Provenance: Galerie Flechtheim, Berlin(?); "Groom Place" label on reverse indicates 1930s for date of acquisition by Cooper.

The Douglas Cooper Collection
(Owned by Churchglade Ltd.)

Ausstellungen/Exhibitions: Bern, Kunstmuseum, *Juan Gris*, 1955, no. 160.

Literatur/Literature: Carl Einstein, *Die Kunst des 20. Jahrhunderts*, Berlin, Im Propyläen Verlag, 1928, plate X (lists Galerie Flechtheim as owner).

OTTO GUTFREUND

21

(Kopf; Head) (1911)

Schwarze Tusche auf Papier/
Black ink on paper.
Blatt mit gerissenem Rand/
Irregular sheet of paper:
20.5×22.8 cm

Herkunft/Provenance: Gutfreund family, Prague; purchased by Grosvenor Gallery, London, 1965–1966; gift of Eric Estorick, Grosvenor Gallery, to Cooper 1966;

The Douglas Cooper Collection
(Owned by Churchglade Ltd.)

DAVID HOCKNEY

22

(Porträt Douglas Cooper;
Portrait of Douglas Cooper) 1974

Farbstift/Colored pencil.
43.3×35.5 cm

Widmung und Signatur (unleserlich) mit blauem Farbstift u.l./ Inscribed l.r. in blue pencil: *for Douglas/with love/from (illegible).../29 March 74*

Herkunft/Provenance: gift from the artist.

Collection William McCarty Cooper.

PAUL KLEE

23

Der Berg der heiligen Katze
(The Mountain of the Sacred Cat) 1923

Aquarell und Oelfarbezeichnung mit Bleistift auf Ingres Papier aufgezogen auf Karton bemalt mit Gouache/ Watercolor and oil transfer drawing with pencil on Ingres paper mounted on cardboard painted with gouache
Blatt/ Mounted sheet: 48.6×31.8 cm

Beschriftung auf dem Karton mit Tusche/ Inscribed beneath image on mount in ink: *1923 120 Der Berg der heiligen Katze*;
Signiert mit schwarzer Gouache direkt auf dem Werk u.r./ Signed l.r.in black gouache directly on the paper: *Klee*.

Herkunft/Provenance: Purchased by Cooper in 1945 (directly from the artist's widow or, more likely, from the Klee Gesellschaft).

The Douglas Cooper Collection
(Owned by Churchglade Ltd.)

Ausstellungen/Exhibitions: London, National Gallery, *Paul Klee, 1879–1946*, December 1945–February 1946, no. 68 (organized by the Tate Gallery; sponsored by the British Arts Council, the exhibition toured England); Newcastle-on-Tyne, King's College, *Paul Klee*, March-May, 1949(?); Paris, Musée National d'Art Moderne, *Paul Klee*, November 1969–February 1970, no. 62; Saint-Paul, Fondation Maeght, *Paul Klee*, July 9–September 30, 1977, no. 71 illus.

Literatur/Literature: "At the Klee exhibition," *New Writing and Daylight*, VII, London 1946, repr. after p. 12; Herbert

Read, *Klee (1879–1940)*, London, Faber and Faber, 1948, color illus pl. 3 p. 7; Douglas Cooper, *Paul Klee*, Harmondsworth, Middlesex, England, Penguin Books, 1949, color plate 9; Carola Giedion-Welcker, *Paul Klee*, New York, The Viking Press, 1952 bw illus, no. 46, p. 55.

24

*(Seiltänzer; Tight Rope Walker)** 1923

Lithograph on Japan paper
Blatt/ Sheet: 52.4×37.8 cm
Plate: 43.1×26.8 cm

Mit Bleistift signiert u.r./
Signed in pencil l.r.: *PKlee*; Numeriert mit Bleistift auf dem Rand u.l./ numbered in pencil l.l. beneath image: *23 138*

Herkunft/Provenance: One of 80 printed on Japan, signed and inscribed "23 138" which appeared in a portfolio, *Kunst der Gegenwart*, München, R. Piper & Co., 1923; acquired by Cooper in 1970s (?).

The Douglas Cooper Collection
(Owned by Churchglade Ltd.)

*Dieser Titel ist nicht auf dem Werk. Es ist jedoch dieselbe Komposition wie der *Seiltänzer*, mit Bleistift (1923, 215) und Aquarell und Oel (1923, 121)./
This title is not written on this work. It is, however, the same composition as that entitled *Seiltänzer*, produced in pencil (1923, 215) and in watercolor and oil (1923, 121). In this regard see: Eberhard Kornfeld, *Verzeichnis des graphischen Werkes von Paul Klee*, Bern, Kornfeld und Klipstein, 1963, no. 95; and Jürgen Glaesemer, *Paul Klee: Handzeichnungen 2: 1921–1936*, Bern, Kunstmuseum, 1984).

25

Blume und Früchte (Flowers and Fruits)
1927

Schwarze Tusche auf Ingres Papier aufgezogen auf dünnen Karton/ Black ink on Ingres paper pasted on thin cardboard
43.6×35.6 cm

Signiert mit Tusche auf dem Papier u.m./
Signed on paper in ink l.m.: Klee

Beschriftung mit Tusche auf Karton/
Inscribed on mount: *1927.Oe.5 Blume und Früchte*

Herkunft/Provenance: Purchased from Klee Gesellschaft 1946 (Cooper's notes, however, indicate gift from Lily Klee).

The Douglas Cooper Collection
(Owned by Churchglade Ltd.)

Ausstellungen/Exhibitions: London, National Gallery, *Paul Klee, 1879–1940*, December 1945–February 1946, (organized by the Tate Gallery), no. 88 (sponsored by the British Arts Council, the exhibition toured England).

Literatur/Literature: Will Grohmann, *Paul Klee: Handzeichnungen, 1921–1930*, Potsdam & Berlin: Müller & I. Kiepenheuer, 1934, plate 42; Jürg Spiller, *Paul Klee, Unendliche Naturgeschichte, Schriften zur Form und Gestaltungslehre*, Basel/Stuttgart, Schwabe, 1970, illus p. 120; Jürgen Glaesemer, *Paul Klee: Handzeichnungen 2: 1921–1936*, Bern: Kunstmuseum, 1984, illus 61a, p. 106 (Paul Klee Stiftung Oeuvre no. 275).

HENRI LAURENS

26

(Kopf; Head) 1919 (?)

Geklebtes Papier, Graphit und Kreide auf Karton/ Pasted papers, graphite and chalk on cardboard
52.5×29.5 cm

Signiert und datiert mit Bleistift u.r./ Signed and dated in pencil l.r.: *HL 1919* (17?).

Herkunft/Provenance: the artist to Galerie Simon, Paris; Jacques Zouboloff, Paris, before 1935; André Lefèvre, Paris, until 1962; Lefèvre estate, 1962–65; 2nd Lefèvre sale, Palais Galliera, Paris, 25 November 1965, lot 12, purchased by Douglas Cooper.

The Douglas Cooper Collection
(Owned by Churchglade Ltd.)

Ausstellungen/Exhibitions: Paris, Musée national d'art moderne, *La collection André Lefèvre*, no. 139; London, The Tate Gallery, *The Essential Cubism*, 1983, no. 207; Paris, Centre Georges Pompidou, *Henri Laurens, le Cubisme, Constructions et papiers collés, 1915–19*, 1986, no. 96 (incorrect work reproduced p. 107); Fort Worth, The Fort Worth Art Museum, *Henri Laurens, Cubist Constructions and Collages, 1915–18*, No. 96.

27

(Kubistischer Kopf; Cubist Head) 1919

Bleistift, Tusche und Gouache auf Papier/ Pencil, ink and gouache on paper
31.6×22.7 cm

Monogramm und Datum mit Bleistift u.r./ Signed with monogram and dated l.r. in pencil: *HL. 1919*

Herkunft/Provenance: Undetermined.

The Douglas Cooper Collection
(Owned by Churchglade Ltd.)

FERNAND LEGER

28

(Stehender Akt; Standing Nude) (1911)

32.6×23.7 cm
Tusche auf Papier/Ink on paper

Mit Tusche signiert u.r./ Signed l.r. in ink: *FL*

Herkunft/Provenance: Purchased by Cooper from Galerie Simon, Paris, November 1938.

The Douglas Cooper Collection
(Owned by Churchglade Ltd.)

Literatur/Literature: Douglas Cooper, *Fernand Léger – le nouvel espace*, London, Lund Humphries & Co., 1949, p. 39 illus (dated 1908)

29

(Studie für eine "Abundantia"; Study for an "Abundance") (1912)

Tusche auf Papier/Ink on paper
30.8×19.2 cm

Herkunft/Provenance: the artist to Galerie Kahnweiler, 1912–14; sequestered Kahnweiler stock, 1914–21; sold in an unidentified lot at one of the Kahnweiler sales, 1921–23; whereabouts unknown, 1923–67; James Wise, Paris, by 1967; Galerie Louise Leiris, Paris (photo no. 30503, stock no. 14931), 1967–69; Galerie Berggruen, Paris, 1969; Parke Bernet, New York, 17 December 1969, lot no. 30, sold to Douglas Cooper.

The Douglas Cooper Collection
(Owned by Churchglade Ltd.)

Ausstellungen/Exhibitions: London, The Tate Gallery, *The Essential Cubism*, 1983, no. 105.

Literatur/Literature: Albert Gleizes and Jean Metzinger, *Du Cubisme*, Paris, Figuière, 1912, repr; Christopher Green, *Léger and the Avant-garde*, New Haven and London, Yale University Press, 1976, p. 32, illus.

30

Nature morte (Stilleben; Still-life) 1913

Gouache und Öl auf Papier/
Gouache and oil on paper
47.7×59.3 cm

Signatur und Beschriftung u.r. mit Tusche (Titel mit Bleistift)/
Signed and inscribed l.r. in ink (title in pencil):
F.L.13/ nature/morte

Herkunft/Provenance: The artist to Galerie Kahnweiler, Paris (no stock or photo no. available), 1913–14(?); sequestered Kahnweiler stock, 1914–21; sold in an unidentified lot in one of the Kahnweiler sales, 1921–23(?); Galerie de l'Effort Moderne (Léonce Rosenberg), Paris (no photo no.), c.1923 until 1936; purchased by Cooper 1936.

Private collection.

Ausstellungen/Exhibitions: London, The Tate Gallery, *Fernand Léger*, February 17 – March 19, 1950, no. 48 (arranged by the Arts Council of Great Britian and the Association française d'action artistique; Cooper wrote introductory essay); Leeds, City Art Gallery, *Fernand Léger*, April 1950, no. 40 (?); Lowestoft Art Centre, *Exhibition of Contemporary Paintings from the Private Collection of Douglas Cooper*, January 1951 (?); London, The Tate Gallery, *The Essential Cubism*, 1983, no. 108, illus. p. 227.

31

Les Foreurs
(Die Sappeure; The Sappers) (1916)

Aquarell und Tusche auf Papier/
Watercolor and ink on paper
23×14.5 cm

Signiert und beschriftet u.r. mit brauner Tusche/ Signed and inscribed l.r.in brown ink: *Verdun/ Les Foreurs/ F. Léger.* Gestempelt u.l./Stamped l.l.: Paul Adamidi Frasheri Bey.

Herkunft/Provenance: Paul Adamidi Frasheri Bey, Geneva, before 1945; to Douglas Cooper in 1945 (Collection records indicate however: Paul Adamidi Bey; to Galerie Benador, Geneva; bought 1954, Heinz Berggruen, Paris)

The Douglas Cooper Collection
(Owned by Churchglade Ltd.)

Ausstellungen/Exhibitions: London, The Tate Gallery, *The Essential Cubism*, 1983, no. 110, pp. 228–229.

Literatur/Literature: Douglas Cooper, *Fernand Léger, dessins de guerre*, Paris, 1956, pl. I; *Fernand Léger*, Berlin, Staatliche Kunsthalle, 1980, p. 96, color illus.

32

Les deux tués (Die zwei Getöteten;
Two Dead) 1916

Braune Tusche und Bleistift auf Postkarte/
Brown ink and pencil on paper post card
12.3×8.9 cm

O.l. mit brauner Tusche/ U.l.in brown ink: *Verdun/Route de Fleury/Les deux tués/24–10–16/FL.*

Herkunft/Provenance: Collection Dangel, Paris; acquired by Cooper at unknown time

The Douglas Cooper Collection
(Owned by Churchglade Ltd.)

Literatur/Literature: Douglas Cooper, *Fernand Léger – Dessins de guerre 1915–16*, Paris: Berggruen and Cie., 1956, illus no. 42; Bradley J. Nickels, *Fernand Léger – Paintings and Drawings, 1905–1930*, Indiana Univeristy, doctoral thesis, 1966, illus VI-23, p. 183; Jean Cassou et Jean Leymarie, *Fernand Léger – das graphische Werk*, Tübingen, Verlag Ernst Wasmuth, 1973, No. 33, bw illus. p. 40; Christopher Green, *Léger and the Avant Garde*, New Haven and London, Yale University Press, 1976, no. 59; *Fernand Léger 1881–1955*, Berlin, Staatliche Kunsthalle, 1981, p. 132 illus in Christopher Green's "Légers Krieg, die Kriegszeit-Avantgarde und 'La partie de cartes';" Peter de Francia, *Fernand Léger*, London and New Haven, Yale University Press, 1983, illus. 7.22, p. 144.

N.B.: Text auf Rückseite/ Léger's text on verso written to Yvonne Dangel, 195 Boulevard Péreire, Paris Ternes: *Chère Mademoiselle, Cette carte peut-être vous changera un peu de nos gros canons. En tous cas, elle porte une date célèbre, celle de jour de la reprise de Douaumont. Le croquis a été fait le jour même au milieu d'un concert d'artillerie peu banal. Avec tous mes remerciements pour votre aimable carte, ayez celle-ci et mon bon souvenir que je vous prie de partager avec Madame votre mère et notre vieil ami Louis.*

33

Dessin pour "La Partie de Cartes" Zeichnung für "Das Kartenspiel"; Drawing for "The Cardplayers") (1916–17)

Tusche und Bleistift auf Papier/ Wash and pencil on paper
52.7×37.8 cm

Signiert und beschriftet mit Tusche u.r./ Signed and inscribed l.r.in ink : *dessin pour "la partie de Carte/Fragment./ FLeger*

Herkunft/Provenance: Purchased by Cooper December 1937 from Léonce Rosenberg.

Private collection.

Ausstellungen/Exhibitions: London, The Tate Gallery, *Fernand Léger*, February 1950, no. 52 (arranged by the British Arts Council with the Association française d'action artistique; introductory essay by Cooper); Leeds, City Art Gallery, *Fernand Léger*, April 1950, no. 44 (?).

Literatur/Literature: Bradley J. Nickels, *Fernand Léger, Paintings and Drawings, 1905–1930*, Indiana University, Doctoral thesis, 1966, illus VI-29, p. 185; Christopher Green, *Léger and the Avant Garde*, New Haven and London, Yale University Press, 1976, illus no. 83 p. 133; *Fernand Léger 1881–1955*, Berlin, Staatliche Kunsthalle, 1980, p. 132 illus in Christopher Green's "Légers Krieg, die Kriegszeit-Avantgarde und 'La partie de cartes'."

34

(Mann in mechanischer Landschaft; Man in a Mechanical Landscape) 1918

Tusche mit Bleistift, Aquarell und Gouache auf Papier/ Ink and wash, with pencil, watercolor and gouache on paper
24.5×32.7 cm

Signiert und datiert mit Tusche u.r./ Signed and dated l.r.in ink: *FL/18*

Bleistiftskizze auf Rückseite/ Pencil sketch on reverse.

Herkunft/Provenance: Date and source of acquisition by Cooper not determined.

Private collection.

35

Zwei Figuren; Two Figures) (1920)

Tusche auf Papier/
Ink and wash on paper
38×31.2 cm

Signiert u.m. mit schwarzer Tusche/ Signed l.m.in black ink: *FL.*
Signiert und beschriftet direkt darunter mit brauner Tusche/ Signed and inscribed directly below in brown ink: *cordialement/29/F. Léger*

Herkunft/Provenance: Purchased by Cooper in 1938.

The Douglas Cooper Collection (Owned by Churchglade Ltd.)

Ausstellungen/Exhibitions: London, The Tate Gallery, *Fernand Léger*, 1950, no. 56; Leeds, The City Art Gallery, *Fernand Léger*, 1950, no. 48 (?); Berlin, Staatliche Kunsthalle, *Fernand Léger*, 1980, illus. p. 162, cat. no. 167.

36

(Drei Frauen; Three Women) 1921

Bleistift auf Papier/ Pencil on paper
31.4×41.8 cm

Mit Bleistift signiert und datiert u.r./ Signed and dated in pencil l.r.: *F.L. 21*

Herkunft/Provenance: Date and source of acquisition by Cooper not determined.

The Douglas Cooper Collection (Owned by Churchglade Ltd.)

Literatur/Literature: Jean Cassou and Jean Leymarie, *Fernand Léger – das graphische Werk*, Tübingen, Verlag Ernst Wasmuth, 1973, no. 99, bw illus p. 78.

37

(Studie für "Mutter und Kind"; drei Figuren in einer Landschaft; Study for "Mother and Child"; Three Figures in a Landscape) (1922)

Bleistift auf Papier/ Pencil on paper
23.8×31.3 cm

Herkunft/Provenance: Musée Fernand Léger, Biot; Galerie Louise Leiris by 1958 (photo no. 30047; no. D.427); date and source of purchase by Cooper undetermined.

The Douglas Cooper Collection (Owned by Churchglade Ltd.)

Ausstellungen/Exhibtions: Paris, Galerie Louise Leiris, *F. Léger, Dessins et gouaches, 1909–1955*, February 19 – March 22, 1958, no. 24 bw illus.

Literatur/Literature: Bradley J. Nickels, *Fernand Léger – Paintings and Drawings 1905–1930*, Indiana University, Doctoral thesis, 1966, illus. VIII-34, p. 261; Gaston Diehl, *Fernand Léger*, München, Südwest Verlag, 1985, illus p. 47.

38

(Zwei Männer auf der Treppe; Two Men in a Stairway) 1924

Bleistift auf Papier/ Pencil on paper
29.3×25.5 cm

Beschriftet mit Bleistift u.r./
Inscribed l.r.in pencil: *F. L. 24*

Rückseite: Bleistiftskizze, zwei Männer in einer Landschaft/ Verso: pencil sketch of two men in a landscape.

Herkunft/Provenance: Date and source of acquisition by Cooper is undetermined.

The Douglas Cooper Collection
(Owned by Churchglade Ltd.)

39

Stilleben mit Kaffeekanne; Still-life with Coffee-pot) 1924

Bleistift auf Papier/ Pencil on paper
31.8×23.9 cm

Beschriftet mit Bleistift u.r./
Inscribed l.r. in pencil: *FL/24*

Herkunft/Provenance: Artist to Kahnweiler 1926 (?); purchased by Cooper from Lionel Prejger, Paris, 1970s.

The Douglas Cooper Collection
(Owned by Churchglade Ltd.)

Literatur/Literature: Maurice Jardot, *Léger dessins*, Paris, Editions des deux mondes, 1953, illus no. 26; Jean Cassou and Jean Leymarie, *Fernand Léger – Das graphische Werk*, Tübingen, Verlag Ernst Wasmuth, 1973, no. 12, bw illus p. 91.

40

(Die Siphonflasche; The Siphon) (1924)

Graphit und Farbstift mit Aquarell auf Papier/ Graphite and colored pencil with watercolor on paper
21.1×19 cm

U.r. mit Bleistift/ L.r.in pencil: *FL*

Widmung und Signatur auf Karton auf die Rückseite des Rahmens geklebt/ Inscription adhered to reverse of frame: *A ... (illegible) pretty girl./Amicalement/ FLeger.*

Herkunft/Provenance: Date and source of Cooper's acquisition undetermined.

The Douglas Cooper Collection
(Owned by Churchglade Ltd.)

41

Studie für "Stilleben mit Büste"; Study for "Still-life with Bust") 1924

Bleistift, Farbstift und Aquarell auf Papier/ Pencil, colored pencil and watercolor on paper
31.4×25.2 cm

Beschriftet mit Bleistift u.r./ Inscribed l.r.in pencil: *F.L-24*

Rückseite: Bleistiftskizze mechanischer Formen/ Verso: pencil sketch of mechanical shapes.

Herkunft/Provenance: Galerie Simon, Paris; Collection G.F. Reber, Lausanne; purchased by Cooper from Erna Reber, 1945;

The Douglas Cooper Collection
(Owned by Churchglade Ltd.)

Literatur/Literature: Carl Einstein, *Die Kunst des 20. Jahrhunderts*, Berlin: Im Propyläen Verlag, 1928, p. 333 bw illus.

42

(Komposition mit Pfeifen; Composition with Pipes) 1925

Bleistift auf Papier/ Pencil on paper
40.4×30.8 cm

Beschriftet mit Bleistift u.r./ Inscribed l.r.in pencil: *F.L/25*

Herkunft/Provenance: Purchased from Liongel Prejger, Paris, by Cooper in 1970s.

The Douglas Cooper Collection
(Owned by Churchglade Ltd.)

43

(Komposition mit Damebrett; Composition With Checker Game) 1926

Gouache auf Papier/
Gouache on paper
43×36.9 cm

Beschriftet mit schwarzer Gouache u.r./
Inscribed l.r.in black pigment: *F.L.26*

Herkunft/Provenance: Date and source of acquisition by Cooper undetermined.

The Douglas Cooper Collection
(Owned by Churchglade Ltd.)

44

Les gants (*Die Handschuhe; Gloves*) 1933

Schwarze Tusche auf Papier/
Black ink on paper
32.4×25.1 cm

Beschriftet mit Bleistift u.l./ Inscribed l.l. in pencil: *les gants/33 FL*

Herkunft/Provenance: Date and source of acquisition by Cooper undetermined.

The Douglas Cooper Collection
(Owned by Churchglade Ltd.)

45

(Bauarbeiter, Beine; Construction worker, Legs) 1951

Tusche/Ink and wash
63.5×48.5 cm

Beschriftet u.r./ Inscribed l.r.: *F.L-51*

Herkunft/Provenance: Acquired by Cooper from Galerie Louise Leiris, Paris, (no. 04106/6736) March 1958 in exchange for Léger *Composition*, 1937, gouache.

The Douglas Cooper Collection
(Owned by Churchglade Ltd.)

Ausstellungen/Exhibitions: Paris, Galerie Louise Leiris, *Fernand Léger, dessins et gouaches, 1909–1955*, 1958, no. 71 illus.

Literatur/Literature: Maurice Jardot, *Léger dessins*, Paris, Editions des deux mondes, 1953, no. 75 illus; Jean Cassou and Jean Leymarie, *Fernand Léger, drawings and gouaches*, Greenwich, New York Graphic Society, 1973, no. 273; Peter de Francia, *Fernand Léger*, New Haven and London, Yale University Press, 1983, illus 9.4, p. 202.

46

(Maquette für Katalogtitelblatt; Maquette for catalogue cover), (1950)

Gouache und Bleistift auf Papier/
Gouache and pencil on paper
32×24 cm

Innerhalb der Komposition/ Inscribed within composition: *Fernand Léger.* Bemerkung auf der Rückseite mit Bleistift in Cooper's Handschrift / Inscribed on reverse in pencil in Cooper's handwriting: *Design for catalogue cover for exhibition/ in London Feb. 1950.*

Herkunft/Provenance: Acquired from the artist.

The Douglas Cooper Collection
(Owned by Churchglade Ltd.)

47

(Maquette für Katalogtitelblatt; Maquette of catalogue cover), (1950)

Gouache und Bleistift auf Papier/
Gouache and pencil on paper
32×24 cm

Beschriftet innerhalb der Komposition/ Inscribed within composition: *Fernand/ Léger*; Bermerkungen auf der Rückseite mit Bleistift in Cooper's Handschrift/ Notes on reverse in pencil in Cooper's handwriting: *Design for catalogue cover for exhibition/ in London Feb. 1950.*

Herkunft/Provenance: Acquired from the artist.

The Douglas Cooper Collection.
(Owned by Churchglade Ltd.)

48

(Maquette für Katalogtitelblatt; Maquette for catalogue cover), (1956)

Gouache auf zusammengefaltetem Papier/Gouache on folded paper
30.6×18.5 cm.

Der Text innerhalb der Komposition/ Text within composition: *F. Léger/ Dessins/ de Guerre/ 1915–16;* Anmerkung mit Bleistift unter der Komposition/ Note in pencil at bottom: *Cette maquette est trop forte/ pour ce livre;* Weiterer Bemerkungen auf der Innenseite des gefalteten Blattes/ Notes within folded paper in ink: *Reproduire un dessin/ à l'encre que tu edits/ dans le livre/ en trait plus fort si possible/ et ce dessous/ ces lettres d'imprimerie/ F. Léger/ dessins de guerre/ 1915–16. ou Léger au dessins/ a toi devoir au mieux.*

Herkunft/ Provenance: Acquired from the artist.

The Douglas Cooper Collection
(Owned by Churchglade Ltd.)

JOAN MIRO

49

Programme, Ballets Russes de Monte-Carlo, New York, 1933–34 (Maquette)

Gouache auf Papier/
Gouache on paper
31.8×25 cm

Signiert und datiert u.l. mit schwarzer Gouache:/ Signed and dated l.l.in black pigment: *Miró/9–33.*; Direkt darüber, dem linken Blattrand entlang, Widmung mit Bleistift:/Directly above, along left edge, inscribed in pencil : *A Cooper/très amicalement/Miró/4/34.*

Rückseite: Farbskala des Künstlers, mit genauen Tönen:/ Verso: artist's color key indicating proper values for: *noir, outremer clair, vermillon inaltérable, citron*.

Herkunft/Provenance: Gift to Cooper from the artist, April 1934(?).

The Douglas Cooper Collection
(Owned by Churchglade Ltd.)

N.B.: Brief Miró's an Cooper/ Letter from Miró to Cooper, 2 January 1934: "J'ai en ce moment une exposition à New York chez Pierre Matisse qui coincide avec les ballets russes de Monte Carlo qui passent actuellement là-bas."

PABLO PICASSO

50

(Stehender weiblicher Akt; Standing Female Nude) (1906–07)

Schwarze Tusche und rote Gouache laviert auf Papier/ Black ink and red gouache with wash on paper
61.5×42.4 cm

Signiert u.l. mit Bleistift:/
Signed l.l. in pencil: *Picasso*

Herkunft/Provenance: Purchased by Cooper from Georges Reber in 1939.

The Douglas Cooper Collection
(Owned by Churchglade Ltd.)

Ausstellungen/Exhibitions: Zürich, Kunsthaus, *Picasso*, 11 September–30 October, 1932, no. 281.

Literatur/Literature: John Richardson, *Picasso / Aquarelle und Gouachen*, Basel, Holbein Verlag, 1956, no. 7 color illus.

51 a, b

(Zeichnung für die "Demoiselles d'Avignon"; Study for "Les Demoiselles d'Avignon") Rückseite/verso: (Amazone) (Spring 1907)
Kohle auf Papier/ Charcoal on paper
48×63.5 cm; zwei Papierstreifen beigefügt, l. und r./two strips of paper added, l. and r.: 63.5×48 cm.

Signatur und Widmung u.r. mit Tusche:/ Signed and inscribed l.r. in ink: *Pour mon/ cher ami/ Douglas Cooper/ Picasso/ 20.2.59*

Herkunft/Provenance: Gift of the artist to Cooper presumably in 1959; Bequeathed by Cooper to Kunstmuseum Basel in 1984.

Kunstmuseum Basel.

Ausstellungen/Exhibitions: Cambridge, The Fogg Art Gallery, *Master Drawings by Picasso*, 1981, no. 27a and 27b.

Literatur/Literature: Christian Zervos, *Pablo Picasso, Œuvres de 1912–1917, II***, Paris, Cahiers d'Art, 1932 to present, no. 644; Rückseite/ Verso: *(Amazone): Z, II**, 685;* Gunter Bandmann, *Les Demoiselles d'Avignon*, Stuttgart, Philipp Reclam. Jan., 1965, illus no. 7; Franco Russoli and Fiorella Minervino, *L'Opera Completa di Picasso Cubista*. Milan, Rizzoli Editore, 1972, illus no. 9; Leo Steinberg, "The Philosophical Brothel, Part I," *Art News* 71, September 1972, pp. 20–29, illus no. 12; Leo Steinberg, "The Philosophical Brothel, Part II," *Art News* 71, October 1972, pp. 38–47, illus no. 45; Ulrich Weisner, *Zeichnungen und Collagen des Kubismus*, Bielefeld, Kunsthalle, 1979, illus no. 12.

52

(Männerkopf; Head of a Man)
(late 1908)

Tusche und Kohle auf Papier/ Ink and charcoal on paper
61.6×47.4 cm

Signiert u.r. mit Kohle oder Bleistift:/ Signed l.r. in charcoal or heavy lead pencil: *Picasso*

Herkunft/Provenance: Pierre Loeb, Paris, by 1938; purchased by Cooper February 1938.

Private Collection.

Ausstellungen/Exhibitions: London, The Tate Gallery, *The Essential Cubism*, 1983, no. 158.

Literatur/Literature: John Richardson, "Au Chateau des Cubistes," *L'Œil*, no. 4, April 15, 1955, repr p. 22; Christian Zervos, *Pablo Picasso, Œuvres de 1912–1917, II***, Paris, Cahiers d'Art, 1961, no. 715.

53

(Stilleben mit Schokoladenkanne; Still-life with Chocolate Pot)
(early 1909)

Aquarell auf Papier/
Watercolor on paper
61.7×47.5 cm

Signiert o.r. mit schwarzem Aquarell:/ Signed u.r.in black pigment: *Picasso*

Herkunft/Provenance: The artist to Ambroise Vollard, ca.1909 until 1939; Madame de Galéa, Paris, 1939–52; Reid & Lefevre Gallery, London, by 1953; acquired by Cooper in 1953.

Private Collection.

Ausstellungen/Exhibitions: Milan, Palazzo Reale, *Picasso*, September 20 – November 20, 1953, no. 16 bw repr; London, The Tate Gallery, *The Essential Cubism*, 1983, no. 159.

Literature: Christian Zervos, *Pablo Picasso, Œuvres de 1906–1912, II**, Paris, Cahiers d'Art, 1944, no. 131; John Richardson, *Picasso*, Basel, Holbein Verlag, 1956, no. 12 color illus; Pierre Daix and Joan Rosselet, *Le Cubisme de Picasso, 1907–1916*, Neuchâtel, Ides et Calendes, 1979, no. 223, bw illus.

54

(Frauenkopf, Schatulle und Apfel; Head of a Woman, Casket and Apple)
(1909)

Bleistift auf Papier/ Pencil on paper
22.9×31.6 cm

Signiert u.l. mit Bleistift:/
Signed l.l.in pencil: *Picasso*

Herkunft/Provenance: Léonce Rosenberg, Paris, by ca. 1919 (?); Richard Wyndham, London, by the late 1920s; Rudolf Stulik, London; Gallery Arnold Haskell, London, 1933; Purchased by Cooper in 1933.

The Douglas Cooper Collection
(Owned by Churchglade Ltd.)

Ausstellungen/Exhibitions: London, The Tate Gallery, *The Essential Cubism*, 1983, no. 161, pp. 326–327.

Literatur/Literature: Arnold Haskell, *Black on White, An Arbitrary Anthology of Fine Drawings*, London, Arthur Barker, 1933, illus pl.20; Christian Zervos, *Pablo Picasso Œuvres de 1912–1917, II***, Paris, Cahiers d'Art, 1961, no. 714.

55

(Stilleben: Zuckerdose und Fächer; Still-life: Sugar Bowl and Fan)
(1909–1910)

Aquarell auf Ingres Papier/
Watercolor on Ingres paper
31.5×43 cm

Signiert u.r. mit Bleistift:/ Signed l.r.in pencil: *Picasso*

Herkunft/Provenance: Elsa Appelberg-Ulfsparre, Stockholm(?); Gosta Olson, Stockholm(?); Heinz Berggruen, Paris; purchased by Cooper at Sotheby Parke Bernet, New York, November 16, 1983, lot. no. 59.

The Douglas Cooper Collection
(Owned by Churchglade Ltd.)

Ausstellungen/Exhibitions: Stockholm, Svensk-Franska Konstgalliert, *Picasso*, 1959, no. 28 repr(?); Kassel, *Documenta III, Picasso* (drawings), 1964, no. 1 repr, after p. 186; Frankfurt, Frankfurter Kunstverein, Steinernes Haus, *Picasso: 150 Handzeichnungen aus sieben Jahrzehnten*, 1965, no. 39 repr(?); Paris, Knoedler, *Picasso: Dessins et Aquarelles 1899–1965*, 1966, no. 3 repr; Paris, Galerie Berggruen, *Œuvres cubistes: Braque, Gris, Léger, Picasso*, 1973, no. 5 repr; Paris, Fondation Maeght, *Exposition Reverdy*, 1970 not illus.

Literatur/Literature: Wilhelm Boeck, *Pablo Picasso*, Stuttgart, Verlag W. Kohlhammer, 1955, no. 52 bw illus p. 462; Jean Leymarie, *Picasso: Dessins*, Geneva, Skira, 1967, illus p. 36; Christian Zervos, *Pablo Picasso, Supplément, Œuvres de 1907–1909, XXVI*, Paris, Cahiers d'Art, 1973, no. 405; Pierre Daix and Joan Rosselet, *Picasso: le Cubisme, 1907–1916*, Neuchâtel, Ides et Calendes, 1979, no. 313, illus p. 249;

56

(Stehende Frau; Standing Woman) (1911–1912)

Tusche auf Papier/ Ink and wash on paper
55.2×21.7 cm

Signiert u.r. mit Bleistift:/ Signed l.r.in pencil: *Picasso*

Herkunft/Provenance: The artist, 1912–36(?); Galerie Renou et Colle, Paris; purchased by Cooper February 1936.

Private Collection.

Ausstellungen/Exhibitions: London, The Tate Gallery, *The Essential Cubism, 1983*, no. 167, pp. 332–333.

Literatur/Literature: Christian Zervos, *Pablo Picasso, Œuvres de 1912–1917, II***, Paris, Cahiers d'Art, 1961, no. 725.

57

(Stilleben mit Marc-Flasche; Still-life with Bottle of Marc) (1912)

Kaltnadel Radierung/ Drypoint etching
Plate:49.8×30.5 cm;
Blatt/ Sheet: 72.2×54.9 cm

U.r. mit Bleistift, auf Blattrand:/ L.r. in pencil, outside of plate: *Picasso*; U.l. auf Rückseite mit Blestift:/ L.l. verso in pencil: *no. 32* (edition no?)

Herkunft/Provenance: One of 100 copies published by Kahnweiler, pulled by Delatre; date and source of acquisition by Cooper undetermined.

The Douglas Cooper Collection
(Owned by Churchglade Ltd.)

Literatur/Literature: Bernhard Geiser, *Picasso peintre-graveur,* 2 volumes, Bern, Chez l'auteur, 1933 and 1968, no. 33b; Georges Bloch, *Pablo Picasso, Catalogue de l'œuvre gravé et lithographié*, volumes i-iv, Bern, Kornfeld und Klipstein, 1968, 1971, 1979, no. 24; Douglas Cooper and Gary Tinterow, *The Essential Cubism*, London, The Tate Gallery, 1983, no. 186, pp. 354–355; Brigitte Baer, *Picasso the Printmaker: Graphics from the Marina Picasso Collection*, Dallas, The Dallas Museum of Art, 1983, no. 7, p. 40–41.

58

(Stilleben mit Tisch und Birnenschale; Still-life with Table and Dish of Pears) (1912)

Kohle mit Graphit auf Ingres Papier/ Charcoal with graphite on Ingres paper
62×47.3 cm

Signiert auf Rückseite o.r. mit Bleistift:/ Signed verso u.r. in pencil: *Picasso*

Herkunft/Provenance: Purchased by Cooper from Renou et Colle Gallery in 1937.

The Douglas Cooper Collection
(Owned by Churchglade Ltd.)

Ausstellungen/Exhibitions:Paris, Petit Palais, *Les maîtres de l'Art Indépendant, 1895–1937*, June–October 1937, not in cat.; Bielefeld, Kunsthalle, *Zeichnungen und Collagen des Kubismus, Picasso, Braque, Gris*, March 11-April 29, 1979, no. 79 illus;

Literatur/Literature: John Richardson, "Au Château des Cubistes", *l'Œil*, no. 4, April 15, 1955, repr p. 21; Christian Zervos, *Pablo Picasso, Œuvres de 1912–1917, II***, Paris, Cahiers d'Art, 1961, no. 781.

59

(Komposition mit Violine; Composition with Violin) (1912)

Bleistift, Kohle, Gouache(?) und Zeitungsausschnitt auf Papier geklebt/ Pencil, charcoal, gouache(?) and pasted newspaper on paper
61.1×46.5 cm

Signiert mit Bleistift auf Rückseite o.l.:/ Signed in pencil on reverse, u.l.: *Picasso*

Herkunft/Provenance: Artist's studio late 1912 (Pictured in photo of artist's studio; see literature below); Galerie Kahnweiler, Paris (see label on verso: *No. 1278/ Galerie Kahnweiler/ 28, rue Vignon, 28)*; Date and source of acquisition by Cooper undetermined (probably 1950s).

Private collection.

Literatur/Literature: William Rubin, *Picasso in the Collection of The Museum of Modern Art*, New York, Museum of Modern Art, 1972, object at l.r. in photo of artist's studio, Boulevard Raspail, 1912–13, p. 207, no. 51; Pierre Daix and Joan Rosselet, *Le cubisme de Picasso, 1907–1916,* Neuchâtel, Ides et Calendes, 1979, photo of artist's studio, p. 358, illus 242.

60

(Eine Flasche "Bass" und Gitarre; Bottle of "Bass" and Guitar) (1912–13)

Pastell, Kohle und schwarze Tusche auf Ingres Papier/ Pastel, charcoal and stenciled black ink on Ingres paper
47.7×63.5 cm

Signiert auf der Rückseite o.l. mit Bleistift:/ Signed on verso u.l.in pencil: *Picasso*

Herkunft/Provenance: The artist to Galerie Kahnweiler, Paris, 1913–14 (stamp on verso: *Galerie Kahnweiler/ photo no. 287*; and u.r. in blue pencil: *287*); sequestered Kahnweiler stock, 1914–21; probably sold in an unidentified lot in one of the Kahnweiler sales, 1921–23; Dr. G.F. Reber, Lausanne, from the mid-1920s until 1939; purchased by Cooper in 1939.

The Douglas Cooper Collection
(Owned by Churchglade Ltd.)

Ausstellungen/Exhibitions: Cambridge, The Fogg Art Museum, *Master Drawings of Picasso*, 1981, p. 122 repr p. 123; London, The Tate Gallery, *The Essential Cubism*, 1983, no. 169, pp. 336–337 color repr.

Literatur/Literature: John Richardson, "Au Chateau des Cubistes", *l'Œil*, no. 4, April 15, 1955; repr p. 22; Christian Zervos, *Pablo Picasso, Œuvres de 1912–1917, II***, Paris, Cahiers d'Art, 1961, no. 376; Pierre Daix and Joan Rosselet, *Picasso: le Cubisme, 1907–1916*, Neuchâtel, Ides et Calendes, 1979, no. 511, repr p. 287; Franco Russoli and Fiorella Minervino, *L'Opera Completa di Picasso Cubista*, Milan, Rizzoli Ed., 1972, illus no. 547; Winthrop Judkins, *Fluctuant Representation in Synthetic Cubism*, New York, Garland, illus p. 376.

61

Stilleben: glas und eine Flasche "Bass"; Still-life: Glass and Bottle of "Bass") (1914)

Bleistift, Gouache und geklebtes Papier auf Papier auf Karton/ Pencil, gouache and pasted paper on paper mounted on cardboard
24.3×19.2 cm

Signiert u.l. mit Bleistift:/ Signed l.l. in pencil: *Picasso*; Signiert auf der Rückseite mit Bleistift:/ signed verso in pencil: *Picasso*

Herkunft/Provenance: Galerie Kahnweiler, Paris(?); sold amidst sequestered Kahnweiler stock (?); Collection Pierre Jeanlet, Brussels(?); Collection Marcel Mabille, Rhode-Saint-Genèse(?); Date and source of acquisition by Cooper undetermined.

The Douglas Cooper Collection
(Owned by Churchglade Ltd.)

Ausstellungen/Exhibitions: Brussels, Galerie Giroux, *Art français contemporaine*, 1947 no. 67 (?); Verviers, Gand and Brussels, Société Royale des Beaux-Arts Verviers, Cercle Royal artistique et littéraire de Gand, Palais des Beaux-Arts Bruxelles, *Sous le signe d'Apollinaire*, 1950, illus p. 16; Paris, Musée National d'Art Moderne, *Le Cubisme, 1907–1914*, 30 January–9 April 1953(?); Brussels, Palais des Beaux-Arts, *Panorama de l'art contemporain dans les musées et collections belges*, 1953, no. 43(?); Paris, Musée national d'art moderne, *L'ecole de Paris dans les collections belges*, 1959 no. 121(?); Brussels, Palais des Beaux-Arts, *Métamorphoses de l'objet*, 1971(?).

Literatur/Literature: Herta Wescher, *Picasso. Papiers Collés*, Paris: Hazan, 1960, no. 11 color illus; Christian Zervos, *Pablo Picasso, Supplément, Œuvres de 1914–1919, XXIX*, Paris, Cahiers d'Art, 1975, no. 18; Pierre Daix and Joan Rosselet, *Picasso, Le Cubisme, 1907–1916*, Neuchâtel, Ides et Calendes, 1979, no. 686.

62

(Stilleben mit Pfirsichen und Spielkarten; Still-life with Peaches and Playing Cards) 1914

Bleistift und Aquarell auf Ingres Papier
Pencil and water color on Ingres paper
48.3×62.3 cm

Beschriftet u.l. mit Bleistift:/ Inscribed l.l.in pencil: *Avignon 1914 Picasso*

Herkunft/Provenance: Galerie Simon (Label on verso: Galerie Simon, no. 0519; photo no. 653); purchased by Cooper in 1937.

The Douglas Cooper Collection
(Owned by Churchglade Ltd.)

Ausstellungen/Exhibitions: Paris, Petit Palais, *Les maîtres de l'art indépendant, 1895–1937*, June–October 1937 (not included in catalogue); Arles, Musée Réattu, *Picasso. Dessins, gouaches, aquarelles, 1898–1957*, July 6–September 2, 1957, no. 34; Cambridge, Fogg Art Museum, *Master Drawings of Picasso*, February 20–

April 5, 1981, no. 49 bw p. 131 (travels to the Art Institute Chicago and the Philadelphia Museum of Art).

Literatur/Literature: John Richardson, *Picasso/Aquarellen und Gouachen*, Basel, Holbein Verlag, 1956, no. 14 color illus; Pierre Daix and Joan Rosselet, *Picasso, le Cubisme, 1907–1916*, Neuchâtel, Ides et Calendes, 1979, no. 796.

63

(Der Kartenspieler; The Card Player) 1914

Bleistift auf Papier/ Pencil on paper
31.5×23.3 cm

Beschriftet u.r. mit Bleistift:/ Inscribed l.r. in pencil: *Picasso/14*

Herkunft/Provenance: Purchased by Cooper from Galerie Renou et Colle, Paris, June 1937.

Private Collection.

Ausstellungen/Exhibitions: New York, Valentine Gallery, *Drawings, Gouaches and Pastels by Picasso*, April 12–24, 1937, no. 35 (?).

Literatur/Literature: Christian Zervos, *Pablo Picasso, Œuvres de 1912–1917, II***, Paris, Cahiers d'Art, 1961, no. 507.

64

(Bärtiger Mann, Gitarre spielend; Bearded Man Playing a Guitar) 1914

Bleistift gehöht mit Aquarell und Gouache/ Pencil highlighted with watercolor and gouache
48.9×37.2cm

Signature, Ort, Datum u.r. mit Bleistift:/ Signed, dated and inscribed l.r. in pencil: *Picasso/Avignon 1914*

Herkunft/Provenance: Galerie Berggruen, Paris, by 1954(?); acquired by Douglas Cooper at undetermined date.

Private Collection.

Ausstellungen/Exhibitions: Bielefeld, Kunsthalle, *Zeichnungen und Collagen des Kubismus, Picasso, Braque, Gris*, March 11–April 29, 1979, no. 117; Cambridge, Fogg Art Museum, *Master Drawings of Picasso*, 1981, no. 48, p. 128–129 illus.

Literatur/Literature: Christian Zervos, *Pablo Picasso, Supplément aux vols. 1–5, Œuvres de 1895–1925, VI*, Paris, Cahiers d'Art, 1954, no. 1244; Wilhelm Boeck, *Picasso*, Stuttgart, Verlag W. Kohlhammer, 1955, no. 254, bw illus. p. 482 (as *L'homme masqué à la palette*); Pierre Daix and Joan Rosselet, *Le cubisme de Picasso, 1907–1916*, Neuchâtel, Ides and Callendes, 1979, no. 761, bw illus p. 166.

65

(Frau und Harlekin; Woman and Harlequin) 1915

Aquarell und Bleistift auf Papier/ Watercolor and pencil on paper
21.1×12.5 cm

Signiert auf der Rückseite o.l. mit Bleistift:/ Signed on reverse u.l. in pencil: *Picasso/1915*

Herkunft/Provenance: G.F. Reber, Lausanne, 1938.

The Douglas Cooper Collection (Owned by Churchglade Ltd.)

Literatur/Literature: John Richardson, *Picasso/ Aquarelle und Gouache*, Basel, Holbein Verlag, 1956, no. 16, color illus; Christian Zervos, *Pablo Picasso, Œuvres de 1912–1917, II***, Paris, Cahiers d'Art, 1961, no. 559; Douglas Cooper, *Picasso et le Théâtre*, Paris, Editions cercle d'art, 1967, no. 61; Pierre Daix and Joan Rosselet, *Picasso. le Cubisme, 1907–1916*, Neuchâtel, Ides et Calendes, 1979, no. 846, repr p. 348;

66

Je t'aime Gaby 1916

5 ovale Aquarelle und 2 ovalle Photographien, je: 4.2×3.5 cm; Rechteckiges Blatt mit Text und ornamentalem Rand: 6.5×17.5 cm; Rechteckiges Blatt mit Text: 3×13.2 cm.
5 oval watercolor and 2 oval photographs, each: 4.2×3.5 cm; rectangular sheet with text and decorative border: 6.5×17.5 cm; rectangular sheet of text: 3×13.2 cm

Texte: in farbiger Zierschrift: *Je/t'aime/ Gaby* (Verwoben mit *Picasso*); mit schwarzer Tusche: *J'ai demandé ta main au Bon Dieu/Paris 22 Fevrier 1916*. Texte auf der Rückseite der 4 ovalen Medaillon Bilder: 1) mit gelber ver-

blasster Tusche: *A toi/Gaby/de/toute mon/âme/Picasso/1915*; 2) mit rötlicher Tusche: *Gaby/Tu ne m'oublieras/jamais/Picasso*(?); 3) mit rosa Tusche: *Gaby/mon/amour/plus fort/pour toi*; 4) mit blauer Tusche: *je/suis toujour[ ] avec toi/Gaby.*

Inscriptions: In ornate colorful script: *Je/t'aime/Gaby* (interlaced with *Picasso)*; in black ink: *J'ai demandé ta main au Bon Dieu/Paris 22 Fevrier 1916*
Texts on the reverse of the four oval pictures. 1) in yellow faded ink: *A toi/Gaby/de/toute mon/âme/Picasso/1915*; 2) in reddish ink: *Gaby/Tu ne m'oublieras/jamais/Picasso*(?); 3) in pink ink: *Gaby/mon/amour/plus fort/pour toi*; 4) in blue ink: *je/ suis toujour[ ] avec toi/Gaby.*

Herkunft/Provenance: Given by Picasso to Gaby Lespinasse; purchased by Cooper in 1978 from Madame J. Blanchet, niece of Mme. Lespinasse (via Daniel Malingue?).

Collection William McCarty-Cooper.

67 a, b, c

(Drei Briefe mit provenzalischen Intérieurs; Three letters with Provencal Interiors) (1916)

Aquarell und Tusche auf Papier/
Watercolor and ink on paper
3 rechteckige Seiten: a) Schlafzimmer, 17.5×13 cm; b) Küche, 17.5×15.3 cm; c) Esszimmer, 17.5×11 cm
Three rectangular pages: a) bedroom interior, 17.5×13 cm; b) kitchen interior, 17.5×15.3 cm; c) dining room interior, 17.5×11 cm

Brieftexte: Text/Inscriptions: Text of sheet a) fast gänzlich getilgt, ausser den verschlungenen Namen: *Gaby* und *Picasso*;/
a) almost completely effaced except for interlaced names in decorative script: *Gaby* and *Picasso*;
b) *Gaby mon amour [ce par]le petit escalier que on monte/dans la chambre ma vie je t'aime toi ma douceur/ je suis si heureux avec toi mon ange. Toujours/ toujours à moi et pour toutjours je ne demande/ que en je te le jure. Je veux que je te ecrire encore/ que je t'aime et de toutes les couleurs Je t'aime/ Je t'aime Je t'aime Je t'aime Je t'aime/ Je t'aime Picasso*;
c) *Ma vie Gaby mon amour mon ange./ Je t'aime ma chérie et je ne pense que à toi/ je ne veux pas que tu sois triste et pour te faire oublier regarde la petite/ salle à manger. Je serais si heureux/ de vivre avec toi. [Prenez] mes lettres quand/tu es seule et pense combien je/ t'aime. Si tu savais combien et tu [ ] comme je t'aime./ A demain mon amour [je] /dans la nuit. Tout mon coeur. Picasso.*

Herkunft/Provenance: Given by Picasso to Gaby Lespinasse; purchased by Cooper in 1978 from Madame J. Blanchet, niece of Mme. Lespinasse (via Daniel Malingue?).

Collection William McCarty-Cooper.

68

Ton amour est pour moi ma vie (1916)

Aquarell auf Papier/
Watercolor on paper
62.8×5.8 cm

Inschrift: in Blockschrift: *Ton/ Amour/ Est pour/ Moi ma/ Vie*; die verschlungenen Namen: *Gaby* und *Picasso.*
Inscriptions: In block letters: *Ton/ Amour/ Est pour/ Moi ma/ Vie*; interlaced in decorative script: *Gaby* and *Picasso*

Herkunft/Provenance: Given by Picasso to Gaby Lespinasse; purchased by Cooper in 1978 from Madame J. Blanchet, niece of Mme. Lespinasse (via Daniel Malingue?).

Collection William McCarty-Cooper.

69

(Porträt Madame Eugenia Errazuriz; Portrait of Mme. Eugenia Errazuriz) 1918

Bleistift auf Papier/ Pencil on paper
33.4×25.4 cm

Widmung mit Bleistift u.r.:/ Inscribed l.r. in pencil: *Eugenia/Picasso/Biarritz 1918*

Herkunft/Provenance: Acquired from Heinz Berggruen(?).

The Douglas Cooper Collection
(Owned by Churchglade Ltd.)

Literatur/Literature: Douglas Cooper, *Pour Eugenia*, Paris, Berggruen & Cie., 1976, fig. no. 1.

70

(Pierrot) 1918

Bleistift auf Papier/ Pencil on paper
27.3×19.4 cm

Signiert und datiert u.l. mit Bleistift:/
Signed and dated l.l.in dark pencil:
Picasso/1918

Herkunft/Provenance: Date and source of acquisition by Cooper undetermined.

The Douglas Cooper Collection (Owned By Churchglade Ltd.)

71

(Pierrot und Harlekin; Pierrot and Harlequin) 1920

Gouache auf Papier/ Gouache on paper 21×26.5 cm

Signiert und datiert mit Bleistift u.l.:/ Signed and dated l.l.in pencil: *Picasso/20*

Herkunft/Provenance: Collection Léonce Rosenberg; Paul Rosenberg; purchased by Cooper, Sothebys, London, 3 July 1979, no. 15.

The Douglas Cooper Collection (Owned by Churchglade Ltd.)

Literatur/Literature: Christian Zervos, *Pablo Picasso, Œuvres de 1920–1922, IV*, Paris, Cahiers d'Art, 1951, no. 64; John Richardson, *Picasso – An American Tribute*, New York, Public Education Association, 1962, no. 20 bw illus; Douglas Cooper, *Pablo Picasso et le Théâtre*, Paris, Editions cercle d'art, 1967, no. 238.

72

(Stehender Weiblicher Akt mit Faltenwurf; Standing Female Nude with Drapery) (1920)

Tusche auf Papier/Ink on paper 24.1×15.7 cm

Signiert mit Tusche u.l.:/ Signed l.l.in ink: *Picasso*

Herkunft/Provenance: Date and source of acquisition by Cooper undetermined.

The Douglas Cooper Collection (Owned by Churchglade Ltd.)

73

(Stilleben mit Mandoline auf einem Tisch; Still-life with Mandolin on a Guéridon) 1921

Aquarell, Gouache und Graphit auf Papier/ Watercolor, gouache and graphite on paper 27.6×21.2 cm

Datiert mit brauner Gouache o.l.:/ Dated u.l. in brown pigment: *12–1–21*; und signiert direkt darunter mit schwarzer Gouache:/ and signed directly below in black pigment: *Picasso*

Herkunft/Provenance: Galerie Simon, Paris (?); Collection G. F. Reber; purchased by Cooper November 1938.

The Douglas Cooper Collection (Owned by Churchglade Ltd.)

Ausstellungen/Exhibitions: Zürich, Kunsthaus, *Picasso*, 11 September – 30 October 1932, no. 308; Cambridge, Fogg Art Museum, *Master Drawings of Picasso*, 1983, no. 66 repr p. 165;

Literature: John Richardson, *Picasso / Aquarelle und Gouache*, Basel, Holbein Verlag, 1956, no. 20 color illus; Christian Zervos, *Pablo Picasso, Œuvres de 1920–22, IV*, Paris, Cahies d'Art, 1951, no. 234.

74

(Knabe mit Eis-Lutscher; Boy with a Popsicle) 1938

Kohle auf Papier/Charcoal on paper 67.5×44.5 cm

Signiert und datiert mit Bleistift u.r.:/ Signed and dated l.r. in pencil: 23.7.38/Picasso.

Herkunft/Provenance: Galerie Pierre, Paris; Gustav Zumsteg, Zürich; Galerie Berggruen, Paris; acquired by Cooper at unknown date.

The Douglas Cooper Collection (Owned by Churchglade Ltd.)

Ausstellungen/Exhibitions: Lyon, Musée de Lyon, *Picasso*, 1953, no. 117 illus no. 20; Paris, Galerie Berggruen, *Picasso – dessins d'un demi-siècle*, 1956 illus; Arles, Musée Réattu, *Picasso, Dessins, gouaches, aquarelles, 1898–1957*, 6 July – 2 September 1957, no. 54 illus; Fort Worth and Dallas, Fort Worth Art Center Museum and Dallas Museum of Fine Arts, *Picasso, Two Concurrent Retrospective Exhibitions*, 1967, no. 198; Cambridge, The Fogg Art Museum, *Master Drawings of Picasso*, 1981, no. 85 illus.

Literatur/Literature: Christian Zervos, Pablo Picasso, Œuvres de 1937–39, IX, *Paris, Cahiers d'Art, 1958, no. 187; Cahiers d'Art*, vol. 13, no. 3–10, Paris, 1938, p. 163.

75

(Liegender weiblicher Akt; Reclining Female Nude) 1961

Bleistift mit weisser Ölkreide gehöht, auf dickes Notizblockpapier/ Heavy

lead pencil with white oil crayon highlights on heavy paper torn from notebook
24×32 cm

Oben datiert mit Bleistift:/ Inscribed at top in pencil: *24.12.61 I*; Widmung mit blauem Kugelschreiber:/ and in blue ball point: *pour Douglas Cooper son ami Picasso/le 25.8.63.*

Herkunft/Provenance: Gift from the artist, August 25, 1963.

The Douglas Cooper Collection
(Owned by Churchglade Ltd.)

Diese Zeichnung kommt wahrscheinlich aus dem Notizbuch No. 159, in *Je suis le cahier, The Sketchbooks of Picasso.* Andere Skizzen dieses Notizbuches sind Frauenporträts und mindestens zwei anderen liegende weibliche Akte, einer mit dem gleichem Datum wie diese Skizze.
Drawing probably pulled from Notebook no. 159, in *Je suis le cahier, The Sketchbooks of Picasso*, New York, The Pace Gallery, 1986. Other sketches in this notebook include female portraits and at least two other reclining female nude, one dated the same day as this sketch: 24.12.61 II.

Das ist eine von fünf Skizzen welche Cooper am 8. August 1963 gegeben wurden, und welche an der Loggia Wand im Garten des Château de Castille, in Grossformat mittels *Betograve* Technik, ausgeführt wurden.
This is one of five sketches given to Cooper, August 8, 1963, and which had been executed on loggia wall in garden of Château de Castille, in enlarged format, using *Betograve* technique (completed April 1963).

76

(Zeichnung für "Déjeuner sur l'herbe"; Study for "Déjeuner sur l'herbe") 1962

Bleistift auf Notizblockpapier (oberer Rand mit Perforierung)/ Heavy pencil on paper torn (at top edge) from spiral note book
27×42.5 cm

Datiert u.l. mit Bleistift:/ Dated l.l. in heavy pencil: *14.6.62./XVI*; Widmung mit blauer Tusche:/ Inscribed l.r. in blue ink: *Pour Douglas Cooper/son ami Picasso/25.8.63.*

Herkunft/Provenance: Gift from the artist, August 25, 1963.

The Douglas Cooper Collection
(Owned by Churchglade Ltd.)

Diese Zeichnung kommt wahrscheinlich aus dem Notizbuch No. 161, in *Je suis le cahier, The Sketchbooks of Picasso.* Andere Skizzen dieses Notizbuches beziehen sich ebenfalls auf das Bild *Déjeuner sur l'herbe* nach Manet, 1960, Z, XIX, 204.
Drawing probably pulled from Notebook no. 161, in *Je suis le cahier, The Sketchbooks of Picasso*, New York, The Pace Gallery, 1986. Other sketches in this notebook, relate as well to the painting, *Déjeuner sur l'herbe* after Manet, 1960, Z, XIX, 204.

Siehe Katalog Nr. 75 betreffend die Loggia Wand im Garten des Château de Castille./ See catalogue No. 75 concerning the wall in the garden at the Château de Castille.

77

(Zeichnung für "Déjeuner sur l'herbe"; Study for "Déjeuner sur l'herbe") 1962

Bleistift auf Notizblockpapier (oberer Rand mit Perforierung)/ Pencil on heavy paper torn (at upper edge) from spiral notebook
27.3×35 cm

Datiert mit Bleistift u.r.:/ Dated in pencil l.r.: *16.6.62 II*; Widmung u.l. mit blauem Kugelschreiber:/ Inscribed l.l. in blue ball point ink: *Pour Douglas Cooper/son ami Picasso le 25.8.63*

Herkunft/Provenance: Gift of the artist, August 25, 1963.

The Douglas Cooper Collection
(Owned by Churchglade Ltd.)

Diese Zeichnung kommt wahrscheinlich aus dem Notizbuch No. 163, in *Je suis le cahier, The Sketchbooks of Picasso.* Andere Skizzen dieses Notizbuches, dessen Anfang- und Schlusseite mit *15.6.62/7.6.62* beschriftet sind, beziehen sich ebenfalls auf das Bild *Déjeuner sur l'herbe* nach Manet, 1960, Z, XIX, 204.
Drawing may have been pulled from Notebook no. 163, in *Je suis le cahier, The Sketchbooks of Picasso*, New York, The Pace Gallery, 1986. Other sketches in this notebook, with front and back covers inscribed: *15.6.62/7.6.62*, relate as well to the painting, *Déjeuner sur l'herbe* after Manet, 1960, Z, XIX, 204.

Siehe Katalog Nr. 75 betreffend die Loggia Wand im Garten des Château de Castille./ See catalogue No. 75 concerning the wall in the garden at the Château de Castille.

78

(Zeichnung für "Déjeuner sur l'herbe"; Study for "Déjeuner sur l'herbe") 1962

Fettstift und Farbstifte auf Notizblockpapier (oberer Rand mit Perforierung)/ Oil pencil and colored pencils on paper torn (at upper edge) from notebook
24×32 cm

Datiert o.l. mit Bleistift:/ Dated u.l.in heavy black pencil: *1.8.62/II*; Widmung u.r. mit Bleistift:/ Inscribed l.r. in pencil: *Pour mon ami:/D. Cooper/ Picasso*

Herkunft/Provenance: Gift from the artist.

The Douglas Cooper Collection
(Owned by Churchglade Ltd.)

Diese Zeichnung kommt wahrscheinlich aus dem Notizbuch No. 165, in *Je suis le cahier, The Sketchbooks of Picasso.* Andere Skizzen dieses Notizbuches, auf dem Deckel: *17.6.62* beschriftet, beziehen sich ebenfalls auf das Bild *Déjeuner sur l'herbe* nach Manet, 1960, Z, XIX, 204.
Drawing probably pulled from Notebook no. 165, in *Je suis le cahier, The Sketchbooks of Picasso,* New York, The Pace Gallery, 1986. Other sketches in this notebook, inscribed on front cover: *17.6.62*, relate as well to the painting, *Déjeuner sur l'herbe* after Manet, 1960, Z, XIX, 204.

79

(Achilles) 1962

Bleistift auf Notizblockpapier (linker Rand mit Perforierung)/ Pencil on paper torn (at left edge) from spiral note book
27.5×21.3 cm

Datiert o.l. mit Bleistift:/ Dated u.l.in pencil: *28.10.62. III*; und direkt darunter mit Kugelschreiber:/ and directly below in ball point ink: *Pour mon ami/ Douglas Cooper/Picasso/le 25.8.63.*

Herkunft/Provenance: Gift from the artist, August 25, 1963.

The Douglas Cooper Collection
(Owned by Churchglade Ltd.)

Diese Zeichnung kommt wahrscheinlich aus dem Notizbuch No. 162, in *Je suis le cahier, The Sketchbooks of Picasso.* Andere Skizzen dieses Notizbuches, datiert und beschriftet auf der Anfangs- und Schlussseite mit: *N.D. de V./ 26.10.62/ 3.11.62*, sind Frauenköpfe, Pferdestudien, weinende Frau mit Kind, und ein Mann eine Frau verfolgend; alle diese Skizzen beziehen sich auf das Bild, *Der Raub der Sabinerinnen*, 1963, Z, XXIII, 121.
Drawing probably pulled from Notebook no. 162, in *Je suis le cahier, The Sketchbooks of Picasso,* New York, The Pace Gallery, 1986. Other sketches in this notebook, dated and inscribed on the front and back covers: *N.D. de V./ 26.10.62/ 3.11.62*, include female heads, studies of horses, a woman crying over a baby, and a man chasing after a woman, all relating to the painting *Rape of the Sabines*, 1963, Z, XXIII, 121.

Siehe Katalog Nr. 75 betreffend die Loggia Wand im Garten des Château de Castille./ See catalogue No. 75 concerning the wall in the garden at the Château de Castille.

80

(Reiter; Cavalier) 1962

Bleistift auf Notizblockpapier (oberer Rand mit Perforierung)/ Heavy lead pencil on paper torn (at top edge) from spiral notebook
20.7×27.3 cm

Datiert o.r. mit Oelkreide:/ Dated u.r. in crayon: *1.11.62./VI./VI.*; Direkt darunter Widmung mit blauem Kugelschreiber:/ Directly below in blue ball point ink: *pour/Douglas/mon ami/Picasso/ le 25.8.63.*

Herkunft/Provenance: Gift from the artist, August 25, 1963.

The Douglas Cooper Collection
(Owned by Churchglade Ltd.)

Diese Zeichnung kommt wahrscheinlich aus dem Notizbuch No. 162, in *Je suis le cahier, The Sketchbooks of Picasso.* Andere Skizzen dieses Notizbuches, datiert und beschriftet auf der Anfangs- und Schlussseite mit: *N.D. de V./ 26.10.62/ 3.11.62*, sind Frauenköpfe, Pferdestudien, weinende Frau mit Kind, und ein Mann eine Frau verfolgend; alle diese Skizzen beziehen sich auf das Bild, *Der Raub der Sabinerinnen*, 1963, Z, XXIII, 121.
Drawing probably pulled from Notebook no. 162, in *Je suis le cahier, The Sketchbooks of Picasso,* New York, The Pace Gallery, 1986. Other sketches in this notebook, dated and inscribed on

the front and back covers: *N.D. de V./ 26.10.62/ 3.11.62*, include female heads, studies of horses, a woman crying over a baby, and a man chasing after a woman, all relating to the painting *Rape of the Sabines*, 1963, Z, XXIII, 121.

Siehe Katalog Nr.75 betreffend die Loggia Wand im Garten des Château de Castille./ See catalogue No. 75 concerning the wall in the garden at the Château de Castille.

GRAHAM SUTHERLAND

81

(Porträt Douglas Cooper; Portrait of Douglas Cooper) 1966

Bleistift und Farbstift auf Papier
Pencil and colored pencil on paper
31×23 cm

Signiert und datiert o.r. mit Tusche/ Signed and dated u.r.in ink: *Sutherland/26 V 66*

Herkunft/Provenance: Gift from the artist, May 26, 1966.

Collection William McCarty-Cooper

Study for oil portrait of Cooper signed and dated *9.II.67*, 130.5×81 cm.

BIBLIOGRAPHIE
der Schriften von Douglas Cooper
BIBLIOGRAPHY
Douglas Cooper's writings

Bemerkung:
Es wird hier nur eine Teil-Bibliografie von Douglas Coopers Schriften vorgestellt, welche nur eine Auswahl seiner Buchkritiken (Kubismus betreffend) und keine seiner zahlreichen Leserbriefe. Die folgenden Abkürzungen wurden hier verwendet: *B = Burlington Magazine; BB = Books and Bookman; L = The Listener; TLS = The Times Literary Supplement*. Douglas Lord ist ein Pseudonym für Douglas Cooper.

Note:
Only a partial bibliography of Douglas Cooper's writings is presented here, including only selected book reviews (concerning Cubism) and none of his many letters to the editor. The following abbreviations are utilized: *B = Burlington Magazine; BB = Books and Bookman; L = The Listener; TLS = The Times Literary Supplement*. Douglas Lord is a pseudonym for Douglas Cooper.

Bücher/Books

Letters to Emile Bernard from Vincent van Gogh. Edited, translated, and with a foreword by Douglas Lord. New York: Museum of Modern Art, 1938 (English edition, 1938).

The Road to Bordeaux. By C. Denis Freeman and Douglas Cooper. London: Cresset Press, 1940 (American edition, 1941).

Panic. By C. Denis Freeman and Douglas Cooper. London: The Cresset Press, 1941.

Georges Seurat: "Une Baignade, Asnières", in the Tate Gallery, London. London: Lund, Humphries, 1946.

Georges Braque: Paintings, 1909–1947. Introduction. London: L. Drummond, 1948.

Juan Gris, ou le goût du solennel. Paris and Geneva: A. Skira, 1949.

Fernand Léger et le nouvel espace. Text in French and English. London: Lund, Humphries, 1949 (Swiss edition, 1949).

Paul Klee. Harmondsworth, England: Penguin, 1949.

Edouard Manet: Paintings. Introduction. London: L. Drummond, 1950 (French edition, 1950).

Rousseau. Paris: Braun & Cie, 1951 (English edition, 1951).

Henri de Toulouse-Lautrec. New York: H. N. Abrams, 1952.

Pastelle von Edgar Degas. Selected and with an introduction. Basel: Holbein Verlag, 1952 (American edition, 1953).

The Courtauld Collection: A Catalogue and Introduction. By Douglas Cooper, with a Memoir of Samuel Courtauld by Anthony Blunt. London: Athlone Press for the University of London, 1954.

Drawings and Watercolours by Vincent Van Gogh. A selection of 32 plates in colour, with notes. New York: Macmillan, 1955 (Swiss edition, 1955).

Marino Marini: 15 lithographies. Introduction. Paris: Berggruen & Cie, 1955.

Henri de Toulouse-Lautrec. New York: H. N. Abrams, 1956 (Austrian edition, 1956; Dutch edition, 1957).

Fernand Léger: dessins de guerre, 1915–1916. Paris: Berggruen & Cie, 1956.

Juan Gris: Letters, 1913–1927. Collected by Daniel-Henry Kahnweiler. Translated and edited by Douglas Cooper. London: privately printed, 1956.

Pablo Picasso: Carnet Catalan. Preface and notes. Paris: Berggruen & Cie, 1958.

Marino Marini. Greenwich, Connecticut: New York Graphic Society, 1959.

César. Amriswil: Bodensee-Verlag, 1960.

Paul Valery, Degas, Manet, Morisot. Translated by David Paul. Introduction. New York: Pantheon, 1960.

The Work of Graham Sutherland. London: Lund, Humphries, 1961 (American edition, 1961).

Nicolas de Staël. London: Weidenfeld & Nicolson, 1962 (American edition, 1962).

Pablo Picasso: Les Déjeuners. Paris: Editions Cercle d'art, 1962 (German edition, 1962; Spanish edition, 1962; American edition, 1963).

Great Private Collections. Edited by Douglas Cooper, with an introduction by Kenneth Clark. London: Weidenfeld & Nicolson, 1963 (American edition, 1963; German edition, 1963; French edition, 1963).

Picasso, Women: Cannes and Mougins, 1954–63. Preface. New York: H. N. Abrams, 1964 (English edition, 1965).

Great Family Collections. Edited and with an introduction. London: Weidenfeld & Nicolson, 1965 (American edition, 1965; French edition, 1965; Italian edition, 1966; German edition, 1967).

Picasso, théâtre. Paris: Editions Cercle d'Art, 1967 (Italian edition, 1967; English edition, 1968; American edition, 1968; Spanish edition, 1968).

Sunshine at Midnight: Memories of Picasso and Cocteau. By Geneviève Laporte. Introduction and translation by Douglas Cooper. London: Weidenfeld & Nicolson, 1975 (American edition, 1978).

Pour Eugenia: Une Suite de 24 dessins inédits exécutés en 1918 par Pablo Picasso. Preface and commentary. Paris: Berggruen & Cie, 1976.

Juan Gris: Catalogue raisonné de l'œuvre peint. With the collaboration of Margaret Potter. Paris: Berggruen & Cie, 1977.

Paul Gauguin: 45 lettres à Vincent, Theo et Jo van Gogh: Collection Rijksmuseum Vincent Van Gogh, Amsterdam. s'Gravenhage: Staatsuitgevereij; Lausanne: La Bibliothèque des Arts, 1983.

Ausstellungskataloge/ Exhibition Catalogues

Unit One. Includes essay, "Edward Burra." London: Mayor Gallery, 1934.

William Turner, 1775–1851. Paris: Braun & Cie; London: Soho Gallery; New York: Erich S. Hermann, 1949.

Fernand Léger: An Exhibition of Paintings, Drawings, Lithographs and Book Illustrations. Introduction. London: Tate Gallery, 1950.

Renato Guttuso. Preface. London: Hanover Gallery, 1950.

Impressionistes de la Collection Courtauld de Londres. Catalogue. Paris: Musée de l'Orangerie, 1955.

Juan Gris. Bern: Kunstmuseum, 1956.

Gauguin: An Exhibition of Paintings, Engravings and Sculpture. Organized by the Arts Council of Great Britain in association with the Edinburgh Festival Society. London: Tate Gallery, 1955.

G. Braque. Organized by the Arts Council of Great Britain in association with the Edinburgh Festival Society. Includes essay, "Georges Braque: The Evolution of a Vision." London: Tate Gallery, 1956.

Picasso – dessins, gouaches, aquarelles, 1898–1957. Arles: Musée Reattu, 1957.

Dora Maar, paysages. Preface. Paris: Berggruen & Cie, 1957.

Claude Monet: An Exhibition of Paintings. Organized by the Arts Council of Great Britain in association with the Edinburgh Festival Society. Includes essay, "Claude Monet." London: Tate Gallery, 1957.

Picasso Ceramics. London: Arts Council of Great Britain, 1957.

Guttuso. Text by James Thrall Soby, Douglas Cooper, and Roberto Longhi. New York: American Contemporary Arts Heritage Gallery, Heller Gallery, 1958.

Guttuso. Rome: Vetrina di Chiurazzi, 1958.

Degas: Monotypes, Drawings, Pastels, Bronzes. London: Lefevre Gallery, 1958.

Nicolas de Staël, 1914–1955. Preface. Arles: Musee Réattu, 1958.

Joan Miró. Bois gravés pour un poème de Paul Eluard. Paris: Berggruen & Cie, 1958.

Edward Middleditch. Preface. London: Beaux Arts Gallery, 1958.

Picasso. Marseille: Musée Cantini, 1959.

Vilato. Includes essay, "Pour Javier Vilato." Paris: Galerie de l'Elysée. 1959.

Masterpieces of French Painting from the Emil Bührle Collection. Organized by the Arts Council of Great Britain in association with the Edinburgh Festival Society. London: National Gallery, 1961.

20 disegni di Pablo Picasso. Rome: Galleria La Nuova Pesa, 1961.

Picasso: Le Déjeuner sur l'herbe, 1960–61. Paris: Galerie Louise Leiris, 1962.

Fernand Léger: Contrastes de formes 1912–15. Introduction. Paris: Berggruen & Cie, 1962.

Georges *Braque: Pradikat des ICOM: "agréée"*. Introduction. Munich: Haus der Kunst, 1963.

Ennio Morlotti. Foreword. New York: Galleria Odyssia, 1964.

Sutherland. Curated by Douglas Cooper, Franco Russoli and Vittorio Viale. Includes essay, "La Lotta eterna". Turin: Galleria Civica d'Arte Moderna, 1965.

Fernand Léger. Preface. Marseille: Musée Cantini, 1966.

Picasso deux époques. Lucerne: Galerie Rosengart, 1966.

Morlotti. Essays by Giovanni Sangiorgi, Douglas Cooper, Franco Russoli. Rome: Palazzo Barberini, 1966.

César: Œuvres de 1955 à 1966. Cannes: Galerie Madoura, 1966.

César. Preface. Marseille: Musée Cantini, 1966.

Graham Sutherland. Basel: Kunsthalle, 1966.

Ennio Morlotti. Essay. Basel: Kunsthalle, 1967.

Graham Sutherland. Munich: Haus der Kunst; The Hague, Gemeentmuseum; Berlin, Haus am Waldsee; Cologne: Wallraf-Richartz-Museum, 1967.

Picasso: Two Concurrent Retrospective Exhibitions. Fort Worth: Fort Worth Art Center Museum; Dallas: Dallas Museum of Fine Arts, 1967.

The Cubist Epoch. London: Phaidon, in association with the Los Angeles County Museum of Art, and the Metropolitan Museum of Art, New York, 1970.

Four Americans in Paris: The Collections of Gertrude Stein and her Family. Includes essay, "Gertrude Stein and Juan Gris". New York: Museum of Modern Art, 1970; Ottawa: National Gallery of Canada; San Francisco: Museum of Art, 1971.

Selections from the Nathan Cummings Collection. Introduction. Washington, D.C.: National Gallery of Art, 1970; New York: Metropolitan Museum of Art, 1971.

Braque: The Great Years. Chicago: Art Institute, 1972; English edition, 1973.

Joan Miró. Includes essay, "Miró: Painter-Poet of Catalonia." New York: Acquavella Galleries, 1972.

Sutherland. Foreward, Zürich: Marlborough Gallery, 1972; London: Marlborough Gallery, 1973.

Œuvres cubistes: Braque, Gris, Léger, Picasso. Introduction. Paris: Berggruen & Cie, 1973.

Ennio Morlotti. Includes essay, "My Friend Morlotti." New York: Marlborough Gallery, 1973.

Juan Gris. Curated by Douglas Cooper and Hans Albert Peters. Baden-Baden: Kunsthalle, 1974.

Joan Miró: Œuvres de 1925 à 1960. Preface. Paris: Galerie Melki, 1974.

Alex Reid & Lefevre 1926–1976. Includes introduction, "A Franco-Scottish Link with the Past." London: Lefevre Gallery, 1976.

César: Rétrospective des sculptures. Overzichtstentoonstelling von Sculpturen, 1953–1966. Includes excerpts from critical writings by Cooper. Geneva: Musée d'Art et d'Histoire/Musée Rath, 1976.

Picasso: 19 plats en argent par François and Pierre Hugo. Includes essay, "La Maîtrise des Hugo au service de Picasso." Amsterdam: E. J. Van Wisselingh & Co., 1977.

Henri Matisse, das Goldene Zeitalter. Includes essay, "Matisse und Gauguin." Bielefeld: Kunsthalle, 1981.

Braque: The Papiers Collés. Includes essay, "Braque as Innovator: The First 'Papier Collé'." Washington, D.C.: National Gallery of Art, 1982.

The Essential Cubism: Braque, Picasso, and Their Friends, 1907–1920. Curated by Douglas Cooper and Gary Tinterow. London: Tate Gallery, 1983.

Guttuso. Includes essay, "La Natura Non Come una Forza Ostile." Bologna: Galleria La Casa Dell'Arte, 1983.

Picasso – Todesthemen. Includes essay, "Picasso und der Tod." Bielefeld: Kunsthalle, 1984.

Artikel / Articles

"Edward Burra." *Unit 1: The Modern Movement in English Architecture, Painting and Sculpture.* Herbert Read, ed. London, Cassell & Co., 1934: 56–60.

"Modern Art." (Douglas Lord) *Tomorrow: The Journal of Living and Learning* 3 (Nov 1934): 14.

"Les Peintres de la Réalité en France au XVIIe Siècle." Review of an exhibition at the Musée de l'Orangerie, Paris. (Douglas Lord) *B* 66 (Mar 1935): 138–141.

"The Impressionists at the Palais des Beaux Arts, Brussels." (Douglas Lord) *B* 67 (Aug 1935): 84–88.

"Corot." Review of an exhibition at the Musée de l'Orangerie, Paris. (Douglas Lord) *B* 68 (Apr 1936): 192–195.

"Paul Cézanne." (Douglas Lord) *B* 69 (July 1936): 32–35.

"Juan Gris." (Douglas Lord) *Axis* 7 (Autumn 1936): 9–12.

"Rubens: Humanist, Painter and Diplomat." Review of an exhibition at the Musée de l'Orangerie, Paris. (Douglas Lord) *L* 17 (Jan 7, 1937): 18–20.

"Chefs-d'œuvre de l'art français." (Douglas Lord) *B* 71 (Aug 1937): 93.

"Van Gogh exhibition in Paris." (Douglas Lord) *B* 71 (Sept 1937): 140.

"The Artist Speaks – The Wisdom of Georges Rouault." (Douglas Lord) *L* 18 (Sept 29, 1937): 677–678.

"Une exposition d'art français du XVIIe siècle à Bristol." (Douglas Lord) *L'Amour d'art* 19 (1938): 394.

"France Looks at English Painting." Review of an exhibition of 18th and 19th century English painting at the Louvre, Paris. (Douglas Lord) *L* 19 (Mar 30, 1938): 673–674.

"Goya des Collections de France." Review of an exhibition at the Musée de l'Orangerie, Paris. (Douglas Lord) *B* 72 (Mar 1938): 143.

"Nineteenth-Century French Portraiture." (Douglas Lord) *B* 72 (June 1938): 252–263.

"Le Paysage à travers les Ages." (Douglas Lord) *B* 73 (July 1938): 38.

"A Juan Gris Exhibition." (Douglas Lord) *B* 73 (July 1938): 38.

"Rappel à l'ordre." Review of the exhibition "Cross-Section of English Painting 1938." (Douglas Lord) *London Bulletin* 4–5 (July 1938): 39.

"Honderd Jaar Fransche Kunst, Stedelijk Museum, Amsterdam." (Douglas Lord) *B* 73 (Sept 1938): 131–132.

"Van Gogh and John Russell: some unknown letters and drawings." (Douglas Lord) *B* 73 (Nov 1938): 227.

"The Art Galleries." Review of current exhibitions in London. (Douglas Lord) *L* 20 (Nov 10, 1938): 1010.

"French Art in Bristol." Review of an exhibition of French 17th century art at the Bristol Art Gallery. (Douglas Lord) *L* 20 (Dec 1, 1938): 1174–1175.

"Views of Paris: An Exhibition at Knoedler's in New York." (Douglas Lord) *B* 74 (Jan 1939): 40–41.

"Sequeira: a neglected Portuguese painter." (Douglas Lord) *B* 74 (Apr 1939): 152–163.

"War Artists' Exhibition at the National Gallery; R.A.F. Exhibition of Photographs at the Building Centre." *B* 77 (Oct 1940): 128–133.

"Paul Klee: A Memorial." Review of an exhibition at the Leicester Galleries. *L* 25 (Mar 13, 1941): 381.

"Harold Gilman: 1876–1919." Review of an exhibition at the Lefevre Galleries. *L* 30 (Sept 30, 1943): 384.

"Deux Automnes." *France Libre* 7 (Nov 15, 1943): 23–29.

"The Problem of Wilson Steer: A Study in British Painting." *B* 84 (Mar 1944): 66–71.

"Henri Rousseau: 1844–1910." *L* 31 (May 25, 1944): 584.

"Henri Rousseau: Artiste-Peintre." *B* 85 (July 1944): 158, 160–165.

"Encore Le Dix-Neuvieme..." Review of the exhibition "From Constable to Cézanne" at the Wildenstein Galleries, London. *France Libre* 9 (Dec 15, 1944): 115–116.

"George Moore and Modern Art." *Horizon* (London) 11 (Feb 1945): 113–130.

"Musées d'Europe." *France Libre* 10 (Sept 1945): 364–366.

"L'exposition de la collection du roi de Grande Bretagne." *Labyrinthe* 22–23 (1946): 22–23.

"Picasso-Matisse Exhibition." Review of exhibition at the Victoria and Albert Museum, London. *Phoebus* 1 (Jan–Febr 1946): 45–46.

"Lucien Pissarro." *B* 88 (Febr 1946): 45–46.

"Old Museums and Modern Masters." (unsigned editorial) *B* 88 (Feb 1946): 29–30.

"James Ensor." *B* 88 (Apr 1946): 97.

"Bonnington and Quentin Durward." *B* 88 (May 1946): 112–117.

"Georges Braque: l'Ordre et le métier." Review of Braque exhibition at the Tate Gallery, London. *France Libre* 12 (May 15, 1946): 63–66.

"Modern Art in Italy." *L* 35 (June 20, 1946): 820.

"Paris: les Chefs d'Œuvre des collections privées françaises retrouvés en Allemagne." *B* 88 (Aug 1946): 199–201, 228.

"The Re-organisation of the Louvre." *B* 88 (Oct 1946): 252–255.

"Select Acquisitions of the Contemporary Art Society: an exhibition at the Tate Gallery." *B* 88 (Dec 1946): 309–310.

"The Arts: A Survey" *Architects' Year Book* 2 (1947): 24–35.

"The Art of Primitive Peoples." Review of exhibition at the Berkeley Galleries, London. *B* 89 (Jan 1947): 22.

"Van Gogh exhibition: Musée de l'Orangerie, Paris." *B* 89 (Apr 1947): 104.

"Aspects of Modern Painting (2): Cubism." *World Review* (Apr 1947): 48–54.

"Sickert: Three Exhibitions at Agnew, Mayor and da Vinci Galleries." *B* 89 (July 1947): 194–195.

"A New Museum of Modern Art." On the new Musée d'Art Contemporain, Paris. *L* 38 (July 17, 1947): 110.

"The Musée de l'impressionisme and the Musée d'art contemporain." *B* 89 (Oct 1947): 283–284.

"Swedish Van Gogh Studies." *B* 89 (Dec 1947): 356–357.

"Van Gogh's The Yellow House: Part I, The Painter." *L* 39 (Jan 8, 1948): 57–59.

"The Iconography of Richard Wilson." *B* 90 (Apr 1948): 109–118.

"Les amis de Gustave Courbet." *B* 90 (May 1948): 148–149.

"A Painter's Painter." An assessment of the art of Delacroix on the 150th anniversary of the artist's birth. *L* 39 (May 13, 1948): 771.

"The Courtauld Collection at the Tate Gallery." *B* 90 (June 1948): 170–173.

"Delacroix et l'Angleterre – Exposition, Atelier de Delacroix, Paris." *B* 90 (Sept 1948): 268–269.

"Italian Futurist and Metaphysical Painting." *L* 40 (Sept 16, 1948): 407–408.

"Italian Painters of Today." *L* 40 (Sept 23, 1948): 444–446.

"Jacques-Louis David: A Bi-Centenary Exhibition." *B* 90 (Oct 1948): 277–280.

"24th Biennial Exhibition, Venice." *B* 90 (Oct 1948): 293.

"Richard Wilson's Views of Kew." *B* 90 (Dec 1948): 346–348.

"The Father of English Landscape." Review of Richard Wilson exhibition at the Birmingham City Museum. *L* 40 (Dec 2, 1948): 854.

"Art" Review of Jacques-Louis David exhibition at the Tate Gallery. *Spectator* (Dec 17, 1948): 806.

"David and the Neo-Classic Style." *L* 40 (Dec 23, 1948): 963–964.

"Visite à Fernand Léger." *Pour l'Art* 6 (1949): 6.

"The David Exhibition at the Tate Gallery." *B* 91 (Jan 1949): 21–22.

"Utrillo: The Story of a Modern Painter Who was Changed by Marriage and Religion." *Leader* (Jan 8, 1949): 10–11.

"G. Braque." *Town and Country* 103 (Mar 1949): 43, 92, 95–96, 99.

"Art Treasures of Lombardy». Review of exhibition at Kunsthaus, Zürich. *L* 41 (Mar 31, 1949): 538.

"French Pictures in London Galleries". *B* 91 (July 1949): 202–205.

"Baudelaire's Critical Outlook and Vocabulary." *L* 42 (Aug 4, 1949): 185–187.

"Baudelaire's Aesthetic Conclusions." *L* 42 (Aug 11, 1949): 233–235.

"'Trois siècles de peinture française' at the Musée Rath, Geneva." *B* 91 (Oct 1949): 289–290.

"Some Exhibitions of French Art." *B* 91 (Nov 1949): 320–223.

"The Books of Albert Skira." *Penrose Annual* 44 (1950): 28–31.

"Die Zukunft der Malerei: Ausländische Stimmen zur Debatte um Herbert Read." Essays by Cooper and others. *Der Monat* 2 (Apr 1950): 89–99.

"Two Schools of German Art." *L* 43 (Apr 13, 1950): 645–647.

"London-Paris: At the New Burlington Galleries." Review of exhibition at the Institute of Contemporary Art, London. *Eidos* 1 (May–June 1950): 46.

"Buildings and Museums in Copenhagen." *L* 43 (June 1, 1950): 954.

"The Biennale Exhibition in Venice." *L* 44 (July 6, 1950): 12–14.

"Art and Architecture in Stockholm." *L* 44 (Aug 31, 1950): 314–315.

"Pointillists and their Period." Review of exhibition at Redfern Gallery. *Eidos* 3 (Nov–Dec 1950): 41–43.

"Les Peintres et les Spectacles." *L* 45 (June 7, 1951): 909–911.

"The Yellow House and its Significance." *Mededelingen van de Dienst voor schone Kunsten der gemeente 's-Gravenhage* 8 (1953): 94–106.

"Homage to Van Gogh." Review of centenary celebrations in Holland. *L* 49 (May 14, 1953): 806–807.

"Cézanne's Studio: American Gift to France." (unsigned) *Times* (July 7, 1953): Arts section, 2.

"Picasso Exhibition in Lyons: Works from the Artist's Early Period." (unsigned) *Times* (July 10, 1953): 5.

"Cézanne in Aix." *L* 50 (July 23, 1953): 150.

"The New Braque Ceiling in the Louvre." *L* 50 (Sept 3, 1953): 369–370.

"Catalogue of the Courtauld Collection: List of Emendations." *B* 96 (Apr 1954): 119–122.

"Cézanne Studio Now National Museum." *New York Times* (July 11, 1954): Art section, 4.

"Reflections on the Venice Biennale." *B* 96 (Oct 1954): 317–322.

"Two Cézanne Exhibitions at the Orangerie and the Tate." *B* 96 (Nov–Dec 1954): 344–349; 378–382.

"La Grande Parade de Fernand Léger." *L'Œil* 1 (Jan 15, 1955): 21–26.

"Derain Exhibition at the Musée d'Art Moderne." *B* 97 (Feb 1955): 51–52.

"Au Jas de Bouffan." *L'Œil* 2 (Feb 1955): 13–16.

"The Painters of Auvers-Sur-Oise." *B* 97 (Apr 1955): 100–106.

"Musées des petites villes du Midi de la France: Musée de Ceret; Musée de Saint-Tropez; Musée de Bagnols." *L'Œil* 7–8 (Summer 1955): 38–45.

"La macchina e il quadro." *Pirelli: Rivista d'informazione e di tecnica* 9 (Mar–Apr 1956): 38–40.

"Nicolas de Staël: In Memoriam." *B* 98 (May 1956): 140–146.

"Cézanne's Vision of Provence." (unsigned) *Times* (July 30, 1956): 3.

"Paul Gauguin." *B* 98 (Aug 1956): 283–284.

"Matisse Without Masterpieces: A Paris Exhibition." (unsigned) *Times* (Sept 15, 1956): 8.

"Two Japanese Prints from Vincent Van Gogh's Collection." *B* 99 (June 1957): 204–207.

"Public and Private: World Art at the Brussels Fair." *Observer* (May 25, 1958): 8.

"Picasso Drawing Identified." *Baltimore Museum of Art News* 21 (June 1958): 1.

"Picasso Chapel Not to Open: Communists Suspect Political Ban." (unsigned) *Times* (June 30, 1958): 9.

"An Outline to the Art of Pablo Picasso." *Sunday Times Magazine* (Sept 28, 1958): 13.

"39-Ton Figure Erected on Pedestal: Moore's Unesco Sculpture." (unsigned) *Times* (Oct 17, 1958): 12.

"Art in the New Unesco Building: Sacrifice of an Ideal." *Sunday Times Magazine* (Oct 26, 1958): 23.

"The Tragedy of Maurice Utrillo." *L* 61 (Mar 1959): 457–459.

"Renoir, Lise and the Le Cœur Family: A Study of Renoir's Early Development." *B* 101. (May; Sept–Oct 1959): 162–171, 322–329.

"In Memory of Léger." *Observer* (May 29, 1960): 16.

"Courbet in Philadelphia and Boston." *B* 102 (June 1960): 244–245.

"The Paris Exhibition: Confusion at the Source: a review of this year's Council of Europe Exhibition in Paris." *Observer* (Nov 13, 1960): 15.

"Graham Sutherland's Religious Subjects." *Encounter* 17 (Oct 1961): 31–35.

"Lettre ouverte" (to Pablo Picasso) *Les Lettres Françaises* (Oct 26 – Nov 1, 1961): 7.

"Primitivism and Bombast." *New Statesman* (Oct 27, 1961): 624.

"The Missing Churchill Portrait." *Sunday Times Magazine* (Nov 19, 1961): 25.

"Absent Genius." *New Statesman* 64 (July 6, 1962): 24–25.

"Manet, Giorgione, Picasso." *Les Lettres Françaises* (June 7–13, 1962): 1, 10.

"How to Collect Pictures and Influence People." *Sunday Times* (July 10, 1962): 14–17.

"Venice Art Fair." *New Statesman* (Aug 17, 1962): 208–209.

"Provence." *Queen* (Sept 18, 1962): 56.

"Matisse Museum." *New Statesman* (Feb 1963): 162.

"Hendy Under Fire: Sir Philip Hendy's 17-year Directorate of the National Gallery." *Sunday Times Colour Magazine* (May 5, 1963): 29–30.

"The Full Glory of Delacroix." *Daily Telegraph and Morning Post* (June 27, 1963): 12.

"Georges Braque." *L'Œil* 107 (Nov 1963): 26–33.

"A Shock Wave from the Whole World of Art." Review of an exhibition of contemporary art at the Tate Gallery. *Evening Standard* (November 18, 1963): 7.

"Goya." *Sunday Times Colour Magazine* (Dec 8, 1963): 20–30.

"Establishment and Avant-Garde." *TLS* (Sept 3, 1964): 823.

"Count of Bohemia." *Sunday Times* (Nov 22, 1964): 32–35.

"Paris 1964." *Art in America* 52 (Dec 1964): 111–112.

"Sutherland, Graham." *Encyclopedia Americana* (1965).

"Ingres The Marvellous Portraitist." Review of exhibition at the Petit Palais, Paris. *Times* (Nov 7, 1967): 14.

"Picasso, Pablo." *Encyclopaedia Brittanica,* 14th ed. (1968).

"Gris, Juan." *Encyclopaedia Brittanica,* 14th ed. (1968).

"The Demise of the Coffee-Table Book." *TLS* (June 20, 1968): 643–644.

"Celebrating the Ingres Cenenary." *Master Drawings* 6 (Autumn 1968): 281–286.

"Monets in The Metropolitan Museum." *Metropolitan Museum of Art Journal* 3 (1970): 281–305.

"Cummings Event in Washington." Review of exhibition at National Gallery of Art, Washington, D.C. *Art News* 69 (Summer 1970): 34–37, 75–76.

"Toulouse-Lautrec, Henri de," *Encyclopaedia Brittanica,* 14th ed. (1971).

"Gertrude Stein and Juan Gris." *Apollo* 93 (Jan 71): 28–35.

"The Temperament of Juan Gris." *Metropolitan Museum of Art Bulletin* 29 (Apr 1971): 358–62.

"Fernand Léger, Galeries nationales du Grand Palais." *L'Œil* 204 (Dec 1971): 26–27.

"Lista d'Urgenza Per Il Futuro Ministro." *BolaffiArte* (May 1972): 16.

"Il Catalano Internazionale." *BolaffiArte* (Dec 1972): 46–51.

"El futuro museo Espanol de Arte Contemporaneo." *Belles Artes* 4 (1973): 25–26.

"Parade." A revival in New York by the Joffrey Ballet. *Dance and Dancers* 24 (June 1973): 20–24.

"Gauguin, Paul." *Encyclopaedia Brittanica,* 15th ed. (1974).

"Early Collectors of Impressionist Painting." *Impressionism and Modern Art: the Season at Sotheby Parke Bernet.* Edited by Michel Strauss. London, New York: Sotheby Parke Bernet, 1974: VII–XX.

"Le Centenaire de l'Impressionnisme." *Revue de l'art* 28 (Nov 1975): 78–85.

"Mon exposition a coulé." *Connaissance des Arts* 286 (Dec 1975): 5.

"Juan Gris: Netteté et Austerité." *Réalites* 374 (Apr 1977): 52–61.

"An Important Gauguin Discovery." *B* 123 (Apr 1981): 195–197.

"Picasso's 'Guernica' Installed in the Prado." *B* 124 (May 1982): 288–292.

"Madrid: Rejuvenation at the Prado." *B* 125 (June 1983): 383–384.

"Lugano: French Paintings from Russia." *B* 125 (Sept 1983): 575–576.

"Moscow and Leningrad: Old Masters from the Thyssen-Bornemisza Collection." *B* 125 (Dec 1983): 788.

"A Juan Gris Discovery." *B* 126 (Febr 1984): 91.

"Baden-Baden: Seurat Drawings." *B* 126 (Mar 1984): 181–182.

Buchkritiken (Auswahl) / Selected Book Reviews

Larrea, Juan, *Guernica, Pablo Picasso. L* 38 (Dec 18, 1947): 1068–1069.

Cirici-Pellicer, A., *Picasso Antes De Picasso. B* 90 (May 1948): 152.

Zervos, Christian, *Dessins de Pablo Picasso, 1892–1948. TLS* (Sept 30, 1949): 635.

The Sculptures of Picasso. Text by Daniel-Henry Kahnweiler. *L* 42 (Nov 10, 1949): 820.

Sabartés, Jaime, *Picasso, An Intimate Portrait. Spectator* (Jan 13, 1950): 50, 52.

Klee, Paul. *Dokumente und Bilder aus den Jahren 1896–1930. TLS* (Jan 27, 1950): 51.

Hope, Henry R., *Georges Braque. B* 92 (Febr 1950): 58.

Klee, Paul, *Pedagogical Sketchbook. TLS* (Oct 9, 1953): 640.

Haftmann, Werner, *The Mind and Work of Paul Klee.* Grohmann, Will, *Paul Klee. TLS* (Mar 4, 1955): 125–126.

Verve. The French Review of Art. Vol. 8, Nos. 29/30. "Suite de 180 Dessins de Picasso. 28 Novembre, 1953, au 3 Fevrier, 1954." *TLS* (Mar 11, 1955): 144.

Kuh, Katherine, *Léger. TLS* (Mar 12, 1954): 164.

Gray, Christopher, *Cubist Aesthetic Theories. TLS* (Apr 29, 1955): 196.

Kahnweiler, Daniel-Henry. *The Rise of Cubism.* Translated by Henry Aronson. *TLS* (June 8, 1956): 340.

Pablo Picasso. Fifty-five Years of his Graphic Work. Introduction and Selection by Bernhard Geiser. Biography and Documentation by Hans Bollinger. Translated by Lisbeth Gombrich. *TLS* (June 15, 1956): 358.

The Intimate Sketchbooks of G. Braque. Introduction by Rebecca West. (Verve 8, Nos. 31–32) *TLS* (June 22, 1956):

Elgar, Frank, and Robert Maillard, *Picasso.* Translated by Francis Scarfe; *Picasso's Vollard, Suite.* Introduction by Hans Bolliger. Translated by Norbert Guterman; Mourlot, Fernand, *Picasso Lithographe.* Volume III; *Georges Braque.* Portraits by Roger Hauert. Text by Andre Verdet. Translated by Frances Richardson. *Pablo Picasso.* Portraits by Roger Hauert. Text by Andre Verdet. Translated by Frances Richardson. *TLS* (Dec 21, 1956): 760.

Picasso. Introduction by Fernanda Wittgens. Translated by Eric Mosbacher; San Lazzaro, G. di, *Klee: A Study of his Life and Work.* Translated by Stuart Hood. *TLS* (Jan 24, 1958): 40.

Leymarie, Jean, *Fauvism.* Translated by James Emmons; Habasque, Guy, *Cubism.* Translated by Stuart Gilbert. *TLS* (Aug 7, 1959): 456.

Golding, John, *Cubism. TLS* (Jan 1, 1960): 4.

Padrta, Jiri, *Picasso: The Early Years.* Preface by Jean Cocteau. Translated by Iris Urwin. *TLS* (Aug 12, 1960): 518.

"Pablo Picasso: The Artist as Subject." Review of 42 books, exhibition catalogues, and periodicals devoted to Picasso. *TLS* (Dec 22, 1961): 905–906, 908. Inklusive die folgenden Bücher/Including the following books:

- Apollinaire, Guillaume, *Chroniques d'Art*, 1960.
- Apollinaire, Guillaume, *Les Peintres Cubistes*, 1913. English translation by Lionel Abel under title *The Cubist Painters*, 1944.
- Barr, Alfred H., *Picasso, Fifty Years of his Art*, 1946.
- Boeck, Wilhelm, and Jaime Sabartès: *Picasso*, 1955.
- Boudaille, Georges, ed., *Picasso, Carnet de la Californie*, 1959.
- Champris, Pierre de, *Picasso, Ombre et Soleil*, 1960.
- Cirici-Pellicer, A., *Picasso antes de Picasso*,1946. French translation, with revisions, under title *Picasso avant Picasso*, 1950.
- Cooper, Douglas, ed., *Picasso: Carnet Catalan*, 1958.
- Dominguin, Luis Miguel, and Georges Boudaille, ed., *Toros y Toreros*, 1961.
- Duncan, David Douglas, *Picasso's Picassos*, 1961.
- Duncan, David Douglas, *The Private World of Pablo Picasso*, 1958.
- Elgar, Frank, and Robert Maillard, *Picasso*, 1955.
- Foster, J. K., *Posters of Picasso*, 1957.
- Geiser, Bernhard, *Picasso, Fifty-five Years of his Graphic Work*, 1955.
- Geiser, Bernhard, *Picasso, Peintre-Graveur*, 1955.
- Golding, John, *Cubism*, 1959.
- Janis, Harriet and Sidney, *Picasso: the Recent Years, 1939–46*, 1946.
- Kahnweiler, Daniel-Henry, *Entretiens*, 1961.
- Kahnweiler, Daniel-Henry, *Picasso, Keramik*, 1957.
- Kahnweiler, Daniel-Henry, *Les Sculptures de Picasso*, 1949.
- Kahnweiler, Daniel-Henry, *Der Weg zum Kubismus*, 1920. English translation by Henry Aronson under title *The Rise of Cubism*, 1949.
- Larrea, Juan, ed., *Guernica*, 1947.
- Matarasso, H., *Bibliographie des Livres Illustrés par Picasso*, 1956.
- Mourlot, Fernand, *Picasso Lithographe*. Three volumes, 1949–56.
- Olivier, Fernande, *Picasso et ses Amis*, 1933.
- Parmelin, Hélène, *Picasso sur la Place*, 1959.
- Penrose, Roland, *Picasso, his Life and Work*, 1958.
- Penrose, Roland, *Portrait of Picasso*, 1966.
- Ráfols, J. F., *Modernismo y Modernistas*, 1949.
- Ramié, Suzanne and Georges, *Céramiques de Picasso*, 1948.
- Rosenblum, Robert, *Cubism and 20th Century Art*, 1960.
- Roy, Claude, ed., *La Guerre et la Paix*, 1952.
- Sabartès, Jaime, *Les Ménines*, 1958.
- Sabartès, Jaime, *Picasso, Documents Iconographiques*, 1954.
- Sabartès, Jaime, *Picasso, Portraits et Souvenirs*, 1946.
- Salmon, André, *Souvenirs sans Fin*. Two volumes, 1955–56.
- de la Souchère, Dor, *Picasso in Antibes*, 1960.
- Stein, Gertrude, *Picasso*, 1938.
- Valentin, Antonina, *Picasso*, 1957.
- Zervos, Christian, *Picasso, Œuvre Catalogue*. Twelve volumes, 1932–61.

Inklusive die folgenden Ausstellungskataloge/Including the following Exhibition Catalogues:

- Barcelona, Sala Parés, *Els Quatre Gats*, 1954.
- Geneva, Musée Rath, *L'Œuvre Gravé de Picasso*, 1954.
- London, Arts Council, *Picasso: Fifty Years of his Graphic Art*, 1956.
- Marseilles, Musée Cantini, *Picasso*, 1959.
- Milan, Palazzo Reale, *Picasso*, 1953.
- Paris, Galerie Louise Leiris, *Picasso, Peintures 1955–56*, 1957; *Picasso, les Ménines*, 1959; *Picasso, Dessins 1959–60*, 1960; *Picasso: 45 Gravures sur Linoleum 1958–60*, 1960.
- Paris, Musée des Arts Décoratifs, *Picasso*, 1955.
- Zürich, Kunsthaus, *Das graphische Werk Picassos*, Zürich, 1954.

Inklusive die folgenden Zeitschriften/Including the following periodicals:

- *The Burlington Magazine*, London, 99 (June 1957), John Richardson, "Picasso's Ateliers and Other Recent Works"; 101 (May 1959), Phoebe Pool, "Sources and Background of Picasso's Art".
- *Cahiers d'Art*, Paris, 1948. Special number devoted to Picasso's ceramics. Also 1939–54, passim.
- *Dance Index*, New York, 5, No. 11 (November 1946), W. S. Lieberman, "Picasso and the Ballet, 1917–45."
- *Verve*, Paris. Nos. 19–20 (1948); 25–26 (1951); 29–30 (1954).

Mackworth, Cecily, *Guillaume Apollinaire and the Cubist Life*. Observer (Jan 22, 1961): 29.

de la Souchère, Dor, *Picasso in Antibes*. Photographs by Marianne Greenwood. *TLS* (Feb 17, 1961): 100.

Klee, Felix, *Paul Klee*. *TLS* (Mar 17, 1961): 164.

Penrose, Roland, *Picasso*. *TLS* (Aug 18, 1961): 544.

Diehl, Gaston, *Picasso*. TLS (Aug 18, 1961): 554.

Leymarie, Jean, *Braque*. *TLS* (Aug 25, 1961): 560.

Duncan, David Douglas, *Picasso's Picassos*. Observer *(Oct 29, 1961): 31.*

Du, October 1961 (issue devoted to Picasso). *TLS* (Dec 15, 1961): 892.

Horodisch, Abraham, *Picasso as a Book Artist*. *TLS* (Aug 10, 1962): 580.

Spiller, Jurg, ed., *Paul Klee: The Thinking Eye. The Notebooks of Paul Klee*. *TLS* (Aug 31, 1962): 652.

Delevoy, Robert L., *Léger*. Translated by Stuard Gilbert. *TLS* (Dec 28, 1962): 1000.

Vallentin, Antonina, *Picasso*. *TLS* (Mar 22, 1963): 196.

Sutton, Keith, *Picasso;* Parmelin, Hélène, *Picasso Plain*. Translated by Humphrey Hare. *TLS* (June 21, 1963): 462.

Olivier, Fernande, *Picasso and his Friends*. *TLS* (Feb 6, 1964): 111.

Arnheim, Rudolf, *Picasso's Guernica*. *TLS* (May 21, 1964): 428.

Foster, Joseph K., *The Posters of Picasso*. *TLS* (Feb 25, 1965): 153.

Lynton, Norbert, *Klee*. *TLS* (Mar 4, 1965): 181.

Gilot, Françoise, and Carlton Lake, *Life with Picasso*. *TLS* (Mar 18, 1965): 208.

Jaffe, Hans L. C., *Picasso*. *TLS* (Apr 1, 1965): 259.

Klee, Felix, ed., *The Diaries of Paul Klee, 1898–1918*. *TLS* (July 8, 1965): 577.

Berger, John, *The Success and Failure of Picasso;* Kay, Helen, *Picasso's World of Children;* Daix, Pierre, *Picasso*. *TLS* (Jan 27, 1966): 56.

Brassaï, *Picasso & Co.; Picasso. Graphic Works 1955–1965*. Introduction by Kurt Leonhard. *TLS* (May 18, 1967): 412.

Frey, Edward, *Cubism*. *TLS* (Oct 12, 1967): 957.

Grohmann, Will, ed., *Paul Klee*. Translated by Norbert Guterman. *TLS* (Dec 28, 1967): 1252.

Daix, Pierre, and Georges Boudaille, *Picasso: The Blue and Rose Periods. A Catalogue Raisonné 1900–1906*. Catalogue compiled with the collaboration of Joan Rosselet. Translated by Phoebe Pool. *TLS* (Feb 8, 1968): 124.

Soavi, Giorgio, *Storia con Sutherland*. *TLS* (Aug 7, 1968): 840.

Mullins, Edwin, *Braque*. *TLS* (Mar 20, 1969): 288.

Blunt, Anthony, *Picasso's "Guernica."* Parmelin, Hélène. *Picasso Says...* Translated by Christine Trollope. *TLS* (Apr 3, 1969): 342.

Chavalier, Denys, *Picasso: The Blue and Rose Periods*. Translated by Stephanie Winston. *TLS* (Oct 30, 1969): 1265.

Crespelle, Jean-Paul, *Picasso and his Women*. Translated by Robert Baldick. *TLS* (May 7, 1970): 501.

Kahnweiler, Daniel-Henry. *My Galleries and Painters*. With Francis Cremieux. Translated by Helen Weaver. *TLS* (July 30, 1971): 911.

Wadley, Nicholas, *Cubism;* Schwartz, Paul Waldo, *The Cubists*. *TLS* (Sept 10, 1971): 1074.

Huggler, Max, *Paul Klee;* Klee, Paul, *Unendliche Naturgeschichte*. Edited by Jurg Spiller. *TLS* (Nov 5, 1971): 1378.

Jaffe, Hans L., *Picasso;* Masini, L. V., *Braque;* Verdet, Andre, *Leger*. *TLS* (Jan 7, 1972): 18.

Berger, John, *Success and Failure of Picasso;* Gilot, Françoise, and Lake, Carlton, *Life with Picasso;* Penrose, Roland, *Portrait of Picasso;* Penrose, Roland, *Picasso: His Life and Work;* Gallwitz, Klaus, *Picasso at 90: The Late Work;* Golding, John, *Cubism*. *BB* 17 (Feb 1972): 6–7.

Roethel, Hans K., *Paul KLee in München*. *TLS* (Mar 31, 1972): 368.

Lecaldano, Paolo, *The Complete Paintings of Picasso: Blue and Rose Periods*. Introduction by Denys Sutton. *TLS* (Apr 7, 1972): 386.

Lasarte, Juan Ainaud de, ed., *Carnet Picasso: La Coruna 1894–1895;* Spies, Werner, *Picasso Sculpture*. *BB* 17 (July 1972): 12–14.

Picasso: Métamorphoses et unité. Text by Jean Leymarie. *TLS* (July 21, 1972): 840.

Chevalier, Denys, *Klee*. Translated by Eileen B. Hennessy. *TLS* (July 28, 1972): 888.

Cirlot, Juan-Eduardo, *Picasso: Birth of a Genius*. *TLS* (Feb 2, 1973): 121.

Cassou, Jean, and Jean Leymarie, *Fernand Léger: Dessins et gouaches*. *TLS* (Apr 27, 1973): 464.

Subirana, Rosa M., ed., *Carnet Picasso: Paris 1900*. *BB* 18 (May 1973): 113.

Ashton, Dore, ed., *Picasso on Art: A Selection of Views*. *TLS* (Aug 17, 1973): 944.

Rubin, William, *Picasso in the Collection of the Museum of Modern Art*. *BB* 19 (Nov 1973): 50–52.

Golding, John, and Roland Penrose, eds., *Picasso: 1881–1973*, *BB* 19 (Apr 1974): 28–31.

Sweetman, David, *Picasso*; Porzio, Dominico, and Marco Valsecchi, eds., *Picasso*. *BB* 20 (Dec 1974): 42–44.

Nuño, J. A. Gaya, *Juan Gris*, Translated by K. Lyons. *Art Bulletin* 58 (Dec 1976): 638.

Malraux, André, *Picasso's Mask*; Duncan, David Douglas, *Goodbye Picasso*; Green, Christopher, *Léger and the Avant-Garde*. *BB* 22 (Mar 1977): 20–23.

O'Brian, Patrick, *Pablo Ruiz Picasso*. *BB* 22 (June 1977): 30–33.

Hayes, John, *Portraits by Graham Sutherland*, *BB* 23 (Dec 1977): 19–21.

Fotonachweis/Photo Credits:

Kunstmuseum Basel (Martin Bühler), Seiten/pages: 10, 36, 37, 38, 39, 40, 41, 42, 60, 61, 65, 66, 68, 69, 73, 81, 82, 83, 85, 86, 89, 94, 95, 97, 103, 104, 107, 109, 110, 111, 113, 117, 118, 119, 120, 122, 123, 124, 125, 126, 128, 129, 141, 142, 146, 147, 153, 157, 158, 159, 161, 162, 164, 166, 168, 169, 171, 172, 173, 174, 176, 184, 186, 187, 188, 191, 194.

Robert Doisneau, Seiten/pages: 16, 17, 20, 21, 23, 24, 27, 135.

House & Garden, Seiten/pages: 74, 189.

Photos NBC, Genève, Seiten/pages: 71, 114, 116, 137, 138, 139, 140, 143, 145, 149, 150, 154.

Unbekannt/unknown, Seiten/pages: 12, 87, 91, 92, 101, 106, 155, 167, 183, 185, 193.